THE HISTORY OF
ADVERTISING
40 MAJOR BOOKS IN FACSIMILE

Edited by
HENRY ASSAEL
C. SAMUEL CRAIG
New York University

A
GARLAND
SERIES

BUILDING
NEWSPAPER
ADVERTISING

JASON ROGERS

GARLAND PUBLISHING, INC.
NEW YORK & LONDON
1986

659.13 R727b 1986

Rogers, Jason, 1868-1932.

Building newspaper advertising

For a complete list of the titles in this series see the final pages of this volume.

This facsimile has been made from a copy in the library of Ohio State University.

The following illustrations appear on a foldout at the end of the book: Department-store Advertising in the *New York Herald* of 1861; Types of Barnum Ads. in the '60's; Circulation and Advertising Rates of 2,166 Dailies Summarized by States.

Library of Congress Cataloging-in-Publication Data

Rogers, Jason, 1868–1932.
   Building newspaper advertising.
   (The History of advertising)
   Reprint. Originally published: New York : Harper, 1919.
   1. Advertising, Newspaper. I. Title. II. Series.
HF6107.R59   1986   659.13'2   84-46059
ISBN 0-8240-6753-3 (alk. paper)

Designed by Donna Montalbano

The volumes in this series are printed on acid-free, 250-year-life paper.

Printed in the United States of America

STANLEY CLAGUE

Manager, Audit Bureau of Circulations. A man who is giving his best to the cause of advertising.

Building Newspaper Advertising

Selling the By-Product of the Newspaper, Printed Salesmanship

Management *and* Organization *of the* Selling Force—Development *of* New Lines *of* Business

by Jason Rogers
Author of "Newspaper Building"

New York and London
Harper & Brothers
m · c · m · x · i · x

BOOKS BY
JASON ROGERS
BUILDING NEWSPAPER ADVERTISING

NEWSPAPER BUILDING

HARPER & BROTHERS, NEW YORK
ESTABLISHED 1817

Copyright, 1919, by Harper & Brothers
Printed in the United States of America
Published April, 1919

D-T

Contents

		PAGE
FOREWORD		xi

PART I

CHAPTER		
I.	THE CHAOS OUT OF WHICH MODERN ADVERTISING GREW	3
II.	SOME FREAKS AND ODDITIES OF EARLY ADVERTISING	14
III.	THE ADVENT OF HEAVY DISPLAY	27
IV.	ADVERTISING FROM THE NEWSPAPER VIEWPOINT	33
V.	CO-OPERATION OFTEN DISCOURAGED BY ADVERTISER	37
VI.	APPEARANCE OF THE ADVERTISING AGENT	44
VII.	THE COMING OF THE SPECIAL REPRESENTATIVE	50
VIII.	INEFFECTIVE NATIONAL ADVERTISING MEDIUMS	54
IX.	ADVERTISING AN AMERICAN PRODUCT	61

PART II

X.	BEST TYPE OF MAN FOR ADVERTISING MANAGER	67
XI.	RELATION OF MANAGER TO REST OF FORCE	76
XII.	HANDLING THE SOLICITING FORCE	81
XIII.	DEMONSTRATION OF PAPER'S PULLING POWER	85
XIV.	CONSIDERATION OF ADVERTISING RATES	89
XV.	MAKING THE RATE CARD	95
XVI.	FALLACIOUS SPECIAL EDITIONS	101
XVII.	SCHEME ADVERTISING INEFFECTIVE	105
XVIII.	POLITICAL ADVERTISING	110
XIX.	TABLE FOR DETERMINING SIZE OF PAPER	117
XX.	SOME OFFICE FORMS AND RECORDS	124
XXI.	DEFINITE PROVED CIRCULATION	131
XXII.	OFFICE CONFERENCES	137

CONTENTS

CHAPTER		PAGE
XXIII.	How to Increase Advertising Rates	141
XXIV.	Sources of Inspiration	145

PART III

XXV.	The Solicitor of Early Days	149
XXVI.	Vital Thoughts for Would-be Solicitors	153
XXVII.	The Peacemaking Solicitor	158
XXVIII.	Wiles of the Space-buyer	162
XXIX.	Silence More Deadly Than Attack	165
XXX.	Weak Spot in the Armor of the Dominant Newspaper	169
XXXI.	Consideration of Sales Methods	173
XXXII.	Meeting Unreasonable Requests	178
XXXIII.	Local Advertising Experience	182
XXXIV.	Shifting Shopping Centers	195

PART IV

XXXV.	Selling Advertising Plus Results	201
XXXVI	Reaching the Distant Manufacturer	206
XXXVII.	Making New Local Advertising	211
XXXVIII.	Selling the Newspapers by States	216
XXXIX.	Map Scheme for Selling Extra Space	233
XL.	Building Up the Classified	235
XLI.	Plan for National Newspaper Organization.	250
XLII.	Proof That Co-operative Effort Will Pay	262
XLIII.	Intensifying Reader Interest in Advertising	276
XLIV.	Local Development.—J. Bernard Lyon	292

PART V

XLV.	The Pioneer Special Representatives	297
XLVI.	The "Special" a Constructive Force.—John B. Woodward	304
XLVII.	Service Rendered the Newspaper.—Dan A. Carroll	308
XLVIII.	Foreign Business at Home.—John E. O'Mara	314

CONTENTS

CHAPTER		PAGE
XLIX.	WHY THE SPECIAL?—G. LOGAN PAYNE	318
L.	MUTUAL CONFIDENCE THE KEYNOTE.—R. E. WARD	324
LI.	ASSISTING SPACE-BUYERS.—CHARLES H. EDDY	328

PART VI

LII.	NEW SORT OF CO-OPERATION WITH ADVERTISING AGENCIES AND WORDS OF ADVICE FROM NOTABLE AGENTS	333
LIII.	THE ADVANCED AGENCY SERVICE OF TO-DAY.—ROBERT TINSMAN	338
LIV.	CO-OPERATION.—STANLEY RESOR	343
LV.	EFFECTIVE CO-OPERATION.—PAUL FAUST	354
LVI.	THE NATIONAL AGENCY.—H. K. MCCANN	376
LVII.	THE VITAL THINGS.—JOHN LEE MAHIN	382
LVIII.	COST OF SPACE IN NEWSPAPER CAMPAIGNS.—WILLIAM H. RANKIN	388
LIX.	SOME IDEALS.—S. WILBUR CORMAN	400
LX.	MAKING NEWSPAPER SPACE PAY.—WILBUR D. NESBIT, VICE-PRESIDENT WM. H. RANKIN COMPANY, CHICAGO AND NEW YORK	412
LXI.	IMPROVED SOLICITATION.—RICHARD A. FOLEY	417
LXII.	RELATIONS BETWEEN AGENCIES AND NEWSPAPERS.—W. B. SOMERSET, OF A. MCKIM, LIMITED, MONTREAL	426

PART VII

LXIII.	ADVERTISING BRILLIANTS	435
LXIV.	HENRY FORD THE SUPER ADVERTISER	437
LXV.	ADVERTISING AN UNKNOWN WANT.—W. R. HOTCHKIN	443
LXVI.	BARNUM AS AN ADVERTISING WRITER.—BERT MOSES	451
LXVII.	SUPERIORITY OF THE NEWSPAPER AS AN ADVERTISING MEDIUM.—THOMAS E. DOCKRELL	459
LXVIII.	THE TIME ELEMENT IN ADVERTISING.—J. F. JACOBS	471
LXIX.	EFFICIENT NEWSPAPER ADVERTISING.—HERBERT CASSON	485
LXX.	SELLING COSTS.—J. GEORGE FREDERICK	492

CONTENTS

CHAPTER		PAGE
LXXI.	Proclamation and Persuasion	496
LXXII.	Killing the Beginner in Advertising	514
LXXIII.	The Law of Repetition.—Thomas E. Dockrell	520
LXXIV.	The Ten Commandments of Salesmanship.—Dr. Frank Crane	523
LXXV.	Successful Advertising.—George C. Sherman	526
LXXVI.	Why the Salesman Fell Down	528
LXXVII.	Elbert Hubbard on Advertising	530
LXXVIII.	Conclusion	534

APPENDIX

Appendix A.—Table of Newspapers by States with Circulation, by Harry Pruden . . 545
Appendix B.—Who Was the First Advertising Agent? 547

Illustrations

STANLEY CLAGUE		*Frontispiece*
AN AD. OF GEORGE WASHINGTON IN *The Maryland* AND THE *Baltimore Advertiser*, OF AUGUST 20, 1773, NOW *The Baltimore American*	*Facing p.*	4
ADVERTISEMENTS OF R. H. MACY IN THE *New York Times* DURING 1861	"	10
A *New York Herald* COMPOSITE LETTER PAGE IN THE '80's	"	14
DEPARTMENT-STORE ADVERTISING IN THE *New York Herald* IN 1855	"	16
DEPARTMENT-STORE ADVERTISING FROM THE *New York Times* OF 1861	"	16
A SAMPLE COLUMN AD. OF BONNER'S *Ledger* IN 1861 .	"	20
ANOTHER BONNER AD. SHOWING HOW HE ADVERTISED THE GOODS BACK IN THE '60's	"	20
TYPES OF BARNUM ADS. IN THE '60's	"	26
CIRCULATION AND ADVERTISING RATES OF 2,166 DAILIES SUMMARIZED BY STATES	"	58
HARRY MILHOLLAND	"	68
ARTHUR FREEMAN	"	76
A. G. NEWMYER	"	82
FLEMING NEWBOLD	"	90
REPRODUCTION OF THE RATE CARD OF THE *Hartford Times*	"	96
SECOND PAGE OF THE RATE CARD OF THE *Hartford Times*	"	96
Philadelphia Evening Bulletin, AND *Washington Evening and Sunday Star* RATE CARD	"	96
REPRODUCTION OF THE RATE CARD OF THE *Chicago Daily News*	"	96

ILLUSTRATIONS

New Standardized Rate Card (*New York Globe*) as Adopted by the American Advertising Agents' Association	Facing p.	100
Harry J. Grant	"	106
Lines of Dry Goods Advertising in New York Newspapers	"	128
Localized National Advertising	"	214
"The Gilt Edge Newspapers"	"	218
Map of Alabama, Showing Towns in Which Newspapers Are Published	"	230
Map of Lake Michigan, Showing How It Was Used for Advertising Exploitation	"	234
Harry Doorly	"	236
John B. Woodward	"	304
John E. O'Mara	"	314
G. Logan Payne	"	318
R. E. Ward	"	324
Charles H. Eddy	"	328
First-prize Ad. of the *New York Globe's* Advertising Agency Competition	Page	334
Robert Tinsman	Facing p.	338
Stanley Resor	"	344
Paul E. Faust	"	354
H. K. McCann	"	376
John Lee Mahin	"	382
Wilbur D. Nesbit	"	412
Richard A. Foley	"	418
W. B. Somerset	"	426
Series of Trade-paper Advertisements Inserted for the Purpose of Stimulating Newspapers to Closer Co-operation with Advertising Agents	"	430
W. R. Hotchkin	"	444

Foreword

NEWSPAPER advertising is without doubt the greatest selling force which the best modern business and commercial efficiency have at their command. But only a very small part of our business men have yet learned how to use it effectively, although thousands who do not know "how" have grown enormously through its use. Newspaper advertising even to-day is practically like an untouched mine of wealth lying just without the door, ready to do wonders for any business enterprise. Intelligently used, newspaper advertising can be readily made to produce vastly increased traffic or to influence public opinion.

I know these things because I have lived, breathed, dreamed, and studied advertising in close proximity to printers for over thirty-seven years; I have watched its development from the crudities of the late '70's to its best modern refinements and efficiencies. I have seen many wonderful successes scored and likewise many millions of dollars hopelessly sunk in futile and defectively constructed campaigns.

Not posing as an advertising expert in any sense of the phrase, my purpose in attempting to set down on paper my personal experiences in manufacturing advertising, in selling it, and making it produce results for the advertiser, is wholly, I hope, to give con-

FOREWORD

structive help and suggestion to those who are inclined, by the study of past performances, to accomplish with efficiency and profit the tasks they are called upon to undertake. To know the pitfalls is to be on guard against accident in many situations, while to know the lines of least resistance is useful in developing plans for expansion. In this book I am actuated by the same desire to be of help to the craft which prompted me to write the previous book, *Newspaper Building*, last year.

In my experience I have found that too many business men view with aversion the approach of advertising solicitors from newspapers seeking to render them a service, guarding themselves against any possible raid on the dollars in the cash-drawer; too many newspaper solicitors fail to understand and properly explain the magic power of the service they can render, and thus lose opportunities every day for demonstrations which would multiply many times the present volume of advertising in the columns of their newspapers.

Whether or not the recording of what is to follow will prove of value to those vitally interested in advertising and to those who come fresh to the fray I cannot foretell and must leave to them. I am confident, however, that could I have had at my service at an earlier period in my life all the experience since acquired, put in get-at-able form, I should have gone much farther than I have.

Newspaper advertising in the past has been too largely experimental and cumbered with too much guesswork and lack of definition. All of our modern efficiencies and refinements are but the result of past experience; we are even now only beginning to under-

FOREWORD

stand why great successes are made in some cases, and why failures result from the practice of almost the same methods in others.

We have discovered that, except in peculiar cases requiring only a sale for a short period, no matter how perfect and wonderful the advertising, no lasting success can be produced unless the article will repeat and the whole selling and merchandizing plan is sound.

Our great department stores and specialty shops have proved beyond a doubt that the courageous use of advertising will produce double the sales that could be made without its use. We have proved that it is those large advertisers who have been honest in their advertising, building institutional confidence, who get greatest results per dollar for advertising.

Henry Ford's discovery, that the man who can supply a public demand better, in larger quantities, and at a smaller price than any one else, commands success if he will make known what he has to offer should provide the inspiration for those who would go farthest through advertising. To advertise the *unusual* for quality or value will double the results which advertising the *ordinary* brings.

The wonderful feat of the makers of B. V. D. underwear likewise stands as a monument to what can be done by intelligent advertising. We all wore underwear before the B. V. D. goods were known. Yet from a standing start a new, cheap, serviceable line was introduced to us all, until to-day people are inclined to call all undergarments B. V. D.'s, and through the sanitary suggestions put forth in the advertising a large additional sale of other lines of underwear was created.

The great success of houses like Marshall Field &

FOREWORD

Co., of Chicago, and B. Altman & Co., of New York, representing the very highest type of desirable big-store business, in contrast with the flamboyant splurges of Siegel, Cooper & Co. in New York and Chicago, O'Neill's, Adams, Simpson Crawford, The 14th Street Store in New York, ending in failure, is proof that the public in the long run demands dependable service and cannot forever be exploited.

It is my purpose here merely to indicate the value of past sound experience shown by the story of successes and failures, in both local and general campaigns, which have come under my observation. Success, either as the result of moderate copy often repeated or heavy dominating campaigns of comparatively short duration, would seem to indicate that the buyer and seller of advertising must apply sound principles in each case.

Handicapped as it has been by ignorant and dishonest practices of many pretending to be experts, newspaper advertising has nevertheless been richly successful in the main. Many of our advertising idols of the past have been proved as false and hollow as the patent-medicine faker at the circus, when we view their performance in the light of best present-day practices.

Unscrupulous advertisers flimflammed the reader with fake bargain offerings until the remark, "Oh, that's just advertising," became general; the mediums had to clean house to protect the industry. Likewise, false claims on the part of solicitors regarding circulation and ridiculous promises regarding wholly impossible results killed off thousands of our best prospects.

Notwithstanding all these things, newspaper advertising has grown better and more effective from

FOREWORD

year to year, until to-day it stands in a class by itself among all other methods; to-day it can be used with absolute certainty as to results by those who know how and are willing to make the reasonable and consistent investment known to be essential.

In this book we shall consider various means for the stimulation of result-producing advertising, the various services that newspapers may render to make advertising more effective and productive, and how, through more cordial co-operation with the advertising agencies, we can materially assist them in developing a new and vastly enlarged volume of business for our columns.

We shall consider where the advertising agent fits into the general fabric, how he performs services for the advertiser for which no newspaper is equipped, and then study the suggestions of leaders in the agency business regarding the best modern service as rendered by them, and how we can best co-operate.

The day is gone by, never to return, when it is safe to count on a sucker being born every minute. A pleased customer for whom we secure steady returns is a far greater asset than any amount of business obtained by paying the heavy toll incident to stirring up new crews to go out and plunder the unwary.

JASON ROGERS.

NEW YORK, *January, 1919.*

Building Newspaper Advertising

PART I

Building Newspaper Advertising

I

The Chaos Out of Which Modern Advertising Grew

THE first advertisement, according to historical records, appeared in London in 1648.

The first American newspaper, *Public Occurrences*, was printed in Boston, September 25, 1690, by R. Pierce for Benjamin Harris, its editor. Its publication created such a stir that the legislative authorities "strictly forbade anything in print without license first obtained from those appointed by the government to grant same," so there was no second appearance of the first paper.

In the beginning, newspaper advertising was looked upon by newspaper editors as an intrusion upon the space dedicated to the subscriber. It did not make any difference whether the reading-matter they desired to print was fresh news reports, lengthy discussions of uninteresting subjects, or clippings from exchanges; advertising was commercialism from their point of view.

Early newspaper efforts were most of them very short-lived because they reflected nothing more than efforts of mere journeymen printers to make a profit out of printed gossip or to serve political or other special interests. These newspapers were frequently owned by postmasters, who had facilities in the way of transportation not possessed by others.

On April 24, 1704, John Campbell, postmaster at Boston, issued the *News-Letter*, printed sometimes on a single sheet, foolscap size, and oftener on a half-sheet, with two columns on each side. No subscription price was mentioned. It was "printed by authority" and the following was the prospectus, advertisement as Campbell called it, as it appeared in the first number:

Advertisement

The News-Letter is to be continued Weekly; and all Persons who have any Houses, Lands, Tenements, Farms, Ships, Vessels, Goods, Wares, or Merchandise, etc., to be Sold, or Let; or Servants Run-away, or Goods Stole or Lost; may have same inserted at a Reasonable Rate, from Twelve Pence to Five Shillings, and not to exceed; Who may agree with John Campbell, Postmaster at Boston.

All Persons in Town or Country may have said News-Letter every week yearly upon reasonable terms, agreeing with John Campbell, Postmaster, for same.

"The *News-Letter* was the only paper in existence and had no rival for upwards of fifteen years," and, as Hudson put it in his *History of Journalism*, "it did not appear to have thrived abundantly from a

Mount Vernon in *Virginia, July* 15, 1773.

THE Subscriber having obtained Patents for upwards of TWENTY THOUSAND Acres of LAND on the *Ohio* and *Great Kanhawa* (Ten Thousand of which are situated on the banks of the first-mentioned river, between the mouths of the two *Kanhawas*, and the remainder on the *Great Kanhawa*, or *New River*, from the mouth, or near it, upwards, in one continued survey) proposes to divide the same into any sized tenements that may be desired, and lease them upon moderate terms, allowing a reasonable number of years rent free, provided, within the space of two years from next October, three acres for every fifty contained in each lot, and proportionably for a lesser quantity, shall be cleared, fenced, and tilled; and that, by or before the time limited for the commencment of the first rent, five acres for every hundred, and proportionably, as above, shall be enclosed and laid down in good grass for meadow; and moreover, that at least fifty good fruit trees for every like quantity of land shall be planted on the Premises. Any persons inclinable to settle on these lands may be more fully informed of the terms by applying to the subscriber, near *Alexandria*, or in his absence, to Mr. LUND WASHINGTON; and would do well in communicating their intentions before the 1st of October next, in order that a sufficient number of lots may be laid off to answer the demand.

As these lands are among the first which have been surveyed in the part of the country they lie in, it is almost needless to premise that none can exceed them in luxuriance of soil, or convenience of situation, all of them lying upon the banks either of the *Ohio* or *Kanhawa*, and abounding with fine fish and wild fowl of various kinds, as also in most excellent meadows, many of which (by the bountiful hand of nature) are, in their present state, almost fit for the scythe. From every part of these lands water carriage is now had to *Port Pitt*, by an easy communication; and from *Fort Pitt*, up the *Monongahela*, to *Redstone*, vessels of convenient burthen, may and do pass continually; from whence, by means of *Cheat River*, and other navigable branches of the *Monongahela*, it is thought the portage to *Potowmack* may, and will, be reduced within the compass of a few miles, to the great ease and convenience of the settlers in transporting the produce of their lands to market. To which may be added, that as patents have now actually passed the seals for the several tracts here offered to be leased, settlers on them may cultivate and enjoy the lands in peace and safety, notwithstanding the unsettled counsels respecting a new colony on the *Ohio*; and as no right money is to be paid for these lands, and quitrent of two shillings sterling a hundred, demandable some years hence only, it is highly presumable that they will always be held upon a more desirable footing than where both these are laid on with a very heavy hand. And it may not be amiss further to observe, that if the scheme for establishing a new government on the *Ohio*, in the manner talked of, should ever be affected, these must be among the most valuable lands in it, not only on account of the goodness of soil, and the other advantages above enumerated, but from their contiguity to the seat of government, which more than probable will be fixed at the mouth of the *Great Kanhawa*. GEORGE WASHINGTON.

BUILDING NEWSPAPER ADVERTISING 5

pecuniary point of view, not sufficiently to enable its proprietor to publish a paper as he planned in his dreams. Appeals for support were repeatedly made to the public. There were more readers than paying subscribers." He admitted he had only three hundred circulation, though many thought he had three thousand or four thousand.

In 1719 Campbell was removed from the post-office. William Brooker was appointed in his place. He started the *Boston Gazette*, the second regular newspaper in America.

Very early in the history of our country, before the Revolutionary War, our ambitious editors realized that a certain amount of advertising was essential to security. But this advertising was as defective, judged by modern standards, as the newspapers. Circulations were small and the prices received for advertising were seldom enough to care for the cost of publication.

As late as January 1, 1797, American journalism was a sickly, poorly supported industry. In an announcement the *Boston Gazette* contained this over the signature of Benjamin Edes:

> The aged Editor of the Gazette presents the compliments of the Season to his generous benefactors and invites all of those who have any demands on him to call and receive their dues. He likewise requests of his customers, who are two, three and more years in debt, to discharge their arrears, as he finds it impossible to live upon the wind, and promises equally uncertain. The former number of subscribers to the Gazette (in times which tried men's souls, and bodies too) were upwards of Two Thousand; nearly three fourths of which are no more. But being now reduced to 400, and not advertisements enough weekly to procure Paper, he is necessitated to publish it any longer than the time before mentioned.

On September 17, 1798, Edes gave up the task of continuing the *Boston Gazette* in a farewell address, brimful of pathos and patriotism, which I reproduce in full from Hudson's *History of Journalism* as a human document, and so that those of the present day may know what hardships the pioneers had to deal with.

The Editor's Farewell.

The Editor of the Boston Gazette, after repeated attempts to prosecute his professional occupation, in the declining period of his life, is at length obliged to relinquish his exertions, to which misfortune has consigned him.

While passing through the gloomy valley of old age and infirmity, his consolation still rests on that staff, which can support a mind conscious of its own rectitude; and though he often feels the thorns and briers on the road, goading him in his passage, yet he patiently suffers under these afflictions, hoping that ere long he shall arrive at that peaceful abode, "where the weary are at rest."

During upwards of 43 years of hard labor in that "art which supports all arts," he has uniformly attempted to vindicate the Rights of the Country. He early made himself conspicuous as the scourge of tyrants. His press was the asylum of the distressed—through that medium an injured people could ever express their wrongs, or plan measures for their deliverance. At that afflicting crisis, when America lay groaning under the unnumerable tortures of a relentless nation, the Boston Gazette was employed as the Herald to sound the alarm through the most remote parts of the Continent.

The Patriots of our Country, at those "times which tried men's souls" were constantly assembled within the confines of his office, and their manuscripts were displayed as with a Telegraph, in legible characters, within the columns of his periodical publications.

Adams, Hancock, Warren, with a train of co-patriots, were his chosen intimates; under their guidance and direction, he stood on the Watch Tower, and like a faithful soldier in the cause of freedom, ever held himself ready, and willing, to Fall and Rise with the Ruin or Happiness of his country.

But, alas! The cause of Liberty is not always the channel of preferment or pecuniary reward. The little property which he acquired has long since fell a sacrifice; the paper evidence of his service were too powerful to be resisted, though he fed them with property at four shillings and sixpence in the pound, which he faitnfully and industriously earned at twenty shillings.

However, it is beneath a patriot to mourn his own misfortunes. The Independence of America being obtained, he enjoys the pleasing contemplation, that the same virtuous sentiments which led to the acquisition will not cease to operate for its continuance —That his fellow citizens will ever revere the First Principles of the Revolution; and it was his earnest prayer to Heaven, that the Rising Generation will remember the exertions of their fathers, in opposing the lawless attempts of Britain for their subjection.

Let the citizens of America reverance themselves. Let them strive to maintain the Republican Principles of their own Constitution; and while practicing these duties, we may trust the Guardian Angel, which has conducted us through dangers, the most alarming and distressing.

And now my fellow citizens, I bid you farewell! Maintain your virtue—Cherish your Liberties—and may the Almighty protect and defend you.

B. Edes.

Boston, September 17, 1798, and in the forty-fourth year of the Independence of the Boston Gazette.

There [as Hudson puts it] at the age of seventy-five, this over-influential journalist passed from affluence and big position, with a few old type, and an elderly daughter as an assistant, to the attic of an old wooden building in Boston, there to eke out five more years of life on a miserable pittance earned at a case in a small job office in the Athens of America.

Casual examination of the weeklies published during the eighteenth century shows that advertising then consisted largely of official notices, ship-sailings, articles for sale, and rewards, published as standing cards and devoid of interest.

Although this business helped pay running expenses, pay-rolls and paper bills, editors of those days, like some of the present day, were still inclined to regard advertising as an intrusion on their rights which they must resent as calculated to influence their judgment on questions of the day.

The increasing volume of this advertising saved the editor the labor of filling the space it occupied, but he looked upon it as a dangerous perversion of his art, and to this day, left to his own inclinations, the editor almost habitually discriminates in the treatment of news items against the advertiser. Anything said regarding an advertiser is an "ax," to be discarded or buried, while he will gladly print a similar item regarding a non-advertiser without grudging the space.

Nothing pleased the old-time editors so much as to prove their independence by throwing out a mass of advertising to make room for news or other reading-matter, and, strange to say, many of them thought they were justified in such action, while in reality they were only proving their own inefficiency.

An interesting bit regarding the development of the weekly into the daily is reported in Hudson's *History of Journalism* in connection with the *Worcester* (Mass.) *Spy's* celebration of its hundredth birthday on July 17, 1870, as follows:

When the Spy was started, one hundred years ago, there were six other papers in Massachusetts, but they all disappeared before the beginning of the present century. The Boston News-Letter, the first paper printed in America, might be living now if it had not become a malignant tory and fallen under the influence of the royalists, at the beginning of the Revolution. Its first number was printed in 1704. For a long time it had no competitor; it became strong and prosperous; but when the

BUILDING NEWSPAPER ADVERTISING

Revolution approached it took the way to death, and, instead of living to hold its centennial celebration nearly seventy years ago, it died of toryism as soon as the British army left Boston. The Spy is living yet because it received life from the ideas that created the revolution and the nation, and preserved this life. It was established by a patriot whose integrity could not be corrupted.

At that dinner ex-Editor Earle, "the founder of the Daily Spy," made some remarks of interest to newspaper men generally regarding the changing from weekly to daily.

The publication of the Daily was begun in 1845. It seemed to him that the city and its business and the commercial interests warranted such an enterprise. He had published and edited the Massachusetts Weekly Spy since 1823, and during that time it had been well supported by the people; but when the question of a daily was brought up, many discouraging objections were made, especially by business men. On the morning of July 31, 1845, the first number was issued. One reason urged by merchants against starting the Daily was that the cost of advertising would be increased. To meet this, he adopted the policy of inserting in the Daily, without charge, the advertisements sent in for the Weekly; and when their customers came, inquiring for articles advertised in the Daily, they began to see that it was greatly to their interest to advertise in the Daily. Then he left out of the Daily their advertisements sent for the Weekly. The result was, that in a short time, they cared much less for the Weekly than for the Daily.

The coming of the daily newspaper made advertising an even greater necessity for successful publication than it had been for the weeklies. The daily also gave advertising a flexibility that made it superior to anything previously conceived.

In place of the old stereotyped routine "cards," called advertising in the early days and sometimes indulged in even to-day, a few wide-awake merchants cashed in on the new possibilities of advertising.

Volume I, No. 1, of the *New York Sun* in 1833

showed advertising rates of $30 per year for a standing card. In some cities the basis was one inch space, single column, while in others the ten-line "square," as it was called, was the unit.

Until about forty years ago newspapers made no intelligent or serious effort to secure advertising through solicitation, except by political support or specific service. They would print anything that was offered at so much per inch or line, regardless of whether it was dependable or not.

Many newspapers did not employ any advertising solicitors, on the ground that to ask for advertising was demeaning. The advertising agents who first worked as the paid representatives of the newspapers did the earliest work of this kind. As late as 1883 the *New York Herald* did not employ a solicitor.

The newspapers merely printed the ads. for so much a line per year, and apparently did not have any further interest in the matter, except to see that the bills were paid. Much as they needed the money, they still thought it would weaken their position to seem to go after it.

There are still a few publishers of daily newspapers who adhere to these old traditions and pride themselves on not knowing or having any contact with advertising or advertisers. These men wish to decide all policies impersonally and think they can do so by holding themselves aloof.

In offices managed by such men nearly all attempts to make advertising productive or to render service calculated to produce increased volume of advertising are nipped in the bud by active discouragement or stolid refusal to undertake anything new.

During the early '90's newspaper advertising took

WESTWARD! HO!!

"*Westward the Star of Empire takes its way!*"
So does the Star of Fashion and the Graces;
Judging, at least, by the vast crowds, each day,
Rushing to MACY'S.

Broadway no longer tempts with costly glare,
With fancy shop fronts, and still fancier prices;
Cheapness—if good and tasteful for the fair—
Is what entices.

Therefore, we find SIXTH-AVENUE to grow,
Daily, in favor with all sects and classes,
And not a Broadway palace, people know,
MACY'S surpasses.

Look at his GLOVES! while other folks elsewhere
Charge for their gloves a price almost fictitious,
For SIXTY-THREE CENTS MACY robes the fair
In kids delicious!

See what a rich assortment, too, he brings
Of LINENS, FLOWERS, EMBROIDERIES and LACES,
RIBBONS, HEAD-DRESSES, and a thousand things
For pretty faces!

Hither flock mothers with their pets, and beaux
Come with the objects of their hearts' devotions,
To see the startling wonders MACY shows
In YANKEE NOTIONS.

Bedecked by him the very plainest lass
Is Venus—in her beau's imagination.
And youngsters, too—in mamma's eyes—surpass
All in creation!

"*Westward the Star of Fashion takes its way!*"
That it should poise o'er MACY'S is not funny;
'Tis that he SELLS GOODS EQUAL to BROADWAY,
FOR MUCH LESS MONEY!

R. H. MACY,
Nos. 204 and 206 6th-av.,
Two doors from 14th-st.

AT MACY'S.
EMBROIDERED LACE CURTAINS,
EMBROIDERED LACE DRAPERIES, by the yard.
NOTTINGHAM LACE CURTAINS,
NOTTINGHAM LACE DRAPERIES, by the yard,
LACE TIDIES, &c.
From the CASH AUCTIONS of LAST WEEK, at VERY
LOW PRICES.
R. H. MACY,
Nos. 204 and 206 6th-av., two doors below 14th-st.

R. H. MACY,
SELLS LADIES' DOLLAR KID GLOVES,
All colors and sizes, for 63 cents; free by mail, 69 cts.
Nos. 204 and 206 6th-av.
No connection with any other store in the City.

HAPPY NEW-YEAR.
AT MACY'S.
ALL THE BALANCE OF OUR CHRISTMAS
TOYS, CHINA ORNAMENTS,
Fancy Boxes, now closing at cost and
Less than cost, to clear them out by
New-Year's.
Everybody made happy at MACY'S.
Full stock or Ribbons, closing low.
Complete stock of French and Scotch Embroideries,
Bands, Flouncings, Needle Work Handkerchiefs,
Points, Collars, Guipure Collars, Thread Veils,
Coiffures, Barbes, Sleeves, Capes, Night-
Caps, Dress Caps, Head Dresses, Fancy
Fans, French Flowers, Ladies' Made-
Up Under-clothing, &c., closing at prices
Certain to make everybody happy.
Full stock of Gents' Handkerchiefs, plain and Hem-
Stitched and colored Bordered.
Full stock of Hosiery, Gloves and Under-Wear,
Splendid assortment of
Embroidered Lace Curtains,
Embroidered Lace for Curtains, by the yard,
Nottingham Lace Curtains,
Nottingham Laces for Curtains, by the yard,
Tidies, &c., adapted to the New-Year.
NOW OPENING
1,000 dozen white, light colors, mode colors and blacks
of our celebrated Kid Gloves, 63 cents a pair.
R. H. MACY,
Nos. 204 and 206 6th-av., 2d door below 14th-st.

DRY GOODS.

CLOAKS AND SHAWLS.
E. S. MILLS & CO.,
OFFER TO CASH BUYERS GREAT BARGAINS IN
CLOAKS AND SHAWLS.
At Nos. 342 and 344 BROADWAY.

R. H. MACY,
NOS. 204 AND 206 SIXTH-AV.,
NOW OPENING,
FROM THE CASH AUCTIONS,
FALL STYLES HAT RIBBONS,
NEW EMBROIDERIES,
LACE GOODS, VEILS, &c.
FULL STOCK FALL STYLES FRENCH FLOWERS,
HEAD-DRESSES, RUCHES, &c.
ENGLISH and GERMAN HOSIERY and GLOVES,
LADIES' UNDER-CLOTHING, WHITE GOODS,
LINENS,
HOUSEKEEPING GOODS, TARLATANS, &c.
FULL STOCK YANKEE NOTIONS, &c.
N. B.—1,000 doz. BEST QUALITY LADIES' PARIS
KID GLOVES—ALL THE FALL AND WINTER COL-
ORS—63 CENTS A PAIR.
R. H. MACY.

Advertisements of R. H. Macy in the *New York Times* during 1861.

BUILDING NEWSPAPER ADVERTISING

on many important and radically new features. The old style standing ad. was dropped for ads. changed every day and made as full of news interest as the news columns by the introduction of specific offerings for sale on the following day.

Barnum's circus ads., Bonner's *Ledger* announcements, patent-medicine ads., political, theatrical notices, auction sales, and lost-and-found ads., had shown the way. People wondered why the old *Herald*, containing all the death notices, was read by everybody. The reason was that its ads. were as interesting as its news matter.

When the new era opened the brightest and most alert reporters found a new and profitable field for their abilities. They, among others, entered the service of the advertisers in constructing advertising which was news, and produced results beyond the most sanguine expectations of those accustomed to standing cards.

Old-time newspaper rates, as previously stated, put a premium on advertising which ran without change of copy. Hand composition was expensive and newspapers did not operate on modern sound cost systems. The man furnishing a plate for his ad. was looked upon as yielding 100 per cent. profit. Many of our country papers still adhere to the old practice of charging one price for set matter and a much lower one for plate matter.

As late as 1897 in a New England city of some importance a leading daily newspaper made a rate of 10 cents per line for the first insertion of any ad., with a rate of 2½ cents per line for every subsequent insertion of the same matter. The result was that most merchants ran the same copy for a week or two under the impression that they were buying space cheaply. To-day it would seem ridiculous to have a department-store sale with goods and prices marked to stand a whole week.

The early experimenters who discovered the magical powers of newspaper advertising, whether for the sale of merchandise, real estate, fake financial offerings, nostrums, or anything else, reaping rich harvests, overdid the thing until they brought themselves into disrepute or the hands of the law.

A get-rich-quick result was often produced by advertising large prizes for answers to puzzles and other semi-lottery schemes. They would draw the same results to-day, for the mass of the public would rather spend their money for a chance at something for nothing than keep it safely in banks, or for articles they needed.

I well remember the heavy advertising of so-called suburban lots during 1892 and other years, at from $50 to $500 a lot, which unloaded thousands of glittering promises on the innocent but ignorant portion of the public whose descendants are probably holding the lots, which to-day represent but a part of what was paid for them twenty-five years ago.

Marvelous as are the results that can be obtained, advertising has scarcely become an exact science, known and understood by any one man who can positively say that for a certain sum he can produce definite returns.

If it were otherwise, modern business would cease to be speculative and all any fool would have to do to become as rich as a Rockefeller would be to advertise something and keep advertising it.

In the development of the modern newspaper at

one cent per copy, before the advance to two cents forced by war conditions, it became imperative to develop new lines of revenue from advertising and the more progressive newspapers sought to stimulate growth by various devices.

Meantime it was found that a large part of the public objected to offensive and fraudulent advertising; that the men in honest lines of business hesitated to advertise in competition with frauds and quacks; and that the newspaper that encouraged confidence in the good faith and reliability of its advertising produced the best results.

This opened new possibilities in all sorts of business through newspaper advertising, only a small part of which has yet been utilized to the full extent.

The thing looks too good to be true from the standpoint of both advertiser and newspaper publisher, and only the department stores and a limited number of retail shops have discovered the great advantages of advertising. As for the newspapers, many of them have been too prone to reap before the harvest was ripe.

Later on I shall analyze some of the best ideas that have been used along lines of business promotion through advertising, and point out the weakness of our present-day newspapers in their relation to it. In *Newspaper Building* I indicated what the *New York Globe* has done in such development in food, fashion, and miscellaneous advertising.

The subject is one which should be carefully studied by every ambitious newspaper man, for by the effective stimulation of advertising I am certain that our newspapers, using sound co-operative methods with advertisers and advertising agents, could double the volume of advertising in a year.

II

Some Freaks and Oddities of Early Advertising

As I look back over the scenes of my boyhood in the newspaper business, when advertising was "mere advertising" in a crude and vulgar sense, I cannot but wonder that those who then used it for business promotion secured profitable results; they did so only because it was the best advertising they knew of.

Newspaper advertising must possess inherent virtues that none of us yet understand and appreciate, else it could not have been effective in spite of obvious deficiencies, ignorance of decencies, and false practices which surrounded it in its inception.

These early advertisements are interesting not only as curiosities, but also because all stores which advertised as shown here over half a century ago are still in business, among the leading concerns of their class in the city and in the nation, very much larger now, of course, than they were at the time they were using thirty- and forty-line ads.

In fifty-seven years the R. H. Macy of 1861, then at 204 and 206 Sixth Avenue, has become R. H. Macy & Co., now at Thirty-fourth Street and Broadway; A. T. Stewart & Co., then at Broadway and Chambers Street, has become John Wanamaker's at Broadway and Tenth Street, while Lord & Taylor then at 461 to 467 Broadway, Arnold Constable & Co., then at Canal and

BUILDING NEWSPAPER ADVERTISING 15

Mercer Streets, and others have moved up-town, some first to the Grand Street shopping district, then up about Union Square, and later to Fifth Avenue.

The leading advertising medium in New York City during the 'seventies was the *New York Herald*. A foolish and crippling regulation which it inflicted on its advertising and rigidly adhered to too persistently and too long proved its own undoing, providing, as it did, the opportunity for Pulitzer in 1883 to come forward with the *New York World* with modern ideas and eclipse the *Herald*.

I refer to the old *Herald* rule that all advertising had to be set in agate type, with no display other than that which could be produced by assembling small agate caps in the form of large letters, with no lines or borders except certain marks produced by periods, hyphens, and asterisks. Here is a sample:

Of course no effective or convincing argument could be made attractive to the eye by such typographical compositions, but the advertisers of that day were compelled to use the *Herald*, and they got results. Another curiosity of that time was the peculiar way in which two of the best old-time advertisers used space, namely, Robert Bonner, of the old *New York Ledger*, a weekly story paper, and P. T. Barnum, the circus man.

Bonner would take a full page in the *Herald* to advertise this way:

16 BUILDING NEWSPAPER ADVERTISING

ROBERT BONNER'S	ROBERT BONNER'S	BORERT BONNER'S	ROBERT BONNER'S
ROBERT BONNER'S	ROBERT BONNER'S	ROBERT BONNER'S	ROBERT BONNER'S
ROBERT BONNER'S	ROBERT BONNER'S	ROBERT BONNER'S	ROBERT BONNER'S
NEW YORK LEDGER	NEW YORK LEDGER	NEW YORK LEDGER	NEW YORK LEDGER
NEW YORK LEDGER	NEW YORK LEDGER	NEW YORK LEDGER	NEW YORK LEDGER
NEW YORK LEDGER	NEW YORK LEDGER	NEW YORK LEDGER	NEW YORK LEDGER
BIG NEW STORY	BIG NEW STORY	BIG NEW STORY	BIG NEW STORY
BIG NEW STORY	BIG NEW STORY	BIG NEW STORY	BIG NEW STORY
BIG NEW STORY	BIG NEW STORY	BIG NEW STORY	BIG NEW STORY
BY	BY	BY	BY
BY	BY	BY	BY
BY	BY	BY	BY
NED BUNTLINE	NED BUNTLINE	NED BUNTLINE	NED BUNTLINE
NED BUNTLINE	NED BUNTLINE	NED BUNTLINE	NED BUNTLINE
NED BUNTLINE	NED BUNTLINE	NED BUNTLINE	NED BUNTLINE
STARTS	STARTS	STARTS	STARTS
STARTS	STARTS	STARTS	STARTS
STARTS	STARTS	STARTS	STARTS
NEXT SATURDAY	NEXT SATURDAY	NEXT SATURDAY	NEXT SATURDAY
NEXT SATURDAY	NEXT SATURDAY	NEXT SATURDAY	NEXT SATURDAY
NEXT SATURDAY	NEXT SATURDAY	NEXT SATURDAY	NEXT SATURDAY

DRY GOODS, &C.

$100,000 STOCK OF DRY GOODS, ALL NEW—Find all wool twilled blankets.
Elegant plain counted stella shawls.
Gents travelling shawls, cheap.
Rich cashmeres and de laines.
Fine 4-4 real French prints.
Welsh flannels 3-4, 7-4 and 8-4 wide.
Red twilled bath-mixed flannel, (a new thing.)
Cassimeres for boys and men, from 4s. to $4.
Cloths for ladies' and gentlemen' swear.
Satinets and jeans of all kinds.
Linen handkerchiefs, good, at 6c., fine do., very fine 1s. 6d.
Gents' do., bordered, at 6s. to $4 per dozen.
Prints for comforters, by the piece or case, 6c.
French merinoes as low as 7s. and up to 10s.
Paramattas of every kind, color and quality.
An excellent assortment of linen goods.
Towels, napkins, diapers, &c., by the quantity.
Table cloths $1 25, once sold at $3.
Domestic goods by the yard, piece or bale.
Every article marked in plain figures, price affixed.
The Bowery Savings Store, 126 Bowery,
F. W. & W. F. GILLEY.

$10,000 WORTH OF RICH VALENCIENNES LACES at uncommonly low prices, being the late purchases of Mr. Roberts while in Europe; just received.
PETER ROBERTS & CO., 375 Broadway.

596 BROADWAY—MANUFACTURER'S DEPOT OF Brussels and chantilly laces. The agent has received a large assortment of the above rich laces, ready to be offered at retail. JULES DELCROIX, 596 Broadway, near Metropolitan Hotel.

ANOTHER NEW STYLE OF MOURNING COLLAR AND sleeves, BAILEY, FARRINGTON & LESLIE. 623 Broadway, received per steamer Pacific, an entirely new material of their own design, for mourning sets which they will offer on Monday, October 8, in collars and sleeves of their own styles, which are entirely new. The material and style are something never before seen, and cannot be found at any other house in the city.

AT THE STORE OF PETER ROBERTS & CO., 375 BROAD-way, will be found the largest and most varied stock of lace goods ever offered in this market by any one firm. Many of the styles are entirely new and never before shown here. The above extensive assortment has been selected with much care by Mr. Roberts while in Europe.

BULPIN'S SHAWLS—JUST RECEIVED, DIRECT from the manufacturers in Paris, Lyons and Vienna, six cases of superb cashmere and French camel's hair long shawls, imported expressly for Broadway retail trade—all at moderate prices. GEO. BULPIN, 361 Broadway.

BULPIN, 361 BROADWAY, WILL OPEN THIS WEEK, in all, twenty cases of Stella, Broche and other shawls, the whole of which he will sell at moderate prices, and to which public attention is invited.

BULPIN'S CLOAKS AND MANTILLAS—THE LADIES of New York, and the United States generally, are respectfully informed that BULPIN'S store is now replete with the usual variety of fall and winter fashions in cloaks and mantillas, and which, in consequence of his vastly increasing trade, he can offer at prices hitherto unheard of for first class articles. Paris Mantilla Emporium, 361 Broadway.

CLOAKS, CLOAKS, CLOAKS! Ladies in pursuit of an elegant cloak will find the largest and most superb stock in the city at
MOLYNEUX BELL'S, 58 Canal street.

CURTAIN DAMASKS, LACE AND MUSLIN CURTAINS, window cornices, bands, pins, loops, &c., of the newest, richest and best styles, at wholesale or retail, by CHILDS & SMITH, 449 Pearl street, corner of William.

DRY GOODS FROM AUCTION—2,000 YARDS ALL wool delaine, at 2s. 6d., worth 4s.; debege, 1s.; curtain muslins, at 1s. 6d., lace curtains, elegant curtain damasks, black and colored silks, paramettas, merinoes, French cloths; 800 French corsets at 3s.; flannels, blankets, shawls, &c.
THOMAS TATE, 80 Canal street, corner of Greene.

ENGLISH AND AMERICAN OIL CLOTHS. Full assortment of widths, designs and prices at LORD & TAYLOR'S, 255, 257, 259 and 261 Grand st.

EUREKA! EUREKA!—FORD'S EUREKA SHIRT IS universally worn by the citizens of the United States, also by the aristocracy, gentry, merchants, tradesmen, and people generally of Europe, the British colonies, India and China, &c. being unrivalled for its superiority of fit, work, pattern, and durability. Manufactured and sold only by W. T. FORD, 438 Broadway. Shirts and collars made to order.

ELEGANT DISPLAY OF CARPETINGS.
Including the very latest European designs of
ROYAL VELVET, TAPESTRY, BRUSSELS,
INGRAINS AND THREE-PLYS; ALSO, R. VELVET
AND AXMINSTER MEDALLIONS,
All of which will be sold at
REMARKABLY LOW PRICES.
FORD & TAYLOR, 255, 257, 259 and 261 Grand st.

ECONOMY IN CARPETS. Auburn, Lowell, and low priced carpetings of every description. Also, druggets, mattings, &c., &c., &c.
LORD & TAYLOR, 255, 257, 259 and 261 Grand st.

FALL AND WINTER FASHIONS.
The attention of connoisseurs, and those who are particularly anxious of possessing a neat and beautiful fabric of symmetrical proportions and artistic finish, are respectfully invited to examine the stock of unsurpassed millinery and millinery goods, at
SIMMONS' FRENCH MILLINERY EMPORIUM,
544 Broadway.

FIVE HUNDRED STELLA SHAWLS—AT $6, $10, $12 and $14—all entirely new in style and coloring—on sale this week at BULPIN'S, 361 Broadway.

MOSAIC AND TAPESTRY RUGS. An immense variety of entirely new and beautiful patterns at
LORD & TAYLOR'S, 255, 257, 259 and 261 Grand st.

MOLYNEUX BELL'S FALL GARMENTS.—Fine gray cloth talmas, trimmed stosie moire antique galloons—just the thing for the present season.
Heavy French beaver cloth talmas, trimmed with velvet, and the largest assortment of velvet talmas, adapted to fall wear, that can be found in the city, and at prices to suit the million. 58 Canal street.

NOTICE.—NEW DRESS GOODS,
CLOAKS AND MANTILLAS,
Also two cases of the fashionable
MANTEAU CASTOR,
Received by the pacific, will be opened on Tuesday October 9. A. T. STEWART & CO.,
Broadway, Chambers and Reade streets.

NEW FALL GOODS.
Upholstery, Curtain materials,
and
French paper hangings.
SOLOMON & HART,
No. 243 Broadway,
are now receiving
a full supply of fall goods,
suitable for
Curtains, Furniture Coverings,
and Interior decoration,
which they offer
wholesale and retail
upon the most favorable terms,
To which they invite the attention of the
TRADE AND PUBLIC.
Store closed on Saturdays.

NOTICE.—LADIES GETTING NEW FALL DRESSES, IN order to insure a good fit, should procure a pair of Mrs. Gaynor's celebrated and elegant fitting French woven corsets. Her prices are only half usually charged. GAYNOR, importer of corsets and embroideries, 45 Third avenue, near Tenth street.

ONE THOUSAND BROCHE DOUBLE SHAWLS—FROM $16 and $16 each; the cheapest and most desirable shawls in the city—all beautiful coloring—are now on sale at
BULPIN'S, 361 Broadway.

PARIS EXPOSITION SHAWLS.—THE SUBSCRIBER has just received from his French agents a case of very beautiful broche long shawls, exact copies of those now exhibited at the Palais d'Industrie in Paris, at very moderate prices. GEORGE BULPIN, 361 Broadway.

POPULAR TRADE—
A. T. STEWART & CO.
Will open on Monday, October 8,
a large lot of extra rich
BROCADE, STRIPED AND SATIN PLAID SILKS,
In robes, at $20 each, (original cost from $40 to $60,) purchased in Paris, at a great sacrifice, and received by recent steamers.
Broadway, Chambers and Reade streets.

RICH PARIS DRESS TRIMMINGS AND MILLINERY goods.—I have much pleasure in announcing to my friends that I have purchased at the late auctions from the failures of two French houses, a very heavy quantity of the choicest ribbons, millinery goods, dress and cloak trimmings, ever exhibited in this country, and that we will dispose of them at the smallest advance on auction prices.
M. H. LICHTENSTEIN,
90 Bowery, corner Hester street.
P. S.—Store closed every Saturday.

SHAWLS!! SHAWLS!!! SHAWLS!!!—LADIES IN SEARCH of really pretty and fashionable stella shawls, at moderate prices, will find them at BULPIN'S, 361 Broadway.

TO MANUFACTURERS AND OTHERS.—THE ADVERTISER, having on hand a large assortment of old and new samples of dry goods, foreign manufacture, would be willing to dispose of same. They embrace a great variety of very new styles. To a manufacturer, or a party in the habit of getting up new styles, they would prove an invaluable purchase. For particulars and inspection of the lot, address H. B., box 183 Herald office.

THE SALE OF CHEAP
PLAID AND STRIPED SILKS,
At 68 cents per yard,
And the BLACK RICH WARP LUSTRE
At 8s. per yard,
Will continue during the week.
A. T. STEWART & CO.,
Broadway, Chambers and Reade streets.

WHALEBONE SKIRTS OF IMPROVED PATTERNS for ladies and girls, together with crinoline, muslin, stitched, corded, hair cloth, merino, Cuzco hemp, &c., for sale or made to order, and a complete assortment of flounces, Valenciennes, Mecklin, and Guipure laces.
E. THOMAS, 706 Broadway.

Department-store Advertising in the *New York Herald* in 1855.

DRY GOODS.

FAMILY AND HOTEL LINENS,
OF EVERY DESCRIPTION, SERVICEABLE AND CHEAP.
ALSO, HOUSE-FURNISHING GOODS,
CURTAIN MATERIALS, WINDOW SHADES, OIL, RUGS, CARPETING, OIL-CLOTHS, RUGS,
&c. &c. AT VERY LOW PRICES.
LORD & TAYLOR,
Nos. 461 to 467 BROADWAY.
Nos. 255 to 261 GRAND-ST.
Nos. 47 and 49 CATHARINE-ST.

IRISH POPLINS, PARIS MERINOS,
PRINTED VELOURS, REPS,
DELAINES and
FASHIONABLE DRESS GOODS
Of every kind—fine assortment now ready.
LORD & TAYLOR,
Nos. 461 to 467 BROADWAY.
Nos. 255 to 261 GRAND-ST.
Nos. 47 and 49 CATHARINE-ST.

NEW FALL DRESS SILKS,
RICHEST STYLES OF THE SEASON,
JUST RECEIVED.
ALSO, LOW-PRICED SILKS,
NEW AND DESIRABLE, IN GREAT VARIETY,
LORD & TAYLOR,
Nos. 461 to 467 BROADWAY.
Nos. 255 to 261 GRAND-ST.
Nos. 47 and 49 CATHARINE-ST.

LADIES' AND CHILDREN'S CLOTHING
IN THIS DEPARTMENT OF OUR STORE,
Nos. 461 to 467 BROADWAY,
which is under the direction of
LADIES OF ADMITTED GOOD TASTE,
may be found all the newest Patterns and Shapes of Up
Garments, for
LADIES, CHILDREN, AND INFANTS,
At very reasonable prices. Orders promptly attended to.
LORD & TAYLOR.

FASHIONABLE CLOAKS AND SHAWLS.
MOST ELEGANT ASSORTMENT OF
THE SEASON,
LOW PRICES, AT RETAIL,
LORD & TAYLOR,
Nos. 461 to 467 BROADWAY.
Nos. 255 to 261 GRAND-ST.
Nos. 47 and 49 CATHARINE-ST.

REAL INDIA CAMELS' HAIR
SHAWLS AND SCARFS.
ARNOLD, CONSTABLE & CO.
Will open their Fall
Importations of the above Goods on
MONDAY, Sept. 29.
These goods have been purchased during the present depressed state of the market, and will be offered at moderate prices.
Canal-st., corner of Mercer.

FANCY SILKS,
AT FIFTY CENTS PER YARD.
A good assortment in
PLAIDS AND STRIPES
Will be offered on
MONDAY, Sept. 29.
ARNOLD, CONSTABLE & CO.,
Canal-st., corner of Mercer.

CLOAKS AND SHAWLS.
E. S. MILLS & CO.,
OFFER TO CASH BUYERS GREAT BARGAINS IN
CLOAKS AND SHAWLS,
At Nos. 342 and 344 BROADWAY.

A CARD.
W. JACKSON, No. 551 Broadway, having purchased a
large lot of Bombazines at panic prices, is offering them
at retail at less than cost of importation.
Also, Black and Second Mourning Silks, in every style
and quality, at unusually low prices, together with a large
and general assortment of desirable Mourning Goods,
purchased during the recent panic, which he is offering
at little more than half cost of importation. Special attention is called to Black Silks at 4s and $1 per yard.
W. JACKSON, Importer of Mourning Goods,
No. 551 Broadway, between Spring and Prince sts.

E. BOUTILLIER BROTHERS beg leave to call unusual advantages in selecting NEW DRESS
GOODS for this season. And beg to request an inspection of their OTTOMAN REPS, MERINOES, WOOL PLAIDS, PRINTED DE LAINES, EMMELINES, POULARD DE LAINES, (a new material,) FOIL DE CHEVRE, and other desirable goods.
ALSO,
AN IMMENSE ASSORTMENT OF SHAWLS,
In various styles and of the BEST QUALITIES
No. 309 Canal-st., near Broadway.

CURTAIN MATERIALS.
NEW IMPORTATIONS,
BROCATEL, SATIN and DE LAINE,
DAMASK, &c.
KELTY'S, No. 360 Broadway.

ZEPHYR WORSTED FROM 12½c. Also,
Knit Worsted articles, trimmings, buttons, hosiery,
small wares, fancy goods. Wm. 1140 Broadway, between Sixth and 25th sts., block above Fifth-avenue Hotel.

DRY GOODS.—A BANKRUPT STOCK SELLING
At sacrifice, to close the season, at No. 37 Chamber-st. Silks, Merinoes, Hosiery, Shawls, Laces, Dress Goods, Back Gloves, Mourning Kid Goods, &c. Merchants are invited to call.

MILLINERY.

DRY GOODS.

BALMORAL SKIRTS AND HOOPS
Of every kind, at low prices, during the Holidays.
LORD & TAYLOR,
Nos. 461 to 467 Broadway.
Nos. 255 to 261 Grand-st.
Nos. 47 and 49 Catharine-st.

OUR ENTIRE STOCK OF CLOAKS,
INCLUDING BLACK CLOTH AND
VELVET CLOAKS in great variety, will be offered on
MONDAY, Dec. 30, will be continued, and during the
Holidays,
BELOW COST!!!
A large lot of FANCY CLOTH CLOAKS, at the following low prices:
100 Fancy Cloth Cloaks at $2, formerly $6
200 Fancy Cloth Cloaks at $3 50, formerly $8.
100 Fancy Cloth Cloaks at $7, formerly $12.
100 Fancy Cloth Cloaks at $8, formerly $20.
50 Fancy Cloth Cloaks at $14, formerly $25.
ALSO,
One case RICH EMBROIDERED VELVET CLOAKS
and short SAQUES, of the prevailing Paris styles, received per steamer Europa,
SUITABLE FOR HOLIDAY PRESENTS,
will be sold at less than the cost of importation, owing to
the advanced season.
LORD & TAYLOR,
Nos. 461 to 467 BROADWAY.
Nos. 255 to 261 GRAND-ST.
Nos. 47 and 49 CATHARINE-ST.

PARIS KID GLOVES AT 62½ CENTS.
500 DOZEN LADIES' PARIS KID GLOVES,
RETAILED AT 62½ CENTS PER PAIR.
LORD & TAYLOR,
Nos. 461 to 467 BROADWAY.

RICH PARIS DRESS SILKS,
SUITABLE FOR PROMENADE,
DINNER, CARRIAGE and EVENING DRESSES.
VERY CHOICE STYLES—CHEAP!
LORD & TAYLOR,
Nos. 461 to 467 BROADWAY.
Nos. 255 to 261 GRAND-ST.
Nos. 47 and 49 CATHARINE-ST.

GENTLEMEN'S TIES, SCARFS, HDKFS.,
GLOVES, HOSIERY, SILK AND
WOOL DRAWERS, &c., &c.
LARGE ASSORTMENT—CHEAP!
LORD & TAYLOR,
Nos. 461 to 467 BROADWAY.
Nos. 255 to 261 GRAND-ST.
Nos. 47 and 49 CATHARINE-ST.

EMBROIDERIES FOR THE HOLIDAYS,
IN SETS, COLLARS, HANDKERCHIEFS,
CAPS, WAISTS, &c., &c.
Also, low-priced and
RICH LACES IN GREAT VARIETY.
LORD & TAYLOR,
Nos. 461 to 467 BROADWAY.
Nos. 255 to 261 GRAND-ST.
Nos. 47 and 49 CATHARINE-ST.

TARLETONS FOR EVENING DRESSES,
SPANGLED, EMBROIDERED AND
PLAIN, at one-third
THE COST OF IMPORTATION.
LORD & TAYLOR,
Nos. 461 to 467 BROADWAY.

FASHIONABLE DRESS GOODS.
AN IMMENSE ASSORTMENT AT
low prices.
FOR HOLIDAY PRESENTS.
LORD & TAYLOR,
Nos. 461 to 467 BROADWAY.
Nos. 255 to 261 GRAND-ST.
Nos. 47 and 49 CATHARINE-ST.

Department-store Advertising from the *New York Times* of 1861.

BUILDING NEWSPAPER ADVERTISING 17

A strong feature of such advertising was that, whether it occupied a full column or a full page, it created a sensation by the mere fact that any one would spend so much money for an advertisement. No one had done this before, so Bonner, by taking a page for an announcement or for the publication of the opening chapters of a new serial, amazed the town and so got its attention. Needless to say, he was a great believer in publicity and had courage to use it far in advance of his time, but he rigidly refused to sell any of the space in his own publication.

He decided to give the people articles and stories written by famous people and to advertise these specialties more largely than anything had ever been advertised before. Naturally he made a great success.

At first he would buy a full column to announce the contents of his paper, an almost unheard-of use of advertising space. Then he would use half a page, then a full page, and finally all the advertising space a newspaper would sell him, which in itself created so much talk throughout New York and the country that his advertising was doubly effective.

As Bennett of the *Herald* would allow no display, Bonner ordered his ads. "run in," giving one sentence announcing a story which was repeated throughout a full column. This also made a lot of talk. He is said to have spent $27,000 for one week's advertising and over $150,000 in a single year, which was an enormous sum in those days. He even paid the *Herald* $2,000 for a single advertisement.

When this advertisement was printed the pastor of the church which Bonner attended is reported to have become very much agitated, says Hudson's *History of*

Journalism. Upon looking over the *Herald* at the breakfast-table he said to his wife:

"I must call upon Mr. Bonner immediately after breakfast; I am really anxious about him."

"Why, what is the matter? Is he sick?"

"I don't know that he is sick," replied the kind-hearted clergyman, "but I think he must be insane. Just look at the *Herald;* it is Bonner on every page. If he has paid for that he will be ruined. Give me my hat."

Mr. Bonner was surprised at an early call from his spiritual adviser.

"I have called," said the clergyman, "to talk to you about the advertisement, or, rather, series of advertisements which appeared in the *Herald* this morning. May I ask if you paid the regular rate for them?"

"I gave my check for two thousand dollars for a single insertion," answered Bonner.

The clergyman, with a deep sigh, wiped his forehead with his handkerchief, remarking: "Two thousand dollars! Two thousand dollars!"

After a moment's reflection, as if overcome by the magnitude of the sum thus recklessly thrown away, he said:

"Mr. Bonner, I have called upon you as a friend. You know that I am one. I felt that there was something wrong. What a waste of money! Two thousand dollars for one advertisement in one publication! Would not a single square like this, for instance," pointing out a ten-line advertisement—"would not that, at a cost of a few dollars, have answered your purpose as well as all that display and costly space?"

Much amused at the perplexity of his amiable

pastor, Mr. Bonner replied: "I see how it strikes you, my good friend. But if I had put in the single square you mention, would you have taken the trouble to call upon me to remonstrate?"

"Why, no! I don't think I should have noticed the matter at all!"

"Then," said Mr. Bonner, triumphantly, "you have demonstrated the correctness of my policy. Every other reader of *The Herald* is as much astonished as you are. This is the secret of advertising. Eureka!"

One of Bonner's ideas was to get the three best-known editors of the daily press in New York—Bennett, Greeley, and Raymond—to write for *The Ledger*. The public was astonished to learn through an advertisement in all the papers what he had done.

Then he induced twelve distinguished clergymen to write twelve stories. Afterward he obtained twelve contributions from college presidents. "Norwood," a novel by Henry Ward Beecher, costing $20,000, had a famous run. "The Life of General Grant," by his father, Jesse Grant, not only sold thousands of copies of the *Ledger*, but obtained many votes for the general for the Presidency.

Bonner was a courageous pioneer. He kept doing things and advertising them so that nearly anything he did was advertising, which made more readers for *The Ledger*. He paid large sums for the sort of reading-matter his imagination led him to believe the people would buy.

One day when asked whether he kept Dexter, the most famous race-horse in the world, and an expensive stable, and did all the remarkable things he did in *The Ledger* for advertising purposes, he replied:

"I never engaged a writer or bought anything or did anything as an advertisement. What I have done has been natural to me and because I wanted to do it, but never was the impelling motive the notoriety that was likely to follow. When I want advertisements I pay for them as advertisements."

Whether this was true or not, he got results, and stands as a unique figure in American advertising.

Barnum was another great advertiser of that time, besides being the first really shrewd free-publicity grafter. His press agent, Tody Hamilton, created a style for the Barnum advertising which was as unique as it was effective. Alliteration and exaggerated statements played the leading part in his copy, which was printed in advance of the show all over the country.

Hamilton had a way of doing things which would not be tolerated to-day that made town talk. For example, during the week previous to the opening of the show a story would get out that one of Barnum's wild beasts had escaped, and every mother would keep her children close at home until the danger had been removed.

His exploitation of the "sacred white elephant," the "dog-faced boy," and a long chain of other features, heralded by columns of advertising and free publicity, reached the people, and induced them to pay millions of dollars for admission to his show.

In this connection I remember an odd experience, showing how Tody Hamilton sought to break down *The Herald*'s rule regarding display. He tried to get that paper to set up a huge figure of an elephant composed of the letters "Barnum," one-sixth the

AN ORIGINAL LETTER OF LOUIS NAPOLEON IN TO-DAY'S LEDGER.—Outside of our country there is no other person whose opinion and disposition in regard to our Southern rebellion are so important, in our own estimation and that of the world, as Louis Napoleon's. So far as his declarations go, he seems to be inclined to let us alone, and that is all we ask of him. Not only have we his disavowal of any intention to intermeddle with our affairs, recently addressed to the French Chamber of Deputies, but to-day Mr. Bonner places before the readers of the LEDGER a copy of an autograph letter, which has not previously been published, written by Louis Napoleon to the Hon. Edward Everett, and which has been procured expressly for the LEDGER. This letter will be read with the deepest interest at the present time, and everybody will be gratified by the friendly feeling which it expresses. The LEDGER will be ready at 12 o'clock to-day, (Monday,) and for sale at all the book stores and news dépôts.

A Sample Column Ad. of Bonner's *Ledger* in 1861.

Another Bonner Ad. Showing How He Advertised the Goods Back in the '60's.

space up and down being occupied by each of the letters.

The Herald, in accordance with its then independent policy, declined to set up the ad. Hamilton came over to me in the old *Sunday Mercury* office and asked me to set it up and lend him the type. We did the job, and he took it over to the *Herald* office, but it was refused on the ground that all *Herald* ads. must be set up in the *Herald* office.

Only a few men of this type live in a generation. In ours, Tom Lipton to a limited extent and Henry Ford as a shining light, are among those who understand the wonderful possibilities of advertising and have the courage to use it. Yet any one with the goods, the know how, and the courage can win fame and fortune by buying the commodity we sell—newspaper advertising.

It is a remarkable fact that nearly all the great enduring successes in advertising were built up by the use of newspaper circulations much lower than can now be bought for about half the price paid for the smaller ones. Until the coming of the high-speed perfecting press in the 'eighties, anything like our present daily newspaper production was an utter impossibility.

In my boyhood we printed from flat sheets fed into a huge central drum, first running one side through and then the other. We got better printing, but no speed. Then came the perfecting press delivering flat sheets, and then the folder delivering the paper printed, packed, folded, and counted with an accuracy and speed never previously thought possible.

The advertiser has derived most benefit from the great improvements in mechanical production, for he can buy his space to-day in papers of over 200,000 circulation for less than was charged by those of 50,000 or 60,000 in the 'eighties. Competition among newspapers and foolish efforts to lead in volume of advertising carried have provided great opportunities for the ruthless space-buyer.

To indicate the progress of newspaper circulation in New York City, I have made a few extracts from Hudson's *History of Journalism*. In May, 1816, the circulation of the New York daily newspapers was as follows:

Mercantile Advertiser....	2,000	*Courier*...............	920
Gazette.................	1,750	*Columbian*............	825
Evening Post...........	1,600	*National Advocate*......	875
Commercial Advertiser...	1,200		

Only two of these newspapers still survive—*The Globe and Commercial Advertiser* and *The Evening Post;* the former established in 1793 and the latter in 1801.

"In 1833, the year *The Sun* was started," says Hudson, "we find that the total number of copies of all papers printed in New York City was 6,000,000 to 8,000,000 in that year." This meant a total sale of between 20,000 and 28,000 a day. Also:

The population of New York in 1835 was 270,089. The population of the United States was, in round numbers, 15,000,000. Only one paper in 1835 circulated 6,000 copies daily. All the others were far below 5,000 and running down to 500.

In the cities of New York and Brooklyn, containing a population of 300,000, the daily circulation of the penny papers is not less than 70,000. This is nearly sufficient to place a newspaper in the hands of every man in the two cities, and even of every boy old enough to read.

BUILDING NEWSPAPER ADVERTISING 23

NEW YORK PAPERS IN NOVEMBER, 1842

Cash Papers		Wall Street Papers	
Herald—2 cents	15,000	*Courier and Inquirer*	7,000
Sun—1 cent	20,000	*Journal of Commerce*	7,500
Aurora—2 cents	5,000	*Express*	6,000
Morning Post—2 cents	3,000	*American*	1,800
Plebeian—2 cents	2,000	*Commercial Advertiser*	5,000
Chronicle—1 cent	5,000	*Evening Post*	2,500
Tribune—1½ cents	9,500	*Standard*	500
Union—2 cents	1,000		
Tatler—1 cent	2,000		

In 1847 *The New York Tribune*, feeling proud of its circulation, challenged *The Herald* to a show-down for $200 to go to two orphan asylums. On the audit *The Herald* proved 28,946 to 28,195 for *The Tribune*, and *The Tribune* paid.

In 1851 Horace Greeley, in testifying before a committee of the House of Commons regarding the effect of the stamp tax on advertising in Great Britain, gave these figures:

Average daily circulation of all New York newspapers, 130,000, of which 60,000 were circulated in the city, which then had 700,000 population.

The New York Sun had 50,000 circulation, *The Herald* 25,000.

Total circulation of daily newspapers in London was then 60,000 a day.

The daily circulation of newspapers in the United States was about 1,000,000, divided among 250 daily newspapers.

There were 2,500 journals published in the United States.

In May, 1870, *The New York Sun* inserted the following advertisement in *The New York Herald:*

BUILDING NEWSPAPER ADVERTISING

TWO AND A HALF MILLIONS A MONTH.

THE NEW YORK SUN
AHEAD OF ALL COMPETITORS.
The Circulation of
THE SUN
is many thousands larger
than that of any other daily newspaper.
The aggregate daily editions of
THE SUN
last week were
SIX HUNDRED AND TWENTY-TWO THOUSAND
FOUR HUNDRED
(622,400)

The daily circulation of THE SUN for the four weeks of May was as follows:

First week...........................	611,800
Second week..........................	620,100
Third week...........................	614,600
Fourth week..........................	622,400
Total in four weeks................	2,468,900

or nearly two millions and a half. This is equal to a daily average of 102,870 (one hundred and two thousand eight hundred and seventy) for the twenty-four days of publication. This simple statement of facts is sufficient evidence of the immense and growing popularity of the SUN. It demonstrates conclusively that the Sun is no servant of a clique or class, but

THE GREAT ORGAN OF THE PEOPLE

As such it will continue to uphold with all its might that which is good and true, while it will fearlessly expose knavery, corruption, and imbecility in high or low places, wherever their practice imperils public safety or private virtue.

THE SUN IS THE BEST AND MOST READABLE NEWSPAPER published. Its news is the freshest, most in-

BUILDING NEWSPAPER ADVERTISING 25

teresting and sprightliest current, and no expense is spared to make it just what the great mass of the people require.

As a matter of information for such as may not be aware of the fact, we may mention that the Sun sheds its genial beams upon all at the

MODEST PRICE OF TWO CENTS.

Another glimpse of old-style advertising of newspapers is that of *The Weekly Sun* or *"Dollar Sun,"* as it was called in 1869, as follows:

THE DOLLAR SUN.
Chas. A. Dana, Editor.

The cheapest, smartest, and best New York newspaper. Everybody likes it. Three editions: DAILY $6; SEMI-WEEKLY, $2; and WEEKLY, $1 a year. ALL THE NEWS at half price. Full reports of markets, agriculture, Farmers' and Fruit-growers' Clubs, and a complete story in every Weekly and Semi-Weekly number. A present of valuable plants and vines to every subscriber; inducements to canvassers unsurpassed. $1000 Life Insurances, Grand Pianos, Mowing Machines, Parlor Organs, Sewing Machines, etc., among the premiums. Specimens and lists free. Send a Dollar and try it.

I. W. ENGLAND, Publisher Sun, New York.

Through the years from 1870 to, say, 1900 numerous proprietary medicines and a variety of trade-marked articles were forced to enormous sales by the use of two-, three-, and four-inch copy, running every other day by the year, but only a few of their proprietors have continued such advertising to the present day.

The newspapers made special discounts for 156-time advertisements of this character, and found them an important source of revenue. That the advertising was resultful was proved by the enormous business created by the constantly repeated copy, which, aside from causing large sales, made the names used familiar in every household throughout the country.

Thirty or forty years ago the use of big black Gothic type and the exploitation of nostrums and fake sales, which to-day would not be tolerated in any self-respecting newspaper, seriously interfered with legitimate advertising and created the general remark, "Oh! that is just advertising!"

Some of these practices, long discarded in our larger cities, are still in vogue among the smaller newspapers in certain sections of the country. Newspapers carrying such copy are shunned by large national advertisers having legitimate goods to sell, for no one wishes to have his advertising topped by or alongside of an offensive medical ad., or seen in such company.

III

The Advent of Heavy Display

EXAGGERATION and false pretense thus marked the first growth of newspaper advertising, and our newspapers, contemplating only the increasing revenue, ignored all responsibility for what they printed. Flash one-night-only sales of junk, quack medicines, fraudulent real estate, and mining promotions had their day.

The direct result of this gross misuse of the advertising columns, which ran parallel with blatant sensationalism and black heads on news articles, made it extremely difficult for legitimate advertising to be seen.

Money came to the newspapers in chunks, and the yellow papers, with their cheap popularity contests for quantity circulation, overturned all old-time practices, until the reputable and sound advertisers commenced to take stock and, in concert with readers, demand a change.

Restrictions directed against the offering of quack medicines and habit-forming drugs were invoked, and the newspapers made for decent people gradually eliminated first one variety of offensive business and then another, generally finding that honest business more than replaced the offensive business they had thrown out.

All of us who went through the period recollect the

vast number of so-called tonics and cures, composed primarily of alcohol, narcotics, or other drugs, which gave the ignorant who bought them a hard kick for their money. There were advertisements of abortion medicines, venereal-disease cures, consumption cures, and such with vulgar and offensive black type and nasty crude cuts to arrest the eye and mar the newspaper page. The Louisiana and other lotteries likewise appealed for the hard-earned dollars of the poor.

I do not say these things for the purpose of showing that the newspapers were depraved or soulless, but to bring out in contrast the great successful newspapers of the present day which carry three or four times the volume of advertising appearing in these old days, free from all offensive or fraudulent announcements.

As shown by specimens of advertising during the '80's and early '90's, our newspapers had yet to come into their own. The use of full-page copy by retail merchants, with occasional double trucks, had not yet arrived in the East from the Central West.

Advertising rates were too high in comparison with circulations to make profitable such large use of space as was being indulged in in the smaller Western cities, where publishers fairly gave away their space and merchants early discovered the pulling power of real advertising.

With the arrival of Joseph Pulitzer in the East, with *The New York World*, imbued with the progressive Western spirit of his *St. Louis Post-Dispatch*, and the low rates made by him to stimulate volume advertising in his New York newspaper, the trick was done, and big advertising became popular among the New York merchants.

The Herald had the big business of that day, having had virtually a monopoly of it for years, so Pulitzer hired Bill Henry, the business manager of that paper, who knew all the New York advertisers, and told him to "get the business" and to make a rate "that would get it." If my memory serves me correctly, the rate fixed for *The World* in May, 1883, was 2½ cents per line.

At this low price, merchants accustomed to using one full column in *The Herald* took larger space in *The World* for less money than they paid *The Herald*, but it was not until well into the '90's that pages and double pages came into vogue. It did not take Pulitzer long, with his yellow-newspaper methods, pictures, and gift enterprise, to pass *The Herald* in circulation and to carry through successfully the advertising campaigns which he created and pushed.

He stiffened his rates as his circulation increased. His progress was rapid and for years he held a record unprecedented in New York journalism. From the very start he sold advertising on the basis of proved circulation, with "circulation books open to all," while the old *Herald* and other newspapers sold "high-water mark" and mere claims.

In the light of later experience, Pulitzer was a sure winner, with the others gradually slipping back into the moribund class, sooner or later to go through the hands of sheriff or receiver. The Pulitzer type of journalism at the start was sensational enough to appeal to thousands who had probably never before bought any newspaper; but through it all he made a real newspaper.

Pulitzer had the New York morning newspaper situation all his own way until 1896, when William

R. Hearst landed in town and bought the old *Morning Journal*, which he changed to *The American* and by similar and more despicable methods secured an even greater circulation than Pulitzer, by going farther afield for it.

It was a cruel race for supremacy between these two new-type adventurers in yellow journalism, but incidentally it produced new newspaper readers by the hundred thousand. It was particularly painful for the old-line newspapers which adhered to old standards, with their lights growing dimmer day by day in comparison with the great leaders.

The good old *New York Times* was driven far up on the rocks into the hands of a receiver. Then came Adolph S. Ochs from Chattanooga, with a sounder kind of journalism than New York had ever known, which he applied slowly but surely, until to-day he has as much circulation as and more display advertising than either the *World* or *American*.

Up to 1896 the great independent evening newspaper had not been known in New York. Lawson had shown the way with his *Chicago Daily News*, Nelson with his *Kansas City Star*, Sir Hugh Graham with his *Montreal Star*, and Pulitzer with his *St. Louis Post-Dispatch*. But New York had not felt the impulse.

In 1897 Pulitzer decided to start an evening edition of *The World*, and Hearst, not to be outdone, promptly launched his *Evening Journal* with 200,000 circulation overnight. Such a circulation start had never been seen anywhere. Advertisers who had established their business on newspaper circulations of less than 100,000 now had opportunities for broader appeal thrust on them in a way that made them fairly dizzy.

During this period what we know as newspaper

BUILDING NEWSPAPER ADVERTISING

advertising really had its birth in New York and became general throughout the country. A highly competitive market enabled advertisers to buy space at a lower rate per line per thousand than ever before and to secure wonderful increase in traffic.

The two great yellow evening newspapers grew like mushrooms, *The World* to nearly 400,000 and *The Journal* to 600,000 and even 800,000 on occasions.

As in the morning field, a group of three better-grade evening newspapers gradually came forward during 1903 and 1904—*The Evening Sun, The Evening Mail,* and *The Globe.* The latter two formerly sold for two cents per copy, and made a strong bid for popular favor.

The Mail changed its price from two cents to one cent in 1903, and the old *Commercial Advertiser* changed its name to *The Globe* and its price to one cent in 1904. New York was ripe for such newspapers, which grew by gradual process as *The New York Times* had done, and they had among the three in 1917 over 500,000 circulation.

The success of the decent journalism practised by *The New York Times, The Evening Sun,* and *The Globe*, making papers that reached 750,000 purchasers a day and refusing to print offensive or fraudulent advertising, marked the opening of an important era in the development of modern effective advertising.

War necessities made all daily newspapers go to two cents per copy in January, 1918, which by the end of that year found themselves with net daily sales almost if not fully equal to those previously enjoyed at one cent the copy, with other and less worthy journals showing striking slumps in sales.

Consciously or unconsciously, New York had swung

into line with the best experience in Chicago, Philadelphia, St. Louis, Kansas City, Washington, Minneapolis, and other cities, and succeeded in establishing high-grade newspapers with large enough circulation to cover the field.

In my opinion the foolish quest for mere quantity of circulation is more largely responsible for our newspapers going so far afield for circulation growth as to make such distribution of questionable value to the advertiser, and put a premium upon much false pretense.

Newspaper circulation of the most useful kind is local sales—in the trading zone immediately surrounding city of publication. Such circulation reached with advertising in connection with the names of local dealers when the goods can be seen and bought is most effective.

In the case of *The New York Globe* we could easily add from 50,000 to 100,000 circulation by going far afield for it with pre-dated editions or special offers, but we never have done so, for we recognized that there was no money in it for us or our advertisers. Our sale is over 94 per cent. in Greater New York and immediate suburbs.

IV

Advertising from the Newspaper Viewpoint

It may be set down as a fundamental principle that the newspaper which sells its advertising space except as a by-product—the right for a definite consideration to appeal to its readers—can never become a community institution with the full confidence of the people.

The experiment has been tried times without end, but history clearly proves that those who have gone farthest have first made their newspapers and then sold advertising space. The one-cent newspaper of yesterday, with a heavy volume of advertising a prime necessity, made the advertiser entirely too important a factor.

Neither Victor F. Lawson with *The Chicago Daily News*, Colonel W. R. Nelson with *The Kansas City Star*, W. L. McLean with *The Philadelphia Bulletin*, Joseph Pulitzer with *The New York World*, nor Adolph S. Ochs with *The New York Times* ever had any delusion regarding the proper relationship.

Even Hearst, with all his deplorable methods, has always been willing to devote enormous sums to give his various sheets a large circulation before making any serious efforts to secure advertising for them on any basis which would or might give the advertiser a strangle-hold.

No single advertiser or group of advertisers is so important to a newspaper as the newspaper is to the advertiser. Too often have the advertisers of a town, by combination, sought to discipline a newspaper, only to find that in the end they had lost more than they had gained in the process.

The sooner our newspaper-advertising men learn to appreciate the fact that their newspapers are made primarily for the reader and to serve the best interests of the public, regardless of the likes or dislikes of any advertisers, the better and more effective advertising men they will be.

No sane person expects more of a club, a restaurant, or a store than he pays for on the same basis as any one else, yet through our own weakness and lack of backbone some of us have brought many to the idea that they can, at least measurably, control our utterances if we allow them to buy a few lines of our space, and that often at too low a rate.

Until our newspaper men are brought to a sounder basis of ordinary commercial understanding or intelligence I suppose they will look upon every thousand dollars received over the counter for advertising as one thousand dollars profit. When they learn, through the application of accurate cost figures, that many of the one thousand dollars they earn yield only one hundred dollars of net profit or perhaps none at all, they will not be so apt to tolerate the indignities they have submitted to in the past.

By the same token, we should all understand that even in the case of the most successful department stores they figure that without advertising they could secure only one-half of the business they now do. In other words, without advertising they could not live.

BUILDING NEWSPAPER ADVERTISING 35

In Chicago in 1898 there was a stereotypers' strike which forced all the daily newspapers to suspend publication for eight or ten days. Practically all traffic in the great State Street stores ceased. After a few days the merchants told me that if the thing continued for thirty days many of them would fail.

This was the most notable and definite demonstration of the power of newspaper advertising ever coming within my experience and gives one a world of confidence in dealing with advertisers who would have us think that they alone keep us alive.

When there is a strike, or an elevator falls in one of our stores, the management's first move is to call up the newspaper offices in an effort to keep the news out of the papers, for fear knowledge of it might deter women from entering the establishment. People who live in glass houses should be very careful whom they stone. If our newspapers were to tell the truth regarding the working conditions in some of our lower-grade retail shops, some of those who now pose as philanthropists would prove to be mere slave-drivers, buying goods and labor regardless of decencies, to sell at the highest price the traffic will bear.

I say this without any intention of casting aspersions at the thousands of upright merchants doing a clean and reputable business, but for the purpose of bringing to the forefront the type who cause newspapers a large amount of trouble.

To withstand the subtle influence of advertisers and others who seek to get from us thousands of dollars' worth of free publicity is to make our newspapers sounder business institutions which will command greater respect.

When merchants give away their goods to some on

request and charge others our newspapers may be justified in permitting one man with more cheek than others to secure publicity free of cost, while the others are obliged to seek similar results through costly advertising.

Newspapers have yet to establish and maintain rigid standards that will eliminate the clever work of the press agents, who, as a rule, are renegades from the ranks of honorable journalism. I know of corporations which pay thousands of dollars a year to put stuff over on the newspapers and figure that they save heavy expense for advertising by so doing.

Our great independent newspapers long ago adopted the policy of no "free puffs" for anybody under any circumstance. They boost all worth-while community or charitable enterprises, but do not permit themselves to be used for the exploitation of commercial efforts for profit.

Such newspapers are the best advertising mediums. The public gradually learns that they are sound and dependable. Every advertiser appreciates that no one else gets free publicity, which is the same as a preferential discount, as bait for business.

V

Co-operation Often Discouraged by Advertiser

IN the light of my experience, it is not what newspaper advertising costs the advertiser so much as what results he gets for every thousand dollars spent in advertising that should concern him. As long as price remains the large consideration in the mind of the buyer, he is going to limit the service the seller can afford to deliver to him.

If the advertiser desires to secure even an approximation of what is within the possibilities for him he should seek to get the best service obtainable, and appreciate that to do so he must be willing to pay for it, where he can buy it.

This is said without any purpose of criticism, but only to stimulate the spirit which should exist between the buyer and seller of advertising. There are to-day only a very few newspapers in the whole country which sell the sort of service I have in mind.

Only too often continuous support of those who have demonstrated their willingness and ability to render this service has been refused by those who have most profited by it. If the advertiser fails to appreciate the sort of service best calculated to produce the most profitable results for him, of what use is it for the publisher to seek to maintain the service?

Some are inclined to think that the advertising agent is largely responsible for this attitude. They think the agent, in his attempts to justify his own service, inclines to minimize the effective service of the newspaper.

In this I believe that they are mistaken, but in a statement before the New York Advertising Club in January, 1916, Stanley Resor said he would rather have the amount spent by the newspapers for co-operative service made available for the use of agents to stimulate definite accounts.

Of course the agent, like any other human being, wants to emphasize the service he renders his client. If the newspaper encroaches upon the service the agent has marked out for himself, we can't blame him for looking upon this as rather interfering with him than helping him.

In this respect there has been a marked change in the viewpoint of most agents and newspaper publishers through a growing feeling of good faith and co-operation. Our modern up-to-the-minute agencies welcome the co-operation of newspapers, as will be shown in other chapters. It stands to reason that, through the machinery of a multiplicity of newspapers, data and local information can be collected more quickly than in any other way.

As we shall see later, a spirit of mutual understanding is growing which I am confident is going to be highly beneficial to all concerned—advertisers, agents, and newspapers. Our newspapers may not be able to secure the exact kind of data an agent may want, but they certainly can assemble sufficient dependable information for a preliminary survey of a **campaign.**

BUILDING NEWSPAPER ADVERTISING 39

It is nonsense for any one to contend that the vast sums of money spent by *The Chicago Tribune* in its promotional department have been wasted or could have been used more advantageously. James Keeley in 1913, when general manager of *The Chicago Tribune*, stated:

> We are endeavoring to show and demonstrate to various advertisers the opportunities that exist for them in the territory in which *The Chicago Tribune* is printed. We have set aside a fund of $50,000 for use this year for the purpose, this being in addition to the $100,000 or more that we will spend in advertising our advertising.

In connection with *The New York Globe's* food advertising we have had frequent and abundant opportunity during the last four years to study the matter in many very interesting variations. Notwithstanding the repeated evidence of lack of appreciation and continued support, we were not discouraged in our efforts to prove a theory by repeated demonstrations.

For example, we have taken an unknown sound article and, by putting back of it all the power and consumer demand we could, given it a substantial distribution and sale, only to get as our sole reward the satisfaction of having accomplished the result, the manufacturer, thinking we could be of no further use to him, quitting our council.

In *Newspaper Building* I presented a closer study of some of the demonstrations by *The Globe* than I can give here. We have had customers, whom we have made in a business way, come to New York with subsequent campaigns and use other mediums which have paid no attention to pure foods, for the reason that they knew *The Globe* was fighting their battle, regardless of their advertising.

It should be obvious to any advertiser that the newspaper which specializes in any particular field is read by people in the community interested in that subject, and that it will produce quicker and more profitable results for their advertising. No newspaper could afford to carry on a feature unless it had an important following. Yet there are many who waste their money, ignoring such co-operation and using other newspapers in which they must till the soil by heavy expenditures before they can secure any sort of a crop.

This *The Globe* has proved most convincingly in many different directions. During the year 1913, when it was conducting its great initial campaign for pure food, it accumulated upward of 50,000 letters from readers asking what foods were sound and where they could be bought.

When we devised our Pure Food Directory and permitted the manufacturers of honest foods that were approved by Mr. McCann to advertise, it was as if we had taken down the service gates of a dam. Thousands of people immediately rushed to these dealers, demanding their products.

Without premeditation we had overturned all practices and traditions of the trade, and proved that consumer demand sufficiently intensified can force distribution despite the opposition or reluctance of jobbers or dealers. We cut out all chance of substitution, for our readers were acting on the advice of Mr. McCann and not on that of the corner grocer.

I touch upon this phase of the matter only to

indicate that I am not merely considering a theory, but actual experience.

My object is to drive home to advertisers and newspaper publishers alike the conviction that through sincere co-operative effort newspaper advertising can be brought to produce results far beyond anything coming within the ordinary experience of those merely trafficking in space.

The book publishers long ago found out that they got best results from those newspapers which specialized in book reviews. It was obvious to them that a constituency which read such matter regularly—and the newspaper could not long continue to print such matter if it was not read—was ever on the lookout for new books.

Likewise the newspapers which devote much space to real estate, financial, insurance, and legal news are always the most effective mediums for advertising along these lines. It seems almost absurd to have to prove such self-evident truths, but some of our badly advised advertisers operate without regard to them.

It is almost impossible for a single newspaper to specialize in every direction and to be equally effective for all advertising, much as we publishers would like to make people believe the contrary of our own publications.

This leads us to the point of my argument, that advertisers, advertising agents, and publishers can get together to accomplish results far beyond our fondest dreams. If the advertiser will support with his advertising the efforts of publishers specializing in his field, he will get greater results and enable the newspaper to render even greater service as support justifies.

For example, regarding food advertising in New York, *The Globe* carries twice as much as any other evening newspaper, and many times as much as any of the morning newspapers. As a result we can afford to maintain an expensive service and devote much space to the subject.

It should be obvious that in the circumstances no food campaign in New York should be attempted without *The Globe*. Its readers are interested in foods and will respond to food advertising, while the readers of a newspaper that devotes no special attention to the subject may pass such advertising by.

Likewise with respect to advertising addressed to women, such as that of the large retail shops, *The Globe* among the evening newspapers and *The Times* in the morning, reaching the class with money to spend, and specializing in genuine fashion departments read by women, to-day carry the largest volume of the better-grade business.

The Times by its long and faithful presentation of the news of Wall Street, the courts, and business, stands in a class by itself among the morning papers for advertising appealing to people interested in those affairs. Likewise, *The Times*, by its capable and reliable book news and reviews, has built up book advertising and merits larger support from book publishers for their announcements than any other New York morning newspaper.

Purposeful specialization by important newspapers is entirely different from pretended specialization by weak journals seeking advertising in exchange for free publicity.

Some advertisers fail to perceive the difference between newspapers and newspaper service. I have

BUILDING NEWSPAPER ADVERTISING 43

in mind one very small newspaper which is made for a class which probably never bought anything through an advertisement. Yet there are those too dense to realize that they can produce no more tangible results by using it than by changing their money from one pocket to another.

There are still many advertisers who think that because they advertise in a journal they can control its policy, and others who withdraw their business because the newspaper may editorially touch upon their enterprise in a way that does not sit well on their stomachs.

Business men advertise to the readers of a newspaper. By buying advertising they cannot prevent a worth-while newspaper from handling any subject in any way it wants. If they withdraw their business they are the losers, for they lose their opportunity, and the newspaper more often than not loses nothing by the omission.

VI

Appearance of the Advertising Agent

COUPLED with advertising as an important factor in all business promotion for our newspapers came a middleman between the seller and buyer of space, in the shape of the advertising agent. Being paid a commission by the newspaper, he was for a long time supposed to represent the publisher in securing and clearing business.

For example, when the business of an advertiser justified the use of several newspapers, and particularly in other cities throughout the country, he naturally went to an advertising agent representing a large number of newspapers for advice, service, and information.

His space cost him no more than it would if tendered over the counters of the various newspapers used, for the newspaper publisher by the allowance of a commission paid the advertising agent for the service rendered to the client, just the same as the insurance companies pay the agent to whom a man goes for insurance.

All of this was very simple and effective until too many newspaper men entered the advertising-agency business, agents began to extract large profits from the traffic, and too many newspapers with aching

BUILDING NEWSPAPER ADVERTISING 45

voids commenced to bid for business by extra inducements in the way of special rates.

Those of us in the business during the '80's in New York well remember W. L. Beadnell, W. H. H. Hull, Lyman D. Morse, George Norman, Daniel Clark, Richard Bell, N. W. Ayer, G. P. Rowell, and scores of others who, by faithful service, helped clients to increased traffic through their special knowledge of the sort of advertising that brought results.

But in spite of the sincere agents, conditions grew worse, as almost any one who wanted to do so could hang out a shingle, get credit from the newspapers, and bamboozle the would-be advertiser. Practices grew up which it has taken a generation to live down, so that even to-day certain newspapers view with suspicion any overtures from all but a few advertising agents.

I want to say here that in my opinion the newspapers by their own foolishness and weakness were largely responsible for what happened to them. It took them years to start standardizing the recognition and credits of advertising agents and advertisers.

George P. Rowell, one of the pioneer agents and the creator of *Printers' Ink*, established Ripans Tabules by securing thousands upon thousands of dollars of advertising in exchange for advertising space in that trade paper during its early days.

Dr. R. V. Pierce, of Buffalo, likewise secured thousands upon thousands of dollars of very cheap space by offering the newspapers machinery and such articles upon which he made enormous profits, in exchange for space for advertising his "Golden Medical Discovery."

Everything from jack-knives to stoves and dogs were handed to the newspapers for space. It got so that an advertising agent would make you a bet that by attaching a dollar bill to a piece of copy and furnishing a cut a certain percentage of newspapers would finally accept it and run the ad.

Then again there developed the man who secured blanket space in a number of newspapers for money or trade or various promises, and peddled it about for the highest rate he could get, more frequently than not failing to make good payment to the newspaper.

After a time, even in the early days, some of the advertising agents began to think of themselves as advertisers' representatives. Instead of stimulating business for the newspapers they sat back and compelled the newspapers to solicit them for business, and many of them added service exactions on the publisher.

The so-called newspaper directory, the first of which to become an important factor being Rowell's (now N. W. Ayer's American Newspaper Directory), was a source of annoyance and a means of graft for the advertising agents. Every year the publishers were urged to take a page in the directories at high rates, to be deducted from business given them.

The agents in many cases went so far as openly to state that they would give preference to the papers giving business to their directories. This, of course, caused resentment among the newspapers, which refused to be blackmailed, and advertisers, whose money was spent to feather the agents' nests and not where it would do the advertiser the most good.

Despite all these handicaps, the business of commercial stimulation grew by leaps and bounds, for

BUILDING NEWSPAPER ADVERTISING 47

newspaper advertising was too powerful an instrumentality to become ineffective merely because those who handled it were partially corrupt or ineffective.

Around this business grew up men who learned more and more about effective advertising. Wonderful progress was made in copy-writing, illustration, and typographical presentation. Many agencies developed men who, through experience, could turn out the sort of product that brought results. They were forced to take on merchandizing experts and study of distribution to meet the demands for service by the advertiser.

Likewise the advertiser, oftentimes with his own advertising manager, began to demand a slice of the agent's commissions through a rebate to the client, on pretense that he used the agent only to clear through. Certain prosperous concerns were said to scale the thing down to the bone, allowing the agent merely 2, 3, or 4 per cent. of the 15 to 25 they got.

Other large advertisers built up their own advertising agencies and bought space at net rates, while competitors paid gross prices.

Out of the chaos came the American Newspaper Publishers' Association, with its official recognition of agencies with sound financial standing, the Advertising Agents' Association, with its effort to standardize agency practices, and the Advertising Managers' Association to regulate relations all along the line.

Through the Quoin Club, composed of the magazines, all agents who split commissions were subject to loss of recognition. Increased demands by advertisers on the agents for service have made the cost of handling business encroach dangerously upon the commission, until to-day many agents who render all the service required frequently demand and receive extra compensation.

Without any doubt a determination by agents to bill all customers at full card rates, as in the case of their traffic with the magazines, would remove a most dangerous and disastrous condition in their business.

All this, as will be seen, tended to line up the advertising agent closer to the advertiser and farther away in some respects from the publisher, whom he started out to serve in return for a commission. This is perhaps a logical evolution produced by long experience, but modern practices would seem to be drawing agent and newspaper closer together again for new cooperation, as will be shown in a later chapter.

In New York and only a few Eastern cities is the advertising agent recognized in the case of local business. Elsewhere he is limited to foreign or general business—advertising placed generally throughout the country and originating outside of the city where the newspaper is published. The line between foreign and general advertising leads to endless disputes in many places where the newspapers have failed to adopt and adhere to the simple fundamental rule above indicated.

In one city there is a never-ending dispute between publishers and agents because the newspapers claim that residence of a general advertiser in their town makes the business of his concern local to them. This is absolutely silly. If a business has grown out of its home town so that it spreads out far afield, it is general, and the agent is entitled to compensation in the way of commission for the service he renders.

Likewise, an agent is entitled to his commission

on all business he develops and places with the newspapers, even though printed in connection with the names of local dealers, for herein lies the great superiority of newspaper advertising over other so-called general advertising.

VII

The Coming of the Special Representative

L. H. CRALL was the first special representative to come to New York on behalf of out-of-town newspapers in 1875. He responded to a change in conditions in the advertising world and represented the medium after it became obvious that the advertising agents had become representatives of the advertiser and not of the publisher.

The out-of-town newspaper discovered that if it were to secure its share of the growing volume of advertising appropriations going out from the agencies it would have to have a man constantly at the great advertising centers to represent it intelligently.

Among the pioneers I remember, besides Crall, A. Frank Richardson, S. C. Beckwith, Teddy Eiker, Sam Perry, Lester Smith, C. J. Billson, E. Katz, Henry Bright, Perry Lukens, J. E. Van Daren, E. T. Perry, Louis A. Leonard, N. M. Sheffield, Frank S. Gray, J. Martin Miller, Thaddeus Eiker, and a score of others who made big money when the going was good.

At the start the newspaper publishers figured that it was a sounder business proposition to allow the special representative a commission on all foreign business rather than to pay him a decent living salary, office rent, and expenses. This seemed cheaper and more effective than having a home-office man make frequent trips about the country, which got him into bad habits, and, as the home-office man was a comparative stranger to the plutocrats in the agencies, the latter more often than not showed that they were too important to devote much time to strangers in the big city.

By securing a list of newspapers to represent, the special agent found himself in clover. Those were the days of real sport in the advertising business. More men went on the rocks through drink and other dissipation, because their prosperity came too quick, than at any other time or in any other business that I have ever heard of.

Many of the specials seemed to think that the easy way to increased business was by buying it through lavish entertaining. Some of the early specials rolling in easy money traveled like princes, as if to prove by their wastefulness that their mediums were the greatest on earth.

In the middle '90's these merry times ended, as a large number of the publishers by general consent changed the relation with their representatives and put effective men on straight salary and expense basis, and demanded a fixed ratio of business per dollar spent.

Toward the end of the profligate days in the special-agency business many advertisers resented the added cost of advertising to them represented in maintaining the men who sought to corrupt their employees.

These readjustments brought into the special field a group of men fresh from the home offices of the most successful newspapers, men of sound training who knew their mediums and the towns in which they were published.

Among them were men of the type of Dan Carroll and John Woodward, who took their calling seriously and commenced to build up definite plans of service to the advertisers to make their advertising more effective than it ever had been.

Such effort was a novelty, but it took years for the specials to educate their newspapers regarding what it would really mean to them in increased business. The fact that they represented successful newspapers made the task only the more difficult.

If any one will show me a tougher nut to crack than getting a successful newspaper publisher to do new things I should like to see it. Filled with a false pride in his strength, the average successful publisher goes out of his way to prove his independence of an advertiser. It is this strange psychological phenomenon on the part of newspaper owners which generally provides the opportunity for the new-comer with real brains, newspaper instinct, and a willingness to serve, to supersede them. Pulitzer with *The World* proved the truth of the thing in New York in 1883, as did Ochs with *The Times* in 1897.

It was against such a wall that the new specials worked. Their theories of how to stimulate new and permanent business were sound and practical and would not be denied. First of all, the specials commenced to give the distant advertiser more intimate facts regarding the merchandizing possibilities of the cities in which the newspapers they represented were published. They produced masses of statistical data carefully arranged for instant reference.

They brought to the hand of the advertiser the very

sort of information he most needed for the planning and carrying through of successful campaigns. It was information and service more quickly obtainable and more dependable than anything he had ever been able to secure at any price regardless of the element of time.

These service specials were a sound breed of men whom advertisers found they could take into their confidence and depend on to help them score success with their campaigns. They were men respected by both advertisers and advertising agents, for they displaced no one, helped every one in the situation, and were as much interested in the success of the advertiser as he could possibly be himself.

VIII

Ineffective National Advertising Mediums

WITH the development of advertising have come all sorts of mediums as often as not primarily designed to separate the would-be advertiser from his money by the most painless method. Everything from the covering of lead-pencils and blotters to bill-boards, etc., has been used to get money for "advertising," and is still used upon those willing to exchange dollars for "conversation" and "chance shots."

For a period, likewise, the monthly magazines and weekly periodicals became dangerous competitors of real advertising—newspaper advertising. Grossly inflated circulations obtained by cutting prices to ten cents and five cents and publishing sensational muckraking and sex-problem matters, made these so-called mediums look mighty good to some people. In this group I include those attracted by artistic copy, good printing, and plausible salesmanship.

At the peak of the day of general mediums, now three or four years past, when they employed the greatest and most expensive exponents of hot-air salesmanship ever developed, many manufacturers could and undoubtedly did force distribution for their products on the strength of heavy campaigns in the magazines and weeklies.

BUILDING NEWSPAPER ADVERTISING 55

As the dealers gradually learned to know that general advertising "at all dealers" would not move the goods off their shelves, and that they had to use local newspaper advertising to get their money out of the goods, they declined to stock up on the strength of campaigns in the magazines, and of course the bubble burst.

Magazine advertising had a legitimate place before the days of its inflation, and has to-day. The pretense, indulged in by the hot-air salesmen, that the so-called national advertising was advertising and all other kinds merely supplemental, helped bring their downfall, for its increasing cost started people checking them up.

The advertising agents soon learned that so-called national advertising was most profitable to them temporarily, for they could easily exhaust an appropriation among a few mediums and save all the bother and expense of handling hundreds of widely scattered newspaper accounts, with the constant necessity of verifying insertions and keeping tabs on changes in rates.

But magazine and general advertising is falling back into its old place—supplemental service to keep a widely newspaper-advertised article before the people. It has not the flexibility of newspaper advertising, which can be adjusted overnight to meet changed conditions regarding price or territory.

Likewise, general advertising is extravagant and wasteful for any article not having an effective general distribution, which it cannot produce. Newspaper advertising can be used in exact accord with distribution by city, state, or nation. The so-called zone theory of the magazines is almost as wasteful as general presentation, except for occasional articles in special demand in one section, such as furs for the Northern states and other things especially bought in the South.

Slow-acting national advertising, involving the release of copy months in advance of its distribution in the printed periodical, defeats its successful use except for merely keeping a name or trade-mark before the public. If, during the period between release and day of publication, circumstances change conditions the advertiser has no escape from paying the bill.

The era of national advertising is filled with annihilations of hundreds or perhaps thousands of manufacturers who were induced to seek increased traffic on the strength of pages in the magazines and general mediums bought at heavy expense, before the manufacturers had any such distribution as would warrant the attempt. Many a promising prospect was forever lost to advertising through the greed of the solicitors, who were compelled to keep the magazines' pages bristling.

General advertising which cannot be hooked up closely with the local dealers in all of the towns where the goods are on sale is wasteful and ineffective. Such a relation is impossible within the commercial possibilities of general advertising. This is the rock upon which the golden galleon of the magazine went to smash. The newspaper with the much sought dealer relation has come in for greater recognition and larger use than ever before.

Magazine advertising costs from three to four times as much per line per thousand as newspaper space. The argument that magazine advertising has longer life is more than offset by increased cost, lack of definiteness as to where the goods can be bought, and the low percentage of magazine readers who can be influenced to buy through advertising.

This brings up a most interesting point worth consideration regarding the class of people most easily influenced to buy through advertising. My investigations indicate that the class given to the reading of the best grade of magazines do not read or directly respond to advertising. Investigation represented by interviewing several hundred women of the well-to-do households convinces me that my statement is justified.

In our every-day experience it is not routine general advertising which induces the buying idea. Who has not frequently glanced at an ad. and made up his mind that he wanted the goods advertised, only to lose all recollection of his wish in a minute because the ad. was not definite selling talk linked with a local dealer's name?

The percentage of loss in advertising calling for a letter is many times as great as it would have been if the ad. had stated that "John Doe" of our home town had the article on sale. Here is another obstacle that magazine and general advertising have never been able to overcome. Many hesitate to cut an ad. from a magazine as a reminder to buy who habitually would tear the same ad. from their newspaper. Even an ad. cut from a magazine stating that the article is "For Sale by All Dealers" is only the starting-gun in the race.

We all know of the substitution evil, and how many dealers will try to switch the prospect from "Cheney silk" to some other kind which they say is "just as good." The magazine reader in the absence of a definite list of local dealers (an impossibility) bumps up against the substituting dealer who is glad something brought a customer to his shop so he could sell him something else.

My only surprise is that magazine and so-called national advertising lasted as long as it did. Had it not been for the friendly and "interested" influence of advertising agents out for the easiest money, who, under pretense of getting some business for the newspapers, worked them for free notices, it would have died long before it did.

Who ever heard of the magazines giving their advertisers "free publicity"? They left that for the newspapers to do and took nothing but real money for their space, and as much as they could get. Unless an agent gave the bulk of all appropriations to them they cut off his recognition. Those were the days of strong-arm methods until the advertisers became convinced that such advertising was not effective.

It can be easily demonstrated that magazine circulation provides too thin a distribution to possess any practical advertising value. In nearly any city it will be found that only a very small percentage of the newsdealers carry a stock of the monthly periodicals. There is not sufficient traffic in them to make them profitable for the general run of newsdealers to handle. They spend enormous sums of money proportioned to sales to secure representation on enough stands at business centers to make the careless advertiser think they do the same everywhere.

Magazine advertising space, as I have said, costs many times as much per line per thousand as newspaper circulation. It can be easily demonstrated that a considerable intensive campaign of the kind that produces large sales could be carried on in the leading dailies of twenty-seven big cities for less money than would be needed for a page in only eight of our leading magazines. All of the newspaper advertising would be joined to local dealers, and reach probably 80 per cent. of the prospective purchasers, while the magazine space would be scattered like shot-gun fire at the whole United States and reach maybe 5 or 10 per cent. of the right people in the towns where the article had distribution, and even then without the very essential dealer relation.

When John Jones, our local dealer in men's attire, advertises in our local paper that he carries some new article of wearing apparel which is a great improvement over anything of the kind previously sold, he makes a far more direct appeal of the sort to induce me to purchase than when the same article is advertised in a magazine. I may want the article in either case, but one is a statement from a fellow-townsman whom I know, and the other is "just advertising" and involves too much uncertainty and an effort that defeats much of its efficiency.

Bill-board and paint-sign advertising, which has enabled many men to grow rich on the plunder taken from those seeking advertising, is an outrage on the scenic beauties of our cities. Its advocates claim that it is local advertising, but very seldom can it be used in conjunction with local dealers. Our big local stores use such methods only occasionally for a flash, not for regular selling service.

Our modern bill-board solicitors, in order to pretend to legitimatize their trade, talk "circulation" for their alleged medium, counting, or rather pretending to count, the number of people who pass a given point as "circulation." Every one who passes in a street-car, automobile, school-children, those who cannot read, and the blind are counted in their so-called circulation. If our newspapers wanted to match up they would start counting their circulation with those who cut the wood from which the paper was made clear through to final carriers of the box-board into which old print waste finally goes.

Likewise, street-car advertising falls only in the general-publicity class, without the flexibility or complete covering of the newspaper advertising. At best it catches only a wandering eye cast up from the newspaper to the one or two cards that happen to be opposite the passenger. Our car-advertising solicitors fail to reveal the limited number of cars in steady operation and the small range of passenger vision in any one of them, and the advertiser pays just as much for space in cars which make a few trips a day during the rush hours as if they were kept busy throughout the twenty-four hours.

Newspaper advertising is the only sort which is looked upon by our people with almost as much interest as the daily news reports in their newspapers, provided the advertiser uses his space to full advantage.

A newspaper gives the advertiser admitted to its columns the right to address regularly every day an audience greater than could be crowded into all the theaters and amusement-halls in its town. The appeal can be made as loud as desired by huge copy, or as quietly as preferred, by the use of small artistically arranged matter.

IX

Advertising an American Product

NEWSPAPER advertising is an American product. For some reason newspaper advertising in other countries has never been developed as it has been in this country.[1] The greater prosperity of the United States and more general distribution of money here may partly account for the phenomenon.

It has been claimed by economic experts and investigators that advertising in the United States is one of the primary causes of the high cost of living, but, on the other hand, we have conclusive proof that advertising by increasing traffic and turn-over reduces selling costs.

In England, France, Germany, and in all other countries I know of, advertising still continues hidebound and stilted, as it was in this country a century ago. Very high rates maintained by newspaper men perhaps sounder in commercial training, but certainly less progressive than ours, may account for the absence of growth.

The French policy of printing paid reading matter and editorial opinion is the short route to quick profit, but is not as well calculated to create good-

---

[1] See article from the London Times on this point in Part VII.

will values for newspapers. In the hands of unscrupulous editors the border-line between decency and honesty and corruption and blackmail becomes very faint at times.

In Germany before the war newspaper advertising was crude and unrefined, with huge black blotches announcing questionable eating-places, patent medicines, and cures. The better classes of business refrained from competition or association with such "advertisers."

In England, Harry Selfridge, formerly of Marshall Field & Co., of Chicago, endeavored to show how to boom a department store with heavy display advertising, and it is reported that he has done exceedingly well; but the English business man has been too conservative to follow suit.

It would seem to me that those operating the newspapers in these countries are more to blame for the lack of growth of advertising than the advertisers. A newspaper in any American city, conducted as the European newspapers are, would not carry much copy.

If our newspapers had adhered to the hidebound methods of a century ago, as the European papers have done, our rates would probably be as prohibitively high as they are overseas. Whether or not lower rates which would draw the European advertiser from his shell would solve the problem I do not venture to say.

None of the American newspaper men who have ventured to enter the newspaper business abroad have been sound enough in their understanding of the basic principles involved, or probably solid enough in their backing and support, to carry through the long campaign of education that is necessary.

BUILDING NEWSPAPER ADVERTISING 63

Bill-board, paint sign, and periodical advertising has been highly developed and successful in England, proving that human nature is about the same all over the world, so I feel reasonably sure that it has been newspaper practices and desires that have held English newspapers back.

The development of newspaper advertising in the United States and Canada has been slow. It has taken thirty years to get our newspapers out of the tame surroundings of the late '80's to the full glory of the present day. If anybody in the '80's had tried to reach modern practices overnight he would have met with the same defeat he would meet in London to-day.

Being brought up in the old school myself, I sympathize with those unable to get away from the old rule-of-thumb principle that advertising rates are an arbitrary exaction regardless of cost of production and whether they are profitable to the advertiser or not.

While I am a firm believer in the theory that advertising is a by-product to be sold without interference with the business of publishing the news, I am certain that on our success in selling the by-product must depend our ability to reach our best all-around newspaper.

Instead, therefore, of arbitrarily specifying that my rate was three or four shillings a line, I should go about the proposition from another angle. I should estimate my total expenses, deduct my probable circulation receipts, and divide the remainder by a liberal estimate of the lineage I expected.

If my circulation was about 200,000, my total expenses, say, £300,000, my circulation revenue, say,

64 BUILDING NEWSPAPER ADVERTISING

£120,000 and my estimate of possible lineage 5,000,000, I would fix my rate at one shilling per line net, and then go ahead.

If the advertising is estimated to be, say, 3,000,000 lines a year, the rate must be increased one and sixpence to cover cost and provide the same margin of profit.

I should by these processes have a talking point of greatest possible potency in my solicitation of advertising, make money for my stockholders, and sell advertising on a demonstrated basis which long experience has proved is profitable to the advertiser.

This is why the United States and Canada lead the world in newspaper advertising. We have made newspaper advertising effective by making its use at fair prices profitable to those who buy it. Many have stumbled into the place they now find themselves in and some few knew whither they were headed.

It might take months and it might take years to make an impression on merchants and others in old Europe, but, once they had tasted the wonderful growth they could secure by effective newspaper advertising, they would follow the example of Americans with a rush.

PART II

X

Best Type of Man for Advertising Manager

GIVEN a newspaper with a definite proved quantity of circulation, our problem is to secure for it as large an advertising earning power as the possibilities of its field provide. The best type of man to put in charge of the promotional work is one who has had the advantage of the broadest possible commercial and merchandizing experience.

The usual product of newspaper-office training is impracticable or a mere space-seeker. He may be a good slave-driver, but can seldom measure up to the man who has bought and used much advertising and been part of a big commercial selling organization. So much depends upon his ability to secure the intelligent co-operation of his force, to train them to think and study along the lines of making the advertisers' copy produce results, that he must be able to draw on his own experience and talk as an authority.

There are thousands and thousands of men who have had big department-store training who would be glad to shake off their daily grind under hard taskmasters and take up the much more interesting and satisfactory work of selling advertising for a newspaper. Some of these would make ideal advertising managers and solicitors. They know advertising as a selling force and can be depended upon to do their best to make the business they secure profitable to their customers.

Installed as advertising manager, the right man, after a survey of his ground and a careful estimate of the solicitors he inherits, will seek to reduce the organization to an effective basis. He will cover all necessary fields of revenue with men who know the customers, or substitute new salesmen he has confidence in.

Having been through the mill myself, not once but several times as advertising or business manager, I hesitate to advise any rule for all cases. There are old organizations which will endeavor to kill the efforts of a new man in the office, and others which will get in behind him as they would never work for the former management.

I incline to the idea that the best course is to make the force recognize that the new manager will favor the old force in reconstructing his department, but that each will be compelled to prove that he is a profitable investment.

This can be done by making each man fill out a card like the one on page 70 for each of his customers, giving a record of the business from each, and a report showing the state of those accounts on which he is still working. With these cards in hand each man can be induced by considerate treatment to prove by the statements he makes whether he is a mere salary-grabber or an intelligent, effective salesman. He should then be frankly told that he is effective only as long as his salary represents, say, 10 per cent. of the net to the office in new business.

HARRY MILHOLLAND
Advertising manager of the Pittsburg *Press*, whose motto is, "We'll beat the world again this year."

DESCRIPTION OF RECORDS USED IN ADVERTISING DEPT.

1—Card (3x5) made out as memorandum of clipping given solicitor, which, in addition to the name, address and line of business of advertiser, contains the name of solicitor and the day and date he received clipping. This card is kept on file on the manager's desk for the purpose of checking up report on every clipping distributed.
2—Slip on which solicitor makes report of call.
3—When solicitor's report indicates future activity of an assignment, details are indicated on card which is placed in permanent file for further action.
4—Sheet on which solicitor makes a report of the amount of business done on such of his assignments as have appeared during the past week.
5—Contract card, (3x5) on one side of which is indicated the details of the contract and on the reverse side of which is posted each month the amount of space used.

Advertiser		Business
Address		
Solicitor	Day	Date

Form No. 1

	Date
Account	
Address	
Business	
Whom to See Direct	
Whom to See Agency	
Will they use the Paper?	
When?	
What did they say?	

Form No. 2

Permanent file
Advertiser
Address
In Charge
Advtg. Agent
Solicitor   Date

Form No. 3

SOLICITOR'S WEEKLY REPORT				
SOLICITOR		Date		1917
ADVERTISER		Lines	Rate	Amount
New Contracts				
Expenses				

Form No. 4

Advertiser
Agent
Commenced   Expires
Rate   Lines
Remarks

Form No. 5—Front

74 BUILDING NEWSPAPER ADVERTISING

MONTH	LINES
January	
February	
March	
April	
May	
June	
July	
August	
September	
October	
November	
December	
January	
February	
March	
April	
May	
June	
July	
August	
September	
October	
November	
December	
TOTAL	

Form No. 5—Back

The old notion that as long as an advertising solicitor brought in more business than his salary he was profitable has gone by. Cost figures prove that it is only the last few cents of any dollar earned that are profit. So an advertising solicitor who costs 50 per cent. of his traffic, except in rare cases, is not a good investment and should be replaced by one who on the year's average can produce on the 10 per cent. basis.

XI

Relation of Manager to Rest of Force

THE advertising manager should be able himself to sell the goods he is seeking to market. Unless he can do this and occasionally prove it his men will not accept without reservation his directions to them for selling the same goods. I am a great believer in the rule that the commanding officer should be able to do anything he asks his men to do.

There are advertising managers who pride themselves on the fact that they seldom go out to see an advertiser or call on advertisers only once a year to renew contracts. Such men are not advertising managers, but rather obstructionists maintained for the purpose of making a show of independence.

The advertising manager should be a good executive, a good salesman, a good mixer, and a man of sufficient education and intelligence to understand at least the big purposes of his newspaper and to keep in touch with all the worth-while activities it engages in.

He should be on cordial terms with the editor and circulation manager and work in the closest harmony with the business manager and publisher. Unless he can command the co-operation of every other man on the newspaper his effectiveness is impaired.

ARTHUR FREEMAN

Advertising manager of Gimbel Brothers, New York, for three years, after having previously held the same position with R. H. Macy & Co. A progressive, constructive advertising go-getter of the first water.

This is said without purpose to suggest any degree of editorial favor as a stimulator of business, but only with respect to advice, comfort, and encouragement.

It is well enough for publishers and editors to look upon advertising managers as overpaid entertainers who commercialize a high profession. The publisher is often too small in his ideas to pay large enough salaries to secure effective men. The chief earning end of any business usually pays those able to produce satisfactory results highest rewards. Why not the newspaper business?

The advertising manager should be able to meet big men of affairs on a basis of equality. Unless he is an all-around man of good experience he cannot hold up his end in the big conferences in which, by one process or another, he should get mixed up. The cheap man appears to disadvantage in such affairs and is estimated largely by the impression he creates.

A two-by-four advocate is likely to make the newspaper he represents look like a mutilated Mexican dollar, where a hundred-per-center, by demonstrating a masterful grasp of things, and a willingness to coöperate, can frequently, secure for a tail-end newspaper greater consideration than the top-notcher.

In other words, it is desirable to employ the best quality of service available. The money required to secure a competent executive and salesman is well spent. If our newspapers generally adopted a sound policy in this respect, the volume of newspaper advertising would be substantially increased and all-around relations with our advertisers put upon a better footing.

Some years ago I came across an advertising manager, who, thinking only of his own advancement, continually sought to belittle the work of his solicitors, claiming all growth and new business as his own. He did not get very far. The property with which he was connected was an ultimate failure and passed into new ownership. Meanwhile, solicitors he had employed drifted to other newspapers, where they came through to high recognition.

This manager had trained them effectively, but failed as an executive through depriving the producers of their just rewards. An advance of five dollars a week would have held most of the men, but he rather sought a thousand-dollar advance in his own salary as more to the purpose.

Another advertising manager made the same mistake, but in a different way. This fellow was a crackerjack salesman who could sell practically any one anything. He failed as an executive because, while he would show a solicitor how to close a piece of business and permit him to bring the negotiation up to the closing point, he would jump in at the end and close it himself. His fondness for taking credit for the work of others proved his own undoing, for he failed to justify the maintenance of a big force used only to raise birds for his own gun.

The effective advertising manager takes more pleasure in having one of his men close an account than in doing it himself. He will gladly help the solicitor make a contract and feel the glow of successful effort. Good management is shown in team work with star performers all out for the big result for the newspaper for which all are working.

Whether the newspaper is a small-town daily or a huge metropolitan sheet makes no difference; much

BUILDING NEWSPAPER ADVERTISING 79

of its success and prosperity depends on the contact between those who sell its most profitable product and the publication office. The advertising manager must be able to sell more than mere space; he must sell institutional service and the right of legitimate business men to address the newspaper's constituency.

No man incapable of fully appreciating the broad purposes back of any worth-while newspaper should occupy this responsible position. When confronted with false arguments and the usual plays to secure broken rates, the advertising manager must rise superior to mere space-selling and convince the customer that the business is not so important to the newspaper as it is to him as an advertiser.

In casting this new rule, I have in mind the sort of work being done by a large number of wonderful men filling such positions. In many cases these men are performing miracles only too often unappreciated by selfish and ignorant publishers and business managers.

In drawing my picture I have especially before me the work of three men, and am seeking to present a composite of their methods. When we get close enough to penetrate the defensive shell, we find fellows so keenly interested in producing results for their newspapers and their advertisers that they never realize how poorly they are paid for the service they render.

While I see these men doing remarkable and often novel things, I see, too, publishers of other papers seeking men who can do the same class of work, but unwilling to pay enough to attract the talent they require. I incline to the conclusion that a newspaper publisher gets about the quality of service he deserves. If he is mean and narrow he is apt to defeat the efforts of an effective man if he gets him.

One Middle West newspaper owner recently asked me if I knew a good man to take charge of his advertising department. I inquired what he would pay. He dodged the issue by saying the man he wanted must have confidence in the future of the newspaper, start low, and depend upon the success of the enterprise for increases.

I told him he did not want a man of proved ability, but rather sought to prove out a lot of doubtful timber. The simple fool expected a proved man to leave a sound job to take a gamble with all the cards stacked against him. He wanted a world-beater for less than the pay of a good solicitor.

XII

Handling the Soliciting Force

IN organizing an advertising department probably no two men will exactly agree as to methods and policy. One manager will contend that he can produce results with three or four good men, while another has found greatest success by using a large quantity of cheap men. Then, again, the possibilities of a field have much to do with the sort of a force required.

Regardless of the potential of the newspaper, I think too many advertising managers err in failing to appoint an assistant to be on the job in case of illness and also to help the solicitors in many of the situations they meet during the year. It is always well to have some one in touch with what all are doing, ready with advice, assistance, and support.

In taking charge of a department I would carefully check up each of the men on the pay-roll by the methods mentioned in Chapter X, Part II, and appoint the best on record as assistant advertising manager. This would give me the benefit of best experience, induce this man to renewed activities, and make the other solicitors hustle to prove up to the job in case the man elevated failed to make good.

I would then offer moderate prizes every week or

every month to the man producing the largest value in new business consistent with the maintenance of satisfactory volume from old accounts in his hands. I would make it understood that, regardless of past regulations, the sky was the limit in that office as far as salary to solicitors was concerned. The more money we pay a man, if he earns it (and it is our business to see that he does), the more valuable he is.

This is the spirit to get best results. If it cost a certain percentage to carry on an advertising department and to promote and develop new sources of revenue, it is far better to be liberal with the men who secure the business than to train and develop them and then see them skip out to other jobs or go into business for themselves.

I know of one publisher who is so mean that he is forever up against the sheriff. He will take business at practically the best rate he can get. He would rather lie regarding circulation than tell the truth. He will not pay any advertising man over, say, $20 a week and everybody else in proportion.

A number of years ago he had on his pay-roll, at combined salaries of less than $75 per week, three men who to-day earn better than $700 a week. Chance brought this combination under his roof, but his meanness shortly shook them apart. The advertising manager drew $15 salary and a commission.

After a short time the advertising manager got the business coming and his commissions amounted to from $30 to $40 a week, whereupon the owner kicked and repudiated the arrangement by stating that he would not stand for any payment for services in excess of $25 a week. In four weeks all three men had gone and the owner can have none but unpleasant

A. G. NEWMYER
Business manager of the New Orleans *Item*. An advertising man of wonderful constructive ability.

dreams about what might have happened to his moribund sheet had he been smart enough to have held on to that trio.

For advertising solicitors of greatest efficiency I believe, as I have said, in seeking men who have had sound commercial training in selling merchandise. There are plenty of drummers who are tired of "drumming" and anxious to settle down at home. As a class they are accustomed to selling goods as commodities, of good approach, and with hearts of stone when it comes to discussion of rates.

The best solicitor I ever employed was a drummer who floated into my office one day and asked whether there was any future in advertising for a man of his experience. I staked him for a few weeks' trial. Within a month he was a star, could reach any one on a business basis, and generally brought home the game he went after without any serious injury to his hide.

Another brilliant star was produced by the same methods in the Middle West. He came fresh off the road and made good from the start. He made good too quickly for his own well-being. He rose to highest recognition within a few years, and, blinded by his own success and high earning power, went on the rocks by the booze route. I could mention case after case of successful use of ex-drummers or ex-salesmen.

Our advertising departments offer peculiar attractions for men of this training. We want real salesmen and not mere copy-chasers, product of the ordinary newspaper office. A good job that will enable him to settle down looks very attractive to the well-qualified traveling salesman, usually away from his family most of the time.

Herein lies our greatest opportunity for building up an organization which can sell space on a business basis. If such men are told that they can make whatever they can earn on a sound basis, they will perform work, under competent directions, that will carry the average newspaper owner off his feet. I don't say this to advance a theory, but to record actual experience.

In a subsequent chapter I shall consider the use of the soliciting force in connection with various special activities, from the stimulation of large local business, small local business, special efforts, classified, and foreign advertising.

XIII

Demonstration of Paper's Pulling Power

IN handling my force of canvassers I should discourage what I have called copy-chasing, that hand-me-down of past ineffective advertising solicitation. Of course we must clip the competing newspapers to note what the other fellows are getting that has got past us. Likewise we must try to get that copy if we hope to hold our job, for the business manager, publisher, and editor watch for opportunities to ask nasty questions.

But our newspaper is not worth while if we cannot solicit business confident of results to the advertiser. If it does not and will not produce results, we are not selling advertising, but peddling space. Therefore, I long ago made up my mind that ads. clipped from other papers that we did not have were proofs of our paper's ineffectiveness or of poor salesmanship.

How any self-respecting man of the caliber required by an advertising manager can day after day manage a crew of men who take money from advertisers which he knows is not going to be productive I cannot understand. Such work is more in accord with the gentle arts of the seller of fake mining and oil stock, the bunco-steerer, or other get-rich-quick experts.

According to my theory and experience, advertising

in any newspaper can be made profitable at a price. While, of course, the advertising manager is hired to sell the space of the newspaper filling his pay-envelop, he should realize that his work must come to naught unless by one process or another he can produce results for his customers.

It is well enough to assume that in a highly competitive field few of the regular big advertisers know exactly which papers produce the results they get. But sooner or later solicitors who go on this assumption will get an unwelcome jolt. There are ways of checking up the best newspapers and spotting the weak sisters. It is all right to talk off-day and blame the copy, but our friends the advertisers make a longer range test than a day or a week and can get an accurate line on us if they know how.

Not many years ago a leading merchant in New York sprang a surprise on me by offering to use a page a day every day for two months to earn a certain rate. I little suspected how important the offer was to be to the future of *The Globe*. We closed the deal. While running the page a day with us he practically discontinued all other advertising. I was not prepared for such an ordeal, especially during December and January.

I quaked in my shoes. To expect one newspaper with less than 200,000 circulation at that time of year to fill the hole made by cutting off others with probably 1,000,000 daily sales seemed too much. But we made good. The store not only did the biggest Christmas business in its long career, but ran into record figures during January. If the paper had not produced, such a test would have been disastrous. But the paper did produce, and so it was made as an

BUILDING NEWSPAPER ADVERTISING 87

advertising medium, and ever since has carried the largest volume of advertising from the big retail shops. I cite the incident only to prove my point that there are ways of checking up newspaper pretense if the advertiser thinks it worth while.

The keenness of a force of solicitors can be increased so much by demonstrations of their paper's pulling power that it pays to go after them. I would almost recommend the carrying of certain business for next to nothing if the advertiser would let me make a big go for him on a tail-end newspaper with no record of achievement. Then if my paper did not produce I would discharge the whole soliciting force until I had found a way of getting results.

After I had found the way I would so fill the minds of my men with the institutional value of the medium that they would not try to sell a single ad. (copychasing), but only a permanent long-haul relation with the newspaper. Each newspaper solicitation should be a complete demonstration of results. A solicitor should stick to his customer until he gets provable results for him.

I am aware that these suggestions are at variance with the views of men connected with well-established prosperous newspapers. They don't have to do such things and naturally feel safe in their leadership if the other fellow sticks to copy-chasing of ads. clipped from their columns.

Joseph Pulitzer, when he took hold of *The New York World* in 1883, as described in Chapter IV of *Newspaper Building*, did not depend upon copychasing. Neither have any of those who have really come through. If we at *The Globe* office had depended upon such a process we should still be groveling in the mud instead of constantly creating new business for all the other newspapers and leading the procession in many important lines.

By instilling the fighting, constructive spirit into the hearts and souls of your soliciting force, your advertising manager will fully earn his keep and render invaluable service. As I said before, if rates are too high to enable the newspaper to produce results, reduce them for a season and then stiffen them up when you have made good.

Too many of us look upon the touching of advertising rates as we would the handling of dynamite. Not so with the merchants to whom we sell. They are used to changes in prices. They put up a pretty stiff fight against any advance, but if our paper produces for them they know their protest is in vain and that a temporary withdrawal of their business means more loss to them than to us.

XIV

Consideration of Advertising Rates

IN the formulation of any effective plan for the development of advertising for a newspaper not yet enjoying full-volume copy in its field, the basis of rates often plays an important part. Only too frequently the advertising manager is up against the arbitrary and ignorant ideas of some foolish owner. Regardless of failure in the past, such an owner insists on such and such a rate, not justified by circulation or result-bringing possibilities.

As indicated in previous chapters and in Chapters XXVII and XXXVIII of *Newspaper Building*, I am not a believer in low rates or broken rates. The rate must be one that can be demonstrated to be fair, and one which will produce results to the advertiser. Then and then only can the advertising be sold as a commodity desired by the business men of the community.

Determining what rate should be asked by a newspaper which has not arrived and secures only a small part of the business often presents problems beyond the comprehension of the ordinary newspaper executive. He is inclined to base his rate on what others are getting rather than to ascertain what he should ask to meet local conditions and put his property on a commercial basis. I know how it is, for I for many years worked in the dark and wondered why it was difficult to secure for my paper business that stuck, while others got and held it without trouble.

In establishing a rate for a newspaper I would first make a careful estimate of the total operating expenses for a year, with full allowance for circulation and advertising, promotion, and for interest, taxes, depreciation, replacement, and such. Some would prefer to charge off promotion expense to investment, which can be done when the plan of financing the enterprise permits, but as the advertiser gets the results of the money spent in promotion we are not unfairly transferring a burden to him by making it a part of our cost.

With the total figure before me I would calculate the volume of advertising carried each year for the last three years, say, 3,000,000 lines. Then I would estimate the total value of space printed in all the papers without duplication, say, 8,000,000 lines.

Assuming that my total operating expense was $60,000 a year, I should divide $60,000 by 4,000,000 lines (adding a million lines to my record), and find my production cost to be 1½ cents an agate line, or 21 cents per inch. This cost plus a manufacturer's profit of, say, 10 per cent. would figure 1.65 cents per line, or 23.1 cents per inch, as the average rate I must secure to be solvent.

To find the net advertising rate per line during the previous year, divide the total earnings by the number of charged lines printed. Comparing the result with the cost figure, I should find out in an instant whether the rate earned during that year

FLEMING NEWBOLD
Business manager of the Washington *Star* and Chairman of the Bureau of Advertising of the American Newspaper Publishers' Association.

BUILDING NEWSPAPER ADVERTISING 91

was justified or not. If the rate was too high, there are ways of taking advantage of the situation to secure heavier volume; and if too low, there are other ways of bringing it up without disrupting the whole machine.

Before considering ways and means for producing changed conditions, I want briefly to consider what is known as the flat-rate theory compared with the sliding scale. There are strong believers in both standards, and great successes have been scored each way. By flat rate we mean a fixed rate for any and all space, of so much per line or per inch, regardless of volume used or frequency of insertions. By sliding scale we mean base one-time rates for various classifications, with discounts for time and space, or either.

Theoretically the flat rate is simplicity itself and wholly desirable from every newspaper standpoint. It puts the manufacture and sale of advertising space on the standardized basis of street-car fares, packages of chewing-gum, and such—one or a thousand at the same price. It encourages the small advertiser by giving him the same rate as the department store, and permits the distant general advertiser to try out experimental campaigns without assuming the obligation of a contract to advertise for a long period to earn a fair rate. Those are big inducements and make easier the sale of space.

On the other hand, there are, it would seem, very serious drawbacks to the flat rate which make it of doubtful benefit. Inasmuch as we have to publish our newspapers every day in the year, it is a distinct advantage to have in our safes contracts which assure us certain definite volume throughout the year. Some of us are able to reduce from 40 to 75 per cent.

of our total advertising to this basis. These contracts are just as good an asset as so much money in the bank. Some may fall down for various causes, but the larger part of them, probably 95 per cent., will be carried out to the letter like any other contracts with reputable business concerns.

It may be asked what would happen to our contracts in the case of a huge financial depression, when many concerns foolishly curtail advertising. The answer is that short-rate collections from those failing to earn contract discounts would partially equalize the loss, but in any case we should be better off than if we had been trading on the flat-rate basis, when any and all our customers could stop without notice or discussion. There is practical experience to prove the point in a number of cities.

In one town I have in mind there are two newspapers of about the same potential, one using the flat rate and the other the sliding scale. The depression of 1908 came along and the paper with the flat rate found itself running with bare columns, while its competitor continued to carry a reasonable volume simply because the advertisers had to go on with nominal space or expose themselves to heavy loss through short rating. This may or may not be sound economics, but I believe that anything that will make an advertiser advertise can do him no harm. Too many of our advertisers are apt to get chilly feet for imaginary causes, like men who trade in Wall Street.

In other words, our friends the advertisers in the town referred to, instead of standing by the man who offered them the advantage of the flat rate, forsook him in the storm, and he suffered for his own liberality and fairness. If our newspapers were endowed institutions I should be a strong advocate of the flat rate, but even then I should seek by experience tables to fix that flat rate at a much higher point than my estimated cost on a sliding-scale basis, in order to protect myself against the increased risk involved by the rights given the advertiser.

I believe the thory of a flat rate fixed on a higher costing basis, with a discount to be earned at the end of each year in the way of a reasonable or small rebate for full copy, might work satisfactorily. A 10 per cent. rebate would be quite an inducement for a man to stick through an off season with as much business as he gave to a competitor with regular contracts. It would be a mere question of pad-and-pencil figuring for the buyer and we could trust him to see the advantage of using the space if the rebate offset what he thought he could save by taking out his business.

It is well to consider one other disadvantage in the flat-rate program for an existing newspaper. It is next to impossible to get the big users of space to stand for an arbitrary advance in rates. It is all right for the little fellows who get the advantage, but when it comes to showing the large stores what they gain by paying as much as the man who buys a single inch, the job is a hard one. Unless your present rate is too high, it is well to approach cautiously so radical a step.

Nearly all advertisers buy their stocks on quantity basis. They expect a better price for goods bought by the car-load than by the dozen. They like to sell on the unit basis, but buy most readily where, through exercise of large purchasing power and turnovers, they can earn discounts and allowances. From my viewpoint, the man who will contract to use two columns every day, 150,000 lines in a year, and so on, is entitled to a lower rate than one who merely uses space occasionally at his convenience and generally at seasons when the pressure of other business is most severe. The transient user should pay a much higher rate, for we could not maintain the medium for him without the support of the steady advertisers.

The transient should pay two or three times as high a rate as the contract advertiser. The one-time advertiser should be discouraged, for he is of the type that expects to get rich quick by a single insertion and should be guarded from his own folly by the intervention of a prohibitive rate. The flat rate makes the use of space as liquid as water from the faucet.

XV

Making the Rate Card

THE making of a rate card which will produce the average net rate we must have is more like the actuarial work for a life-insurance company than anything else. There are flat-rate newspapers supposed to get the same price from all comers, which do nothing of the sort, those which at least try, and those which would like to do so. With the best of them inconsistencies develop. For example, the theaters may pay more than others, political advertising a shade more than run of paper, and so on down the line; while, on the other hand, certain large users sometimes have been known to get allowances.

I say these unkind things only to show the desirability of fixing fair and just variations of rates for different volumes and kinds of business, rates which can be maintained. It is comparatively easy and it is equitable to establish and rigidly enforce rates which can be justified as sound. I know, for I have sold thousands of dollars' worth of space under widely differing conditions and studied conditions in nearly all our leading cities.

It is a comparatively easy thing to secure a record showing the volume of business done in a year by those in highly generalized lines. If the data do not exist, it is high time they were dug out or some system started to keep tabs on the use of space hereafter for future analysis. In New York we keep records of these subdivisions for each of our newspapers:

Amusements	Men's Furnishings
Art	Miscellaneous
Automobiles	Musical Instruments
Boots and Shoes	Newspapers
Building Material	Non-intoxicating Beverages
Candy and Gum	Office Appliances
Charity and Religious	Proprietary Medicines
Deaths	Public Service
Druggists' Preparations	Publishers
Dry Goods	Railroads
Financial	Real Estate
Food Stuffs	Resorts
Furniture	Sheriff Sales
Hotels and Restaurants	Steamships and Travel
Instruction	Tobacco
Jewelry	Wants
Legal	Women's Specialty Shops

We also keep record of:

Total National advertising
" Local "
" European "
" Brooklyn "
" Harlem & Bronx "
" New Jersey "

For the purpose of my calculations in arranging a new rate card I should want not only a table of my own newspaper record, but another showing the total volume of each kind of business in any other newspaper in the same town. This would show my

The Hartford Times
ESTABLISHED 1841
Every Afternoon Except Sunday
3 Cents a copy $8.00 a year
MEMBER A. B. C.

ISSUED AUGUST 1, 1918
EFFECTIVE AUGUST 1, 1919

DISPLAY RATE
7c. FLAT
PER AGATE LINE

PREFERRED LOCATION.
Pages 2 or 3, if available, 33 1-3 per cent. additional.

Pages 2, 3, 4 or 5, publisher's option, 25 per cent. additional.

POSITION CHARGES.
Next reading matter, 15 per cent. additional.

First following and alongside reading, 25 per cent. additional.

Advertisements ordered in full position must be at least 28 lines deep.

CLASSIFIED ADVERTISING.
Wanted, For Rent, For Sale, Etc., set in solid nonpareil, one cent a word each insertion, minimum 20 cents.

READING NOTICES.
Reading Notices, body type (minion) with letters "Adv." attached, 50 cents per count line, each insertion. Headlines to count double.

Reading Notices (nonpareil) with "Adv." attached, 25 cents per count line, each insertion. 500 lines used within one year, 15 cents per line. Headlines to count double.

Reproduction of the Rate Card of the *Hartford Times*.

INFORMATION.

Agate measure—
- Column width 12 1-2 ems.
- 306 lines to a column.
- 2,448 lines in a page.
- 8 columns to the page.

Contracts are accepted for one year from date of contract.

No contract will be made for display advertising occupying less than 14 agate lines.

Advertisements must be one inch deep for every column in width.

The Hartford Times does not publish on Fourth of July, Thanksgiving, Christmas.

Advertisements not accepted for first, last and editorial pages.

No telegraphic reader advertising accepted.

Get-rich-quick schemes and objectionable medical advertisements not admitted.

Commission to advertising agents, 15 per cent.

Cash discount of 2 per cent. given on all accounts, paid on or before the 20th of the month.

POPULATION.

Hartford—1910 Census, 98,915.
Estimated 1918, 125,000.
Hartford and Trading Territory, 250,182.

SPECIAL REPRESENTATIVE
KELLY-SMITH CO.,

220 Fifth Ave.,   Lytton Bldg.,
New York.   Chicago.

Second Page of the Rate Card of the *Hartford Times.*

GENERAL ADVERTISING RATES

OF

THE CHICAGO DAILY NEWS

15 NORTH FIFTH AVENUE,

CHICAGO.

GENERAL EASTERN OFFICE:

ROOM 710 TIMES BUILDING, NEW YORK CITY

Represented by all Responsible Advertising Agents

In Effect January 1, 1917

Reproduction of the Rate Card of the *Chicago Daily News*.

SCHEDULE OF GENERAL ADVERTISING RATES

DISPLAY RATES

Per agate line, per insertion	$0.50
1,000 lines or more within 1 year	.43

Either party to a contract may terminate it when the amount of display space specified has been used, or at any time thereafter.

SPECIAL DISPLAY CLASSIFICATION RATES
NO DISCOUNTS

Amusements, per agate line, per insertion	$0.55
Automobiles, " " " "	.36
Financial, " " " "	.36
Publishers (except newspapers), "	.36

Reading Notices, per nonpareil line, marked "adv."	$2.00
Business Topics, " " "	.75
Business Mention, per agate line	.50
Special Notices, " " "	.45

SPECIAL CLASSIFIED DISPLAY RATES
WITH TIME DISCOUNTS

Resorts and Travel (including Hotels and Restaurants) 1 time	$0.36
30 consecutive insertions, not less than twice a week	.30
Schools and Colleges, 1 time	.36
30 consecutive insertions, not less than twice a week	.30
Once a week one year	.30

Regulations Governing the Sale of Advertising Space

Changes of matter will be made whenever desired without extra charge, provided the copy is delivered at THE DAILY NEWS counting room before 9 P. M. preceding the day of publication. The number of insertions to be given it, the day or days on which it is to appear, the advertising, if any, which it is to replace, and the number of lines it is to make, must be stated in writing on the copy. If the advertiser at any time fails to furnish copy and directions for the regular and uninterrupted insertion of his advertisement on a contract for a specified number of insertions, it is understood and agreed that the last copy furnished and the space therewith ordered shall be repeated until new order and copy are given as above stated. Verbal orders or orders by telephone will not be accepted.

Notice of typographical errors must be given in time for correction before the second insertion, otherwise no repetition of publication shall be claimed or allowed.

Rate Card of the *Chicago Daily News* (*Continued*).

ERRORS IN ORDERS

Agents and regular customers are advised that, to avoid delay and annoyance to them, the forwarding of an order will be construed as an acceptance of all the rates and conditions under which advertising space is at the time sold by the paper. A failure to make the order correspond in price, or otherwise, with the schedule in force will be regarded only as a clerical error, and publication will be made and charged for upon the terms of the schedule in force, without further notification.

POSITION

No special location will be assigned—all locations are at the option of The Chicago Daily News Co.

Two or more separate advertisements by the same advertiser are not considered as one announcement, and are not guaranteed location in adjacent columns, but are treated as distinct advertisements.

CUTS, HEAVY TYPE, ETC.

Cuts and electrotypes must be on flat metal base.

In display advertising, illustrative cuts on flat metal base, designs, heavy faced type, borders, etc., subject to the approval of The Chicago Daily News Co. and space without column rules may be used by the advertiser so long as they are permitted in the columns of the paper to any other advertiser, but the advertiser must assume all risk of the cut not printing distinctly in the paper.

The Chicago Daily News Co. reserves the right to outline or tool engrave any cut or part of cut or white letters on solid black background which, because of its size and unusual blackness of face, is regarded by it as a disfigurement of the paper.

Any fraction of a line upon cuts or electrotypes in excess of space named in orders will be charged for as one line.

The style of type and setting shall in all cases be within the discretion of The Chicago Daily News Co.

COMPOSITION

No column rule is omitted from an advertisement in THE DAILY NEWS less than fifty lines deep, nor two column rules for less than seventy-five lines deep, and a larger number in same proportion, except advertisements, seven and eight columns wide which must be at least one hundred and fifty lines deep.

Any advertisement more than one column wide must be of uniform depth in all its columns.

Reading matter has "adv." appended to final line of all articles or paragraphs measuring 30 lines or less, and [ADVERTISEMENT] preceding all articles or paragraphs measuring more than 30 lines.

Rate Card of the *Chicago Daily News* (*Continued*).

SPACE LIMITATIONS

No display advertisement is counted less than five lines, except special classified display, which may be two lines.

No classified advertisement on contract is counted less than three lines.

Advertisements over 255 lines in depth are accepted only as a full column in depth.

The Chicago Daily News Co. reserves the right to decline any advertisement for any given issue whether offered by an advertiser with or without an advertising contract with THE DAILY NEWS when the space allotted to advertising in that issue has all been taken by other advertisers.

Advertisements written to read across column rules are not accepted.

The Chicago Daily News Co. reserves the right to revise or reject, at its option, any advertisement which it deems objectionable, either in its subject matter or phraseology.

MEASUREMENT

The Standard for Display, Special Notices and Business Mention is agate, 14 lines to one inch, and of Business Topics and Reading Matter, nonpareil, 12 lines to one inch.

The column width is 25 ems nonpareil, or 12½ ems pica, which equals 2 1-12 inches. 8 columns of 305 agate lines to a page.

CONTRACTS

It is expressly understood and agreed:

1. That The Chicago Daily News Co. reserves the right to cancel a contract at any time upon default by the advertiser in the payment of the monthly bills, or in the event of any persistent violation on the part of the advertiser of any of the conditions herein named, and upon such cancellation all advertising done thereunder and unpaid shall become immediately due and payable.

2. That the advertiser shall do a substantial amount of advertising under a contract during every period of thirty days within the time herein limited, and in the event of the failure of the advertiser so to do, The Chicago Daily News Co. shall have the right to cancel the contract without notice.

3. That if at the end of the advertising period named, or upon a prior termination of a contract for any cause, it shall appear that the advertiser has not used advertising to the full amount ordered, the advertiser shall pay to The Chicago Daily News Co. such additional sum on each and every line of advertising so done as shall be equal to the difference between the price applicable to the amount of advertising ordered and the price applicable to the amount of advertising actually so done according to the above schedule of advertising rates, and upon such expiration or termination said additional sum shall become immediately due and payable.

4. That any statement rendered to the advertiser by The Chicago Daily News Co. shall be conclusive as to the correctness of the items therein set forth, unless the advertiser shall in writing call the attention of The Chicago Daily News Co. to any alleged inaccuracies in such statement within ten days from the rendering thereof, and receive from The Chicago Daily News Co. a written acknowledgment of such complaint.

5. That during the life of a contract all advertising done thereunder shall be paid for at the office of The Chicago Daily News Co. not later than the fifteenth day of the month following that in which the advertising is done.

6. That no verbal changes or modifications of these conditions will be recognized.

Rate Card of the *Chicago Daily News* (*Continued*).

weak points and the total would prove the total possibilities.

By tabulating the average rates for the different classifications I could carry forward on each line the probable earnings from each source, and by totaling the columns, cross check the accuracy of estimates of earnings from the different lines of business. Now I should want a list of all contracts or agreements made by the larger users of space. For example, if the largest customer used 100,000 lines in a year at a certain rate I should head my list with as many of these contracts as the paper had, each figured as producing so much. Next the 50,000-line customers, then the 25,000-line, the 10,000-line, and the 5,000-line ones.

These sheets would show how much business was carried at a loss, if any, and how much at various degrees of profit, and afford a side check on many activities which in the absence of such information have been supposed to be successful. Analyzed in the search-light, many an old sore spot would be uncovered. With such information in hand the suffering members could be cured and made producers or dropped for new ones more promising. Business to-day is too near a science to work in the dark through the lack of effective data regarding costs and returns.

By these processes we have reached the point of beginning. We know:

1. The average rate we must have to live.
2. The average net rate earned last year.
3. The classifications that paid their way and those that did not.
4. We can make a definite estimate as to volume and returns from possible increased business.

5. Where to expend time and money for most profitable results.

6. A chart which will enable us to adjust rates to a higher basis without disturbing business.

Regarding the last of the six points the reader may require further light. It may be found that the volume from some classification, while highly profitable in line rate, is not what it should be. Here is an opportunity for a proposition that will be attractive. Perhaps a slight concession in price for definite, even small, quantities of business may draw. Then again, perhaps in cases where business may have been taken at too low a rate, we can raise prices a notch to-day and another in a month or two, so that in a year or eighteen months we shall have what we sought.

A study of the frequently boosted rate cards of *The New York Globe* during 1917 to meet the increased print-paper prices referred to in Chapter XXVI of *Newspaper Building* will show what can be done in this respect. There need be no loss of volume, and it can be done anywhere if it is done correctly.

It may be thought that I have here generalized too much and not given enough specific information. My defense is that it is impossible definitely to outline any rate card that will fit all conditions. To meet the difficulty I present reproductions of the rate cards of some of the most successful newspapers in the country.

Best experience, as shown at a recent conference of business managers of a score of our most substantial newspapers, indicates that the ideal rate card should show a good stiff rate for one-time business, make a heavy discount for small contractural relations, and provide a small final discount in the shape of a rebate to be earned by those who use certain specified large copy.

We in *The Globe* rate card, which is reproduced on other pages, showing the new standardized form recently recommended by the National Association of Advertising Agents, seek to conform to the above standard as nearly as practicable in providing a heavy discount for the man who uses as little as 2,500 lines during the year—100 lines more than a full page. We did this purposely so that the man buying a single page for one insertion would not earn the discount. That the plan has been successful is proved by the fact that before the new form went into effect we had a much smaller percentage of advertising under contract than we have to-day. Incidentally our relations with the many small advertisers enjoying the advantages of the 2,500-line contracts are much more satisfactory than they were.

Many publishers make the great mistake of permitting advertisers to buy or secure positions for their advertising which result in serious handicap in the production of a newspaper that will be sound enough to command the respect and confidence of its readers.

By this I mean the printing of advertising up the front side of the page, the sale of "island" positions, top or bottom, with reading matter on three sides, and such.

Best experience proves that the sale of anything beyond "next following and alongside reading" is unprofitable.

The pyramid form of make-up from the right-hand lower corner, with each page starting with reading

New York City
New York

The Globe

Issue—Evening—Daily, except Sunday
Rate Card No. 2
Date of Issue—Jan. 15th, 1919
Date in Effect—Feby. 1st, 1919

1. GENERAL ADVERTISING
(Display)

a. Base rate 50 cents a line.
b. Time discounts:
                     Per Line.
  E. O. D. for 1 year 25% .37½
  Twice a week for
    1 year ....20%   .40
  One time a week
    for 1 year......15% 42½
e. Space discounts:
  2,500 lines in 1 year 22% .39
  5,000 lines in 1 year 24% .38
  10,000 lines in 1 year 28% .36
  20,000 lines in 1 year 32% .34
  30,000 lines in 1 year 36% .32

Discounts apply only on written contract to individual advertisers.

Time discount not allowed when space discount is given

If at least 28 lines of space is not used within thirty days after the beginning date of space contract the contract is void.

d. Rates for Special Position.
  2d or 3d page, double price.
  Other designated pages 20% extra.
  Next following, or alongside reading, 20% extra.
  Top, next, double price.
  Bottom surrounded, triple price.
  If page 2 is ordered, or page 3 ordered, 10 cents per line additional.
  Position charges on time or space advertising subject to same ratio of discount as run of paper charges.
e. Minimum size of advertisements: 7 lines.
  No double-column ad less than 25 lines deep.
  No triple-column ad less than 75 lines deep; four cols., 150 lines; five cols., 200 lines; eight cols., 250 lines.
  Advertisements more than 250 lines must be full columns.

Position top next, not less than 42 lines deep.
f. All contracts are subject to delay and to cancellation by The Globe without notice and without short rate for any cause
The Globe reserves the right to limit the amount of advertising to any advertiser in any issue under any contract.
All advertising that is ordered set, and which for any reason of print paper limitation, strike, fire, or difficulties beyond the control of The Globe, cannot be printed on any given day, may be printed on the following day.
In case any advertisements are omitted under print paper conservation orders by the government, those selected for publication will be taken in the order received in The Globe office and released for publication

((Over)

2

1. GENERAL ADVERTISING (Continued).

All orders for advertising must be accompanied by copy

Right reserved to reject, lighten, or change type, borders, or cuts, or to limit space of advertisements without notice

Claims for allowance for errors must be made within ten days after date of insertion.

Credit for errors in advertisements placed by agents allowed for first insertion only

Time contracts must specify days of week on which insertions are to be given

Space on all advertisements in agate type less than ten agate lines charged actual counted lines; ten lines or over charged by agate measurement.

Drawings or other art work supplied to advertisers at cost Drawings and articles for reproduction accepted only at advertiser's risk

The forwarding of an order is construed as an acceptance of all the rates and conditions under which advertising space is at the time sold by The New York Globe. Failure to make the order correspond in price or otherwise with this rate card is regarded only as a clerical error and publication is made and charged for upon the terms of the schedule in force, without further notification.

Serious errors in advertisements will be rectified by republication without additional charge, but such republication will not be made where the error does not materially affect the value of the advertisement.

"Till Forbid" orders are subject to change in rate without notice. Cancellation of orders over the telephone not recognized unless confirmed same day in writing

2. CLASSIFICATIONS

Display Classified.
a Amusements ....Flat .60
  Automobiles 40
Discounts
  2,500 lines in one year .38
  5,000 lines in one year .35
  10,000 lines in one year .30
  Books and Magazines Flat .30
  Hotels & Restaurants Flat .40
*Lodge Notices, Memorials
  and Vital Incidents Flat .60

Newspapers .... Flat .50
Political .... Flat .60
Religious Notices ..... Flat .25
Undertakers .... Flat .50

* Allow five words lower case to line, as these ads are indented

Flat rate advertising ordered in position pays position premium flat.

Grouped under designating heads, minimum size of advertisements 7 lines.
  Excursions and Travel... .20
  Real Estate .... .30
  Mortgage Loans .... .30
  Resorts .... .30
  Steamships .... .30
Discounts:
  Daily 6 mos. or E. O. D. 1 year .25
  3,000 lines 1 year .... .11
  5,000 lines 1 year .... .23

New Standardized Rate Card (*New York Globe*) as

2. CLASSIFICATIONS (Continued)

1 Auction Sales .... .30
  Discounts, 1 time a week
    for 1 year .... .23
  Schools and Instruction... .30
Discounts:
  26 times consecutively, or
    3 insertions (including
    Saturday) each consecu-
    tive week for 3 months... .28
  52 times consecutively, or
    3 insertions (including
    Saturday) each consecu-
    tive week for 6 months... .27
  156 times consecutively, or
    3 insertions (including
    Saturday) each consecu-
    tive week for 1 year...... .25

*†Pure Food Directory—
14 agate lines three times a week for one year, 39 cents per agate line per insertion.

*Minimum space, one inch single column; maximum space, four inches single column

†All products and copy must be approved by Alfred W McCann

b. **Undisplayed Classified.**
  30 cents per line for solid agate, except "Situations Wanted" 15 cents.
Discounts:
  6 Consecutive times... .28 cents
  26   "   "   .. .27 "
  312   "   "   .. .25 "
Discounts apply only on written contract to individual advertisers.
  40 cents per line if light display is used.
No ad. less than 3 lines. Agate type only permitted. Light display only in ads measuring 7 lines or more.
Only single column advertisements accepted.
Six average words to a line, set in agate type; four average words if all agate caps.
Undisplayed classified advertisements with special agate type "layout" must be at least seven lines.
Change of copy permitted.

Advertisements ordered under other than proper classification, if accepted, pay the higher rate.
Undisplayed Classified Advertising with special "layout" measured 14 agate lines to the inch.
Legal Advertisements:
  *Bankruptcy Auctions.Flat .30
  *Bankruptcy Notices, inc. U.S.
    Referees' notices...Flat .30
  Co-partnership and Dis-
    solution ....Flat .40
  Election Notices......Flat .50
  *Legal Notices (Assignees'
    Notices, Foreclosure
    Sales, Referees' Notices,
    Summonses, Surrogates'
    Citations) ....Flat .30
  Public Notices ....Flat .50
  Proposals ....Flat .50
  Surrogates' Notices (once
    a week; 6 months, 27
    times). $120

*If displayed 50 cents per agate line flat.

(Over)

3. READING NOTICES

Rates for styles and for positions when available:
First page. Per agate line,$2.50
Inside pages.   "   "   2.00

Reading Notices not accepted on Editorial, opposite Editorial, or on last page

"adv." must be affixed

4. COMMISSION AND CASH DISCOUNT

a. Agency Commission, except on Amusements and U. S. Gov't, State, or City Notices or advertising... 15%

b. Agency Cash Discount except on Amusements and U. S. Gov't, State, or City Notices or advertising. 2%

c. Cash Discount date 15th of month following month of insertion

5. MECHANICAL REQUIREMENTS

a. Width of col., 12½ ems pica.
b. Depth of col., 300 agate lines.
c. Number of columns to page, 8.
d. Centre spread space not sold.

e. Size of printed page: 17¼x21⅜ inches.
f. Closing dates, none.
g. Half-tone screen required, 65.

h. Requirements as to originals, electros, and mats: If furnished by advertiser, used at his risk. Can use mats.

6. CIRCULATION

a. Member of A. B. C.
b. Daily evening newspaper. Independent Republican.

c. Circulation Local.
Over 90% in Greater New York and suburbs.

d. See latest A. B. C. Report.

7. MISCELLANEOUS

a. No offensive or objectionable copy accepted or printed. No liquor ads or cures.
b. Established 1793.
(Oldest daily newspaper in U. S.)

c. $7.20 a year. 2c. per copy.
d. No other publications by same owners.

e. Jason Rogers, Publisher.
H. J. Wright, Editor.
O'Mara & Ormsbee, Inc., Special Representatives, New York and Chicago.

(Over)

Adopted by the American Advertising Agents' Association.

matter, is best for the reader and advertiser. Of course, if he can buy and force an island or detached position he will continue to do so.

In our better-grade successful newspapers we try to keep our second and third pages clear from large advertising. We feel that our newspaper is made with the first, second, and third pages, so we seek to keep them clear by establishing prohibitive rates to those who insist on a place in our show windows. Under the operation of such a rule the newspaper is at liberty to give any advertiser an occasional position on the second and third pages when it meets its convenience to do so, free from the demands and dictation of those who seek to dominate such positions.

The heavy advertising of the larger stores which is so distinct and conspicuous that it cannot be buried, and which is usually accepted at lower rates, should be used as filler, as background and underpinning for the smaller ads. which pay higher rates.

The sooner the newspaper demonstrates to its advertisers that its first and primary purpose is to serve its readers, free from the attempted control and unreasonable demands of those who would advertise to the readers, the sooner will that newspaper command the respect and confidence of the sane advertisers.

It is human nature for the buyer of anything to think that his money can buy anything on his own terms, but it is only the weakling or unfortunate who permits the exploitation of what is decent and legitimate by the unprincipled buyer.

XVI

Fallacious Special Editions

SPECIAL editions are a device to be shunned by the advertising manager seeking to build up a strong edifice. The temptation to seek the extra money obtainable from those who most easily bite on artificial bait, in preference to real live worms, is generally strong, but that does not prove that it is good business to take their money on false pretense.

If I were an advertiser I would not go into a special edition if the space were offered free. Representation in the best of them is proof of one's weakness rather than anything else. Yet nearly every day some of my newspaper friends send me copies of big special editions as proof of their ability and enterprise.

From my standpoint it matters not whether a special edition is the product of your regular advertising force or the work of a crew of strong-arm men set loose among your local industries; the result is the same—no satisfactory return to the advertiser. Few readers take the trouble to wade through such publications, whose chief purpose is to puff up those who spend money for their production.

On this point an extract from a recent editorial from *The Emporia* (Kansas) *Gazette*, edited by William Allen White, is pertinent:

The Gazette has received sample copies of a daily newspaper of 228 pages, printed this week in an Oklahoma town. The paper is said by its publishers to be the largest single edition ever printed in the United States. If it is, it also is the silliest single edition ever printed in the United States.

No newspaper in the world can get out a 228-page edition and fill it with reading matter that is worth while to the average newspaper reader, or, for that matter, with advertising which is worth while to the average advertiser.

. . . . . .

The tendency in modern newspaper-making is to fewer pages. The newspaper is becoming a sort of public utility, and it is a reasonably well-established belief that public-utility service should not be duplicated. Another tendency in modern newspaper-making is more concise writing of news, and because the writing is more concise the newspapers are requiring better-trained writers. Any reporter can tell his story in a column, but it takes a real master to get it into the space known to the old hand-set men as a stickful.

The newspaper business is growing away from the sensational. The present-day tendency is news, tersely written, and articles of the news and great world events, at some length, written by past-masters in the art of newspaper and magazine writing.

In my time I have had opportunity to try out almost every kind of special edition ever put over, and on a final review of my experience I must fall in with the views of Mr. White and the policies pursued by such representative newspapers as *The Chicago Daily News*, *The Kansas City Star*, *The Philadelphia Bulletin*, and many others which would no more give house room to a special edition than to paid advertising as reading matter at any figure.

During my earlier days I have seen special-edition men draw down 50 to 60 per cent. of their take from a town, and yet the newspapers figured that they were doing a sound business because in some way or other they were able to figure a small margin of profit for the shop. There are men who to-day make a specialty of such work, openly advertising their trade and newspapers which employ them, and think they are doing legitimate business. And, stranger still, they are the papers who as a rule object to paying advertising agents a commission of 15 per cent. on business sent them if it is linked to the names of local dealers.

Only once or twice since my connection with *The Globe* have we tried out special editions, and every time, regardless of results, we have had a feeling of regret and remorse at having lent ourselves to such childish and foolish makeshifts for real advertising. The only kind of advertising which is profitable to a newspaper (this cannot be repeated too often) is the sort that is profitable to the advertiser. It is much more effective to put in double the effort to get 312- or 365-day a year business into a newspaper than to fool business men into throwing away their money in special editions.

For some reason it is always easy to get ordinary business men to agree to pay for space in a special edition, on the strength of glittering promises made in connection with a hand-made dummy. They seem to like to part with their money for such blarney. I know because I have sold it to them. The same man who will gladly pay good money to see his picture and a puff of himself or his business will balk a block when asked to buy advertising of the kind that will bring him increased sales and new trade.

But it is up to our advertising manager to devote his time and attention to educating merchants and local dealers to the use of legitimate advertising and away from the special-edition idea and other fly-by-night schemes called advertising.

Total space figures produced by special editions provide a fictitious basis for future comparisons, and lead to further special editions or temptation the next year to equal previous records or to establish new high marks. We all know how such things work, and yet too many of us in a moment of weakness listen to the voice of the plausible talker seeking to put over a special or series of specials on us.

Sound experience, I repeat, is against special editions of all kinds under any pretense, yet the best of them, aside from the really successful newspapers, occasionally indulge in twenty-fifth-birthday testimonial benefits. The farther away you keep from such efforts the better will be the appreciation of your newspaper as a community institution.

As a striking example of the more dignified treatment, *The New York Globe* on its 125th anniversary published an eight-page historical section and did not solicit or print a single line of special advertising, though we could have secured $40,000 or $50,000 of it, if we had sought it. The fact that we did not merely take money is worth more to us than the profit we would have made by the other process.

XVII

Scheme Advertising Ineffective

CLASSIFIED directories of various sorts are a delusive phase of activity in stimulating local advertising that has been tried time and again in endless variety, and never, so far as I know, with lasting success. As a rule, such activities furnish a seemingly promising outlet for the pent-up enthusiasm of some solicitor or group of solicitors, and often start off quite successfully for a few weeks or months, before the advertisers commence to tire of spending even small sums without result.

Years ago I had a strong inclination toward this sort of development, on the theory that under a series of general heads such as "Household Necessities," "For the Office," "Dressmaking," and such, it would be easy to secure the small cards of people engaged in such lines who at trifling cost could keep their names before the public and pick up profitable trade. Whether or not in those days the papers I was connected with did not pull, I never succeeded in establishing such a feature for any length of time.

Later I discovered that in trying to make a directory attractive typographically the general head and classified lines ate up too large a proportion of the space to make even a fairly high rate produce the average per column required to make both ends meet. This may have been due to our own weakness in granting classification headings too freely.

To me, at least, these demonstrations stand as striking testimony that no advertising of the standing-card variety can ever be profitable to those seeking definite sales. I tried to get my customers to change their copy and offerings from day to day, but the business in individual cases was so insignificant that it did not pay to give it personal attention.

The Chicago Sunday Tribune has apparently made a success at different times with various specific groupings of small advertisers, but *The Tribune* can do things that probably no other newspaper can do. Carrying a mass of classified advertising in its Sunday issue which its readers have been trained to utilize, the small specialized directories on the women's pages, kept alive in advertising news interest, have gone a long way to disprove the soundness of my theory and to impair the value of my own experience.

On *The Chicago Inter-Ocean* in 1898 we built up a directory of nearly a full page which made a fine showing, and, with space at 10 cents a line, bid fair to be profitable. Before the year was out it had dwindled to such small proportions as no longer to justify the running of the general head.

Likewise, the scheme of presenting a collection of one-inch cards from business houses in a community, a device that has been a bread-winner for many a weak newspaper, has seldom continued beyond the duration of the introductory contracts. Such advertising becomes stagnant in the eyes of the reader, who after a few days or weeks skips it. It is not news-

HARRY J. GRANT
Business Manager of the Milwaukee *Journal*. A newspaper man who has had successful experience as a special representative.

paper advertising in its soundest sense, and is therefore of doubtful value in building up a healthy advertising following.

This brings me to another point of interest in the consideration of newspaper advertising—the comparative value of a full-page ad. and one of six full columns in a newspaper carrying seven columns to the page. John Wanamaker, of New York and Philadelphia, one of the most successful advertisers in the country, has long believed that space on a page with some reading matter was more valuable to him than the full page.

By studying the way people read their newspapers on the street-cars and on the trains I am almost convinced that Mr. Wanamaker's conclusion is sound. More often than not I have seen the reader in public places give a solid page ad. a mere glance to see if there was any reading matter there, and then turn to the next page. If this is a common practice—and I think it is—are not our newspapers making a mistake in seeking full pages and double trucks? It is wasteful and destructive to induce a customer to buy more than he can use at a profit, just as much in selling advertising as in stocking him with goods by means of an over-zealous drummer.

For a long time I have inclined to the notion that our newspapers have sold their advertising so cheaply as to encourage advertisers to wasteful use of space. From every standpoint both the newspaper and the advertiser would be better off if much less space were taken at higher rates.

Only a few years ago we conducted a series of advertising contests in *The Globe*, for the purpose of intensifying reader interest in advertising, which produced a total of over 70,000 letters. An analysis showed that the advertising of Hearn & Co., who use only two full columns every day except Saturday, and three columns on Wednesday, drew as many mentions as the advertising of any large advertiser except John Wanamaker. This was a surprising result, and one which indicates that mere bulk of advertising does not secure increased volume of trade. (See further details in Chapter XLIII Part IV).

Whenever I see the statements of certain newspapers in various cities boasting that they carry upwards of 1,000,000 lines of advertising per month, I make up my mind they are selling their space too cheaply and inducing merchants large and small to shout their heads off with huge copy until the moderate user of space has little or no chance. Most of them could profitably borrow a page of experience from *The Philadelphia Bulletin* with its 400,000 two-cent circulation and rates which hold the big fellows down and give the small advertiser a chance.

I know of several very successful big-volume newspapers which experienced advertisers with means of checking results put down as of doubtful value to them except where they can use dominant copy. As one of them recently told me, "I know the ——— has an enormous circulation and should pay me handsomely, but my small copy gets lost in the shuffle and after a dozen trials I now use other newspapers of less circulation with better results."

Newspapers reach a point of reader saturation. Few people nowadays have the time or inclination to read thoroughly a daily newspaper of over 16 pages, yet there are publishers who pride themselves on crowding from 24 to 36 pages of printed matter on them day in and day out. Sooner or later their sins will find them out. Higher rates and more condensed news and advertising constitute an effective means for the conservation of print paper and the time of readers.

XVIII

Political Advertising

IN the early days many of our newspapers were started for political purposes, supported by contributions either from those who sought official recognition or from those who hoped for franchise grants, and from public funds through election, legislation record, and other governmental printing. Too many newspaper men still look with favor upon such practices, and in my opinion it is leaning on this broken reed that causes more newspapers unsuccess than almost all other factors combined.

Dreamers and impractical journalists have for years looked upon newspapers as correlated to politics and interested control rather than as a legitimate business probably more essential to a community than any other, upon which, indeed, most others are largely dependent for growth and prosperity. Men like the late Col. W. R. Nelson, Victor F. Lawson, W. L. McLean, Adolph S. Ochs, and a hundred others of perhaps less prominence I could name have never played up to or for politics.

The party newspaper is a weak newspaper, for, by the assertion or partizan bias, it cuts off all possible influence among those outside of party lines, who will not buy it. Divested of all pretense, the advertising of a party in its own controlled newspaper is about as effective as would be the offer of warm blankets in the region supposed to be dominated by his Satanic majesty.

The most casual investigation of newspaper conditions in the larger cities of the country convincingly proves that there is absolutely nothing worth while in seeking political or governmental advertising in compensation for inflicting interested propaganda on the readers of a newspaper. The old *New York Star*, *The Chicago Times*, *The Chicago Herald*, *The Chicago Inter-Ocean*, and later *The Chicago Chronicle*, were samples of the policy of such conception and method of newspapering. Others too numerous to specify in nearly every city in the country could be cited as additional proof.

Millions upon millions of dollars have been spent by men in their zeal to serve a party and its cause or to accomplish political ends by backing or supporting newspapers. So many thousands of enrolled citizens composing a party look like real circulation ready made, while the promises of advertising by men enthusiastic for the moment and of public printing seem to prove that the enterprise must be a winner from the start.

After Election Day political enthusiasm peters out like a crowd from a baseball game. Lack of partizan support means circulation materially below glowing estimates, and advertising promised in advance of a campaign fades like a shadow if it does not produce profitable returns. The few exceptions of really worth-while newspapers that have grown out of political sheets have merely happened and serve as bait to lure those with money to burn, trying to prove their patriotism or party zeal.

For the purpose of stimulating political advertising nothing is so effective as an absolutely independent newspaper, pledged to no party, but faithfully serving the best interests of the taxpayers and commending the best men for office regardless of party. Such a newspaper wins the confidence of the community, generally attains largest circulation, and is in the best possible situation to attract political advertising. It is not hampered by the hoodoo badge of partizanship, and provides the ideal medium for all parties and candidates wherein to make their display appeals.

With columns freely open to orderly and sane arguments of any party, such a newspaper, reaching all sorts and conditions of people, facilitates circulation of arguments among the voters. Our newspapers in New York make a higher rate for political advertising than ordinary run of paper copy, probably on the theory that they are entitled to a special revenue from business coming only for a few weeks in a year, in order to make it pay its share of the carrying charge of publication every day in the year.

For example, in the case of *The Globe*, our one-time ordinary rate is 50 cents per line, while we place it at 60 cents a line for political. During the 1917 campaign we eliminated the extra 10 cents a line as an experiment, but the additional business secured was not sufficient to justify the sacrifice. Those who inserted political advertising used certain newspapers regardless of rates, and we had merely lost 10 cents per line of revenue for our willingness to apply common-sense rules to the situation.

Official business from the city and the state in the case of our New York City newspapers pays the usual one-time transient rate, 50 cents a line. This came

BUILDING NEWSPAPER ADVERTISING

largely as the result of politicians of one sort seeking to beat the newspapers down to very low rates for such business, and the politicians of another sort seeking to enrich favored friends by giving them the highest rates they dared for certain business.

Aside from the Brooklyn newspapers, which print a large volume of legislative records, a relic of country newspaper days, none of our New York newspapers receive or seriously seek official advertising. The list of election-district polling-places and results of the official canvass go to a certain number of Republican and Democratic newspapers each year, and a limited volume of small ads. referring to specific offerings in *The City Record*, a government daily, is about all that is out.

Political pap dealt out to the faithful in many cities and states is, as a rule, as illusive and profitless as the bag of gold supposed to be deposited at the end of a rainbow. The little fellows and amateurs continue to look for it as a necessity for support when they could probably dig up twice as much profit by devoting the same amount of time to the quest for legitimate business.

My only personal experience in connection with large-volume official advertising was in Chicago in the '90's, when two or three papers got competing for it on the basis of determining which would take it at the lowest rate. I am not certain regarding the final result, but have a faint recollection that the winner took it for one cent a line, hardly sufficient to pay for setting the type and wear and tear of the metal. I believe the publishers thought there was some small circulation that followed the printing of this matter.

BUILDING NEWSPAPER ADVERTISING

Many of the states have enacted laws regulating political advertising so as to prohibit the old practice of selling paid reading matter printed to influence voters. In Minnesota, for example, the General Election Laws clearly define what may and may not be done, as follows:

SECTION 568. DESIGNATION OF POLITICAL ADVERTISEMENTS IN NEWSPAPERS—PUBLISHER TO FILE STATEMENT WITH SECRETARY OF STATE.—No publisher of a newspaper, periodical or magazine shall insert either in the advertising columns of such newspaper, magazine or periodical, or elsewhere therein any matter paid or to be paid for which is intended or tends to influence directly or indirectly any voting at any primary or general election unless at the head of said matter is printed in pica capital letters the words "Paid Advertisement," and unless there is also a statement at the head of said matter of the amount paid or to be paid therefor, the name and address of the candidate in whose behalf the matter is inserted and of any other person, if any, authorizing the publication, and the name of the author thereof. No publisher of any newspaper, periodical or magazine published within this state shall insert therein in the advertising column of such newspaper, magazine, periodical, or elsewhere therein, any matter whatsoever of a political nature, or any political editorial relative to a candidate for any public office, unless the publisher thereof shall file in the office of the secretary of state of this state within six months before the holding of any primary or general election, or within ten days after the calling of and before the holding of any special election, a sworn statement which shall contain the names of the owners of such paper, and if such paper be a corporation, the names and addresses of the owners of the shares of stock of such corporation.

SECTION 569. PUBLISHER'S STATEMENT TO BE FILED WITH COUNTY AUDITOR.—Every candidate and every member of any personal campaign or party committee, who shall either in his own name or in the name of any other person, own any financial interest in any newspaper or periodical, circulating in part or in whole in Minnesota, shall, before such newspaper or periodical shall print any matter otherwise than as is provided in Sections

2(568), which is intended or tends to influence, directly or indirectly, any voting at any election or primary in this state, file in the office of the auditor of the county in which he resides a verified declaration, stating definitely the newspaper or periodical in which or over which he has such financial interest or control, and the exact nature and extent of such interest or control. The editor, manager or other person controlling the publication of any such newspaper or article, who shall print or cause to be printed any such matter contrary to the provisions of this act, prior to the filing of such verified declaration from any person required by this section to file such declaration, shall be deemed guilty of a violation hereof.

SECTION 570. SOLICITING BY PUBLISHER OR CANDIDATE PROHIBITED.—No owner, publisher, editor, reporter, agent or employe of any newspaper or other periodical, shall, directly or indirectly, solicit, receive or accept any payment, promise or compensation, nor shall any person pay or promise to pay, in any manner compensate any such owner, publisher, editor, reporter, agent or employe, directly or indirectly, for influencing or attempting to influence through any printing matter in such newspaper any voting at any election or primary through any means whatsoever, except through the matter inserted in such newspaper or periodical as "Paid Advertisement," and so designated as provided by this act.

Likewise, in many of our states corrupt-practice laws, compelling candidates and parties to file detailed statements of subscriptions and expenses, are tending to eliminate the outright purchase of votes by money or entertainment, and to foster paid newspaper advertising. Here in New York, during the Presidential election of 1916, our newspapers carried more political advertising than ever before. The ads. were carefully prepared, largely free from abuse, clearly presented the strongest arguments, and were read and studied by the voters.

As previously stated, the modern practice, which places upon independent journalism the highest premiums in circulation and public confidence, also brings the heaviest volume of legitimate political advertising. A newspaper can accept and print non-abusive advertising from both or many sides, and keep free from entanglements as far as editorial conduct goes.

XIX

Table for Determining Size of Paper

THE print-paper shortage of 1916 and 1917 and the higher price of print paper for 1918 compelled newspaper-makers to give more attention than ever to the proportion of news matter to advertising. The subject was touched on in *Newspaper Building*, Chapter XX. Increasing pressure has demanded still further consideration of the situation by newspaper publishers, and hardly a day passes without some query coming to me for additional data.

I have prepared the two tables herewith, covering various standards of news matter from 40 to 76 columns for 7- and 8-column newspapers, which, if reproduced for office use on slips, will save print-paper waste. In *The Globe* office a check mark opposite the standard in force any week or any day, copies of the slips going to the editors and composing-room, eliminates any possible misunderstanding.

In explanation of the tables:

The first column shows the size of the paper determined by the quantity of advertising.

The second column, the number of columns in the number of pages given in the first column.

The third column, the number of columns of reading matter which we may adopt as our standard.

MAKE-UP SCHEDULE

8-COLUMN BASIS

Pages	Total Columns	Columns Reading	Columns Advertising	To go to Next Size
12	96	40	56	60
14	112	40	72	76
16	128	40	88	92
18	144	40	104	108
20	160	40	120	124
22	176	40	136	140
24	192	40	152	156
12	96	44	52	56
14	112	44	68	72
16	128	44	84	88
18	144	44	100	104
20	160	44	116	120
22	176	44	132	136
24	192	44	148	152
12	96	48	48	52
14	112	48	64	68
16	128	48	80	84
18	144	48	96	100
20	160	48	112	116
22	176	48	128	132
24	192	48	144	148
12	96	52	44	48
14	112	52	60	64
16	128	52	76	80
18	144	52	92	96
20	160	52	108	112
22	176	52	124	128
24	192	52	140	144
12	96	56	40	44
14	112	56	56	60
16	128	56	72	76
18	144	56	88	92
20	160	56	104	108
22	176	56	120	124
24	192	56	136	140

BUILDING NEWSPAPER ADVERTISING

MAKE-UP SCHEDULE

8-COLUMN BASIS

Pages	Total Columns	Columns Reading	Columns Advertising	To go to Next Size
12	96	60	36	40
14	112	60	52	56
16	128	60	68	72
18	144	60	84	88
20	160	60	100	104
22	176	60	116	120
24	192	60	132	136
12	96	64	32	36
14	112	64	48	52
16	128	64	64	68
18	144	64	80	84
20	160	64	96	100
22	176	64	112	116
24	192	64	128	132
12	96	68	28	32
14	112	68	44	48
16	128	68	60	64
18	144	68	76	80
20	160	68	92	96
22	176	68	108	112
24	192	68	124	128
12	96	72	24	28
14	112	72	40	44
16	128	72	56	60
18	144	72	72	76
20	160	72	88	92
22	176	72	104	108
24	192	72	120	124
12	96	76	20	24
14	112	76	36	40
16	128	76	52	56
18	144	76	68	72
20	160	76	84	88
22	176	76	100	104
24	192	76	116	120

MAKE-UP SCHEDULE

7-COLUMN BASIS

Pages	Total Columns	Columns Reading	Columns Advertising	To go to Next Size
12	84	40	44	48
14	98	40	58	62
16	112	40	72	76
18	126	40	86	90
20	140	40	100	104
22	154	40	114	118
24	168	40	128	132
12	84	44	40	44
14	98	44	54	58
16	112	44	68	72
18	126	44	82	86
20	140	44	96	100
22	154	44	110	118
24	168	44	124	132
12	84	48	36	40
14	98	48	50	54
16	112	48	64	68
18	126	48	78	82
20	140	48	92	96
22	154	48	106	110
24	168	48	120	124
12	84	52	32	36
14	98	52	46	50
16	112	52	60	64
18	126	52	74	78
20	140	52	88	92
22	154	52	102	106
24	168	52	116	120
12	84	56	28	32
14	98	56	42	46
16	112	56	56	60
18	126	56	70	74
20	140	56	84	88
22	154	56	98	102
24	168	56	112	116

BUILDING NEWSPAPER ADVERTISING

MAKE-UP SCHEDULE

7-COLUMN BASIS

Pages	Total Columns	Columns Reading	Columns Advertising	To go to Next Size
12	84	60	24	28
14	98	60	38	42
16	112	60	52	56
18	126	60	68	72
20	140	60	80	84
22	154	60	94	98
24	168	60	110	114
12	84	64	20	24
14	98	64	34	38
16	112	64	48	52
18	126	64	64	68
20	140	64	76	80
22	154	64	90	94
24	168	64	106	110
12	84	68	16	20
14	98	68	30	34
16	112	68	44	48
18	126	68	60	64
20	140	68	72	76
22	154	68	86	92
24	168	68	102	106
12	84	72	12	24
14	98	72	26	38
16	112	72	40	52
18	126	72	56	68
20	140	72	68	80
22	154	72	82	96
24	168	72	96	110
12	84	76	8	12
14	98	76	22	26
16	112	76	36	40
18	126	76	50	54
20	140	76	64	68
22	154	76	78	82
24	168	76	92	96

(By reading matter we mean everything in the newspaper except paid advertising.)

The fourth column, the number of columns of advertising in a normal paper of the size fixed by the number of pages in the first column.

The fifth column, the point where the size of the newspaper is to be increased. By demanding four additional columns to justify a larger paper, we secure sufficient revenue to justify the additional sheet. For example, a 14-page paper on the 56-column standard becomes 52 columns of reading matter and 60 columns of advertising before we go to 16 pages.

Important newspapers like *The Chicago Tribune*, *The Chicago Daily News*, *The New York World*, and *The Washington Star* have adopted the 60-column standard with success, while newspapers which try to operate on percentage basis are continually in hot water and find their editors needlessly using up paper. Even the modern two-cent paper does not justify the use of the old fifty-fifty standard—half reading and half advertising—or, for that matter, 40 per cent. reading and 60 per cent. advertising.

It is much easier to decide on the quantity of reading matter you will give for the one, two, or three cents paid by the reader, and stick to it, than to be at the mercy of your advertisers regarding the total of your print-paper bill. Where there is a gain of ads., they are run more solidly, but the advertiser must put up with that or stay out if we are to operate on a sound basis and do our part in conserving print paper.

As I recently told a well-known newspaper publisher, the difference between operating on a fixed standard basis and on a fifty-fifty basis is the difference between a smile and a frown. In other words, the man who is on a sound basis smiles, while the one ever at the mercy of factors beyond his control has cause to worry.

If in conjunction with the rigid enforcement of some such sane rule as is here indicated the newspapers would apply the pyramid make-up, advertising starting from the lower right-hand corner of each page, and reading-matter at the upper left-hand corner, they would soon discover how wasteful and profligate they had been in the past.

Nothing so graphically proves a newspaper's apparent weakness as advertising alongside the left-hand edge of pages, hanging freely from the top, or made up above reading-matter. Such treatment is not good for the advertiser or the newspaper. But no one can blame the advertiser or agent for seeking what he thinks he wants if he can get it.

XX

Some Office Forms and Records

For the purpose of keeping track of the volume of advertising inserted by all local advertisers or any group of them, the forms in figures Nos. 1 and 3 may be used as simple and effective. In a highly competitive field like New York or Chicago such data provide the final check-up to ascertain whether our force is getting its share of any business.

Figure No. 1 shows a method of watching the use of space by automobile concerns during the annual show week in New York. It is a summarized report for the ten days or two weeks. Each day a sheet like Figure No. 2 is made up and the totals from the day sheets are brought up to date.

Regardless of trade deals and special inducements, it is interesting to know definitely what the other newspapers are getting from the various manufacturers in detail and in total, both as a check on the efficiency of the soliciting force and to regulate future relations with the manufacturers.

To know exactly what part of its advertising a certain automobile concern is giving to us and to other newspapers is often desirable in the adoption of policy in relation to consideration to be given it.

BUILDING NEWSPAPER ADVERTISING

Following are the specimen tables of automobile show week advertising:

SAMPLE DAILY REPORT
January 6, 1917

	Globe	Mail	Sun	Post	Evening World	Evening Journal
Auto Show GCP	255	500	255	...	255	500
Auto Salon	...	140	...	...	...	...
Abbott	...	...	...	270	...	...
Apperson	...	252	...	240	...	140
Autocar	...	...	...	...	...	70
Braender Tires	110	...	...	...	...	...
Briscoe	196	196	...	...	...	...
Buick	264	264	...	264	...	...
Chadwick-De Lamater	...	...	28	...	...	...
Chalmers	588	588	...	294	...	600
Champion Ignition	...	520	...	520	...	...
Chevrolet	140	255	...	...	...	...
Doble	160	...	...	160	...	160
Dodge	660	660	...	660	...	...
Ford	...	60	...	...	...	...
Grant	42	42	42	42	42	28
General Engineering	...	150	...	...	...	...
Goodyear	...	...	...	780	...	...
Harroun	336	336	...	336	...	336
Haynes	...	full page	...	...	...	...
Houdaille Shock Abs.	...	84	...	42	...	...
Hupmobile	...	620	...	600	...	...
Hamilton Corp	...	800	...	800	...	...
Hurlburt	...	...	140	...	...	...
Interstate	200	200	...	150	...	...
Jeffery-Nash	700	200	200	700	...	200
Kissel	...	420	...	420	...	...
King	...	...	...	640	...	...
Lexington	...	196	...	196	...	...
Liberty	...	...	409	...	...	...
Locomobile	...	...	...	140	...	...
Moline-Knight	300	300	...	300	...	...
Maxwell	...	511	...	...	...	...
Mitchell	...	...	860	...	...	...
Marmon	...	...	...	full page	...	...
Murray	...	...	...	60	...	224
Marion-Handley	...	...	...	...	...	...
National	196	196	...	336	...	...
Owen Magnetic	390	390	...	...	...	...
Oakland	...	420	...	435	...	435
Pathfinder	784	680	...	792	...	...
Peerless	...	720	...	720	...	...
Pierce-Arrow	...	full page	420	420	...	420
Reo	555	546	546	546	...	...
Studebaker	760	748	...	760	...	...
Saxon	100	100	...	100	...	100
Springfield Body	...	full page	...	...	...	...
Republic Motor Truck	...	255	...	...	...	...
Smith Form A Truck	...	792	...	800	...	...
Singer	...	...	...	50	...	...
Scripps-Booth	...	...	...	432	...	330
Velie	...	...	...	...	...	...
White	...	...	330	616	...	...
Willys-Overland	...	double page	...	full page	...	...
	6,736	23,941	3,230	17,737	297	3,543

BUILDING NEWSPAPER ADVERTISING

AUTOMOBILE SHOW (SUMMARY)

	Globe 1917	Globe 1916	Mail 1917	Mail 1916	Sun 1917	Sun 1916	Ev. World 1917	Ev. World 1916	Ev. Journal 1917	Ev. Journal 1916	Post 1917	Post 1916
Auto Salon												
Auto Show GCP	765		280	280	1,020	700	140		1,010	140	140	140
Abbott		1,510	1,265	1,510		1,265	765			1,010	1,010	1,010
Ajax Tires						252	261			168	272	
Allen		320		316		160				320		160
American "8"										338		
Apperson	224		224		224				2,136			
Auburn	140	420	392	140	380	140			532	280	520	
Autocar					908	200				200		
Automatic Carburetor												
Baker, R. & L.					280				927			
Ben-Hur					960				1,120			
Bishop, McCormick & Bishop					100							
Bosch Magneto	168	168	224	224	168	168			952			
Braender Tires	440	1,176							100			
Briscoe	196	1,196	631	800	435	306	390		168	168	264	450
Buick	264	300	264	300	270	300	264		270	600		
Certified Used Car Advertising	888	1,026								300		
Cadillac	300	600	600	600	300	450	150				450	450
Case					600	900						
Chadwick-De Lamater					196				1,494		594	435
Chalmers	888	200	888				300		520	200	520	
Champion Ignition			520	435	1,000							
Chandler			395		280	465			270		140	
Chevrolet	420	465	336	465	1,000							
Cole					168							
Columbia Six					980							
Crow-Elkhart						50						
Daniels	200		1,200						616		666	50
Dann Insert	28		56						28		600	
Denmo Motor Truck					480							
Detroit Electric					3,700		330					
Detroit Weather Proofing			2,440		150		150		166	600	320	435
Doble (General Engineering)	310		300		840				1,092		1,080	
Dodge	1,080	1,052	1,080	1,432	600	1,432			1,180	1,432		1,052
Elgin	100											
Firestone												170
Ford Auto Parts (I. Davega)			120						90			
Ford Dearborn Truck			90						200			

BUILDING NEWSPAPER ADVERTISING 127

(SUMMARY) AUTOMOBILE SHOW—*Continued*

	Globe 1917	Globe 1916	Mail 1917	Mail 1916	Sun 1917	Sun 1916	Ev. World 1917	Ev. World 1916	Ev. Journal 1917	Ev. Journal 1916	Post 1917	Post 1916
Franklin			250		250		250					
Fulton Motor Truck					348		856		856			
Garford	848	840	860	800	860	2,376			840	680	860	680
Goodrich Tires		210		840	780	2,360			800	2,530	780	2,575
Goodyear Tires	42		42	2,800	42	210	42		644	210	42	500
Grant				210	196				435			
Guaranty Sec. Corp	200	160	200		200						200	
Hal			800		780						800	
Hamilton Corp	672		672		336				672		672	
Harroun Motors		684										
Hardman Tires		300	2,360	300	2,400	300				300		336
Haynes		400		400		240				400		
Hartford Shock Absorber	120				120		120		120		120	
H. & N. Carburetor Co			84								42	420
Houdaille Shock Absorber												
Houk Wire Wheels												
Hudson	1,000	1,350	1,000	1,350	1,025	3,076	140		2,000	900	2,055	900
Hupmobile	880		740		2,730	1,800	140		2,490			
Hurlburt					420				140	490	192	488
Interstate	350	400	256	400	448	400	200		156			
Jackson					400	950			1,110	940	900	1,115
Jeffery-Nash Motors	900	300	900	1,236	1,394				1,112			
Jordan												
King	420	587	640	590	640	605			420	230	640	345
Kissel	196	783	420	435	196	200	196			200	420	200
Lexington		200	196	795							196	
Liberty			409								285	
Locomobile				600		1,180	200				140	
Lozier				1,180	220	594	214		220	200	3,658	3,630
Marion Handley		336	1,200	345	2,000							
Marmon		1,000		790					795	1,344		910
Maxfer Truck & T. Co						742			420			
Maxwell		1,046	420	1,642	420		294		378			
Metz						660						
Michelin Tires		300		300						510	224	200
Chas. E. Miller	480		495	196	2,400	196	196		795	2,840		200
Miller Rubber Co		1,200	818	600	1,720	600			1,732		300	
Mitchell	300		300						300		60	
Moline Knight			60									
Murray "8"												
N. Y. Edison Co. Electrics		330		330		330				330		330

AUTOMOBILE SHOW.—*Continued*
(SUMMARY)

	Globe		Mail		Sun		Ev. World		Ev. Journal		Post	
	1917	1916	1917	1916	1917	1916	1917	1916	1917	1916	1917	1916
National	196	350	196	350	700	150	....	....	200	350	336	350
Oakland	700	....	700	750	880	750	....	....	715	750	715	750
Owen Magnetic	780	968	786	965	890	695	....	....	390	625	396	736
Packard	....	....	354	....	....	2,055	....	....	....	....	1,200	....
Paige	....	....	....	....	....	1,225	....	....	....	....	....	....
Pathfinder	784	450	1,190	450	1,395	900	300	....	1,580	330	....	....
Peerless	720	1,550	720	1,050	....	1,550	....	....	720	900	792	1,330
Parker Hydraulic	....	200	....	200	....	200	....	....	....	1,550	720	1,550
Perfection Heater	....	....	....	....	800	700	....	....	....	200	....	....
Perfection Spring Service	....	....	672	....	672	....	....	....	....	....	....	....
Perlman Demountable Rim	825	795	3,605	3,140	825	420	....	....	1,260	420	840	1,215
Pierce-Arrow	....	....	2,320	....	....	....	580	....	2,200	1,200	2,058	....
Premier	....	....	....	....	....	....	....	....	....	....	....	....
Pullman	....	....	....	....	360	180	....	....	....	....	....	....
Rainier	....	....	200	....	200	920	....	....	....	....	....	....
Redden Motor Truck	1,101	1,120	1,092	1,120	1,101	....	100	....	1,110	1,120	1,647	1,618
Remington	200	294	255	294	....	....	....	....	510	....	....	294
Reo	....	....	....	....	....	538	....	....	400	870	600	225
Republic Motor Truck	300	734	500	800	400	450	....	....	510	200	632	360
Russell Motor Axle Co	435	200	435	200	435	....	....	....	224	....	....	....
S. G. V. Co	224	....	420	....	435	....	....	....	....	....	50	....
Saxon	1,000	....	792	....	1,600	....	....	....	1,000	....	800	....
Scripps-Booth	....	....	3,480	....	1,000	2,150	....	....	500	....	....	....
Selden	....	....	700	500	1,160	500	....	....	2,240	....	1,050	....
Singer	....	....	....	150	1,162	100	....	....	....	....	....	....
Smith Form A Truck	1,885	500	1,873	1,800	1,125	2,175	200	....	200	196	1,885	2,175
Sparks Withington	200	150	200	350	635	196	106	....	....	....	200	150
Springfield Body	....	2,175	....	....	1,375	510	2,750	....	2,750	510	2,750	510
Standard (Duffy)	168	346	2,750	510	168	224	168	....	330	448	168	224
Stearns	....	510	168	414	....	620	....	....	....	620	....	620
Sterling	....	414	....	620	....	....	....	....	....	....	....	....
Studebaker	600	620	300	2,770	300	454	....	....	420	....	916	422
Stutz	....	....	5,920	7,720	2,400	3,000	1,200	....	4,640	4,500	4,508	4,500
Union Truck Mfg. Co	....	4,500	330	....	....	....	....	....	....	....	330	....
U. S. Tires												
Velie												
Weed Chains												
Westcott												
White												
Willys-Overland												
Winton												

*Lines of Dry Goods Advertising in New York Newspapers
DURING YEAR 1917
Evening Newspapers

	World	Journal	Globe	Mail	Sun	Telegram	Post	Total
Altman	136,712	134,448	133,429	124,691	136,071	123,455	123,173	911,979
Arnold Constable	15,825	—	147,340	146,117	146,388	—	—	455,670
Best	41,876	106,914	99,711	97,284	99,234	—	13,517	458,536
Bloomingdale	196,923	197,947	6,530	6,569	6,504	11,979	7,152	433,604
Bonwit Teller	47,932	49,042	37,159	—	46,281	—	6,856	187,270
Gimbel	8,810	315,900	435,721	424,040	426,354	—	—	1,610,825
Greenhut	368,684	364,460	81,267	77,652	17,484	79,713	12,209	1,001,469
Hearn	181,996	182,160	161,296	158,219	—	160,586	3,446	847,703
Lord & Taylor	235,730	10,851	183,769	51,019	219,815	42,918	3,815	747,917
McCreery	358,515	68,976	11,754	219,544	325,227	198,631	930	1,184,577
Macy	466,714	—	483,209	415,120	—	24,420	133,170	1,522,633
Oppenheim Collins	123,461	124,983	49,213	48,617	54,483	1,590	5,970	408,317
Stewart & Co.	534	19,773	67,905	—	58,438	—	—	146,650
Franklin Simon	101,883	54,602	80,044	81,512	100,647	—	8,556	428,044
Stern	181,077	56,477	73,262	163,693	155,642	14,348	82,966	727,565
Wanamaker	140,213	322,026	474,655	115,602	450,804	485,888	394,980	2,384,168
Total	2,606,885	2,008,559	2,527,364	2,130,679	2,243,172	1,143,528	796,740	13,456,927

Lines of Dry Goods Advertising in New York Newspapers
DURING YEAR 1917
Morning Newspapers—Six Days, Excluding Sundays

	World	American	Herald	Times	Sun	Tribune	Total
Altman	38,979	61,683	32,224	65,646	31,283	34,765	264,580
Arnold Constable	—	1,096	—	20,442	—	—	21,538
Best	—	3,094	—	9,177	—	130	13,401
Bloomingdale	7,203	6,359	6,388	6,304	6,317	6,381	38,952
Bonwit Teller	1,500	—	—	9,181	—	—	10,681
Gimbel	4,280	33,281	—	112,598	—	—	150,259
Greenhut	5,830	5,390	5,335	59,545	—	—	76,100
Hearn	8,057	6,010	—	11,377	—	997	26,441
Lord & Taylor	48,865	—	985	56,248	20,515	24,514	151,127
McCreery	25,649	—	6,049	26,588	2,320	1,864	62,470
Macy	15,246	420	12,294	150,494	420	—	178,874
Oppenheim Collins	13,465	10,395	2,228	11,359	—	2,312	39,759
Stewart & Co.	1,651	—	—	1,328	—	—	2,979
Franklin Simon	45,186	9,026	10,807	96,087	38,182	48,806	248,094
Stern	35,916	4,589	11,493	41,009	17,676	8,627	119,310
Wanamaker	18,085	44,558	344,384	—	47,845	42,695	497,567
Total	270,012	185,901	432,187	677,383	164,558	171,091	1,901,132

Lines of Dry Goods Advertising in New York Newspapers
DURING YEAR 1917
Sunday Newspapers

	World	American	Herald	Times	Sun	Tribune	Total
Altman	82,043	80,175	83,747	86,301	83,505	82,615	498,486
Arnold Constable	—	77,117	10,143	68,243	—	—	155,503
Best	660	36,523	27,282	59,837	27,523	—	151,825
Bloomingdale	112,859	96,090	6,225	6,310	5,017	4,803	231,304
Bonwit Teller	15,367	6,455	62,108	85,756	—	61,384	231,270
Gimbel	130,671	87,874	—	129,448	150	—	348,143
Greenhut	82,830	78,578	61,300	63,312	—	—	186,069
Hearn	76,150	80,515	35,365	70,731	—	51,171	313,912
Lord & Taylor	162,572	126,682	4,040	166,202	60,829	67,069	587,394
McCreery	225,227	5,810	127,041	225,834	10,628	85,364	679,904
Macy	107,812	76,501	105,148	112,290	—	—	400,951
Oppenheim Collins	54,327	47,868	41,181	55,009	—	10,263	208,648
Stewart & Co.	25,147	—	12,790	7,725	11,830	414	57,106
Franklin Simon	36,605	20,902	80,242	129,581	16,835	102,933	386,298
Stern	73,479	44,788	58,359	88,706	61,387	15,161	342,080
Wanamaker	—	—	—	—	—	—	—
Total	1,185,119	743,336	837,881	1,355,296	276,104	481,177	4,878,913

*See *Newspaper Building* pages 103, 104, for yearly Summary as above for years 1915, 1916.

BUILDING NEWSPAPER ADVERTISING 129

In addition to these summaries there is a record of the number of lines taken by every considerable user of space among local concerns and general advertisers, summarized on the form shown in Figure No. 1. This is printed every month and is watched with much interest by local advertisers.

For each local contract advertiser a card like form No. 5, in Chapter X, is issued and kept in a card-index box. At the end of each month the total space used by each is entered on the back of the card, so that at all times there is an exact record for each account of the amount used and agreed upon.

The form herewith lends itself to easy use in a small loose-leaf book with evening newspapers on one page, morning newspapers on another, and Sunday newspapers on another. I have compiled these records for a number of years, with summaries for the first quarter, for six months, for nine months, and for the full year, and they make a record well worth the study of any one interested in spending money for advertising.

With exact data of this kind the newspaper advertising manager knows more regarding what the advertisers are doing than they do themselves. Armed with this information, on sheets or in loose-leaf form, he can often interest even the largest local advertiser as to what others are doing.

To be able to show a merchant exactly what advertising is being done and to tell him just what he is doing himself puts one in an advantageous position in talking business with him.

I believe in "showing" the customer that I am selling him something more than mere space. I seek to convince him that we study to make his advertising profitable to him as sound business practice on our part. Our advertising manager is most effective when he can brush aside with facts false impressions in the minds of those with whom he comes in contact.

The advertiser who makes a rash statement of what he is doing in another newspaper or regarding his whole advertising policy can be brought to earth by the man armed with facts and positive data diplomatically presented at the proper moment. This is nicely done by some such remark as, "Why, Mr. ———, my impression is so and so. Please let me refer to my records," then take the book from your pocket and let him see the facts.

XXI

Definite Proved Circulation

DEFINITE proved circulation should be the basis of any serious attempt to develop increased advertising for any medium. Victor F. Lawson, who, with *The Chicago Daily News*, has stuck to that principle for upward of forty years, with overwhelming success, has clearly established the soundness of playing fair and square with the advertiser.

In 1911, when *The New York Globe* determined to go from "gross print" as circulation to "net paid," we had to admit that 138,000 gross print meant only 103,000 sold. It was a radical step, but it brought us only increased advertising.

Up to that time only one other New York newspaper had pretended to sell "net paid." They all counted gross print where they took the trouble to count anything. Some of them had traded on "high-water mark" figures, gross print for some big day's sales, far above the net average.

When we came out with net figures our immediate competitors jumped at the chance to overwhelm us with unproved figures against those which we presented after an A. A. A. audit, but it profited them nothing and incited me to activities which resulted in the organization of the A. B. C.

I wrote reams of articles for the trade papers and

traveled widely about the country, talking before newspaper and advertising bodies, trying to produce some better and more generally recognized method for authenticating circulation statements and showing up the pretensions of those who would not tell the truth or submit to audits.

At nearly every newspaper gathering are men ready to throw a brick at the Audit Bureau of Circulations and claim that it costs the publisher members too much money; that in no other business is the seller compelled to pay for such work; that most newspaper publishers are honest and should not be asked for proof.

Of course, all of this is humbug, pure and simple. Many of those who form the knocker brigade remain in it only because they have not given the subject the study which it merits. Before the day of the A. B. C. it was well known to many, whose business it was to get the facts, that the average circulation statement was from 10 to 25 per cent. out of line.

I do not mean that that percentage of inaccuracy came from wilful misrepresentation and fraud, but that, owing to lack of standardized accounting and definite understanding of what part of all printed copies was circulation, there was abundant opportunity for an honest man to err.

All of this has been brushed aside. We know what is net paid circulation, and so does the advertiser, and because he knows this every thousand of net paid circulation is worth more to-day than it was before the A. B. C. standardized circulation figures. As the advertiser pays for whatever service he gets, it is obvious that he and not the newspapers pays for A. B. C. audits. If any newspaper has not adjusted the trifling additional expense of the A. B. C. in recent increases in advertising rates, I have yet to hear about it. Yet there are benighted newspaper men who object on the ground that they and not the advertiser pay for the service.

Colonel Mapes, of the Cream of Wheat Company, has for many years insisted on getting the circulation guaranteed him in the contracts he made for advertising. He has brought many suits and been instrumental in exposing fraud. He was president of the old A. A. A. at the time we changed it over to the A. B. C.

While the Colonel was ever willing to fight to see that he got full measure of what he bought, I was fighting to compel other publishers to maintain the standard of honest net paid circulation statements that we issued. The A. B. C. is the result and I guess the Colonel is as proud of it as I am.

As picturing actual experience I reprint herewith an article by Colonel Mapes in *Printers' Ink* about 1910:

CIRCULATION JUGGLING AND THE ADVERTISER

I have read with much interest the article of P. R. Barney on magazine circulations, and as you request that I give my views on the "pay-for-what-you-get proposition," will do so as briefly as possible, although I fear the ground has been pretty well trodden over before.

The principal objections to the plan, which our company has pursued, of paying for what they get, to judge by the opinions expressed in Mr. Barney's article, seem to be, briefly as follows: First, that it is not "business-like for the buyer to bind himself in accordance with the figures kept by the clerks of the seller," and that it is not feasible, on account of the expense, to audit the publisher's books, and, even if this were the case, it would be easy for the publishers to deceive the most eagle-eyed auditor, if they chose to do so; also that the publishers would never submit to having their books audited, but would combine to refuse it and the poor advertiser would consequently be in the soup.

Answering this: I certainly do not consider it business-like for a buyer to bind himself according to the figures kept by the clerks of the seller, yet this is exactly what ninety-nine out of one hundred advertisers are doing at present when they take the circulation statements of the different publishers without authentication.

As to the impossibility of auditing the publisher's books, will say we have during the past five or six years audited the books of almost every leading magazine and similar publication in the United States and have not found that the expense entailed was in any way prohibitive. In doing so, it is true, we have frequently had the publisher attempt to deceive our auditors, and sometimes with success. In the long run, however, any one attempting to deceive a competent auditor is almost sure to be caught. As a matter of fact, we think, in our case, at least, they have always been caught sooner or later, and we can assure you where that has been the case, that, like the man mentioned in the Scriptures, "their latter state was worse than their first."

As to the publishers combining and refusing to accept the advertisements of those who prefer to pay for what they get rather than to buy gold bricks; this has been tried on us many times, but so far has been unsuccessful. As a matter of fact, there is a great deal of misapprehension among the advertisers as to the absolute necessity to them of any given publication. Almost any large advertiser can put half of them in the discard and still have plenty left, and there are enough publishers who are not selling gold bricks to satisfy the requirements of all advertisers. As a matter of fact, in as far as the writer knows (and that after auditing, as I say, nine-tenths of the leading publications of the United States), there is not to-day a publisher who has got the circulation which he claims who is not perfectly willing to have his books audited, while the contrary is the case with regard to those who are securing money under false pretenses by representing that they have a circulation which they have not. The percentage of padding I usually find about 15 to 20 per cent., although I have frequently known it to run to 50 per cent., and, in very rare instances, as high as 60 or 75 per cent.

As a fair example, I will, without mentioning any name (which is a thing contrary to our practice), cite what I consider a fair illustration:

BUILDING NEWSPAPER ADVERTISING

There is a certain publication ranking high in the publishing world, which during the year 1909 carried approximately $1,400,000 in paid advertising at their card rate, we ourselves furnishing about $40,000 of this, but with a written guarantee as to circulation. Our examination showed them to be short 16 per cent., for which amount they sent us their check. They claimed that we were the only ones to whom they guaranteed circulation or to whom they paid a rebate. Now, if this is the case, they collected from their other customers $224,000 under false pretenses, not one cent of which they were entitled to. This is only an average example (I could cite dozens of them), nor is this an isolated instance. The same publication has been examined by us for the last seven years, with the same average result (one year the shortage was 34 per cent.).

This publication now, however, like many others under like circumstances, says, "Never again," basing their refusal to stand another examination on the ground that it would not be fair to their other customers, which sounds a good deal as though a train-robber should go back and rob the sole remaining passenger whom he had missed on his first rounds, on the ground that it would not be fair to the other passengers to let him escape. I fear, however, that we shall escape.

I am happy to say, however, that our examinations do not always pan out that way. We paid one publication (carrying about $800,000 of advertising) for the same year, approximately $3,000 for overage, and we were glad to do it. In fact, we much prefer paying for overage to receiving rebates for shortage. We simply don't like to be buncoed.

The pleas made by another publisher, that if the advertising business were the same as other business and dealt in tangible things, this pay-according-to-circulation plan might be practical, is very ably answered further on in Mr. Barney's article by the "agency man" when he says, "There is nothing more mysterious about buying space than there is about buying a car-load of wheat." This is so patent that it seems surprising that any man capable of conducting a successful business should not see and appreciate it. The majority of advertisers, however, seem to think that the advertising proposition is something very dark and mysterious—that they must throw their money up in the clouds, and in some inscrutable way they will get returns. There are just two things to consider in buying advertising space, and only two.

First is the question of quality, which varies according to the requirements of each particular advertiser, and must be judged by the advertiser for himself.

Second, the question of price, and this includes the question not only of quality, but also of circulation, as without a standard unit of value (which, in the case of magazines, would be the thousands of circulation) the price cannot be determined.

The further pleas by the successful publisher, that there must be mutual confidence and the advertiser must trust the publisher, would cause any one who has any knowledge of the circulation business to smile with an exceedingly broad smile. There are publishers who can be trusted, and these publishers are willing to have their circulation examined. There may be publishers who can be trusted and who are unwilling to have their circulation examined, but I have never run across one of them.

"PULP-MILL CIRCULATION"

The further statement that press-room figures should be taken as circulation is puerile, from the fact that press-room figures are by no manner of means always circulation, nor anywhere near it. We know of an instance where one of the leading magazines and one of the largest circulation has a news-stand return amounting to 40 per cent., and this news-stand return is sold to the old-rag man and goes to the pulp-mill. Is that pulp-mill circulation valuable to the advertiser? I think not.

As to the truth of Mr. Barney's conclusion: "Nevertheless, the per-circulation plan does not continue to find favor everywhere and the rebate plan is looked upon as clever, but impractical," deponent is unable to say. A prominent advertising manager once said to me, after a somewhat extended discussion, "Well, for the sake of the argument, I will admit that the publishing game is the crookedest thing on God's earth, but you must admit also that the advertiser is the biggest —— fool on the face of the earth who is still engaged in business," and I was speechless.

In the long run, however, honesty has usually been considered the best policy, and, although they say "There is a sucker born every minute," the sucker doesn't last long in the advertising business and we 'av' 'opes.

XXII

Office Conferences

I AM a great believer in advertising-department conferences at which the editor, publisher, business manager, and advertising manager are brought into man-to-man contact with those who daily go forth to sell space. A meeting of this sort every week or every month, if properly conducted, will do more to provide institutional enthusiasm in the heart of the humblest seller of space than anything else that can be devised.

For psychological reasons the advertising manager should preside. The men look upon him as their leader, and if competent for the job he can arrange the programs so as to develop interesting and encouraging business results.

The occasional presence of the editor, publisher, or business manager is desirable both to listen to the matters discussed and personally to explain the purposes of the newspaper, present and prospective. Likewise it is a good plan occasionally to invite the circulation manager and other department heads to listen and to answer questions.

The key-note to be sounded is enthusiasm and loyalty. Develop the idea that in seeking to induce business men to buy space the solicitors are in reality rendering service to the men they are dealing with. It is well to start off with an explanation of the most notable achievement of the force during the last week, telling how it was accomplished and the arguments used.

The advertising manager should give every solicitor a favorable opportunity to tell of his experiences, failures as well as successes, and cheer up each member of the little army with words of advice and explanation. Unless the boys are shown that they can frankly tell of their hard luck without causing merriment, they will lose half the benefits to be derived from such conference.

The most successful solicitors will go on selling without conferences, but the dynamic influence of their victories can be multiplied by having them cheer up those who need inspiration to make them go out and secure similar results. Successful advertising solicitation is contagious. If one man is bringing in orders regularly the others soon realize that they, too, must make good.

Not many years ago I had an experience which left a lasting impression on my mind of the value of advertising-department conferences. A very good feature had been kicking about an office for two months, and no one seemed able to start the thing going. The office kid said he would like to try it. He had listened to the reports of those who had repeatedly fallen down, and had made up his mind the thing could be done if it was started right. He got the chance, and the first day's work resulted in three orders, the second six, and within a week the business was well under way.

At the next weekly conference the "kid" told such

BUILDING NEWSPAPER ADVERTISING 139

a straight, easily understood story of what he had done that the other solicitors each took up some call-backs and brought in contracts. He had sold service while the others had been merely trying to peddle space. The "kid" of the story, who then probably got a ten-dollar retainer per week, is to-day the big man in one of our largest advertising agencies, getting heavy profits as a result of his ability to sell service.

The conference frequently develops a willingness on the part of the advertising manager, publisher, or business manager to make a call or do something else to help the solicitor put over a contract. When the solicitor knows that the whole organization is back of him, he generally approaches every prospect with confidence.

In a well-regulated office it is wise to make the soliciting force understand that no prospect is dead till every man has had a try at it, including the advertising manager, business manager, and publisher. Many a prospect one solicitor thinks hopeless can be brought in by another. It is therefore well to encourage men to turn in accounts they cannot land promptly, rather than sit on them.

Aside from salaries or salaries and commissions, it is well to offer small or substantial prizes, awards, or salary advances for good work, to be announced at the conferences. The acknowledgment of individual success before the whole organization is conducive to general efficiency.

An occasional big conference or dinner of the entire working establishment, with home speakers at one time and big local or national figures at others, will be found to put pep into a force. Good-fellowship begets good work, and when a pressman sits between the editor and the publisher and a compositor or reporter gets up and makes a spirited talk of institutional purpose or even sings a song, every one present feels the stimulus of a common purpose.

When every man on the force understands all about the paper he is working on and sees what others are doing to produce the dollars to fill his pay-envelop, he will be inclined to boost the institution at every opportunity. With the organization widely scattered and never coming together, much of the force of cohesive effort is lost.

XXIII

How to Increase Advertising Rates

THE raising of advertising rates is not half so difficult as many think it, regardless of competitive conditions. Even where the other fellows are silly enough to give away their space, the man with stamina enough to demand a fair return for service rendered will in the long run come out on top.

Notwithstanding the tendency of newspapers to proclaim their superiority by imposing figures of advertising space used, an inclination often yielded to with injurious results, I believe in ignoring such figures among my competitors and demanding a fair and profitable rate.

No newspaper that I know of has the local advertising situation in as satisfactory shape as *The Philadelphia Bulletin*, which has never encouraged heavy use of space by cuts in rates. As described on pages 42, 43, and 44 of *Newspaper Building*, Mr. McLean did not believe in printing more than sixteen pages in a paper sold for one cent, and he established and maintained rates which encouraged the small advertiser and held the big fellows down to reasonable proportions.

No newspaper in the United States ranks higher in the minds of advertisers generally than *The Bul-*

letin, for its circulation covers a territory equal to any, and, thanks to the admirable way the paper is made up, even the little fellows get a chance to be heard. This is in striking contrast to conditions in many other great newspapers where the big ads. completely blanket and nullify the small ones.

The best way to raise advertising rates is to advance them by degrees. Each increase should be so trifling that the stores which reap profits from the use of space will not be likely to question it or drop out at the risk of losing the regular day in and day out appeal to your readers.

During 1916 and 1917 we advanced the rates on *The New York Globe* seven times, with the loss of but one big account. This was done by a series of readjustments throughout the rate card made every two or three months, as described in Chapter XXVI of *Newspaper Building*. At each lift we gave all advertisers the opportunity to go for a full year at the then existing rate, which was fair.

By the time we had made the second or third shift it became a mere matter of bookkeeping with our customers to make a new contract at the new rate or ride along for the remainder of the year at the rate specified in their contracts. After four or five months, instead of the full year, we were getting a fine return in the way of a higher average net rate.

By the time the full year had rolled around most of our old customers were operating under contracts at two or three cents more a line than they or we expected at the time we started boosting rates to meet increasing war costs.

Many newspaper owners hesitate to raise advertising rates for fear of permitting a competitor to swing successfully across the line of success. There are those, too, who believe a rate made years ago is good enough for all time and should not be disturbed.

Such conceptions of business provide opportunities for advertisers to revel in a waste of print paper, and had much to do in bringing about the print-paper shortage of the last two years. Too low advertising rates are as serious a menace as too high rates, such as are exacted by the European newspapers.

Unless a big city newspaper can get at least one-tenth of a cent a line per thousand from the largest buyers of its space, and about one-eighth of a cent a line from smaller users, it is selling its advertising at too low a figure. Present high prices of print paper indicate that even these rates per line per thousand are too low. To get a correct view of the situation, I refer to Chapter XXVII of *Newspaper Building*, where a simple cost-finding formula is presented.

As set up in a previous chapter, it is not primarily what space costs an advertiser, and whether it produces results for him, that should concern him. Of course he will buck like an untamed bronco at any suggestion of an increase in rates, but if convinced that you mean to get the price he will come to his mutton just the same as he does when he pays higher prices for other commodities.

The trick in getting higher rates consists, as I have said, in making the advances by gradual steps, so that at no time is the amount large when figured out in dollars and cents. An advance of one cent a line on a 10,000-line contract is only $100. If you go at the advertiser for a five-cent lift all at once on a 100,000-line contract he says to himself, "$500 increase? I won't stand for it," and the fat is in the fire.

When the fat is in the fire the best course is to let it stay there and sizzle. If you reach in to rescue it you are apt to get your hand burnt. Let the advertiser try to pull it out. Before long he will be back, because in nine cases out of ten, as I have said more than once, he needs your space more than you need the few dollars of profit made from his account.

The way out, then, is to advance your rates gradually and by as painless stages as possible, recognizing that certain very close buyers will kick anyhow and that it is occasionally a good demonstration of independence that So-and-so is out because he will not pay rates.

If all the big advertisers of a town refuse to stand for an increase in rates, the way to their hearts is to announce another more radical advance and special inducements, if necessary, to smaller people. The big fellows are only big if we think them big and take them at their own estimate. In many cases we have made them big by the foolish way we have permitted them to buy space cheaper than others.

XXIV

Sources of Inspiration

ANY man who wishes to be fully equipped as an advertising manager or effective salesman should invest a few dollars in the best books written by men who have devoted their lives to the successful demonstration of advertising and salesmanship.

Among those I would recommend are:

Awakening of American Business, by Edward N. Hurley.
The New Business, by Harry Tipper.
Men Who Sell Things, by Walter D. Moody.
Advertising as a Selling Force, by Paul T. Cherrington.
The First Advertising Book, by Paul T. Cherrington.
Crowds, by Gerald Stanley Lee.
The Manual of Successful Store-keeping, by W. R. Hotchkin.
Thoughts on Business, by Waldo W. Warren.
Advertising — Selling the Consumer, by John Lee Mahin.
Ads. and Sales, by Herbert N. Casson.
How to Reduce Selling Costs, by Paul E. Derrick.
Newspaper Advertising, by George H. E. Hawkins.
Benjamin Franklin, Printer, by John Clyde Oswald.

These are only a few of the scores of excellent books which can be picked up by the man who wishes to build his edifice on the foundations laid down by those who have gone before and to reach higher points of achievement than was possible for the pioneers.

These trade papers and magazines should come regularly to the desk or home of every wide-awake advertising manager if he would keep abreast of the times:

> *Printers' Ink*
> *Advertising and Selling*
> *Editor & Publisher*
> *Forbes' Magazine*
> *Fourth Estate*
> *Judicious Advertising*
> *System*

To clip out and file properly pertinent articles from these and other publications is to build up a background of informatory data which is invaluable as time goes on.

Merely to clip the articles and file them leaves a lasting impression on the mind, which comes into play with powerful effect most unexpectedly at some important moment. One learns to visualize almost anything he has filed away.

PART III

XXV

The Solicitor of Early Days

BEFORE taking up the details of other devices for the development of new lines of advertising, I shall briefly review some of my experiences with advertisers in New York, Chicago, and other cities, for the purpose of providing still further background which may be of value to those brought sharply up against similar situations in their solicitation and constructive work.

The man unqualified by experience in salesmanship and unable to meet almost any situation which skilful buyers can devise is seriously handicapped in the work of selling advertising or any other commodity. With salesmanship of the highest order go an understanding of human nature and knowledge of where to strike hard, when to avoid producing a climax, when to stop talking, and how to leave things in shape for further calls.

Many a solicitor has talked himself out of a sale just the same as many others have failed because their selling talk was mere chatter. As far back as the late '80's I tried to sell space. Looked upon from the standpoint of my present knowledge, I was as little equipped to do that then as I would have been to run an ocean steamer, and yet I was no worse off in knowledge of what I was trying to sell than many of those trying to sell advertising to-day.

I shall relate some of my early experiences analyzed in the light of later-day knowledge for the reader able to profit by frank confession and to avoid the traps and entanglements into which I fell in my quest for business.

I had been brought up in a newspaper office, had worked in nearly every department, and was finally set loose on the advertiser. I knew absolutely nothing regarding salesmanship, and merely called on the prospect for the purpose of asking him to authorize us to print a certain piece of copy. There was no argument beyond my claims regarding circulation and his use of another newspaper and his statement of reasons for not giving me the copy. It was copy-chasing of the crudest sort. I soon found that I could approach business men with a satisfactory degree of ease and secure a goodly proportion of the copy I went after, but sensed something lacking in the whole basis of solicitation.

I did not have a definite statement of circulation to lean upon. When I asked for exact details I found the management dodged the issue and would give me nothing but a cold figure which all must accept as accurate, without analysis or detail regarding distribution or changes from week to week. Being suspicious regarding the circulation figures given out, I made personal investigation and found the statement to be a gross misrepresentation by at least 40,000. When confronted with proof of this the business manager said all papers did the same thing and that it didn't make any difference, anyway. This gave me a new idea of the situation and the determination then formed to correct the abuse I adhered to until, over thirty years later, I was able to play the game on the level with *The Globe*.

I still continued to sell advertising because I had made up my mind to stick to the thing until I had mastered it and got to the top. As I plodded along in more or less intimate contact with advertisers I studied their copy, the results they said they got, and all angles of the business. I did not know how valuable these years of experience among crude conditions were going to be to me later on — I was growing up from youth to manhood side by side with modern effective advertising.

I well remember the first impression made upon me by one of the first brilliant exemplars of spread-eagle advertising. He was a Scotchman from Canada who first set the New York advertising world on fire. He was an all-around good fellow who simply took our local advertisers by storm, literally hypnotized them to use bigger copy than they had ever used, and in many cases produced satisfactory results for them. He didn't last long; drink and the gay life got him, as it has a whole series of others who have since followed in his shoes.

In those days the man who could joyously and agreeably spend most money with the advertiser or agent most frequently got the bulk of the business. Over the bar and round the lunch-table the glib hypnotist got orders which never could have been secured in less genial surroundings. But the pace was devastating.

Dissipation of various sorts got nearly all of the solicitors of this type. Of the men working on advertising in New York during the late '80's and early

'90's in a prominent way, there are not half a dozen left in the ring to-day. Those who have survived now, either in the newspaper business or out of it, are those who kept clear of the barrooms and restaurants where liquor was the lever. The day has gone by, never to return, when wining and dining are a necessary part of advertising solicitation. I have seen many of the most brilliant men entering the business destroyed by booze, and know from experience that the space-buyer views with suspicion the entertainment argument for the business he is placing.

Our more conservative newspapers nowadays will not employ a solicitor who takes a drink during business hours or shows signs of drinking. We don't want that sort of man to represent us in calling on our customers. When we consider that the newspaperman is probably asked to take more drinks by those with whom he comes in contact than almost any one else, it is easy to see why an iron-clad rule is the only protection he has.

I had not intended to make an argument for temperance, but the subject is so important in its bearing upon advertising solicitation and the advertising business in general that I have presented it as a basic principle in my consideration of the pitfalls and things to be avoided in the business. If inclined to drink, give up connection with the advertising business. It has got the best of them and will get you. No man with a weakness that way can survive. The drinking good-fellow advertising solicitor is foreordained to the drunkard's grave.

XXVI

Vital Thoughts for Would-be Solicitors

DURING those early days my solicitation was among the big stores then on Canal and Grand Streets extending well over toward Second Avenue. As I look back upon what passed as big stores those days, our modern specialty shops with their beautiful appointments seem like palaces in contrast, while up-to-date big shops like Altman's, Lord & Taylor's, Arnold Constable's, and Stern Brothers' were beyond the dreams of the merchant prince a generation since. Nevertheless, the old magnates thought themselves even more important than do the executives of our present greatest department stores.

For example, it is much easier to secure access to the big man at R. H. Macy & Co., Gimbel Brothers, or John Wanamaker in New York, or Marshall Field & Co., The Fair, or Carson, Pirie, & Scott's in Chicago, than it was to reach the owner of one of the old-style big shops. Advertising in those days did not mean so much to the merchants as it does now. They rather dodged the issue and purposely made it difficult for solicitors to see them. I well remember my first big experience in tackling the lion in his den during the early '8o's.

My call was upon Mr. Ridley, the head of Ridley

& Co., on Grand Street, for the purpose of asking for a rate increase. As I said before, I was a mere inexperienced boy, but ranked as advertising manager of my grandfather's newspaper. There were no telephones in those days, and horse-cars provided the service now rendered by Elevated roads and Subways. By appointment through the store's advertising manager I put in an appearance at Mr. Ridley's office, presented my card, and was ushered into the den. Without so much as a greeting, I met this: "Well, my boy, we have about made up our minds to reduce our appropriation for advertising, so I don't think there is any use of talking. If you have any better terms to submit through our agent, please do so," and I found myself being led from the operating-room.

To say that I was filled with dismay is to put it lightly. When I made the report to the office, one of the older men most casually said: "Don't take that to heart. The old man was merely making a play for a lower rate." In the light of later experiences I realize I had been made the victim of a scene created for the purpose of buying as cheaply as possible. When I called again a week or two later I did the talking first, but finally got another jolt in a statement that the firm had decided to cut us off. I was told there was no use putting up an argument, and again ushered out into the cold world.

Again I waited a few weeks, the business meanwhile being sent down to us every Saturday at the old rate, and secured another appointment. This time my instructions were to tell him no more business would be taken under old conditions. Of course my little speech produced a pretended storm, and again

I got a cool dismissal from the interview, but two days later the advertising agent called at the office to say, "It is all right; we will pay the new rate," which was as far as we went in the way of making contracts in those days.

I cite this incident only to show the methods resorted to by the buyers of space to continue an old rate as long as possible and to induce some special lower price if possible. Under modern conditions the same results are produced by different methods under new scenic effects and perhaps more effectively. The modern outer office generally has a softer chair. The solicitor is generally very cordially received and told the same story with a touch of regret like a swan-song.

My second experience was with a firm farther uptown, who employed the cleverest buyer of space I have ever had the pleasure of meeting. This fellow outwardly really loved everybody, though I never heard of his lending any money to any one or giving up copy except as bait for some trap. He generally kept you away from the thing you were after with what I now call "exhausted appropriation stuff," by saying: "My boy, there is no use talking, we can't use your paper now. We have spent practically all we are going to." But he would always manage to get in: "I certainly would like to be in the ——. By the way, I just happened to think of a little money we laid aside for program advertising. I might cut off a slice of this if you will make me an inducement."

I fell for this blarney twice, and each time for a "bust" in rates. By playing one newspaper against another and making them all hungry for a piece of the business the man for years bought space from most of the New York newspapers at lower rates than any one else. As I grew older and more experienced in sword-play I enjoyed battling wits with Brother ——, if for no other reason than to sharpen my sword for more worth-while people who would stay put when once we reached an understanding.

Nowadays the up-to-date newspaper keeps a running record of every line of advertising used by all regular advertisers in every competing paper, and thus often really has a better line on what the various advertisers are doing than they have themselves. In my calls on advertisers I always carry a mass of this material, so as to be able to show what other advertisers are doing and hold the prospect down to actual facts regarding his own use of space. My record-book, filed in a small loose-leaf folder, covering many years and in shape for quick comparison by month, by quarter, by six months, and by year, is generally studied with great care by all who see it.

In my early days I had nothing of the kind to attract the interested attention of the buyer, and more often than not was thrown widely off the track regarding the volume he was using in other papers, and could not talk intelligently about what part of his appropriation he should use in the one I represented.

This brings me to another point of inestimable value in solicitation. The solicitor generally confines his talk to a rate for so many thousand lines or inches, with the merchant merely listening to the chatter, but always calculating the total cost as so many thousand dollars. To him a boost of two cents per line may mean $2,000 more money, and while you are confining your talk to justifying the rate per line,

BUILDING NEWSPAPER ADVERTISING

he is figuring whether your paper is worth $2,000 more money for the year. To argue for the money represented by the rate increase is often to hit directly on the bull's-eye and secure the prospect's notice.

I am now firmly of the opinion that if the newspapers as individual units, and collectively by section or state, were to gather this information or other data asked for, and supply it through the advertising agent, we would be using it to better advantage.

The agent naturally desires to make his customer believe that he is rendering the fullest possible service, and, as I have indicated in an earlier chapter, frequently knocks any outside service.

Therefore, if our newspapers would make their service devices functionate through responsible service agencies, they would produce more satisfactory use and recognition of the service they perform.

XXVII

The Peacemaking Solicitor

Looking back upon my early experience, the pleasantest one was in connection with an account which had been badly handled in *The New York Sun* before I took my job as advertising solicitor on that newspaper. If my memory serves me correctly, the Hawes Hat Company had ordered a certain ad. in *The Sunday Sun* which through some mistake was published in *The Evening Sun*. Mr. Hawes properly refused to pay for the erroneous insertion, while the *Sun* office insisted that he must or keep out of the paper.

My job was to get business for *The Sun*. In asking for assignments I happened upon an ad. of the Hawes Hat Company, and was told that there was no use calling there, as the concern had been out of the paper for years because it refused to pay for an ad. I stuck to my knitting, and was finally told I could call on the Hawes people, but that there was no use talking business to them unless they would pay up.

My first call was devoted to listening to a tirade of criticism of the *Sun* management and a rather abusive treatment of my nerve in calling. I went back with the statement that I called in the line of making my living, that I knew *The Sun* would sell hats for them, and that I wanted to get their side of the story

BUILDING NEWSPAPER ADVERTISING 159

to enable me to try to adjust the difference. It was a most difficult diplomatic effort to obtain an interested audience, but I finally succeeded. The advertiser was more positive than the newspaper in his conclusion, and, if I remember correctly, backed up his statement by producing a duplicate of the original order.

When I returned to the *Sun* office on my peace mission my reception was colder than the one I had had with the advertiser. Mr. W. M. Laffan, the publisher, had given the order, and Mr. Paddock, the business manager, was as solid as a stone wall against any compromise. By sticking to my task, first going to the Hawes Hat Company and then back to the *Sun* office, fairly exuding my conviction that both sides were foolishly losing money and opportunity through the misunderstanding, I finally got a contract from Mr. Hawes contingent upon the cancelation of the disputed item, which I got the *Sun* people to accept.

I relate the experience only to show that the solicitor may have as much trouble with the office end of an account as with the prospect. I acted as peacemaker in several other cases for *The Sun*, and ever after have taken particular satisfaction in producing such results by applying horse sense and reason to situations largely produced by innocent misunderstandings that have taken on the proportions of bitter feuds.

Shortly before my work on *The New York Sun* I had had some experience when acting as advertising manager of the old *Chicago Inter-Ocean*. I had joined the paper as a complete stranger to the town, most unexpectedly when on the way farther West. It was an also-ran newspaper which had suffered from bad management for years and, owned by Yerkes, then the local street-car magnate, was hopeless from every standpoint.

Such a thing as a definite fixed rate for local business was about as unknown in the *Inter-Ocean* office as was a definite knowledge regarding circulation. At one time its owner had been called on a circulation challenge by another newspaper, when it was proved that the presses were started with the indicators at 25,000 every day. I found such a variety of rates that I prepared an indexed vest-pocket booklet to refresh my mind before entering the door of the various State Street shops. The rates for Sunday advertising varied from 8 to 40 cents per line, while on week-days they varied from 5 to 30 cents.

All the big stores were supposed to pay 16 cents per line for their Sunday space. It was not until I had been in the place for a month or two and it became necessary to renew contracts that I discovered what conditions existed and prepared my little book. The Fair got a secret rebate of 50 per cent., Siegel Cooper got a rebate of 25 per cent., Mandel Bros., Schlessinger & Mayer, got a rebate of 6 cents per line, and so on, with only one firm, John M. Smyth, paying the full 16 cents without drawback of any kind.

One day the bookkeeper by mistake sent the bill of the Woolf Clothing Co. to Sol Woolf, and there was considerable of a circus to straighten out, for the former had a much lower rate than the latter, and the latter thought he was in on the ground floor. On another occasion Frank Cooper, of Siegel Cooper & Co., discovered that he was getting only 25 per cent. rebate, when he thought he was getting the same 50

BUILDING NEWSPAPER ADVERTISING 161

per cent. as The Fair, and there was a break in relations.

If ever an experience taught a man the great advantage of doing business on a business basis, with fixed rates and definite proved circulation, these few months on *The Inter-Ocean* did so for me. In such a cesspool of false pretense and shallow claim nothing large could find root or grow. In competition with such real newspapers as *The Chicago Daily News* and *The Chicago Tribune*, the old *Inter-Ocean* was logically and surely headed for the scrap-heap.

In the absence of fixed rates rigidly maintained the advertiser is never sure that he is getting the lowest rate and is ever seeking for something lower. It is easier to establish a fixed rate by sticking to it than to restore a sound basis where business has been demoralized by the lure of special inducements. I know because I have tried both ways. When I took hold of *The New York Globe*, the first thing we did was to go on *The Chicago Daily News* basis of fixed rates and definite proved circulation statements, and I am sure it has been much more successful than the other way would have been.

XXVIII

Wiles of the Space-buyer

A FAVORITE dodge of the clever space-buyer for the big stores is to get a newspaper to quote a rate for some enormous volume of space, just for the purpose of seeing whether he will fall for such a play, and then start establishing that rate for a much smaller use. I have had it played on me so often that nowadays I almost laugh in the face of one who thinks that I am so soft-headed as to be caught in such an obvious trap.

For example, only a few months ago the head of one of our large department stores taking, say, 150,000 lines a year, pretended that he would like to consider the use of as much space as is sold to our largest three advertisers—a minimum of 400,000 lines a year. In the first place, he didn't think I would tell him the rate, but I frankly did, coupled with the statement that I knew he could not live up to such a contract. To this he replied, "Well, I think I should get a rate as low as anybody else, for our business means a great deal to the papers we patronize."

This is as far as he had ever meant to go, just a play to get by at car-load rates for gross lots. I did not put it in exactly these words to him, but he saw the point, or, rather, made up his mind that it

BUILDING NEWSPAPER ADVERTISING 163

would be useless for him to continue in his effort to break rates.

In my younger days I listened to the beautiful words of encouragement handed out by the big advertiser willing temporarily to splurge if I would make an "inducement" for him. The word "inducement" so largely used by many advertisers and buyers as a device to justify murder is one to be avoided by the newspaper advertising manager if he is to build an enduring edifice.

Times without end we have all seen the man who would sign a maximum contract without any intention to carry it out, as a means of getting a low rate. The practice grew so general that we learned to study the prospect's possibilities and probabilities before taking him on for more than nominal business at solid rates.

These practices induced some of our strongest newspapers to scale their discounts for open space and make a heavy rebate at the end of the year on the basis of the money value of advertising used. For example:

The following discounts are allowed for advertising in any or all editions of *The New York World* when contracted for:

For $ 5,000 per annum	....	2½	per cent.
" 10,000 "	....	5	"
" 15,000 "	....	7½	"
" 20,000 "	....	10	"
" 30,000 "	....	15	"
" 40,000 "	....	17½	"
" 60,000 "	....	20	"

An additional discount of 10 per cent. will be made to such advertisers each month on local display advertising, unclassified, in the Morning and the Sunday editions of *The World* when the advertiser shall have used during the month as many lines of advertising in such editions as in any other daily Morning and Sunday newspaper.

The same allowance will be made, under similar conditions, in the Evening Edition of *The World*.

Local advertisers must sign agreement in advance to receive space discount.

Some of the irresponsible advertising agents were ready to make contracts for more space than the advertisers expected to use, in the hope that in the exchange of traffic there would be increased profit to them. If by making a contract for 10,000 lines they could get a rate of, say, 9 cents a line, while their customers expected to pay 11 cents for 5,000 lines (the card rate), the agent could legitimately (?) pocket 2 cents per line added profit if the newspaper did not short-rate him.

This led to the practice of short-rating by newspapers interested in the integrity of their rates. Unless we short-rate we place a premium on the practice of overbuying. This no self-respecting newspaper advertising manager can fail to do, for he might just as well cut rates. Newspaper publishers hate to short-rate and agents and advertisers protest most loudly against the practice, but there is no middle course, and the advertiser only pays what he should have done had he correctly gauged his needs at the time he signed his contract.

XXIX

Silence More Deadly Than Attack

ONE of the weirdest conceptions of journalism I heard of in a Middle West city in connection with a newspaper under the control of a notorious character, who later served a term in prison for publishing objectionable advertisements contrary to the Federal law. This man had a theory that what he needed in order to maintain his newspaper was advertising and not circulation. Of course he never got anywhere except into trouble. Those who worked for him said he begrudged the use of every extra roll of print paper.

He had a convincing way with him when he sent a solicitor after copy. If there was any flinching on the part of the prospect he was ever ready with veiled threats of activities along lines of publicity of the undesirable kind. One big store honored his demands for cash in advance of the insertion of the advertising, and no one was ever impertinent enough to demand any proof of circulation.

Strong-arm methods bordering on blackmail have been employed by disreputable characters in the newspaper business and are still indulged in in several parts of the country. Sooner or later such methods bring their just rewards—exposure and convictions—

and are not to be recommended as a basis for advertising development.

In one Western city within the last six years I was invited to a luncheon given me by the leading business men of the town, who wished advice and suggestions as to the possibility of securing the right man to put through a plan for a decent, clean newspaper able to run the owner of an objectionable existing newspaper out of business. I was unable to name a man who I thought would be willing to undertake the job, for nothing short of a lynching-bee seemed practicable to me.

In another Western city I had a similar experience when a group of bankers and leading business men indicated their desire to finance a new newspaper they could take into their homes without the danger of exposing their children to filthy details of crimes and abuse. They did not even ask for control of the new newspaper, but stood ready to extend any required financial support as long as the paper was pledged to decency.

These cases indicate clearly enough that the rough and crude methods of adventurers in the newspaper business are not desirable from any point of view.

A tradesman with a record for sharp practices presents an attractive target for attack when, upon being approached for advertising, he rears up on his hind legs and curses all newspapers. If we will but hold our horses in the face of such abuse and decline to accept any of his business when he wants to return to our columns, he will soon realize that he is losing more in the exchange of civilities than we are.

Giving a sorehead the "absent treatment" for a few months or for a period of a year has in the end

BUILDING NEWSPAPER ADVERTISING 167

been found more effective than anything yet devised. The late Colonel Nelson, of *The Kansas City Star*, did the thing beautifully in a number of noteworthy cases. A theater objected to a criticism and got nasty. Colonel Nelson simply refused its advertising, and gave orders never to mention the theater in *The Star*. That ended the incident and incidentally the theater after a lingering illness.

A group of brewers wanted some unusual facilities or objected to something *The Star* was working for, and threatened to withdraw its advertising if the paper did not change its position. Colonel Nelson's answer was short and to the point—"*The Star* will run no more beer advertising." If all newspaper publishers had the courage and sincerity of purpose of Colonel Nelson in such matters more newspapers would be successful.

It was a hobby of Colonel Nelson's that the only advertising he really wanted in *The Star* was that of local merchants. He figured that the outsider advertising in his paper was reaching in to take money out of Kansas City. His paper, as he put it, "was made for the people who paid ten cents a week for it," and he felt that he could get all the advertising earnings he wanted or needed from Kansas City stores and enterprises. Such a policy was unique and the outside general advertisers seeking business expansion in the Southwest always included *The Star*. If their advertising was reliable and unobjectionable it was accepted, but *The Star* never insulted the intelligence of its readers by opening its columns to the cure-alls and fakes.

In the smaller towns, where everybody knows every one else's business, the advertising manager must exercise great care to avoid permitting outside mail-order concerns to compete with local merchants if he would get best results. Likewise it is well to draw the line against one-night-stand sales by the adventurer who leases an unoccupied store for a week or two and seriously cuts into the trade of regular customers. I have seen these fly-by-nights use pages and half-pages of fake offerings, foolishly accepted by newspapers, which later on wondered at the criticism they richly deserved from regular advertisers.

By adopting a sound policy for the protection of legitimate home industry and making it known you will win the cordial support of local merchants and dealers. It pays in dollars and cents every time to be loyal to your constituency. The advertising manager who permits himself to take a few hundred dollars' worth of irresponsible business which affronts his regular customers is injuring his efficiency as a business-getter.

XXX

Weak Spot in the Armor of the Dominant Newspaper

A RATHER unusual opportunity came to me unexpectedly a number of years ago as a solicitor when calling upon an advertiser. It was one of those chances which, if taken full advantage of, leads to final escape from the drudgery of a solicitor's life. I did my part in completing the thing, but those higher up behind me for various reasons put the skids under it and thereby brought about their own undoing.

It was in the executive office of a department store in Chicago where I had called to try to interest the concern in a contract with my newspaper. I had not got past the usual formalities when this was thrown at me: "You have had New York experience. What are we going to do about this?" handing me a printed notice from a competing newspaper (*The Chicago Daily News*) that on and after a certain date certain regulations previously waived, amounting to 25 or 50 per cent. in rates, would become effective.

Before I had completed reading the notice the merchant said: "We cannot get along without *The News*. It is our bread and butter. It is an outrage for them to take such an advantage of us." I asked him to show me his contract, for the purpose of seeing how he was bound, and found that the newspaper was within its rights. The same provision had been in all contracts for many years, was specified in all rate cards, and the store clearly had to pay the extra amount whenever the newspaper demanded it. *The Daily News* then had a rule providing for a penalty of 25 per cent. extra for cuts and 25 per cent. extra for broken column rules. In the case of large local advertisers the penalty had been temporarily waived.

After seeing the exhibits I replied: "You are up against it and you merchants deserve all you are getting. By building up a huge monopoly and making it impossible for another newspaper to get anywhere near it you have put yourselves in their hands." I then unfolded to him one of my pet schemes by which merchants combining their volume business in a tail-end newspaper, with provision against arbitrary advances in rates, could buy their space more reasonably and certainly more satisfactorily than by the ordinary method.

I showed him how, by getting the four or five other big stores to co-operate in the plan, he would enable the newspaper selected to spend a few thousand dollars in advertising the fact that "it carried all the bargain ads. of the big stores," and so secure increased circulation; how the stores, by displaying placards announcing that "all our ads. appear in the ——," would assist in making their advertising productive, and named a scale of gradually advancing rates assuring him against any arbitrary change.

Before I concluded my story he said, "I am sold and will help you put the plan through." This was too good to be true to me—a solicitor who had not even consulted my superiors regarding the scheme.

I told him I would have to formulate an agreement and would call again next day, when he promised to go with me to call on the other merchants.

On my return to the office my immediate superior, the advertising manager, was out, so, after nearly an hour's wait, I got in to the business manager. I now think he thought I was crazy or drunk as I described my project. Seeing his attitude of doubt, I urged him to call up Mr. Davis, of A. M. Rothschild & Co., to confirm his willingness to go ahead with such an arrangement. He did this and, all smiles, asked me to compose the agreement.

It was a simple affair, that agreement—a rate of 8 cents per line for the first six months, $8\frac{1}{2}$ cents for the second six months, 9 cents for a year, 10 cents for another year, and so on up to 15 at the end of eight years. It provided for full copy and the mutual services briefly touched upon above.

Inasmuch as I was calling on but one of the big stores, I signed up the first merchant while other solicitors tied up three or four others, and everything started in good shape. The stores gave us page copy, and only two to four columns to *The Daily News*. But our business manager did not carry out the plan of outside advertising or provide the placards for the stores. Buyers in the stores commenced to howl because their departments were not represented in the space in the other newspaper. Yet the stores played the game like men, and would have kept it up had it not been for the weak-heartedness and bad faith of the newspaper in carrying out its end of the deal.

In the first place, my arrangement with the newspaper was on a salary and commission basis. When I put in a claim for commissions on the big growth I had produced I was told that "of course your arrangement had nothing to do with State Street business," so I quit on the spot and put my feet under a desk in a rival shop. Meanwhile the business manager, out for an advance in his own salary and bent on keeping down expenses, did not make any of those moves that were so necessary to keep things running smoothly.

I can only add, in justification of the soundness of my plan, that on *The Globe* I have tried the thing out, with improvements, with great success, and found it sound and effective. Such a relation as one can establish by going frankly to his largest customers and putting business on a basis of complete understanding is most satisfactory.

XXXI

Consideration of Sales Methods

REGARDING the salesmanship of advertising involved in the day's work by the solicitor, it may be truthfully stated that probably no two men pursue exactly the same technique. In making this statement I, of course, refer to those who by experience or intuition have built up a scheme which enables them to sell advertising in paying volume. Without some definite plan easily and quickly adjustable to varying conditions in the contact with the customer the solicitor is at a disadvantage.

I am a strong believer in the theory that the salesman should never approach a prospect until he is confident that he has something definite with which to secure his interested attention and not merely glittering generalities; for in my experience, at least, I have always found that the man who was most successful had initiative and a reserve fund of data and information which got attention and brought the business. In making this statement I have in mind the successful efforts of the most efficient business producers who have ever gone out for contracts.

I would rather have a solicitor make two effective calls a day than have him stop in thirty shops merely chasing copy or to talk about the weather or politics. This is why the solicitor of sound commercial instinct and experience, has it all over the man of ordinary newspaper-office training.

One of the very best solicitors in men's retail clothing advertising I ever knew was one who had been advertising manager of two stores in that line in another city. His business had brought him in touch with traveling salesmen from other cities until he had a first-name acquaintance with many of them. As luck would have it, he entered upon the selling of advertising for a newspaper in New York, specialized on retail-clothing advertising, and made a glorious success of it. He knew the line inside out, so to speak, could talk with authority, and in nearly every case was able to show the prospect how to increase his trade and advertising efficiency without giving offense or betraying any confidences.

Likewise in the women's clothing-shop advertising, extending right up to the big department stores, the cleverest solicitor I have ever met was one who knew the business and many of the underlying principles upon which success in it depends. He not only could talk style with any of the experts, but could tell them about the ideas of those who created the styles in Paris. He understood salesmanship and selling plans far beyond the comprehension of mere tradesmen, and was a power for business promotion as long as he stuck to the job.

In my own experience I have found that very few business men whom I have undertaken to interest in a definite selling plan get away without giving me a chance to establish an enduring business relation. I purposely maintain personal contact with many of our customers, large and small, just to keep my hand in and to be able to show our solicitors that I can do what we ask them to put through. Of course, as publisher of a New York newspaper, I get attention much more easily than they do, but no man separates himself from his dollars unless he is made to see how to secure a profit by so doing.

Therein lies the art of selling advertising, which is printed salesmanship. If you sell advertising you are selling salesmanship, pure and simple. If you cannot sell advertising which you know will produce results if properly used, you are no solicitor. In order to sell such advertising you must know what it will do and be able to help the man who buys it to get results from the money he invests in response to your arguments.

The only men in a community on whom I would not waste time are doctors and lawyers, who for what they call ethical reasons would rather get their advertising for nothing. If our newspapers always reported the names of doctors who attended patients who died as they report the names of doctors attending well-known invalids, so that the public would be informed concerning the doctors who fail as well as those who succeed, our ethical friends would probably object to any mention of a doctor's name in print except when he himself was dead. Likewise with the lawyers. They object to advertising, but always seek publicity of the "free" variety.

In the approach to the customer the solicitor should hit upon worth-while topics regarding his business, or local public movements in which he is interested. They are all alike and ever on the lookout for new thoughts and ideas. Study of a man's personal peculiarities and hobbies may come later to secure material seldom needed for the first call.

Good salesmen nowadays don't jump in with "Mr. ——, can't we print your advertising in *The Gazette?* We sell 10,000 a day and can produce more profitable results for you than *The News.*" Not by a mile; that is left for the amateurs and copy-chasers. He does it more like this: "Mr. ——, I would like to have just a few minutes of your time to consider a plan of advertising used by Cammeyer in New York, The Hub in Chicago, etc., which, I am told, is producing most surprising results. We are anxious for some store in —— to try out the plan, and have gone to the trouble of studying it carefully in all its angles for the benefit of some local dealer on the lookout for the latest selling methods. *The Gazette* sells something plus when it sells advertising; it sells results." The chances are that such an opening will produce a hearing.

Any wide-awake solicitor of sound experience, by following the trade papers, studying the various books on advertising, can present ideas and suggestions of inestimable value to the tradesman too close to his shop to keep familiar with what is going on in his line in other cities. In many solicitations the subject of advertising in your own newspaper may not come up until well along in the conversation and more often than not at the suggestion of the prospect.

The biggest and most important advertising contract I ever landed was produced by avoiding direct selling argument. I kept the prospect rising for the fly, but every time I saw him coming I jerked the hook far out of the water before he got to it. It would have been injurious to what I had in mind to let him get a weak hold before he got hungry enough to take a firm hold.

The result was that when he did make up his mind to do business he apparently at least wanted the space more than I wanted to sell it to him. Such a situation is difficult to produce, but the farther we get away from the cold-blooded bludgeon tactics of the mere peddler of space the more satisfactory results we can secure for our customers and for our newspapers.

The solicitor who has conscientiously served the customer has built up an asset for the newspaper worth many times the amount he pays every year for his advertising. So long as he continues to get results nothing will keep him out of the newspaper except its discontinuance. They say that cats have nine lives, but I know newspapers which are practically unkillable, and have survived twenty and thirty years beyond their periods of usefulness.

XXXII

Meeting Unreasonable Requests

ONE of the most discouraging features of advertising solicitation and advertising management is the matter of unreasonable requests and complaints of those who seek through such methods to get minor advantages over those who do not do so.

If I had my life to live over again in the newspaper business the first rule I would adopt would be that of *The Chicago Daily News*, to sell or give position to no one under any circumstances, and stick to it as *The News* has done. In the experience of those who have studied the subject far enough to know, any definite specified position sold involves loss to the newspaper running a heavy volume of business. It frequently causes an increased number of pages, which involves heavier expense than can be made good by many an extra cent per line in rates.

Whenever a newspaper specifies any special positions for sale there are advertisers and agents with enough gall to expect to get them "on request," which is another form of discount from rates to those securing such concession.

Exactly why a man thinks himself privileged to demand, say, page 3 every day he runs an ad, regardless of fairness to others who would like the same treatment, is beyond me, and yet there are newspapers

BUILDING NEWSPAPER ADVERTISING 179

which give and defend the granting of such unusual favors. I have had many an interesting argument with advertisers regarding such matters, and found that it paid in the long run to show them we would not sell them our show-windows except at prohibitive prices.

According to my notion, a newspaper is made by its first, second, and third pages, with protection against serious encroachment of business on the editorial, sporting, and last page. I am perfectly willing to grant certain regular daily users of space certain definite pages as much for their increased value to them as for our own convenience. For example, one firm is assured page 5 or 7; another, the next right-hand page; another, the next right; and another, opposite editorial. Other business, unless specifically paid for, is rotated back of page 4 and as well forward as we can arrange, with none but smaller ads. on pages 2 or 3.

It is much easier to establish a rule of no special or specified position to any one under any circumstances than to try to maintain a standard of no position without extra rate. The buyers of space are so cunning in their devices to secure just the little added bit that the best of us are inclined occasionally to take down the bars for a friend or for some business which we have been seeking for years, and which we can get if we merely promise, as a side talk with the contract, that a "request" for position will get it without extra compensation. This trifling difference given to one agent and not to another has occasionally been instrumental in getting an account away from the one quoting the higher rate. Thus the newspapers often help the price-cutter through their own weakness.

In our larger cities, where we have photo-engraving plants handy, advertisers have often been so spoiled that they demand that we make all their cuts and illustrations for them, and set up two or three times as much copy as they use, for them to edit and select from in laying out their ads. They foolishly think that we do this for nothing, but in the long run, if they made careful analyses of increasing costs, they would find that they finally pay for all service rendered and a slight profit beyond. The advertiser who is most troublesome to a composing-room usually gets the worst service and has no one to blame but himself.

I know of one advertiser in another city who grew so difficult to handle that all the newspapers refused to set his copy, subject to corrections other than typographical errors. He then had a job office attempt the job for him, but finally came back and begged for the opportunity of having the newspapers do the work for him, with penalties for over-set and any unreasonable changes.

Then again we all sooner or later discover the alleged advertising manager and so-called advertising expert who frequently desires to change the sort of type the advertising of the store he writes for is usually set in. Some few of these experts work in league with the type-founders, judged by their ability to select faces not found in any of our newspaper offices. We have long since declined to use any faces not obtainable in mats for our typesetting machines. The day of hand composition is past.

One of the meanest men we meet is the fellow who seeks to make corrections in his ad. between editions or after he has seen the ads. of others, or wishes to kill an ad. without paying for it after it has been run in one or more editions. The first fellow is difficult to cope with, for we have no specific proof and want to give him every opportunity to make good. For the second one the only way out is to charge for the full run as an eventual cure for the nervous condition which he has permitted to grow up in his business system. The cost of the composition and corrections, and of the white paper for the day's paper including the ad., cannot be adjusted in an instant to suit anybody. The pro-rating of the circulation given works a gross injustice to the newspaper.

All of us at some stage in our experience have been up against the perpetually late customer who always gets his copy in at the last moment and wishes us to "railroad" his ad. without corrections so as not to miss an edition. We don't do business that way and have not for years, because we found in one or two cases a tendency to hold us responsible for errors. Nowadays we will not run an ad. until it has been finally approved or ordered in exact accordance with copy with time for us to revise the proofs.

It is needless to go on describing the off-side play of advertisers seeking to exact the last drop of blood our pleasant dispositions will give up without breaking relations. But I cannot quit the topic without again pointing out the error of permitting any advertiser who has made a contract earning a discount for a certain volume of space and failed to use it, to get away without paying a short-rate penalty. If we permit this we put a premium on wilful lying and misrepresentation. The man with the greatest nerve can get the lowest rate regardless of use, unless we compel every one to pay for exactly what he takes.

XXXIII

Local Advertising Experience

In a brief consideration of a few notable successful newspaper campaigns I shall not attempt to do more than view the high spots, leaving it for the student of advertising to go to the sources for further data. Observation of local advertising practices in many cities shows that all follow the same fundamental laws.

Of all the large stores in the country, Marshall Field & Co., of Chicago, and B. Altman & Co., in New York, have best succeeded, by the practice of sound merchandizing and conservative representations in their advertising, in getting fullest returns per dollar spent in advertising.

A simple announcement by either of these two firms will get a larger response from the most desirable class of trade in America's two largest cities than a full-page bargain announcement by other stores. When Marshall Field or B. Altman announces a sale, every one knows it is a real sale.

A reputation for absolutely clean trading, therefore, is a large part of advertising efficiency, and those who make their advertising a medley of bargain offerings, a large part of which are mere pretense, to draw the crowd, are compelled to spend increasing sums and to invent all sorts of novel devices to pull the people out.

I say this without purpose of casting any reflection upon the other reputable merchants doing an immense volume of business in New York and Chicago by means of enormous expenditures for printers' ink, perhaps wasting money by losing opportunities for building up the soundest appreciation of public confidence.

Than John Wanamaker, with his huge stores in New York and Philadelphia, there is no more effective advertiser in the United States. The Wanamaker style of advertising is as individualistic as the whole atmosphere of his stores. The daily signed editorial and the intimate manner of telling the women the news of the store and merchandise make his advertising stand in a class by itself.

Wanamaker is one of the cleverest buyers of advertising space in the world. He fully realizes the circulation and attraction value of his store news to the newspapers of the two cities he trades in. A unit of nearly 500,000 lines of space per year, having a powerful influence upon competitive business, has great attractions for the newspaper seeking volume of advertising.

For many years Wanamaker bought space in the better-grade New York newspapers for less money than his competitors, because he bought in larger blocks, while they sought results from the mass circulation of the yellow press and got a much lower return per dollar invested. Most of the stores which continued the use of the lower-grade papers have gone out of business, while those who were smart enough to read the signs rightly used their heavy advertising where it would be read by people with money to spend.

In line with the basic principles involved in the practices of Marshall Field and B. Altman, the policy of Rogers, Peet & Co., dealing in men's clothing, indicates that huge bombastic copy is not necessary to sell even clothing. Rogers, Peet & Co. seldom use over 120 lines single column, and yet have grown from a very small store to an enormous trade all over the country, with several stores in New York.

The success of such enterprises proves that it pays in dollars and cents to be accurate and reliable in representations in advertising. Such methods, probably a bit slower in developing big business, build along the institutional basis an edifice which ultimately can do business at a lower operating cost than where forced draft is compulsory to keep going.

R. H. Macy & Co., of New York, occupy a unique position among all the big stores of the larger cities in selling strictly for cash, without the overhead expense involved in credits and charge accounts. Their selling argument woven around this point has proved a magnet to attract trade, and their business has grown in wonderfully steady volume.

Now conducted by the three sons of Isadore Straus, who lost his life on the ill-fated *Titanic* in 1912, Jesse, Percy, and Herbert, whose chief purpose in life is to leave the immense institution as a monument to their father in better shape than when they undertook its management, its future growth is watched with great interest.

So obviously sound is the argument that a store which sells for cash only and buys for cash only, after taking every possible discount, can sell cheaper

BUILDING NEWSPAPER ADVERTISING

than one extending credit through charge accounts, that the problem of doubling their present volume of trade is more largely one of accommodating the seasonal traffic than anything else.

Like Marshall Field in Chicago and B. Altman in New York, R. H. Macy & Co. long since discovered that the way to increased response to advertising and to larger traffic was in making their sales real sales and a service to the customer. The public is not slow in discovering where greatest values can be secured.

Involved in the Macy principle of cash only is a problem they have partially solved through their deposit-account department, which, by charging purchases against deposits drawing interest, measurably provides the convenience of charge accounts. Where a concern sells for cash only there is no charge-account relation which tends to bring the customer back to the store.

As proof that service to the customer in the way of values is a stronger magnet than the charge account, nothing further need be urged than the marvelous growth in the annual turn-over of the Macy store. Likewise it disproves the theory that our women folks buy more than they need through the convenience of charge accounts.

Neither Marshall Field nor Wanamaker uses Sunday newspapers in their advertising campaigns, finding that small space in the Monday morning newspapers and the bulk of his other advertising in the evening newspapers produce results most economically. It has been said that these two stores spend less than 1 per cent. of their turnover for advertising, as against 2, 3, and 4 per cent. by competitors.

Sunday advertising, where full pages and double trucks fight for reader attention in competition with the gymnastic stunts of Sunday editors, piling up scores of pages until the reader is reduced to the state where he seeks only titbits for reading among the mass, have had their day. They represent waste to the advertiser.

The longer I live the more I incline to the idea that we have grown profligate in the use of advertising and have sold it too cheaply and thereby made its use too easy. It would be much sounder business for the stores to use smaller space at higher rates. Their advertising would not cost so much and there would be a reasonable margin for profit in the newspaper business.

As described in another chapter, the advertising of Hearn & Co., in New York, two columns four days a week and three full columns on Wednesday, received more votes in 30,000 votes cast as indicating reader preference than the advertising of any other New York store except Wanamaker's and Macy's.

If a big store can keep scoring new high-water marks in traffic when located at a point far removed from the big shopping districts by the use of two columns a day, as Hearn does, it seems to me that those insisting on burning up print paper by their use of larger copy are probably wasting money.

It would seem that, notwithstanding enormous trade established by many big stores in our various cities, newspaper advertising provides the way for the successful building up of new stores and new shopping centers. In our American cities the older stores do not seem to be able to grow fast enough and large enough to care for the increasing population.

There seems to be a limit to the scope of the big emporium beyond which it cannot go. I sometimes think this limit is reached at the point when people cannot shop with comfort on the street-level floor, and where elevators grow uncomfortably crowded. The only way for growth beyond the full block or square is by bridges underground and across the street, as in Wanamaker's in New York.

To spread out beyond the four streets of a block often means prohibitive investment in real estate, while to go on up beyond five or six stories means uncomfortable jamming of elevators and unbearable crowding on the first floor during the rush seasons.

As a well-known department-store man recently told me, the department store has not yet been proved. He admitted the growing success of a few in many cities, but claimed that increasing overhead and service charges were making them too expensive to be real money-makers.

This man thought that the smaller community stores could sell cheaper and give much more satisfactory service than the huge emporium. In the small store the proprietor can keep in touch with the customer, while in the big store the point of contact between store and customer is through "Six-dollar Annie," and very impersonal at best.

A wonderful change has come over retail advertising in New York and other cities during the last ten years. The volume of retail dry-goods advertising in New York has shrunk over 1,000,000 lines for our leading newspapers, while smaller store and specialty-shop advertising has developed more than 1,500,000 lines per year for the same newspapers.

In other words, owing to the failure and closing up

of such stores as O'Neill's, Adams's, Ehrich's, Greenhut, Simpson-Crawford, and The 14th Street Store, over 1,000,000 lines per year of advertising have been lost by each newspaper carrying volume business from them.

On the other hand, the high-grade specialty shops, such as Oppenheim Collins & Co., Franklin Simon & Co., Bonwit Teller & Co., Stewart & Co., Worth, where better goods and better service have been created, have stepped into the shoes of the less worthy and filled the newspaper columns with more interesting advertising than the bald bargain ads. of those who dropped out largely through bad business methods.

A local New York account of recent growth which has interested me more than almost anything else that has appeared in recent papers is that of Worth on Thirty-fourth Street just east of Sixth Avenue. Here is an advertiser who has had the courage to practise what others have preached—always bought enough white space around his ad. to make it stick out, regardless of the position on a page.

His advertising agent, Sigmund Kahn, who has watched the account with the eye and care of a good mother, deserves a place in the Hall of Fame for the successful development of a very prosperous business from a small beginning. For upward of a year Worth advertised in no other newspaper than *The Globe*, so we can justly claim that we put him on his feet.

Worth does not use comparative prices and I have never heard anything but praise for his merchandizing methods. Other stores have now followed the style of Worth's advertising, but this store has continued to grow and is destined in time to become one of the large specialty shops of New York, if I am not mistaken.

Another really notable line of retail advertising which has won national recognition is that of Mark Cross & Co. under the inspiration of Patrick Francis Murphy. The ads. generally run one full column once a week, with a full-page ad. in advance of Christmas. The style of these ads. are distinctive and well known to all.

That the Mark Cross advertising is good advertising and effective is proved by results and the growth of the business, and by the effect it has had in establishing agencies all over the country for the house. The ads. in the New York newspapers were seen by out-of-town concerns, who applied for agencies and then for mats of the advertising.

A feature of the Cross advertising has been that it has not been "English," as it might easily have been, but distinctly "American," intensely human, and has created a desire to buy high quality of leather goods at fair prices. No better proof of the wonderful pulling power of rational newspaper advertising could be given than the success of Patrick F. Murphy's work for Mark Cross.

As Robert S. Tinsman, of the Federal Advertising Agency, once put it in a statement in *Printers' Ink*, "Good advertising, whether personal or written, must contain an element of repression—a certain indefinable reserve that will leave the customer curious to find out what you will say the next time, and that means 'welcome.'"

Now for the aim. Every man must have it—every advertisement must have it—every campaign must have it. One of my customers in the silk trade is such an example. In a recent advertisement to the merchants, he stated, "We give you what they want, when they want it, and we know in advance they will want it," or words to that effect.

The aim of his business is to anticipate fashion to such an extent that his line will always lead in every store that it enters. And because he never loses the sight of this aim he accomplishes results far above the ordinary. Every business you know permits such an analysis. Every advertisement you read should suggest it or it is faulty. The single aim, the single purpose, the grand goal, is what makes every contributing circumstance insure achievement.

In a recent address before the advertising club of Cleveland I tried to draw the distinction between aimed and aimless advertising. I called the one a campaign of character, recalling that Emerson said "character is centrality." Consequently, every part of a character campaign recognizes and observes the center of its circle; the one big fact—the all-dominant reason why the article advertised is superior.

That brings us up to merchandizing advertising—the ability of an advertising campaign to accurately reflect the merchandizing element. This merchandizing idea as applied to advertising is a much-abused term, these days. It goes a lot deeper than the assumption that advertising is merely a salesman. A salesman is a mighty important "cog" in a big wheel; so is an advertisement, but back of the cog and back of the wheel must be the motor, and that motor is the merchandizing instinct, faculty ability which digs down to the fundamental roots of business and makes the wheel go round and the cogs catch, and pays the dividends.

Many a campaign has been doomed to failure because some advertising man, without real merchandise resource, permitted, not to say advised, the customer to do the wrong thing. Similarly, many a great campaign has leaped to success because the merchandizing idea back of it was fundamentally right.

There is Printz-Biederman, who jumped from the ranks of ordinary garment advertisers, with the announcement of a patented lining canvas that was guaranteed to preserve the shape of a garment for two full seasons. Can you figure how each of these campaigns finds immediate reflection of every printed word to the public in the action of the salesman behind the counter and on the road? That is aimed advertising.

BUILDING NEWSPAPER ADVERTISING 191

I'd like to get the goat of old general publicity that so many seem to worship. Compare Kellogg copy with Shredded Wheat, and tell me which the most of you eat. How about Ivory Soap, or Pears? Whose dividends would you rather share? For every general publicity success which is merely the claim of supremacy without supportable reasons or logical merchandizing argument, I will show you one hundred of the other sort. The one may make good if you spend enough money—the other is bound to make good on a reasonable expenditure. Aimed or aimless advertising—which do you recommend?

This is just what Mark Cross advertising does. Every one knows that Mark Cross leather goods are good goods. The ads. are always interesting and the reader is trained to read them for bright sayings and attractive offerings and style suggestions.

The same thing is true of the advertising of Marshall Field & Co., John Wanamaker, B. Altman & Co., Rogers, Peet & Co., and scores of other houses who by years of dependable advertising and square dealing have won public confidence, and hold it despite the efforts of others to win it away from them by bargain inducements.

Regardless of whether it is a repetition or not, I want to say that in my opinion it is the freedom from comparative prices and the genuineness of their "sales" when they announce sales of these stores that make their advertising so wonderfully effective in comparison with that of others pretending to hold sales every day in the year.

For example, when Rogers, Peet & Co. announce their midwinter sales of overcoats at, say, $12.50, there are thousands of New Yorkers who by years of training and experience know that this sale is the opportunity to get a good coat cheap for the next winter. I once bought a $50 coat for $12.50 from

Rogers, Peet & Co., and it was the biggest ad. for them they ever issued. I told scores of my friends about it, and there is nothing in advertising like the praise of a pleased customer.

I am not going to attempt to call attention to the hundreds of national campaigns which have won success through newspaper advertising. All of us know them well through seeing them in our daily newspapers.

But there is one of these which sticks in my mind in a way that leads me to mention its peculiarities, for it represents a wonderful leverage for additional local business, and points a way for other manufacturers with goods in general demand to go and do likewise. I refer to the advertising of the Victor Talking Machine Company.

H. C. Brown, advertising manager and now vice-president of the Victor Company, is a great believer in dominant copy for his concern. He rightly says that there is not a single issue of any daily paper in the country without the ad. of the Victrola through some local dealer. When the company advertises he goes in for copy on a basis which lends itself to combination with ads. of the dealers.

Mr. Brown believes in advertising, whether the product is oversold or not, for he realizes that advertising of the right kind possesses a wonderful cumulative value in an institutional way, does much to keep all agents pepped up, and emphasizes the dominance of his machines over all others in the minds of those who have them and those who sell them.

In F. Wallis Armstrong, his advertising agent, Mr. Brown finds an able lieutenant filled with a fire and purposeful ambition to make Victor advertising stand

BUILDING NEWSPAPER ADVERTISING 193

in a class by itself. I have seen this pair in action, and can vouch for the effectiveness of their methods in doing big things "now" and marvelously well. No wonder their advertising has been successful.

Another most interesting national advertising account in the newspapers was the institutional campaign from Armour & Co., worked out by E. T. Merritt, the advertising manager and myself, three or four years ago. Ed Merritt had been a fellow-solicitor with me on State Street years before, he representing *The Herald*, while I was on *The Inter-Ocean*.

The scheme was to pick out a newspaper in each city where there was an Armour branch house and advertise like a department store, 50,000 or 100,000 lines a year for Armour products. It was a big idea and was carried on successfully in many cities, but, like many another big thing, was not carried out to the maximum because the man higher up got cold feet.

In an interview with J. Ogden Armour he told me that for institutional purposes it would be worth millions of dollars for him to find a method of branding each steak cut from the side of beef with the word "Armour," so as to prevent unscrupulous dealers selling cheaper products as standard goods. We in the newspaper business do not half appreciate how much advertising is killed off or discouraged by the practice of substitutes.

Years and years ago the manufacturers of proprietary medicines inaugurated an extensive campaign against this substitution evil—the attempt of the druggist, when asked for an advertised article, to substitute one of his own by saying, "No, we haven't got that, but we have something of our own make just as good or better," on which he turned an extra profit and defeated the efforts of the advertiser.

The practice grew so extensively that no worthy article could be advertised very long before some firm or firms in the business of making imitations would stock up the druggists with goods that they pretended to make themselves. Regarding the relative merits of the advertised goods and the substitutes, I think it is fair to assume that the former were apt to be better.

So dangerously near did the imitators come to infringing on the trade-marks and rights of the owners that hundreds, if not thousands, of injunction suits were started, all of which made it rather discouraging to the individual or firm to build up a nation-wide or extensive business through advertising.

Expiring trade-marks, such as that of Castoria, were grasped by the vultures lurking around the edges of honorable business, and fortunate was Fletcher to have prolonged his exclusive right to continue as the sole maker of "Fletcher's Castoria" by having added his name as characterizing his individual product.

All of the litigation developed by the struggle against the substitutor helped bring about the era of national advertising in the magazines of standard trade-marked goods, and led many manufacturers to build up erroneous conceptions regarding imagined rights which they thought they could write into Federal statutes giving them the privilege of fixing prices and selling under licenses, now finally decided against them.

XXXIV

Shifting Shopping Centers

As stated in a previous chapter, I have lived to see New York's center move from what is now far downtown—Canal and Grand Streets and along the Bowery, to Fourteenth Street, up Sixth Avenue to Twenty-third Street, toward Broadway, and then to Thirty-fourth Street at Broadway, and east to Fifth Avenue to Forty-second Street and west to Sixth Avenue.

Each move has left those merchants who failed to go with the tide high and dry of trade as the traffic went elsewhere. For example, Ridley & Son died out when they failed to go up-town from Grand Street, and for years Arnold Constable and Lord & Taylor suffered until they moved to their beautiful, modern stores on Fifth Avenue.

Of the big stores remaining at the old stands, that have successfully endured regardless of the departure of nearly all worthy competitors, are Wanamaker's, at Broadway from Eighth to Tenth Streets, and Geo. A. Hearn & Co., still holding the fort on Fourteenth Street. These two great stores by reason of strong individuality and established relations continue to enjoy wonderful prosperity.

Geo. A. Hearn refused to move farther north because he figured there was no logical reason for the change and that he could sell cheaper if he avoided the heavy cost of moving and new investment. He once told me that he considered Fourteenth Street as handier for the mass of his customers than any other point in the city.

When one stops to consider the vastly improved transportation facilities which enable people from the whole metropolitan district to reach Fourteenth Street to-day compared with, say, thirty years ago, when that street was the shopping center of New York, he must concede the force of Mr. Hearn's conclusions. His family are still continuing at the old site, with no sign of a change in policy.

About fourteen years ago, when B. Altman took his store away from Sixth Avenue and Eighteenth Street to Thirty-fourth Street and Fifth Avenue, many a wise and knowing head among the merchants was wagged philosophically, and more than one remark was made to the effect that the beautiful new building would prove a tomb in which Altman's "class" ambition would be buried. Altman's had for years catered to the quality trade of the great city, and to have a charge account at that store meant almost social standing.

Many of the great merchants who for years had been trying to wean away trade from Altman's secretly rejoiced at the move, for they figured that they would now most certainly get a larger piece of the most desirable trade. R. H. Macy & Co. had previously moved from Fourteenth Street and Sixth Avenue to Broadway and Thirty-fourth Street, so those who were left believed that they were now doubly blessed.

Such stores as O'Neill's, Adams's, Ehrich Bros., sub-

BUILDING NEWSPAPER ADVERTISING 197

sequently Kesner & Co., Simpson-Crawford, and Siegel Cooper's remained on Sixth Avenue, while Stern Brothers, Bonwit Teller, McCutcheon, Best, and Le Boutillier stayed on Twenty-third Street. This was a group of great emporiums important enough to justify any reasonable calculation that the neighborhood they occupied would continue a heavy shopping center.

The late Captain Greenhut, of Siegel Cooper, leased the old Altman building and opened Greenhut & Co., to be run as a "class adjunct" to the Big Store, while Henry Siegel bought out Simpson Crawford & Co. and opened The 14th Street Store on the site previously occupied by R. H. Macy & Co.

Altman and Macy took the big traffic up-town with them, and the opening of Gimbel Brothers and Saks & Co. helped the current north, so that to-day there is nothing left of any of the great stores mentioned which did not subsequently see the handwriting on the wall and get out when the getting was good.

Siegel, Simpson-Crawford, and The 14th Street Store went up when Henry Siegel got to the end of his rope; Kesner & Co., the successors to Ehrich Bros., went out, as they deserved; O'Neill's and Adams's blew out; Siegel Cooper & Co., later J. B. Greenhut & Co., and the Greenhut ventures on the Altman site, recently closed their doors; while Le Boutillier just dried up and quit.

Bonwit Teller & Co., Best & Co., McCutcheon, and Stern Brothers went north to increased prosperity, taking over their share of the trade represented by the suspension of operations of those firms unable to see or unable to move with the current.

A factor of great importance to the student of advertising is indicated by this experience. It was the stores given to greatest bluffs and absurd sales that were unable to weather the storm. Forced-draught methods of bargain sales and fakes practised by many of those who failed could not long hold the trade of women intelligent enough to know values.

There can be no question that the present-day great department stores and specialty shops of New York do a sounder business on a firmer foundation than those of any previous period, and there is little likelihood of any further great change in the shopping district. Means have been adopted to keep the sweat shops and wholesalers out, and the Park on the north would seem to limit further progress that way.

Chicago, Boston, and most other American cities, on account of geographic conditions, have never suffered the hardships and expense represented in moving whole retail shopping districts like New York. Many of our present stores have moved, not two, but three, four, and five times, each time involving heavy additional expense and investment.

Chicago's loop district, now extending a block outside on the east to Michigan Avenue, will probably remain its shopping center for years to come. In Boston the big stores still continue to hold their place along Washington Street, nowithstanding Back Bay developments.

Wanamaker and Hearn seem to prove that big, well-conducted stores can go forward to constantly increasing business far removed from other stores, but there are few concerns in the country, aside from perhaps Marshall Field in Chicago and R. H. Macy in New York, which have a strong enough following and prestige to do so.

PART IV

XXXV

Selling Advertising Plus Results

THE advertising manager of sound experience will appreciate that the most difficult obstacle to overcome in developing new business, or stimulating old business through a soliciting force, is getting advertisers to use copy that will produce results which they can see. Here is where modern advertising management is vastly superior to the old-time method with heavy volume of business the only goal.

It requires considerable diplomacy to reach common ground with a man untrained in the use of advertising and unwilling to admit his ignorance. The prospect is on his guard against any attack on his bank-account, perhaps has wasted some money in church programs and other stuff called advertising, and of course has secured no results, and is predisposed to cast no more of his bread upon the waters.

It is all well enough to have aggressive young men of good approach exert their most convincing selling talk, which will eventually get some business, but if we are to reduce our selling costs we must work along lines of less resistance, and offer something that will sell almost on sight and when sold will produce results.

Even our largest advertisers will gladly grasp at

suggestions regarding successful experience elsewhere. Few advertisers have yet reached the point where they are satisfied that their copy is producing as satisfactory results as are possible. When they reach that point, it is best to leave them alone in their fool's paradise.

Therefore it is suggested that the advertising manager, after careful study of the ads. in exchanges, cut out the best specimens of those in different lines, to be later pasted on loose sheets for compilation according to classification of business. By dating each ad. or sheet, a collection of shoe ads., for example, covering a full calendar year will provide constructive and suggestive material of convincing force when shown to a local shoe-dealer and guide him regarding seasonal offerings.

The sheets covering different lines of trade can be arranged in binders and carried by solicitors calling on prospects in any line. It is remarkable how interesting such a collection of ads. is to the dealer who has never advertised effectively. He knows that big business has been created through advertising. His palm itches to get increased traffic and without half the argument necessary in the absence of the sample ads. he will say, "I would like to try ads. like these." It is then up to your solicitor to get him up some sample ads. like the ones which appeal to him, and our prospect is fairly started on an advertising career.

In my opinion, it is during this formative period that the work of our advertising manager and solicitor can do much to make the prospect a permanent customer or kill him as an advertiser for years if not forever. (For fuller detail see Appendix.) After we have induced him to make an appropriation for advertising, we should bring him to a state of mind where he will not expect impossibilities, or he will be discouraged before his advertising can become effective. (See "The Time Element in Advertising" in Part VII.)

There is true art to be exercised at this point. We must not throw a wet blanket on his ardor, but gradually bring him to a realization of what he must do to secure results. We must show him that if all a man had to do was to advertise to-day to reap a heavy profit to-morrow, there would be nothing worth while in business. We must show him that the results of advertising are cumulative, some coming overnight, the greater and more enduring part being in the form of good-will toward his establishment as a going institution.

He must be shown that his advertising at best can only be expected to bring the would-be buyer into the store, where it is up to him to make the sale and a regular customer of the inquirer. If his shop is attractive, his line full, and his salesmanship sound, failure to sell rests with him and not on the advertising. He must be told that even the most successful advertisers experience the greatest difficulty in their contact with the customer through "Six-dollar Annie," and that therein lies a promising opportunity to render a quality of service impossible of duplication in the big store.

It is well to show the prospect that the best advertising experience demonstrates that stores which regularly advertise figure that without advertising they would do about only half the volume of business they now do. In other words, the second half of their turnover, in which is included their whole margin of profit, is produced by advertising. Successful business growth with a determination to attain higher traffic every year is produced only by consistent and persistent advertising.

Our prospect must be pledged, before his first ad. appears, to a definite campaign to run for a season. It will be well to keep in touch with him during the early stages to see that his merchandizing methods are sound and to give him courage to continue. Here is where the advertising manager and solicitors of commercial experience can be of great assistance, helping the prospect over the rough spots usually found during the early stages of any selling campaign.

After a few weeks our prospect will have commenced to see results from his advertising, and we can perhaps help him to even greater returns by showing him how to arrange for a sale that will fill his store for a day and clear his shelves of certain accumulations that otherwise would find their way to much lower prices or the scrap-heap.

If our advertising help has been effective, our prospect will be close on our trail for further assistance and larger advertising. That is the nature of the animal. If our advertising has not been effective it is then up to us to give further consideration to the case for the purpose of trying out some other line of copy and plan of merchandizing.

Unlike the physician whose practice consists in trying first one thing and then another on a patient, with no positive assurance of a cure, we may be pardoned for our experiments, for we know positively that advertising will stimulate any business to increased sales and growth when once we find the way.

Even the largest and most persistent advertisers must confess that they find great difficulty in explaining why they occasionally fail to get satisfactory results from their most productive medium. They recognize that perhaps the reason lies in the fact that people on that day do not want the goods they offer, which is an admission of their own error in judgment regarding merchandise and copy. This does not discourage them in their continuous policy of advertising, but oftentimes proves of value in arranging their further appeals.

I have seen a half-column ad. in a certain Chicago newspaper fill a State Street clothing-store with customers of the buying variety, while I had the same storekeeper tell me that on another day a thousand-line ad. failed to get out a corporal's guard. I have seen the offer of a baseball to every kid for whom a suit was bought on a Saturday crowd a store to standing room only, and those of us who have been in the harness long enough have seen many seemingly miraculous results produced through advertising.

XXXVI

Reaching the Distant Manufacturer

THE development of routine local business by our advertising manager through the use of his soliciting force, through the demonstration to local dealers not inclined to advertise on their own, by advertising secured from distant manufacturers seeking an outlet or larger sales in our city, offers most interesting possibilities. This general field of opportunity is practically as unlimited as the waters of the sea, and can be utilized to dig out new business by the advertising manager who is really competent, and to teach local dealers the value of advertising.

For our purpose here, the use of the Graphic Survey referred to in a previous chapter and described in detail in Chapter XXXI of *Newspaper Building* provides the key. For every present general advertiser entering our field there are thousands of others with products they would like to sell to our people if they only knew an easy and practical way to do so. In many cases, a large percentage of these prospects are shunted to the magazines by the advertising agents for many reasons which are considered in other chapters.

If a newspaper in almost any city or town will but show itself willing and able to help a manufacturer to a distribution among leading dealers handling his line of goods, the manufacturer will gladly appropriate sufficient money to pay for an introductory campaign. If the manufacturer is possessed of an advertising manager of the sort too important in his own eyes to grasp such an offer, or if his advertising agent is loath to co-operate in such work, there are hundreds of others in his line who will jump at the opportunity if it is set before them properly.

Now to come back to the numerous local dealers who perhaps to-day will not advertise. They nearly every one of them are flooded with circular matter from distant manufacturers and hounded by drummers asking them to take on new lines or new articles. By approaching these dealers from the right angle and showing them that if they will co-operate with us we can secure advertising appropriations for them, they will furnish tips as to whom to approach and give us information regarding the comparative sale of different standard goods.

If the advertising manager will but instruct his solicitors how to establish the desired relation with non-advertising dealers and even those who now advertise, he will soon find himself, and such auxiliary force as he may organize for the correspondence and co-operation, so busy in the most interesting work he ever tackled that he will feel happier than at any time in his life.

For example, if the manufacturer he is approaching makes soap of a certain kind or a whole line, the appeal should be to him that —— offers a most promising market for his goods for such and such reasons. It will be comparatively easy to gather data from a number of local dealers regarding the sale of soaps, and to get them to pledge their co-operation with window and counter displays in conjunction with a local advertising campaign, with their own names appearing in the copy as outlets.

I should not advise the giving of dealers' names to the manufacturer in the preliminary correspondence; only state the trade conditions and say that you can get distribution, window or counter display, in so many stores. Experience shows that many a so-called advertising or sales manager has gone the short route directly to the dealer and received orders on unfulfilled promises of advertising, regardless of long-range effects of such shabby treatment of dealer and newspaper.

In many cases it will be found possible to get a local dealer to pledge himself to stand half or one-third of the cost of a reasonable campaign to stimulate the sale of a certain article. The difference between local and foreign rates for the advertising in such a case can be utilized to the advantage of the local dealer in getting him to sign a definite term contract without disadvantage to the interests of or increased cost to the distant manufacturer. *The Globe's* rate is the same for both local and foreign advertising, but many publishers still adhere to the old practice of charging more to those from out of the city on the theory that they are compelled to pay a commission and other expenses for getting it.

If we stop to consider that by such work we are making it possible for the local dealer to do a larger volume of business in his store, and for the distant manufacturer to secure effective distribution and most desirable dealer relation through an advertising campaign that costs him probably less than would be required to make the necessary investigation and

BUILDING NEWSPAPER ADVERTISING

stock up the dealer, we shall appreciate the service we can thus render.

The only drawback to this method of business stimulation is the fact that we must understand in advance that few manufacturers are rigged so as to have time to deal with 2,500 different daily newspapers and 18,000 country weeklies. They, of necessity, must head up the different branches of their operation, and do things along generalized lines. This, however, has never prevented a real red-blooded man from making an exception from the rule where a proposition for the increased sale of his goods struck him as real and worth the experiment.

This brings us to another interesting point for possible development which has been tried out sufficiently at various places to be found sound in principle. I refer to the combined appeal of a group of newspapers willing to render the same degree of service as a group covering a certain section of the country important enough to warrant the consideration of almost any manufacturer. The advertising manager possessed of the big idea which he has demonstrated in a number of cases should invite the co-operation of other newspapers in his section, and the problem of attracting the interested attention of the distant manufacturer will be solved.

Such a group could afford to buy regular space in the trade papers to demonstrate the possibilities for trade expansion in their territory, to circularize unlimited numbers of manufacturers and to pay for effective representation to carry their selling argument directly to the doors of the distant manufacturer. We shall consider this plan in more detail in another part.

In my experience, when it comes to rendering the sort of service I have in mind and which we in the office of *The New York Globe* have done very effectively, the price asked for advertising is a secondary matter to the advertiser if he gets the results he seeks. In the end the advertiser must pay for the service he receives. There is no use trying to deceive him or ourselves in this respect. If our newspaper rates are too low to pay for the sort of service we must render to secure the business we should get, the easiest route to it is higher rates.

This, I appreciate, will be received with merriment by both newspaper-men and advertisers and their agents, for it is at variance with usual rules. Looked at from the broadest constructive angle, it will be found that my conclusion is sound. It resolves itself into the equation of comparative cost of selling goods. If the newspapers can secure data and information for the distant manufacturer for 5 per cent. of what it would cost him to gather it, isn't it obvious that he should be willing to pay them, say, 25 per cent. of the direct saving to him, through a slight advance in rates to cover the cost involved in making many such investigations which do not pan out? I vote yes, and so will the manufacturer, regardless of the likes or inclinations of the buyer of space.

As is indicated in other chapters, I incline to the view that eventually the service that I have outlined will be rendered by the newspapers through recognized and dependable advertising agencies. By so doing the work will be standardized and, passing through the agents, will have their approval and support.

XXXVII

Making New Local Advertising

IN the development of new business from distant manufacturers through co-operative effort with local dealers, I wish to show how the advertising manager can put over many quick-acting measures in conjunction with the larger retail shops and department stores. It is the same thing as indicated for the small non-advertising stores, but in many cases has a particular appeal to certain manufacturers.

A great many makers of various articles for household and general use are particularly anxious to put their line into the big stores, and more often than not find it extremely difficult, if not impossible, to get the buyers to take on their goods. In our relations with the big stores we are brought face to face with ruthless "buying methods" of these concerns. They are past-masters in starting to dicker after the other fellow has quoted his absolutely bottom price. That is where they begin to do business. They will never concede that bottom has been reached.

The big-store buyer probably rightfully believes that in taking on a new line or a new article he is conferring a great service in the way of direct or indirect advertising and recognition. He figures that counter room in his store at locations where traffic is heavy is something which the manufacturer should pay for in the way of special price inducement to him. He also figures that taking on a new line involves a certain degree of risk either in displacing goods which he knows will sell or in the way of possible decreased profit from so many square feet of floor space or counter room.

We must concede some degree of justification for this attitude, but the big-store man often so outrageously overplays his hand as utterly to defeat the ends he really seeks, forcing makers of high-grade one-price goods to find other outlets, which the big stores often attack later on by ruthless price-cutting. The big stores cannot assume to handle only a small percentage of the various lines of goods or articles offered them. They take on only those they want to, those they have to, those they are sure will sell, and those with which they are willing to take on a gamble, more often than not wholly at the manufacturer's expense.

The best of the big department stores openly admit that they must carry any article in general demand, and that it is poor business to keep repeatedly telling customers they do not carry "Pears' soap," for example, but have something of their own "just as good." They have found that such tactics drive a customer to a store that carries what she wants. The big stores have been accused, and justly so, of purposely cutting prices on standard articles to demonstrate the money-saving in buying in their store.

Many manufacturers with standard advertised articles have done everything in their power, by building imaginary protections about their patents and selling plans, to prevent their articles being sold for less than the advertised price. Their claim that price-cutting disorganizes their distribution organization may be justified, but thus far practically all the final decisions of the United States Supreme Court have been against their contentions, and for years they have been valiantly endeavoring to secure the enactment of the so-called Stevens bill through Congress to give them the protection they desire.

The contention is that if the big department stores cut the price of a standard article, the numerous small dealers must meet the cut or give up selling the goods. They claim they should be allowed to stipulate at what price their article should be sold for the protection of the good-will values they have created for their trade-marks, trade names, and patents. In this I agree with them, but not to the extent they seek to secure through the objectionable and dangerous phases of the Stevens bill.

I have wandered far afield for the purpose of defining certain of the underlying factors in the relation between the distant manufacturer and your local department store. In the absence of a knowledge of these conditions the advertising manager and solicitor are at a disadvantage in seeking to bring the two ends of the proposition into harmonious co-operation.

Our local newspaper, through its close relations with the department store, can frequently secure for the distant manufacturer the representation he most desires on the counters of the big stores. We have avenues of approach wholly impossible to the manufacturer. In the first place, we know the owners of the store personally, while the manufacturer must approach the proposition through perhaps a badly equipped drummer seeking an audience with a hard-headed, merciless buyer. It should be comparatively easy for the advertising manager, on the strength of an assured local advertising campaign to be paid for by the manufacturer, to secure the necessary co-operation of the store owner for the display of occasional articles.

From the storekeeper's standpoint the service of the newspaper in securing additional advertising space for his store should be welcomed and grasped as an opportunity. He can well afford to take a very small profit on the goods for the period of the short campaign, because the percentage of selling cost represented by advertising is eliminated.

Likewise the distant manufacturer should be glad to carry on introductory sales in this way, because from his viewpoint the expense of salesmen, railroad fares, hotel bills, and "extras" is cut out, and many very difficult but profitable distributing outlets are established on legitimate price basis.

I know of cases where the manufacturers were so anxious to get into a certain store that they cut prices far below the cost of production on introductory orders, lulled to sleep by the same sort of "buying eloquence" that too many newspaper-men have swallowed whole in selling space to the same clever traders.

Those newspapers which still foolishly adhere to the rule that foreign advertising appearing over the name of a local dealer is "local" advertising upon which they refuse commission to agents stand squarely in their own light and can never expect to receive their full share of business. Let us concede that the man who develops an account, prepares the copy, and guarantees the payment of the bill is entitled to his compensation.

Localized National Advertising

is the coming thought in business promotion through the use of printed salesmanship.

The daily newspaper provides the only medium through which the purposes of the distant manufacturer can be linked up to local dealers everywhere in exact accord with distribution or desire to promote sales.

Localized National Advertising Is National Advertising Over the Signatures of Local Dealers

A STRIKING DEMONSTRATION

In the Editor and Publisher of January 18 it was shown that the 2,166 daily English language newspapers in the United States circulated, per issue............28,625,000

That one line in all the newspapers would cost the advertiser under minimum contract.....................$61.63

That it cost in reaching 1,000 newspaper buyers........21½ cents

That it cost to reach every buyer of a daily newspaper or any appreciable part of them.............1/50 of one cent

To reach these same people with a postal card:

Postal Cards @ 2 cents....................$20.00 per thousand
Addressing @ $2.00 per M...................2.00
Printing @ $1.00 per M.....................1.00
Addresses @ $5.00 per M....................5.00
                                 $28.00 " "

28,625,000 postals at $28 per thousand...............$801,500

Now just glance at these figures:

A 70-line ad (approximately the size of a postal card) inserted in each of the 2,166 daily newspapers every other day (156 times a year) would cost...............$672,999 or $128,000 less than the cost of a single postal to 28,625,000 people if it were possible to get their addresses and mail it to them.

Newspaper advertising is the cheapest and most effective form of advertising and the only medium permitting localized national advertising.

Member A. B. C.   **The New York Globe**   Now 180,000 a Day
JASON ROGERS, Publisher

The Globe allows agents full commission on "Localized National Advertising," and urges all other newspapers to do the same.

*See table opposite page 58, "Circulation and Advertising Rates of 2,166 Dailies Summarized."

BUILDING NEWSPAPER ADVERTISING 215

In the smaller cities, where everybody knows everybody else, where advertising rates are comparatively low, activities along the lines I have indicated should be prolific in results. Even here in New York we, in the *Globe* office, have achieved marked success in a number of instances, most notably, perhaps, in the case of the Gossard Corset described in Chapter XVI of *Newspaper Building* and in connection with many food products referred to in Chapter XV of the same book.

XXXVIII

Selling the Newspapers by States

ASIDE from the service devices suggested in previous chapters and in Chapters XV and XVI of *Newspaper Building*, which are fundamental and can be expanded and elaborated to meet almost any line of endeavor, there are broader and bigger ideas which should be developed to secure the increased use of newspaper advertising by manufacturers and retailers for business expansion and to the profit of our newspapers. In 1912 the writer started a series of short first-page advertising talks entitled "Advertising the Advertiser," by John Fallon, in *The New York Globe*, which attracted so much attention that they were offered free of charge to any daily newspaper which would use them. The result was that within six weeks over 800 newspapers were printing them simultaneously.

Probably nothing short of a Presidential message or some big item of national importance ever received such general and standardized presentation, which shows what could be done if all the newspapers, for a short period, would stand shoulder to shoulder for their own best interests. After a few months, as some of the newspapers insisted on paying their way, I organized the United Newspapers to continue the printing of advertising talks and to do many other

BUILDING NEWSPAPER ADVERTISING

things for the stimulation of advertising for the newspapers.

At one time we had nearly 500 newspapers represented in the United Newspapers. At that time there was a moribund, ineffective organization known as the Daily Newspaper Club, consisting of some twenty or thirty daily newspapers endeavoring by various means to do something in the same line. Conducted by a small coterie of those primarily seeking advantage for themselves (the big papers), it never got out of the would-like-to-be class. Then there was off in the distance the National Newspapers, which never got into action, composed of fifty big city newspapers which pretended that they covered the whole United States.

For the broadest possible benefits to the newspapers of the country as a whole, I, in 1913, got what was left of the two ineffective newspaper organizations to combine with the United Newspapers, then 440 strong, and become the Bureau of Advertising of the American Newspaper Publishers' Association. But no sooner was the thing accomplished than I realized that I had made a mistake. All initiative and forceful purpose was ironed out of the movement before it was taken into the A. N. P. A., and at the first meeting of the committee placed in charge it was decided not to give out lists of members of the bureau and not to recommend any specific newspapers to an advertiser. The 440 members of the United Newspapers who had paid their dues or agreed to pay them were not taken in "as is," but invited to sign a new application for membership, which reduced the number nearly one half.

In June, 1913, I presented to the Board of Control

of the old Association of American Advertisers the plan upon which the Audit Bureau of Circulations was organized. For months I had been the single representative of the newspapers in perfecting the plan in co-operation with the advertising managers of many large national advertisers. When the pressure grew too great for me I organized The Gilt Edge Newspapers, about 300 strong, from which I and a committee, consisting of H. H. Bliss, of *The Janesville* (Wis.) *Gazette;* Milo W. Whitaker, of *The Jackson* (Mich.) *Patriot;* and J. L. Sturtevant, of *The Wausau* (Wis.) *Record-Herald*, produced the very moderate basis of dues of $26 a year for the smaller newspapers.

My experience in studying and developing these organizations had given me unusual opportunities for studying conditions all over the country, regarding the contact between newspapers and advertisers, and to consider improved devices for producing more satisfactory results for all concerned. I beheld the controllers of advertising space calmly sitting in their offices, waiting for business to come to them, and manufacturers wishing to buy and use the space prevented from doing so, owing to the absence of machinery and proper facilities to do so effectively and economically.

Only in a few spots in the whole country had the newspapers of any large enough block of worth-while territory got together for any purposeful effort to sell their goods. It may be said that the advertising agents were there to serve the prospective customer. They were, but more often than not they switched him into the magazines just the same as I would have done had I been in the business, because most newspapers refuse to allow commission on local busi-

THIRD QUARTER, 1913

— THE —

"Gilt Edge Newspapers"

(Not Incorporated)

A GROUP OF LEADING MEDIUMS WHICH "SELL ADVERTISING AS A COMMODITY."

Each of these newspapers plainly states its circulation and has signed agreement providing for quarterly reports with permission to audit and verify its claims by any body of Advertisers recognized by the Gilt Edge Newspapers as an organization.

This first quarterly report is sent out for the purpose of showing advertisers which newspapers in the country wish to be lined up with those standing for circulation verification and has been prepared before certain of the members have had time to furnish circulation data in the form required. In cases where blank lines are shown, the newspaper has joined within a very few days and has not had time to furnish the information we demand Subsequent issues will be complete or the name of the newspaper omitted.

Every circulation figure below will be proved on request.

		CIRCULATION DATA							ADVERTISING RATES						
		Population	Average for year Sept. 30	Average for July	Average for August	Average for Sept.	Percentage Cit'y	Percentage Co'ty	No Cols	Width Col. Pica Ems	Length of Cols Lines	Per Line	1,000 Lines	Per Inch	100 Inches
Albany (N. Y.) Times-Union	E	100,253	42,810	41,623	40,155	46,642	60	40	8	12½	308	6	6	84	84
Alliance (Ohio) Review	E	15,083	4,953	5,053	5,020	4,090	60	40	7	13	280	—	—	21–26	—
Alliance (Ohio) Review	S.-W		3,428	3,163	3,176	3,187	—	100	7	13	280	—	—	21–26	—
Alpena (Mich.) News	E	12,700	2,181	2,124	2,205	2,215	86	14	7	13	280	—	—	10–15	10–15
Amsterdam (N. Y.) Recorder & Democrat	E	31,267	4,106	4,018	4,028	4,095	83	17	7	13	305	—	—	50	25
Anaconda (Mont.) Standard	M	10,134	—	—	—	—	75	25	7	13	278	4	4	—	—
Anaconda (Mont.) Standard	S		—	—	—	—	75	25	7	13	278	4½	4½	—	—
Asbury Park (N. J.) Press	E	10,150	6,190	6,313	6,575	6,420	—	—	7	13	294	—	—	25–30	25–30
Aurora (Ill.) Beacon-News	E	35,000	14,259	14,228	14,171	14,320	51	49	7	13	294	2½	2½	—	—
Beaumont (Texas) Enterprise	M	20,640	11,618	12,270	11,798	11,549	32	68	7	13	280	6	5	—	—
Beaumont (Texas) Enterprise	S		11,618	12,270	11,798	11,549	32	68	7	13	280	6	5	—	—
Beaver (Pa.) Times	E	25,623	—	3,775	3,710	3,991	90	10	7	13	280	—	—	15–18	—
Belleville (Ont.) Intelligencer	E	10,000	1,990	2,232	2,214	2,204	63	37	7	13	287	—	—	35	14
Beloit (Wis.) News	E	15,125	4,610	4,713	4,860	4,774	68	32	7	13	287	—	—	15–20	15–20
Berlin (Ont.) News-Record	E	18,338	—	—	—	—	88	12	7	13	294	—	—	28–31	—
Binghamton (N. Y.) Press and Leader	E	48,443	24,325	24,508	24,312	24,579	53	47	7	13	294	10	6½	—	—
Birmingham (Ala.) News	E	180,000	—	34,269	35,114	36,488	70	30	7	13	308	8	8	1 12	1 12
Birmingham (Ala.) News	S		—	33,853	33,823	35,229	70	30	7	13	308	8	8	1 12	1.12
Bloomington (Ill.) Pantagraph	M	25,768	15,446	15,311	15,304	15,486	40	60	7	13	294	3	3	—	—
Bridgeton (N. J.) News	E	14,209	—	4,796	4,805	4,818	60	40	7	13	287	—	—	15	20
Burlington (Iowa) Hawk-Eye	M	27,000	—	9,061	9,137	8,924	30	70	7	13	297½	2½	2½	—	—
Burlington (Iowa) Hawk-Eye	S		—	10,120	10,115	10,172	30	70	7	13	297½	2½	2½	—	—
Butte (Mont.) Miner	M	39,165	8,435	8,804	8,915	8,733	68	32	7	13	280	—	—	1.00	50
Butte (Mont.) Miner	S		13,791	14,003	13,961	13,985	68	32	7	13	280	—	—	1 00	57
Cairo (Ill.) Citizen	E	14,548	2,663	2,450	2,530	2,465	63	37	7	13	280	1½	—	21	12
Calgary (Alta.) Herald	E	43,704		19,844	19,735	20,380	57	43	8	13	305	5	5	70	70
Cambridge (Ohio) Jeffersonian	E	15,000	5,825	5,890	5,779	5,850	—	—	7	13	276	—	—	22	18
Canton (Ill.) Register	E	10,453	5,651	5,562	5,301	5,266	38	62	7	13	294	—	—	28	21
Carlisle (Pa.) Herald	E	10,303	—	2,280	2,286	2,295	45	55	6	13	280	—	—	11	—
Centralia (Ill.) Sentinel	E	12,250	2,738	2,828	2,766	2,722	70	30	7	13	290	—	—	11–16	—
Charlotte (N. C.) Observer	M	49,500	10,188	9,967	10,065	10,043	30	70	7	13	294	7	5½	—	—
Charlotte (N. C.) Observer	S		14,210	14,025	14,090	14,338	30	70	7	13	294	7	5½	—	—
Charlottetown (P. E. I.) Guardian	M	14,000	3,5 0	3,413	3,423	3,497	60	40	7	13	287	3	1½	42	14
Charlottetown (P. E. I.) Guardian	E		2,633	2,503	2,516	2,601	25	75	7	13	287	3	1½	42	14
Charlottetown (P. E. I.) Guardian	W		3,898	3,720	3,787	3,879	58	42	7	13	287	3	1½	42	14
Clinton (Ill.) Journal	M	6,165	1,911	1,842	1,915	1,995	40	60	7	13	274	—	—	10–15	—
Concordia (Kan.) Blade	E	5,203	1,507	1,507	1,507	1,507	50	50	7	13	308	3	1	10–15	10–15
Concordia (Kan.) Empire	W		1,525	1,525	1,525	1,525	50	50	6	13	280	3	1	10–15	10–15
Connellsville (Pa.) Courier	E	12,845	6,668	6,604	6,621	6,590	45	55	7	13	283½	—	—	30	—
Crawfordsville (Ind.) Journal	E	9,371	—	—	—	—	—	—	—	—	—	—	—	—	—
Coshocton (Ohio) Tribune	M	11,000	—	3,869	3,824	3,892	35	65	7	13	282	—	—	12½	12½
Danville (Ill.) Commercial-News	E	27,871	12,595	12,483	12,529	12,485	42	58	7	13	280	—	—	25	25
Davenport (Iowa) Times	E	45,000	22,168	22,552	22,691	22,778	47	53	7	18	280	3½	3½	—	—
Dayton (Ohio) News	E	116,577	30,736	30,311	30,074	30,089	65	35	7	13	203	4½	4½	—	—
De Kalb (Ill.) Chronicle	E	8,102	2,315	2,492	2,360	2,346	40	60	7	13	287	—	—	10	10
Delaware (Ohio) Gazette	E	10,000	1,713	1,749	1,759	1,787	80	20	7	13	274	—	—	10	5
Des Moines (Iowa) Capital	E	86,368	—	—	—	—	35	65	7	13	305	6	6	—	—
Dubuque (Iowa) Times-Journal	M	38,494	11,396	11,366	11,524	11,692	42	58	7	13	280	3½	3	50	42
Dubuque (Iowa) Times-Journal	E														

ness. We newspapers had not, and have not to-day, made it as easy and profitable for agents to use us for a national campaign as the magazines. Until we do we can expect no better treatment than we get.

It may be urged by some that through their special representatives the newspapers could provide the bridge between the manufacturer and their newspaper. This relation will be treated in more detail in a later chapter. Be as effective as he will, the special representative is chiefly effective in following up the big agency advertisers for copy, and going out from time to time and making occasional calls on advertisers on his trips. He is up against the same handicap as would be a man from the home office. Few business men can afford to give much time to a man representing a single newspaper or, for that matter, any small group of newspapers.

I studied the conditions carefully and made up my mind that the best way to sell the newspapers as a whole to national advertisers and to any manufacturer was through a new style of organized effort. Something bigger, more definite, and more purposeful than the Bureau of Advertising, The United Newspapers, or The Gilt Edge Newspapers, must be created to do the thing, and I devised the plan of Graphic Commercial Surveys described in Chapter XXIX of *Newspaper Building*, offering to provide filing offices in New York and Chicago free of charge if enough newspapers made the surveys. My plan was to create, through the surveys, a background for consolidating and utilizing the best experience of the Wisconsin Daily League, the Inland Press Association, and the Ohio Select List, and organizing similar movements all over the country.

Out of 160 newspapers which promised to prepare surveys, only 31 came through. The ones completed were wonderfully effective and undoubtedly brought satisfactory results to the newspapers making them, and stand as a striking testimonial to the willingness of these newspapers to co-operate.

Before unfolding my later plans for the organization of an effective national advertising-getting body I wish briefly to touch upon the early efforts in this direction as they appear to me or outsiders much interested in watching their progress.

The Wisconsin Daily League, for which H. H. Bliss of *The Janesville* (Wis.) *Gazette*, as secretary, has done really wonderfully effective educational work, according to the support back of his efforts, has fallen short of its goal only through the failure of its men to realize what they were out for. The Milwaukee papers did not co-operate, so the organization was deprived of the financial backing it should have received. Wisconsin provides admirable ground for the demonstration of the plan for sectional advertising promotion, but its papers apparently are not strong enough to stand the expense of a real campaign. They have had valuable experience and will be in fine shape to swing into line as part of a big national campaign when it develops.

The Ohio Select List, of which Robert E. Ward, of Chicago and New York, is advertising special representative, has done big and important work, according to its possibilities, hobbled by the restrictions regarding membership. All newspapers, big and small, in a state or a section should be behind any such movement for the general good of newspaper advertising. What a wonderful showing the state of Ohio

BUILDING NEWSPAPER ADVERTISING

could make if its newspapers all got into line to create trade stimulation through newspaper advertising!

The Wisconsin League is weak because it does not include the Milwaukee newspapers, as the Ohio Select List is because it does not include the daily newspapers of Cleveland, Cincinnati, and other of the larger cities. If our newspapers are ever going to come into their own they must sink petty differences and all boost newspaper advertising, regardless of whether they all get in on an appropriation or not. It is absolutely foolish for the big city papers to pretend that they thoroughly cover territory supporting local dailies. By making such a claim they get into the same class as the magazines which have claimed that they cover the whole country.

The general advertiser, situated in a distant city, is greatly handicapped in any attempt to create demand or increased sales for his goods through newspaper advertising in, we shall say, the state of Texas, for many reasons, which must be clearly understood to be appreciated.

Newspaper men, thoroughly conversant with local conditions and probably representing the greatest power in the various communities, little realize the difficulties of the distant manufacturer, even supposing he is willing to attempt to reconcile several hundred such units as our separate newspapers represent into a national campaign.

In the first place, our friend the manufacturer, who has not the capital or willingness to investigate conditions in each community that we represent, is largely dependent upon the scant and unsatisfactory information he can get through existing conditions.

I have traveled over one million miles in the United

States and Canada during the last ten years, visiting all of the larger cities and many small towns, calling on newspapers, advertisers, and agencies, and feel that I am qualified to view the situation from the broadest possible standpoint.

What I am now going to say is in the interest of all newspaper advertising, and for the purpose of urging the newspapers of the various states to launch campaigns which will be demonstrations of lasting effect on the whole newspaper business and bring direct and immediate results in the way of increased revenue, which I know all most earnestly will welcome.

We will take, for example, the state of Texas, for many reasons, as the starting-point of such a campaign as I shall outline. Viewed from a distance, Texas, on account of its size and widely scattered cities, must ever seem a most bewildering prospect for the man wishing to increase his sales through direct appeal to all the people.

I know the cities and the people and want to show the Texas publishers how, through co-operative effort, they can each of them get more business coming to their newspapers than in any other way that I have ever seen worked out or presented for consideration.

In the first place, the state is rich and prosperous and possesses limitless possibilities. The task of properly presenting the appeal of Texas to the general advertisers of the country is beyond the commercial possibilities of any single newspaper or of any small group of newspapers.

At really trifling expense per paper, they can, through the organization of a state Daily Newspaper Association, in which every daily newspaper in the state should participate, regardless of local rivalries, produce a cohesive force that will be wonderful in its productiveness along lines I shall briefly indicate.

I shall not attempt more than to outline the points which my investigations of advertising conditions have shown me are most desirable for the purpose (through intelligent appeal and service) of securing a larger use of the newspapers.

In the first place, the Texas newspapers should have a central office, preferably in Austin, the state capital, Dallas, or some other centrally located city, with a paid secretary in charge to gather and summarize the information secured by members or to take charge of other activities which we shall get to later on.

The secretary should, by correspondence with the members, and personal investigation, if necessary, produce a set of loose-leaf pages which will reflect business conditions and possibilities of every town in the state, with maps of business centers and lists of reliable dealers in practically every line like Graphic Commercial Surveys, as described in *Newspaper Building*, page 236.

Copies of all these data should be kept on file for the use of prospective advertisers in New York and Chicago, and perhaps later elsewhere, and copies of the whole of it or any part furnished to advertisers at purely nominal rates.

When we consider that, in advance of any state-wide campaign, one manufacturer, say, in New York, should have much of these data before him, and that the newspapers can give him for a few dollars information which would cost him thousands of dollars to duplicate and months of labor to produce, you will realize the importance of this service.

Graphic Commercial Surveys of the business centers of all the cities and towns, indicating by numerals and signs the location of the principal dealers in the many lines of trade, and perhaps later on shaded to show districts according to rental values, would be of inestimable value.

In three months' time these basis data would put Texas at the head and forefront of all the states in the Union as a desirable field for experimental campaigns which would prove the wonderful and superior pulling powers of the newspapers.

Through the organization I am indicating, each state could establish an iron-clad standard of advertising rates which every one would soon learn were as unalterable and substantial as the Rock of Gibraltar, and cut off the traffic of the space-buying jugglers among them.

Each state could establish its own checking bureau, which, under bond, could furnish advertisers' reports as to insertions and positions sold at extra rates, and could, through the organization of a small mat plant, cut out much of the expense of supplying such matter to each individual paper at long range.

There is absolutely no doubt in my mind of the success of such a plan of operations. It is as sound and correct in principle as the science of banking or any other known success. There is not an "if" about it if the newspapers will but get together to put it through.

Through organization of similar state associations throughout the country, all hooked up together in six sectional groupings and then in a national newspaper organization which would be effective and worth while, it would be possible to double, treble, and multiply by a dozen times the present volume of general advertising in the newspapers.

Each sectional unit of representation in a national organization with, say, two directors from each state would give us a body far more effective than the present American Newspaper Publishers' Association with its self-perpetuating policies, giving control to the business managers of a few big city papers. Every subject of newspaper interest could be regulated on a basis of cost fixed on average circulation. In Chapter XLI I give a brief outline for the organization of the new national organization that should succeed the A. N. P. A.

The newspapers, by reason of their close contact with local conditions in practically every city in the country, could (at but a trifling expense to themselves) jointly produce a fund of direct and up-to-the-minute information otherwise unobtainable except at a prohibitive price.

Advertising is fast growing out of the experimental condition in which it has existed for years. It is for us to demonstrate in an unmistakable way that the strength and success of any national campaign must depend upon its influence in bringing the people to local shops in every city through local newspaper advertising.

It is for us as newspaper publishers to try to make it easier for the prospective advertiser to do business with us. If, by a slight adjustment in our rate cards, we can make it easier for him to figure a combined rate for all the newspapers in a state, why not attempt to provide the simple general rate card?

The general advertiser very naturally objects to paying the newspapers twice as much per line for space as his local agent, and we have all heard the arguments of the large agent who wishes to buy bulk space for his clients on the same basis as the department stores.

Of course, it would be out of the question to grant such an absurd request and put any agency in the position of being able to quote a lower rate for our space to a single advertiser than that provided in our rate cards, but the point is well worth considering in the development of state associations.

Let Texas or any other state show the way and sell advertising as a commodity alike to all customers buying the same quantity under the same conditions. We are doing this in the big cities, and it can be done with big profit to the smaller newspapers and great simplification of relations with general advertisers.

I believe that the newspapers of each state should, as an organization, decide upon a uniform basis of discounts for various amounts of space and seek the greatest possible uniformity and simplicity regarding any extra charge for position, which should be rigidly lived up to by every member.

For instance, make rates for one-time business, 26 times, 52 times, etc., and for different volumes of open space to be used in one year, run of paper, and, say, 25 per cent. extra for next following reading, and 50 per cent. next and alongside reading, or, better still, adopt a flat rate.

By devoting a reasonable degree of care to the make-up it will be found that the newspapers can easily take sufficient care of the small general ads. to make them productive. If the customer wants to buy anything special as a "must," make him pay for

BUILDING NEWSPAPER ADVERTISING

it just the same as you would if seeking special service anywhere.

In making it easier for the general advertiser to do business with us, we shall find that it will simplify matters very much if we, as an association, rigidly live up to the literal application of a "no free reading notice" rule. Simply cut out the outrage and make the advertiser pay for everything he seeks, just the same as we have to.

Our friends the magazines never give up a line of free space. The agents realize that they have to pay for what they get in the magazines, and endeavor to work the newspapers for as much better than fifty-fifty as they can get. Just as long as we will stand for being worked they will try to work us.

We have it in our power entirely to eliminate all waste in the matter of a general advertiser wishing to build up or stimulate business in Texas. No general medium can compete with the newspapers as a group. The newspapers can render dependable service and information quicker than any other instrumentality in the world.

Through the sectional organizations I suggest, the newspapers can get direct audience with the biggest manufacturers in the country to submit selling plans and invaluable data. You can dictate your own terms and conditions to the buyer, for your proposals will be of sufficient importance to make any man wishing to do business in your state sit up and take notice.

The average manufacturer has not the time or the inclination even to see a small part of the newspaper representatives that try to see him. He can see but a few important newspaper publishers in the course of a year. If he tried to see them all he could do no other business. He must, therefore, of necessity get his information through subordinates.

Through the state and sectional organization, the newspapers will have a proposal big enough and important enough to warrant the concentrated attention of any business man wishing to do business in your state, just as long as you can give him the sort of information he needs in his business. He will grasp the efficiencies of your service and do what he can to encourage such efforts by giving you business.

The newspapers should be determined in advance to forget personalities and local feuds in trying to get business to come to their state. Fight and struggle as they wish in local matters, but pull together and boost all Texas newspaper advertising in the full confidence that eventually some part of all accounts will come their way.

Texas is an empire in itself. Its newspapers hold the key to the situation. They must jointly exploit the possibilities of their field. No matter how strong any one of them is in its own community, it must recognize that, as a rule, the whole state must be considered as a unit by the general advertiser.

NEWSPAPER STATE MAPS

A year or two ago an idea occurred to me which if carried out by the newspapers would do much to simplify the sale of newspaper advertising, by visualizing them in state groups in convenient form for use on the desks of all space-buyers. It is a little thing which could be done quite effectively by the

Bureau of Advertising of the American Newspaper Publishers' Association or some such body.

My thought was to make a series of maps like that of Alabama herewith, merely showing the towns in which daily newspapers are published, to go on the left-hand side of the booklet, with the statistical form giving details as to the population, circulation, etc., on the right-hand side.

The booklet should be of the loose-leaf variety, printed on strong quality of paper and space left at the right-hand edge of the right-hand page for the space-buyer to jot down data regarding advertising rates.

Brought together in a neat leather cover, newspaper maps and statistical tables covering every state in the Union would be of immense value to men seeking to outline a national campaign in the newspapers, and of greater use to help him convince the advertiser how the newspapers cover the field and can be used in exact accord with distribution.

Such a booklet easily folded for insertion in a traveling-bag or rolled for carrying to meetings or conferences would save much lost motion in making up lists for various campaigns.

At a glance the buyer or seller of space could ascertain the total population of a state or a city, ascertain the number of families, and what proportion of them can be reached by the newspapers and at what cost per reader or per family.

Until the newspapers realize that they each of them are but a unit in a big national medium, which must be bought and sold as such in competition with other media which can be bought much more conveniently, they will never get the share of foreign business which they should get.

ALABAMA

1910 population.......................... 2,138,093

City	Population	Paper	Circulation	Rate
Anniston.....	12,794	*Star & Hot Blast	......	......
Bessemer.....	10,864	Free Press	......	......
Birmingham..	132,685	Age Herald	......	......
		*Ledger	......	......
		*News	......	......
Dothan......	7,016	*Eagle	......	......
		*News		
Enterprise....	2,322	Journal	......	......
Eufaula......	4,259	Citizen	......	......
Gadsden.....	10,559	*Journal	......	......
		*Times News	......	......
Huntsville....	7,611	*Mercury	......	......
		Times	......	......
Mobile.......	51,521	*Item	......	......
		*Register	......	......
Montgomery..	38,136	*Advertiser	......	......
		*Journal	......	......
		*Times	......	......
New Decatur.	6,118	Daily	......	......
Opelika......	4,734	News	......	......
Selma	13,649	*Journal	......	......
		Times	......	......
Sheffield......	4,865	Daily	......	......
Talladega....	5,854	Home	......	......
Troy........	4,961	Messenger	......	......
Tuscaloosa...	8,407	News & Times Gazette	......	......

*Evening.

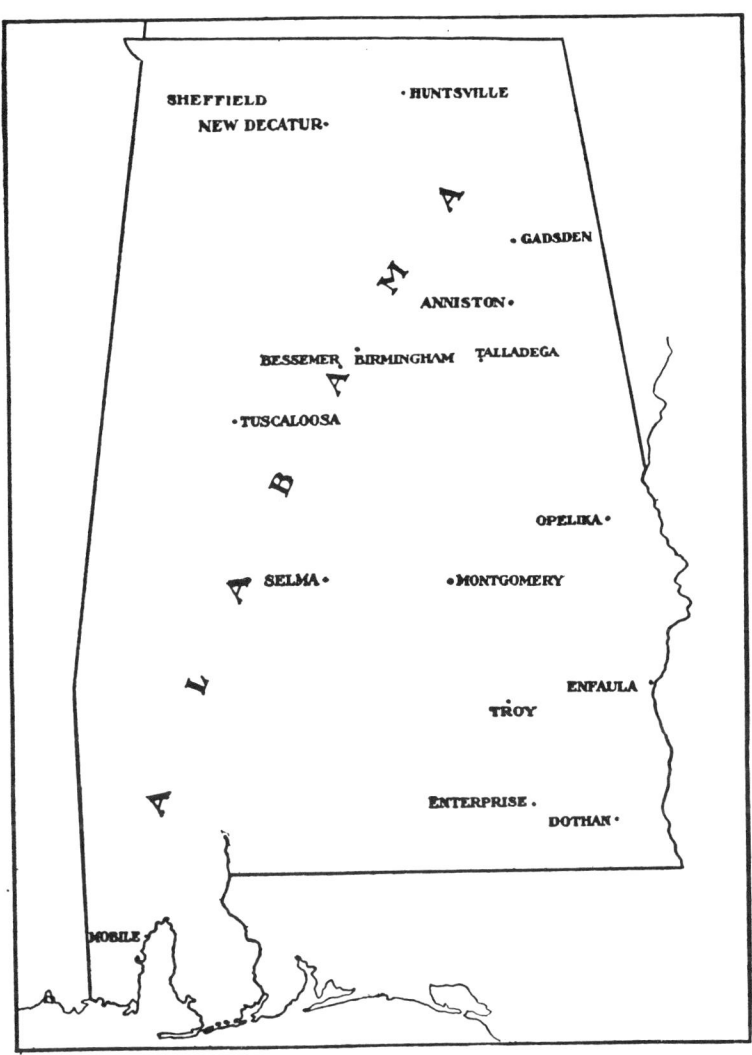

Map of Alabama Showing Towns in Which Newspapers Are Published.
For use in connection with data on page 230.

Aside from the very large cities, the national advertiser seldom has time or inclination to take up newspapers as single units. He decides to cover a state or a section of the country. Before he starts his advertising he arranges his distribution and other details. Herein lies the greatest efficiency of newspaper advertising to him, if we would but co-operate, which we do not.

Maps and statistics such as I am here proposing invite the distant manufacturer to try to stimulate sales or create new sales. It is the sort of information which he desires and seldom can get through existing channels, for as far as I have been able to ascertain the data are not assembled in as easily get-at-able form.

It is after the manufacturer has arranged his distribution and is ready to contract for newspaper advertising space through his advertising agent that we fall down and fall down hard.

The very strength of newspaper advertising is that it enables the advertiser to hook up his copy to a local dealer or local dealers. As soon as he starts to do this too many of our newspapers put up their "keep off the grass" sign and refuse to pay the agent a commission on the advertising on the ground that it is "local business."

A well-known agent recently told me that three years ago, recognizing the superior pulling power of the newspapers when properly linked to local dealers, he got one of his clients to take $100,000 of the $300,000 previously spent in general mediums and try newspapers.

In nearly all cases the foolish newspapers refused to allow him a commission on the business, and he has been trying to get the business back into the magazines ever since. I merely cite the incident as evidence of a weakness in the armor of the newspapers and one of the reasons why rates and conditions regarding local and foreign advertising should be identical.

XXXIX

Map Scheme for Selling Extra Space

A SCHEME page which I got up for *The Chicago Inter-Ocean* in June, 1898, has many possibilities for effective use by newspaper advertising managers to bring in extra earnings from time to time. The beauty of the thing is that it provides good value for the advertiser represented in it, and can be repeated as a seasonal affair in many cases.

In looking ahead to see what figures we had to beat for June, 1898, I discovered a special number in the previous year sticking up like a sore thumb, and, not having any desire for such a thing, nor time to get one up if I had, I conceived the idea of arranging for a full-page map of Lake Michigan and selling representation on it.

I was a comparative stranger in Chicago. I knew there were many boat lines going across the lake and up the west shore to Milwaukee and other points. The steamship lines advertised, but the whole proposition of lake travel was a mystery to me, so I thought it would be a good idea to make some money visualizing it.

As the idea developed I reduced the size of the map to permit a border of thirty-lines space across the top and bottom, and similar space down each side, for the insertion of time-tables of the transportation lines. For $50 we would give a steamship line one of these spaces for its time card and a dotted line on the surface of the lake, with the name of line running along it.

It was a cinch to sell each of the lines representation. Then I thought of letting them run a picture of one of their boats on the dotted line for $25 more. Next we inserted the summer resorts along the lake and put in the railroads. We charged the railroads $50 each for a space for their time-tables and announcements.

In order to make the thing complete we then inserted the names of hotels and boarding-houses at the resorts for $5 each, and inserted outline cuts of the hotels for $25 each. After we published the page in the newspaper I had several thousand copies struck off on good paper, with the top and bottom tinned, which the advertisers were glad to hang in their waiting-rooms and distribute to good advantage. My recollection as to the amount of money we got from that page is dim, but it was a good fat sum, and every one was pleased.

In many situations the same basic idea can be applied to good purpose. Even in the cities the use of page maps for the purpose of visualizing various shopping centers, theaters, etc., offers a phase of new activity for the alert advertising manager. The mere act of seeking to turn up new ground develops an inquiring state of mind apt to develop many other relations with new customers.

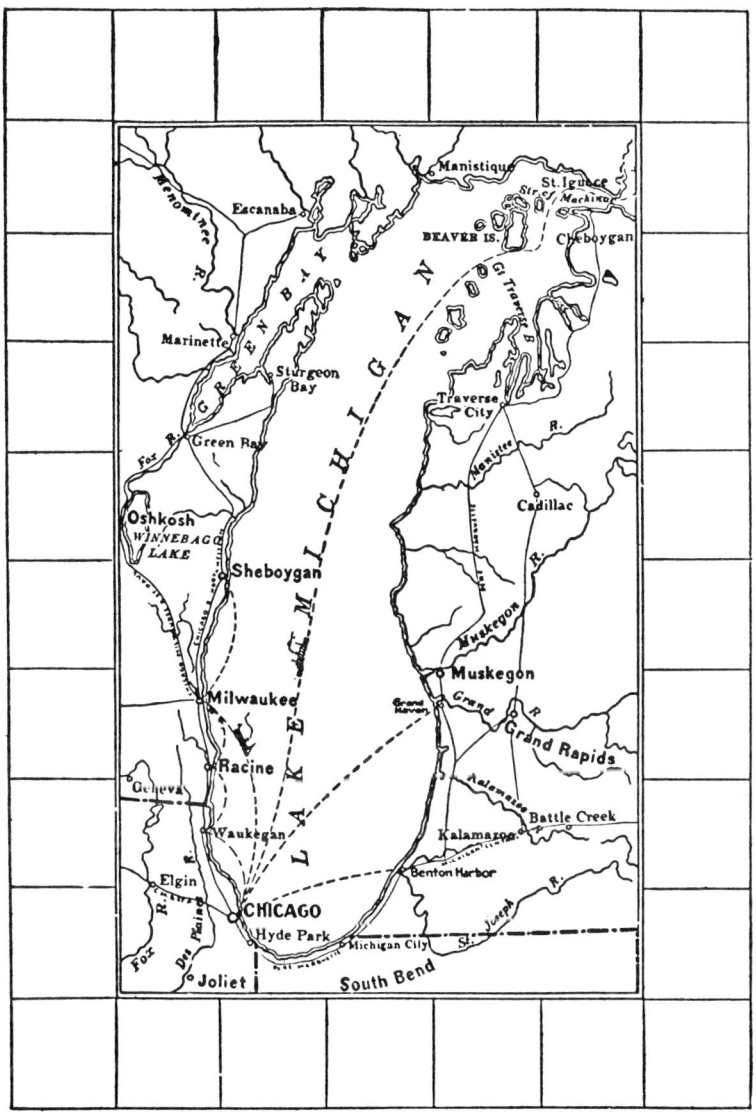

Map of Lake Michigan, Showing How It Was Used for Advertising Exploitation.

XL

Building Up the Classified

BUILDING up the classified advertising columns of a newspaper is either an extremely difficult task or an easy one, according to the way in which we approach the subject. I have watched various efforts to build classified for upward of thirty-five years in New York and other cities, and have no hesitancy in saying that, of all methods, the one so wonderfully put over by Harry Doorly for *The Omaha World-Herald* seems most direct and effective.

Back in the early '80's *The New York Herald* owned the classified advertising of New York, and was probably the leader in that line among all newspapers in the whole world. It was more arbitrary in its regulations than any of our present-day newspapers and demanded rates as high as or higher than are now charged by any newspaper. Up to 1883 there had been many efforts to wrench some part of the business from *The Herald*, but without any serious result.

In 1883 Joseph Pulitzer, who had just bought *The New York World*, started after *The Herald* in a way it had never been tackled before regarding both display and classified, which put him "over the top" in fine style. In Chapter IV of *Newspaper Building* I briefly outlined the methods by which Pulitzer produced the marvelous results which enabled him to pass *The Herald* in display and to later on get the classified leadership.

Limiting ourselves to the mutton before us—classified—the development of that part of *The New York World* to its present magnificent proportions has been produced by resort to every forcing device known to man. Free "wants" for a time filled the columns with masses of trade offerings disguised as "wants," and plenteous first-page boxes and display ads. called attention to the bargains and values represented in the mass of small ads.

It was a long, hard struggle for *The World* to overcome the dominating position of *The Herald*, but in twenty years, or by 1903, *The World* had pulled level, and then went to the front, notwithstanding the additional competition of Hearst with *The American* struggling valiantly for a slice of the business and spending tons of money to get a representation.

I seriously doubt whether it would be possible for another newspaper now to cut in on *The World*, keeping in mind the masses of small ads. run every day and Sunday by *The American* and *Evening Telegram*.

The Telegram's development of classified represents a freakish achievement starting with free "exchange ads." later separated into groups at various rates, and then refined so as to produce a higher rate from dealers and traders than from private individuals. It was a rather peculiar and wonderful finding of a big classified following, but one that it would be difficult to duplicate.

By a more labored and painstaking process *The New York Times* has now developed the nucleus of

HARRY DOORLY
Business manager of the Omaha *World-Herald*, who solved the problem of getting classified advertising.

a real classified department at very handsome rates without spread-eagle or bombastic methods. Starting with so-called "censored wants," advertisements from those in a position to prove their reliability, *The Times* has gradually come into about the highest-grade group of small ads. ever printed in a New York newspaper.

Unlike most other newspapers, *The Times* does not seek or desire want ads. which do not represent a service to the substantial sort of people it is made to please. Questionable rooming-houses, fake business opportunities, and the cheaper classes of stuff filling most other classified pages do not get into *The Times*.

In Chicago, *The Daily News* on week-days and *The Tribune* on Sundays carry the volume of classified advertising, and have done so for years without any serious intrusion from other newspapers spending fortunes to break in and offering to run such stuff at from one to two and a half cents a line.

But in the development of classified advertising for any newspaper the plan successfully worked out by Harry Doorly for *The Omaha World-Herald*, as I have said, seems to me to be soundest and bound to be successful to a degree wherever adhered to.

Based on the theory that the way to get classified is to teach your readers to use the columns of their own newspaper as an exchange for commodities and service, all that is needed is the appropriation of a sufficient volume of space every day for a year or more to get your readers reading classified and sending in business.

Harry Doorly had been up against the usual office experience in getting in office ads. for any particular feature. Every day there was a jam the office ad.

was crowded out, and the editors generally can manage to be in a hole for space about every other day.

To meet this situation Doorly got a stated allowance of half a column of space every day for one year in which to boost classified. The space was charged to the classified department at run of paper rates as a promotional item. That he used it effectively and got results is proved by final conclusions.

Day in and day out Doorly kept hammering at the readers to read and use the classified columns of *The World-Herald*. Small ads., large ads., and readers were used to such purpose that within a year the paper had more than doubled the volume of classified and continued to grow ever since.

At a meeting of the Associated Newspapers I developed the matter of Doorly's experience, and Lafe Young, Jr., of *The Des Moines Capital*, visited Omaha to investigate. He adopted the idea and, carrying it through consistently, more than doubled his classified inside a year.

The plan was so simple and effective that I got Harry Doorly to get out a book showing sample ads. and various forms used, guaranteeing him cost of production. Any one seriously interested may get copies of this book from Mr. Doorly, I think, at $20 per copy, if it is not out of print.

Viewing classified in the light of broadest experience in many cities, the mistake we newspaper-men generally make is in putting too low a price on our space. In classified the cost of a small ad. does not mean anything to the advertiser if we produce results. In Chicago in 1898 I tried to sell *Inter-Ocean* "want" space for 2 cents a line against *The Tribune's* at 30 cents a line, but couldn't keep it sold. The man who paid *The Tribune* 90 cents for an ad. made a profit, while the man we got to use *The Inter-Ocean* for 6 cents got only a receipt and the sight of his adlet in print.

In those days we did not know as much about the "why" of the advertising business as we do to-day. Even the old *Inter-Ocean* could have been made to produce some results had we known "how" to educate our readers to use the columns of their newspaper as a medium of exchange.

It matters not how little circulation a newspaper has, its space at some rate can be made profitable for its advertisers if its regular subscribers are brought to understand its possibilities and learn to co-operate. Every reader of a newspaper can generally be accepted as a friend and booster. If we keep after him long enough he will gladly take the hint and watch our ads.

In the seeking of classified advertising, aside from that coming in over the counter, there are three forms in general use:

1. Personal solicitation.
2. Circulars.
3. By telephone.

Personal solicitation is the most expensive way, but, under the direction of a competent manager, very productive for many lines. Circularization with a coin-card, similar to sample on page 240, is handled very profitably in many places, while solicitation by telephone has been found most effective almost wherever put on in the proper way.

Almost any contract customer of the telephone company is good for the value of a classified ad. If he does not pay his bill within two weeks he is listed among delinquents and not accorded further credit. By using a revolving index system it is very easy for the person in charge almost instantly to ascertain whether the prospect is good or doubtful.

In experience it has been found that less than 5 per cent. of "want" ads. 'phoned in are not paid for. If the items were large enough to be worth following up by collectors the percentage of loss would probably be much lower.

By the same token, it has been found that it is more effective merely to put bad-pay items on the index and forget them than to open regular accounts and bother with labored effort to collect them.

A simple method for handling the entering, checking, and billing of classified advertising is as follows:

PLACE COINS IN SPACES PROVIDED FOR THEM, FOLD PAPER MONEY UNDER FLAP AND MAIL THIS CARD TO THE GLOBE, IN THE ENCLOSED ENVELOPE, SECURELY SEALED.

THE GLOBE

Use this Form to advertise your lost Bank Book.

THE GLOBE
73 DEY ST.

LOST—Bank Book No.................................of Bowery Savings Bank, 130 Bowery, New York. Finder is requested to return it to bank.
If not restored before....................................
application will be made for new book.

This ad., properly filled out, will cost 70 cents in The Globe.

ORIGINAL

To THE GLOBE
73-83 Dey Street, New York City

New York,............1917.

Gentlemen: Please publish all death and memorial notices that we may be able to send to you, for the period of one year from this date, for which we agree to pay you at the rate of $1.00 for the first three lines of each notice, and Fifty Cents (50c.) for each additional line.

You are to allow us as commission for sending such notices to you, thirty-three and one-third (33⅓) per cent. of the cost of such notices, provided they are sent directly to you and not through any advertising agency.

Accounts are payable on or before the 15th day of the month following the charge.

....

....

BUILDING NEWSPAPER ADVERTISING

DUPLICATE

To THE GLOBE
73-83 Dey Street, New York City

New York,...........1917.

Gentlemen: Please publish all death and memorial notices that we may be able to send to you, for the period of one year from this date, for which we agree to pay you at the rate of $1.00 for the first three lines of each notice, and Fifty Cents (50c.) for each additional line.

You are to allow us as commission for sending such notices to you, thirty-three and one-third ($33\frac{1}{3}$) per cent. of the cost of such notices, provided they are sent directly to you and not through any advertising agency.

Accounts are payable on or before the 15th day of the month following the charge.

....

THE GLOBE

TELEPHONE ADVERTISEMENT ORDER AND CHARGE TICKET

Tel. No.......... Lines........ Rate........ Price........

Name.......................... Ad. Telephoned by.........

Address.......................... Our Copy No..........

Dates to be inserted..

Ad. Received by........	Called back for number of insertions by..........	Supervisor's Stamp for Reading and O. K.
Checked to Tel. Directory by		
Checked for Credit by..............	for reading by..........	
	for address by..........	
....	if rejected by..........	

Remarks:...

....

....

....

....

....

....

....

....

THE GLOBE

HELP WANTED

We Can Serve You

You need help.

With the number of people you employ it is natural that there should be many changes from time to time.

Every change, however, costs you money.

Therefore, the fewer changes you have, the better pleased you will be.

The quality and character of the employe has much to do with the question of changes.

If you can secure the stable, sober, industrious employe, the chances are that such an employe will be likely to remain with you permanently.

Your advertisement for HELP WANTED should be placed in a medium which reaches the class of people you want.

The New York Globe is such a medium.

Hereafter, when you need help, if you will try a Globe Want Ad. you will be more than pleased with results.

A Globe Want Ad. is the stepping stone to complete satisfaction.

Rates are low—25 cents a line for a single insertion, 20 cents a line for three or more insertions.

If you want the enclosed ad. to run in The Globe, just fill out the blank below, tear it off, and mail it to The Globe. The ad. will be charged to you.

THE GLOBE

THE GLOBE HAS NO SUNDAY EDITION   Classified Advertising Dept.

....

Globe Want Ads. Produce Results

The ad. below will cost:

1 time...................$........

3 times.................$........

Additional insertions at the three time rate.

RATES: 25 cents per agate line (2 line minimum); Three or more times, 20 cents a line. 4 words capital letters. (Six average words to a line.)

The Globe:

New York City:

Please publish this ad. for......insertions for which I enclose $........ also send Free copy of The Globe showing ad.

Yours truly,

Name..................................

Address..............................

BUILDING NEWSPAPER ADVERTISING

THE GLOBE

IF YOUR OFFERING IS GOOD GLOBE READERS WILL BUY IT

Whether it be to buy or sell, to lease or to serve, Globe readers are in the market for every attractive proposition.

They number over 215,000 of the class which has not only the inclinations but also the means to secure what they want.

Why not address this offering to them? You cannot reach them except through The Globe.

No paper in New York commands the home attention like The Globe. Its Pure Food Campaign, Dr. Crane's powerful articles, its Home Garden Hints, its Bedtime Stories, School News and general conservative, reliable policy have served to establish it as the strongest newspaper in the New York evening field.

Globe Classified Rates are as follows:
    1 time order, 25 cents per line
    6 time order, 23 cents per line   *The Globe Has No Sunday Edition*
    24 time order, 20 cents per line

This is based on agate type, allowing four words to the line for capital letters and six words to the line for small letters.

Trusting to be favored with your orders, we are

THE GLOBE

Return the Attached to Us To-day   Classified Advertising Department

....

Globe Want Ads. Produce Results

The ad. below will cost:

1 time....................$........

6 times a week...........$........

24 times a month.........$........

RATES: 25 cents per agate line (2 line minimum); six times, 23 cents a line; twenty-four times, 20 cents a line. (Six average words to a line in regular type, and four words to a line in agate caps.)

The Globe:
    New York City:
        Please publish this ad. for......insertions for which I enclose $.........
                Yours truly,

Name..............................

Address...........................

THE GLOBE Is the Great Home Paper
YOURS IS A HOME APPEAL

To Sell a Farm

Not only must the person you are seeking have a desire to live in the country, but he must have also the wherewithal to gratify that desire.

The Globe opens the way for you to reach over 200,000 who have the means to gratify that desire.

No paper in New York commands the home attention like The Globe. Its Pure Food Campaign, Dr. Crane's powerful articles, its Home Garden Hints, its Bedtime Stories, School News and general conservative, reliable policy have served to establish it as the strongest newspaper in the New York evening field.

The trend to-day is toward the country. The increasing cost of local apartments, the high cost of food and other commodities, which a city residence demands to a higher degree than does country living, have taught the New Yorker a strong lesson in the advantage of going back to the farm.

Your message to be profitable must be directed to those who consider the solid comforts of life, the healthy up-bringing of their children and wholesome living for themselves. This is the type of reader of which The Globe may justly boast. Let us direct your story to those readers who read the Globe regularly. You *cannot secure their* attention through *any other* paper.

Globe Classified Rates are as follows:

    1 time order, 25 cents per line
    6 time order, 23 cents per line
    24 time order, 20 cents per line

The Globe Has No Sunday Edition

This is based on agate type, allowing four words to the line for capital letters and six words to the line for small letters.

Trusting to be favored with your orders, we are

THE GLOBE

Return the Attached to Us To-day   Classified Advertising Department

---

Country Real Estate—Globe Want Ads Produce Results

The ad. below will cost:

1 time ....$........

6 times a week...........$........

24 times a month.........$........

RATES: 25 cents per agate line (2 line minimum); six times, 23 cents a line; twenty-four times, 20 cents a line. (Six average words to a line in regular type, and four words to a line in agate caps.)

The Globe:
  New York City:
    Please publish this ad. for....... insertions for which I enclose $........

               Yours truly,

Name............................

Address.........................

To check up the results obtained by various methods the following plans are employed: Each solicitor reports nightly his returns. These are entered on a daily sheet on which is also recorded the total business brought in and business appearing in the paper on that day. Credit is given for telephone advertisements to the individual who has originated the advertisement and had it confirmed by call-back.

The daily record of solicitor's business, telephone calls, and results, number of circulars sent out and received, as well as total business brought in and business in paper, serves as an automatic check and helps determine which form of business-getting is the most productive.

Circulars and advertisements placed in the office come under the head of office business.

The separate advertisements of the day are entered on sheets like that marked Form A. The carbon record remains in the classified department. The sheet is then forwarded to bill clerk, who detaches under sheet containing advertisement, retaining top sheet with records and text of advertising. On the under sheet instructions are recorded for the benefit of the composing-room.

The column is checked daily by the billing department to prove publication. The further process is as follows: For short-time orders paid direct by advertisers record is kept only on classified journal. Bills in duplicate are made out immediately for charge advertisements; bill is forwarded at once, duplicate is held for two weeks and then marked for collection. Time advertisements charged to agents follow the same course as display advertising.

In addition to the checking done by the billing

department, a card is made out in the classified department marked for every day on which the ad. is to run. The column is checked up each day, and yesterday's insertions are circled on the card. This not only serves as a check in this department, but also helps as a tickler, as memorandum is given out for renewal several days before the expiration of the ad.

This method of handling classified advertising is as economical and accurate as can be applied where the volume of business is not excessive. However, where classified advertising reaches great proportions, the loose-leaf method is more desirable. The process is about like this: The advertisements brought in for insertion and not identified as regular or known accounts are entered on a loose sheet properly divided as to classifications. Bill for the whole amount is rendered at once. These sheets are allowed to grow during the month, and as payments are effected accounts are checked off. At the end of the month these sheets are handed over to the collection department. Whatever the collection condition may be after allowing a month to effect it, this sheet is then disposed of and the loss written off and swallowed in the great volume of business. Of course a record is kept of the names and addresses of the delinquents, so the paper need not be caught more than once by the same offender.

The Telegram follows a system practically the same as this, and believes it cheap. Certainly records and collections in great numbers representing small amounts can eat greatly into the profits of classified advertising.

As a medium between the small volume of business carried and the large amount of advertising, as men-

BUILDING NEWSPAPER ADVERTISING

tioned in the latter instance, a good staff of quality rather than quantity soliciting advertisements, and effecting payments on the repeated call is desirable. This, of course, to be backed up by strong circular advertising and an equitable commission arrangement with established agents. Regarding the last item, it is cheaper in the end to figure the cost of maintaining solicitors and the uncertainty of their securing the business. It will then be seen that a portion of this expenditure extended to the agents as a commission will go much farther in securing the business than the same amount of money invested in mediocre solicitors.

Furthermore, in this city at least, it is an axiom that if a classified account is worth cultivating, it is already in the hands of some agent, and a large portion of the remainder is likely to be poor credit.

As to the development of classified advertising, of course not all the work should be left to the agent, but a small, well-equipped and well-paid staff will take care of the necessary promotional work. It is also well to confine solicitors to certain classifications. They acquire a knowledge that helps business and collections.

Attached herewith are solicitation forms covering General for Sale, Farms for Sale, and Help Wanted. There is also included the form and coin-card for Lost Bank-book advertising, which is worked in conjunction with the banks. A contract form is also included, showing arrangement to be entered into with large undertakers and burial establishments.

XLI

Plan for National Newspaper Organization

So far as practical results go, my experimentation with plans for the development of more advertising for the newspapers has proved to me that if the newspapers would only get together in some big, worthwhile, and effective national co-operative body, they could secure amazing achievements.

The idea back of my "Advertising the Advertiser" movement, crystallized later into the United Newspapers and later into the Bureau of Advertising of the A. N. P. A., accomplished something definite, and my agitation for increased efficiency of the old A. A. A. at Syracuse in 1913, by the help of the organization of the Gilt Edge Newspapers, made the present Audit Bureau of Circulations.

During all this time I tried to get the American Newspaper Publishers' Association to become a real organization, representative of all the daily newspapers of the United States and Canada. But the old guard of the A. N. P. A. remained wedded to its old inactive policy, firmly convinced that it had little interest in the small newspapers.

If I am not mistaken, the time is now ripe for the newspapers of the country as a whole to organize a new body which will take over the place the

A. N. P. A. pretends to occupy, and put the newspaper business where it should be. I was a director of the A. N. P. A. for five years and resigned in 1918 because I had grown to feel the hopelessness of getting it out of the mutual-admiration class.

I am firmly convinced that the basis of an effective newspaper organization must be the state unit, expanded into sectional groupings, and then a national body built up on strictly democratic principles. This can be done and the whole enterprise operated with much more effective service to all classes of members than by leaving affairs to the control of the business managers of a few big city newspapers, as in the past in the A. N. P. A.

A rough outline of a plan I should like to see tried out is that presented by me in the shape of a circular to all the newspapers of the United States in June, 1918, as follows:

SUGGESTED PLAN FOR STRONG SECTIONAL NEWSPAPER ORGANIZATION

THE DAILY PRESS ASSOCIATION

Which, in Combination with Other Sectional Associations, Would Produce a National Newspaper Organization Really Representative of the Newspaper-making Industry.

OFFICE NEW YORK GLOBE,
73 DEY STREET, NEW YORK, *June 6, 1918.*

To the Daily Newspaper Publishers of America: GENTLEMEN,—
Filled with a confidence that the group of newspapers represented in the various state or sectional organizations have it within their power to develop the degree and kind of constructive co-operative

effort I have been trying to make effective among all the newspapers of the United States. I am taking the liberty of briefly outlining a program for your earnest and serious consideration.

I may say in advance that I feel deeply honored in being elected an Honorary Member of the Inland Press Association, and take this opportunity for assuring the newspapers of the country of my willingness to work with them and for them in making their organizations more effective and working units in a big, efficient, national body.

You represent a field most attractive and profitable to the manufacturer wishing to expand his business through newspaper advertising. Your newspapers cover this vast field in a way to wonderfully lend their use, and informatory and co-operative facilities in accordance with the possibilities of almost any campaign.

I say these things not for the purpose of pleasing you, but to set up the case for you from the standpoint of an outside observer of wide experience in the study of such situations. All that you lack is organization and the practice of a sound degree of co-operative purpose correctly developed and carried out.

For some reason or other the newspaper business develops a degree of destructive competition which in the past has prevented us getting together for maximum results, and permitted other types of mediums to reach in and get many millions of dollars of advertising which, if expended in our columns, would have produced much more satisfactory returns to the advertiser.

In my opinion, the state unit is best calculated as the basis for sectional or national organization. Each state may have its own problems, legislation, legal or otherwise, so it is desirable to take advantage of existing state organizations in building our edifice or to get the newspapers in each state to build up such an organization.

In the Central Division, covered by your Inland Press Association, with its thirteen states, for example, it seems to me to be practicable to ask each state to elect its own representative on the Board of Directors of the Division body, with the officers to be elected from this group at the annual meeting of the sectional body.

Each state organization should be constructed on exactly the same plan as the sectional body, with the same committees, having the same functions, the chairman of each state committee

BUILDING NEWSPAPER ADVERTISING 253

becoming automatically a member of the Inland Press Association committee of the same name, each sectional committee to elect its own sectional chairman.

Organized in this way, the next step in development—a national body—may be developed in the same way, with each chairman of the various sectional committees becoming a member of the national committee of the same name and performing the same functions.

For the purpose of visualizing the proposed organization I have prepared the chart. In the state organizations each of the committees could consist of five members, elected at the annual state meetings. Otherwise the operations are identical.

The divisional groups of the United States and Canada with plans for sectional meetings suggested are as follows:

Eastern Division.—Comprising the states of Maine, New Hampshire, Vermont, Massachusetts, Rhode Island, Connecticut, New York, New Jersey, Pennsylvania, Maryland, District of Columbia, Delaware and West Virginia, with meetings at Boston, Philadelphia, Baltimore, Washington, Providence, Hartford, Springfield, New Haven, or Trenton.

Central Division.—Comprising the states of Ohio, Indiana, Michigan, Illinois, Wisconsin, Missouri, Iowa, Minnesota, Kansas, Nebraska, South Dakota, North Dakota, and Oklahoma, with meetings at Chicago, Detroit, Cleveland, St. Louis, Kansas City, Columbus, Milwaukee, Indianapolis, St. Paul, Minneapolis, or Des Moines.

Western Division.—Comprising the states of Wyoming, Colorado, Montana, Idaho, Nevada, Utah, New Mexico, and Arizona, with meetings at Denver, Salt Lake City, Reno, Boise, Albuquerque, or Phoenix.

Pacific Division.—Comprising the states of California, Oregon, and Washington, with meetings at San Francisco, Los Angeles, Portland, Seattle, Tacoma, Spokane, or Sacramento.

Southern Division.—Comprising the states of Virginia, North Carolina, South Carolina, Georgia, Florida, Alabama, Tennessee, Mississippi, Louisiana, Texas, Arkansas, and Kentucky, with meetings at New Orleans, Atlanta, Birmingham, Richmond, Houston, Dallas, Little Rock, Oklahoma City, Charleston, Jacksonville, Louisville, Nashville, or Chattanooga.

Canadian Division.—The whole of Canada, with meetings at Montreal, Ottawa, Toronto, Winnipeg, or Vancouver.

Chart Showing Proposed Sectional Organization

BOARD OF DIRECTORS
1 Elected by Each of the States

PRESIDENT and VICE-PRESIDENT
*Elected at Annual Meeting From
Directors Elected in States*

SECRETARY and TREASURER
Elected at Annual Meeting

EXECUTIVE COMMITTEE
5 Directors Elected at Annual Meeting

FINANCE COMMITTEE	LEGISLATIVE COMMITTEE	POST-OFFICE COMMITTEE	LABOR COMMITTEE
1 From Each State	*1 From Each State*	*1 From Each State*	*1 From Each State*

ADVERTISING COMMITTEE	EFFICIENCY COMMITTEE	PAPER COMMITTEE
1 From Each State	*1 From Each State*	*1 From Each State*

MACHINERY COMMITTEE	MEMBERSHIP COMMITTEE
1 From Each State	*1 From Each State*

Divided into natural groupings the states with number of daily newspapers and populations would be like this:

Eastern	Division	.. 679	newspapers	31,041,042	population.
Central	"	.. 776	"	33,343,247	"
Southern	"	.. 388	"	26,272,735	"
Western	"	.. 122	"	2,633,517	"
Pacific	"	.. 240	"	4,948,999	"
Canadian	"	.. 139	"	8,000,000	"
	Total........	2,562		106,239,540	

FUNCTIONS OF COMMITTEES

EXECUTIVE.—To be responsible for the conduct of official headquarters staff; to transact business between meetings of the full board; to hold mail votes when desired, and to be an emergency body that can quickly be brought together.

FINANCE COMMITTEE.—To make budgets and levy assessments with the approval of the Board of Directors; to formulate plans for financing any special efforts or activities; to audit and check the accounts of the treasurer or treasurers of state organizations.

LEGISLATIVE COMMITTEE.—To keep track of attempts at adverse legislation in the states or at Washington; to work in conjunction with similar committees from other sectional organizations; to be represented at Washington, or wherever needed, to protect the best interests of the newspapers.

POST-OFFICE COMMITTEE.—To specifically watch and keep informed regarding postal services; to work with the Legislative Committee when required; to gather data regarding post-office carrying costs, and to secure best service for members.

LABOR COMMITTEE.—To act as clearing house for labor disputes between members and labor unions; to codify best practices and forms of contracts; to establish more harmonious relations with the unions; to employ paid manager if necessary.

ADVERTISING COMMITTEE.—To handle and carry out various plans for the development of new advertising for the newspapers; to pass on the recognition of agents; to produce greater harmony between the newspapers and agents; to establish standard rate card; to publish bulletins and information to members, and to employ a paid manager if necessary.

EFFICIENCY COMMITTEE.—To work out for the benefit of all members, through the interchange of information collected from members, best practices in newspaper efficiency; to produce accurate and simple cost-finding data; to ascertain and promulgate best office systems for various groups of members; to engage experts as necessary to install systems for members.

PAPER COMMITTEE.—To handle all the various angles of the print paper situation; to carry out bulk purchases if desired; to produce greater harmony between print paper manufacturers and newspaper publishers; to gather statistics and protect members from unfair treatment by manufacturers; to employ a paid manager if necessary.

MEETINGS COMMITTEE.—To handle the details of all meetings; arrange programs; invite speakers; to arrange departmental conferences for the purpose of giving members best and most authoritative information on all phases of newspaper making, and thus make the meetings most profitable to attend.

MEMBERSHIP COMMITTEE.—To work untiringly until every daily newspaper in the territory is enrolled in the membership, both for what its co-operation will mean to the Inland Press Association and for the great benefits it will be to the new member.

SUGGESTION REGARDING DUES AND ASSESSMENTS

Inasmuch as both a state and sectional organization must be maintained, I suggest a nominal basis of dues—say $10 per year—one half of which will go back to the state body and the other half remain in the treasury of the sectional body.

I suggest that all additional money required be raised by assessments based on post-office circulation statements. This will work in absolute fairness to all and can never be burdensome to even the weakest member, which will receive inspiration and direction how to make up many times what the service will cost.

Later on, as a national organization is perfected, to be operated on the same basis, the pro-rating of expenses can be made by very equitable increases to all classes of members, with the larger newspapers carrying the heavier expense, which they should by reason of their higher advertising rates and greater earning possibilities.

I have estimated that in a national plan organized on this

basis the dues and assessments to a newspaper like *The New York Globe* with 200,000 circulation might become $5,200 a year as against $2,700 during 1918, but that the total cost to the smaller newspapers would be less than A. N. P. A. membership at present.

DEPARTMENTAL CONFERENCES

It is suggested, as a relief from the purposeless and uninteresting, long-drawn-out meetings where everybody feels that his time has been wasted, like those of the A. N. P. A. and others which I have attended, that the committees in charge arrange definite programs through which those in attendance can work out a plan of attendance to enable them to go home with greatest amount of information on subjects of especial interest to them. For example:

1. First forenoon or few hours to be given to reports of officers and committees and election of new officers.

2. First afternoon, three departmental conferences with experts to deliver carefully prepared addresses and to answer questions—for instance:

    2 to 3 P.M.—Circulation problems.
    3 to 4 P.M.—Print paper and paper economies.
    4 to 5 P.M.—Relations with advertising agents.

3. Second morning:

    10 to 11—Development, increased volume local advertising.
    11 to 12—Consideration of advertising rates.
    12 to 1—Press-room production and efficiencies.

4. Second afternoon:

    2 to 3—Office systems and efficiencies.
    3 to 4—Co-operative effort for new national advertising.
    4 to 5—Proportion of news and advertising.

5. Third morning:

    10 to 11—Intensifying readers' interest in advertising.
    11 to 12—Two speeches by well-known advertising agents.
    12 to 1—Two speeches by well-known advertisers.

6. Third afternoon:

    2 to 3—Adoption of resolutions proposed by committees.
    3 to 4—Consideration of new activities for coming year.
    4 to 5—Speeches from well-known publishers, urging all to get together to boost newspaper advertising.

If desirable, any of the departmentals can be extended beyond the hour each, and several departmentals could be held simultaneously in different rooms, so as to produce the greatest possible fund of information for those in attendance.

The preparation of briefs and pamphlets embodying the points brought out distributed at departmental conferences, and later in bulletins, would make membership not only worth more than it costs, but indispensable to any newspaper.

For example, to have Harry Doorly, of *The Omaha World-Herald*, talk half an hour regarding the development of classified and answer questions for another half-hour and distribute the forms he uses, would well repay a trip to New York.

To have Victor F. Lawson, of *The Chicago Daily News*, tell of his early experiences and the success of *The Daily News* and answer questions, would be worth many times the cost of membership for a year and the trouble and expense of a trip to New York.

Such a program would stand in striking contrast with the kindergarten effect produced in the A. N. P. A. on hand-picked purposeless topics, of which less than 10 per cent. are ever reached.

RELATIONS WITH AGENTS

I am positive that through such an organization the newspapers could produce a working relationship with the advertising agencies which would be productive of largely increased business for the newspapers.

1. We could protect reputable agencies from the damaging competition of irresponsible adventurers through co-operation and recognition.

2. We could functionate our service activities through the agents who co-operate with us.

3. We could regulate the degree and scope of service to be asked of or given by our newspapers.

4. We could eliminate many expensive and annoying practices on the part of agents inclined to seek something plus.

5. We could do more effective service for the advertiser with the co-operation of the agent than if we attempted the same things with the agent trying to belittle our activities in order to intensify his service to his client.

6. We could, through the co-ordination of local effort, reduce duplication of expense at present attempted by various newspapers as individual stunts.

So long as the agent is viewed by many as a sort of a parasite on advertising and a needless expense there can be no satisfactory relation. We must learn that our gross rate, less agent's commission, is our net rate, and to enter all business as net so as to eliminate the item "commissions" as an expense.

We must learn that the agent performs a function for the advertiser which none of our newspapers is in a position to render as a continuous facility, and that the commission is finally paid by the advertiser, even though we make ourselves believe through defective bookkeeping that we pay it.

Through an advertising committee, properly selected, or a sub-committee on recognition we can iron out many of the past troubles of the agents, and compel irresponsible upstarts to clear through responsible agents, the same as is done in other lines of business.

In protecting the agent and trying to make it easier and more profitable to sell the commodity we manufacture it is obvious that we will secure a much larger part of the appropriations he handles.

STATE ASSOCIATIONS

Through the state associations working harmoniously through sectional headquarters and thence to national headquarters with branches in several advertising centers all of our newspapers can be sold more effectively to national advertisers.

Instead of national advertising amounting to between 15 and 20 per cent. of our total business it should be worked up to at least 50 per cent. of the total if we could but pull together and really co-operate through some such plan as I have indicated.

Every manufacturer in the country is a good advertising prospect if properly approached. Every newspaper in the country is a good advertising medium at a certain rate if properly used. Variations in cost of production at different points and differences in ability to produce the newspapers efficiently make radical inequalities in rates.

Through our state associations, sectional organizations and the national organization it seems logical that newspaper publishers will be made more effective business men and able to sell advertising which will produce results at a profit to themselves.

The advertiser and the advertising agent agree that these conditions must be met, if the fabric known as newspaper advertising is to endure. Known circulation and one rate to all, with constructive co-operation all along the line and the elimination of petty local jealousies, will work wonders.

In the state associations much of the rivalries between competing publishers can be overcome. Each member must seek first to help get business for his state and then his city and finally, and without petty knocks on his competitor, for his own newspaper.

Through the state association the newspaper which repeats unfair solicitation and knocks after repeated complaint, borne out by investigation, must be suspended from privileges or finally dropped from membership, if the best interests of all newspapers and newspaper advertising are to be served.

JASON ROGERS.

Around such a stem, with the by-laws of the A. N. P. A. as a model, a workable organization could be created which would be worth many times what it cost the newspapers to establish and maintain it.

In operation each of the sectional meetings arranged in circuit should be attended by the president, manager, and as many other national officers as possible to bring to those not going to the national meeting direct messages concerning what the national body is trying to do for them. These sectional meetings, arranged during the fall season so as not to interfere with the annual spring meeting, would be most valuable.

The meetings arranged on the basis of departmental programs, with scheduled topics specified for certain hours, could be made a vast improvement over the purposeless and ineffective practices adhered to in the A. N. P. A., with hand-picked topics selected at random and representing time-worn annuals trotted out for the entertainment of the visitors.

Members would go home from such meetings with

valuable pointers and suggestions for application to situations confronting them, instead of wondering why they had spent time and money in attending, as they have done in the past. If thought necessary, meetings for large-city members and small-city members could be held in different rooms. This in answer to the suggestion often made that all members are not interested in the same sort of problems.

Through the interested activities of well-organized committees, it would be possible to develop a fund of instructive, informatory matter which by effective interchange and publication in bulletins would save the newspapers of the country hundreds of thousands of dollars of waste and useless expense every year.

I have ventured to submit this outline for the consideration of the newspapers of the country in the hope that they will sooner or later awake to the necessity for perfecting an organization that will represent them in a progressive spirit wholly lacking in the past. The newspapers can do wonderful things for the business interests of the country if they will but co-operate.

XLII

Proof That Co-operative Effort Will Pay

As definite examples of what the newspapers of the country could do through co-operative effort to double and treble the volume of general advertising in their columns I present for consideration a few of the many things I have attempted during the last six or seven years, all of which produced some result, but not such as they would have done if backed by a big national association.

In 1916 I prepared a select list of 400 strong newspapers which was printed in *The Globe* several times, as a full-page ad. and likewise in most of the newspapers in the list. Proofs of the ad. were mailed to a large list of advertisers and agents, and later the list was reduced to small pamphlet form and given 30,000 distribution.

In preparing the list I got myself disliked by many newspapers not represented, but, as I stated in the ad. that it could be "supplemented by other newspapers as might be necessary to produce desired results," I think I put over the big idea to good purpose.

Few national campaigns extend beyond the use of 300 or 400 newspapers. In this list I sought to give the prospective advertiser an illustration of the news-

BUILDING NEWSPAPER ADVERTISING 263

papers of the country I would use for a campaign to include 400 of them.

Hundreds of letters came in from advertisers thanking me for the service, backed up by scores of other letters from advertising agents of an unusual quality, from which I shall quote as demonstrating the merit of such work by the newspapers to help the agent in selling their space:

Accept my thanks for the list of 400 newspapers, which I appreciate very much.
C. IRONMONGER,
20 Vesey Street, New York.

Thank you for the "Select List of 400 Newspapers." It is very useful and we are glad to have it in this form.
W. G. BUNNELL,
W. H. H. HULL & Co.,
New York City.

This is a very handy little booklet for pocket use, and we appreciate your sending it to us.
VICTOR H. YOUNG,
PHILIP KOBBE CO.,
New York.

This contribution of yours to advertising agents is worthy of praise.
WILLIAMS & CUNNINGHAM,
Chicago, Illinois.

This is quite valuable, and we appreciate your courtesy in sending a copy to us.
WM. T. MULLALLY,
MCCLAY & MULLALLY,
New York.

This list is very interesting and I am sure will prove profitable.
>
> GEO. A. LITTLE,
>   JAS. A. RICHARDS & STAFF,
>   New York.

These lists are very finely gotten up, and will be of value for ready reference to us.
>
> D. J. HINMAN,
>   STREET & FINNEY,
>   New York.

I want to congratulate you on the manner in which you compiled this list.
>
> V. J. CEVASCO,
>   RUDOLPH GUENTHER, Inc.
>   New York.

Must congratulate you on the completeness of the list.
>
> GORDON BEST,
>   WM. D. MCJUNKIN ADV. AGENCY,
>   Chicago.

I want to send you just a few lines to compliment you on the splendid piece of newspaper publicity. This ought to be productive of good results for you and I certainly think it will.
>
> EDWARD M. CARNEY,
>   CARNEY & KERR,
>   New York.

We thank you for favoring us with this information, as it is very handy and useful.
>
> STACK ADVERTISING AGENCY,
>   Chicago.

We acknowledge with thanks receipt of the copies of a list of selected newspapers in the United States which will be undoubtedly useful to us in making recommendations to our clients.
>
> J. P. HALLMAN,
>   H. K. MCCANN Co.,
>   New York.

I have received two booklets containing selected list of 400 strong newspapers, and I thank you very much for these booklets.

E. T. WELLS,
MORSE INTERNATIONAL AGENCY,
New York.

I must say that this is one of the finest lists ever put out. It is a handy pocket guide and is useful to every advertiser and agent.

H. W. FAIRFAX,
World Building,
New York.

We wish to thank you for sending these to us, as we have looked them over and believe we can make very good use of the list in our daily work, because you have included sufficient data to make it possible to use the list as a working basis.

LEE E. HOOD,
RICHARD A. FOLEY ADV. AGENCY,
Philadelphia.

We think this will be very valuable not only to us but to our clients.

E. V. VAN HOOK,
THE FLETCHER CO.,
Philadelphia.

It is surely a handy book for any agency to be in possession of, and I am taking this means of thanking you for your foresightedness in compiling it.

J. P. STORM,
New York.

In January, 1913, I appeared before the Association of American Advertisers at their convention at Syracuse, and presented the idea upon which I later formulated the foundation of the present Audit Bureau of Circulations. In order to crystallize the idea I sent proofs of my address to some 400 daily newspapers, asking them to print it, and sent marked copies and a letter to a list of 262 national advertisers.

The address was printed from Maine to California and the list of advertisers I had furnished got a deluge of clippings and letters, demonstrating what the newspapers could do more forcibly than could have been produced by any other sort of an effort.

In June, 1913, I submitted to the Board of Control of the Association of American Advertisers the outline of the plan upon which the Audit Bureau of Circulations was built. Letters from the members of the Board of Control may be of interest:

July 5, 1913.

Mr. Jason Rogers,
 % The Globe,
  New York, N. Y.

My dear Mr. Rogers:

Replying to your kind favor of July 1st, will say that my understanding is that the letter to which you refer, and copy of which you enclose, is to be sent out over your signature, and such being the case both myself and the other members of the Board of Control are a little diffident about even suggesting any alterations in a letter so kindly intended towards us.

It rather seems to all of us, however, that it would be better to eliminate Paragraph 1, on Page 2, commencing "It is now planned, etc.," and I would suggest that Paragraph 4 on Page 2 be altered to read as follows:

"It is natural to suppose that papers on this list will be given preference over those refusing to stand for audits, and thus make it more difficult than formerly for the fakers in the business to get as large a share of most general business as they have done in the past."

In the next to the last paragraph on Page 1, I would also suggest the use of a comma after the words "general advertiser," in the second line, and the word "every" between the words "and" and "medium." This latter suggestion is, of course, merely a clerical one and you will readily see expresses your apparent meaning a little more clearly.

I think your suggestion of sending out a slightly modified edition of this letter to a selected list of national advertisers who are not members of the Association is a good one and cannot but result in some good, both to our Association as representative of the advertiser, and yours as representative of the publisher. Our interests are, in reality, identical, but of course the publisher and advertiser frequently have to be approached from a little different angle.

Noting what you say about the article which will be printed in the *Editor and Publisher*, will say I will probably receive a copy of this, at least I hope so, and will read same with a great deal of interest.

In connection with all of the above I wish to thank you most heartily for the interest you have exhibited, and are exhibiting, in this matter. There is absolutely no reason why the interests of the publisher and advertiser should not be identical, but unfortunately many on both sides of the fence sometimes fail to see this.

With very best regards, I am
Yours respectfully,
E. MAPES.

July 7, 1913.

MR. JASON ROGERS,
73-83 DEY ST.,
NEW YORK, N. Y.

DEAR MR. ROGERS:

Replying to yours of the 5th I am sending another one of our Cube circulars.

Regarding your *Editor and Publisher* article, I think this is fine. I want to personally thank you and I know the balance of the Board of Control will also feel grateful to you. This is fine co-operation and want you to feel sure we appreciate it.

Yours very truly,
E. B. MERRITT.

July 12, 1913.

Mr. Jason Rogers,
  New York, N. Y.
My dear Mr. Rogers:

I am in receipt of yours of July 8th, together with copy of proposed letter, which strikes me as being very well draughted. I understand this will go out over your signature, and both in my official and personal capacities wish to thank you very much indeed for the interest which you are manifesting in behalf of the Three A's.

Yours truly,

E. Mapes.

July 11, 1913.

Mr. Jason Rogers,
  Editor, The Globe,
    New York City.
Dear Mr. Rogers:

I have your favor of the 8th inst. enclosing clipping from the *Editor and Publisher* which expounds your plan for exploiting the work of the Association of American Advertisers.

I think this is very comprehensive, and the Association will certainly be indebted to you if this scheme can be made effective, which I surely believe it can.

With kindest personal regards, believe me
Very truly yours,
G. H. E. Hawkins,
Advertising Manager,
The N. K. Fairbank Company.

July 11, 1913.

Mr. Jason Rogers,
  % New York Globe,
    New York City, N. Y.
My dear Mr. Rogers:

Am just this moment in receipt of your letter of July 10th, enclosing copy of your printed letter of July 9th addressed to newspaper publishers; also copy of your proposed letter to selected list of 2,000 general advertisers.

You surely are striking some very telling, forceful blows in the interests of the sale and purchase of advertising as a commodity. If you won't consider it pure cheek, I would suggest that your proposed letter to general advertisers would be all the more effective if with it you would enclose a copy of your printed letter to the newspaper publishers.

Am glad to see that you cut out of your letter to publishers the suggestion that by the publishers coming into the Association it would reduce the dues of the Association members. I don't think the A.A.A. members expect, or ought to expect, any smaller dues, but if we give them more reports for the same dues they now pay, that would be far more desirable.

We certainly are delighted and obligated to you personally for the vigorous, generous way in which you are devoting your time and money to test out and organize the movement.

It will interest you to know that Messrs. Merritt, Squier, and the writer spent yesterday afternoon with the president of the Advertising Agencies Association, who expressed himself as being very much interested in our general plan of having the general agencies admitted as members and to receive full reports. On next Thursday we are going to meet with the Executive Committee of the General Agencies Association and discuss the proposition. With your publishers as a right wing, and the General Agencies Association as a left wing, we ought to be a victorious army in routing the legion of lilliputian liars on circulation.

Sincerely yours,
Louis Bruch.

This circular was sent out to all daily newspapers:

PLEASE READ THIS CAREFULLY—I THINK IT MEANS DOLLARS IN YOUR POCKET

Office New York Globe,
83 Dey Street,
New York, *July 9, 1913.*

TO NEWSPAPER PUBLISHERS:

Dear Sir:—

A clearer understanding between general advertisers and newspaper publishers will bring about a fuller appreciation of the superior selling power of the newspaper over any other medium.

For upward of two years I have been working along this line in the broad general interest of all newspapers.

The United Newspapers, which I organized until it consisted of 460 daily newspapers pledged to co-operation for the development of more advertising for the newspapers, was turned over to the Bureau of Advertising of the American Newspaper Publishers' Association, which is now carrying on a work that will benefit every newspaper in the land.

Incidental to the work which I did in organizing that advertising movement, I was brought into close personal contact with many of the largest general advertisers in the country, and, knowing how they feel regarding business development for the future, I think I see a way of bringing about a profitable and effective co-operation that will SPELL MORE BUSINESS FOR THE NEWSPAPERS.

In response to an invitation I recently attended a conference at Chicago with the Board of Control of the Association of American Advertisers, representing about eighty large general advertisers, and after a long general discussion, during which we viewed the problem from every angle, I was invited to outline a general plan.

Last week I again went to Chicago and met the Board of Control and presented the rough draft of a plan which was very favorably considered by them.

In advance of the final announcement of this plan I am anxious to secure the views and suggestions of newspaper publishers generally, and will now briefly outline it to you, with a sincere hope that you will carefully consider it and let me know what you think of it.

THE PLAN

In a word, the idea is to crystallize the general sentiment that found expression at the recent great Baltimore convention of advertising clubs and associations.

The interest of general advertisers and reputable publishers is identical. The advertisers want to find as many mediums as possible which sell advertising as a commodity, and reputable publishers want to be effectively separated from those who are not awake to modern conditions and who for one reason or another don't believe that advertisers are entitled to information as to what they get for their money.

I have suggested that the Association of American Advertisers enlarge its scope so as to include in its regular and affiliated membership every general advertiser, and every medium that will stand for the verification of its claims and representations.

For upward of twelve years the A. A. A., which consists of about eighty large national advertisers, has been conducting the business of investigating circulations for its members. It has done a good work, but being limited in funds through small membership has only scratched the ground, so to speak.

It is planned to invite every medium that will stand for annual audits and make quarterly reports regarding circulation to become affiliated members on payment of annual dues based on the population of its city, which dues will represent only a part of the expense of making the annual audit of its own circulation, and in most cases less than has formerly been asked for certificates.

It is planned to compile the quarterly reports of all affiliated members and send them out to all advertisers who are members in such form as to make them convenient for reference as to any town, city, or section of the country, and thus provide a gilt-edge list which can be used with full confidence as to value received.

It is natural to suppose that papers on this list will be given preference over those refusing to stand for audits, and thus make it more difficult than formerly for the fakers in the business to get as large a share of most general business as they have done in the past.

A form of "gilt-edge list of newspapers" over the seal of the A. A. A. and the signature of its president containing a full list of affiliated newspapers will be furnished for occasional publication.

The affiliated members will naturally get the largest share of business being placed by advertisers who are members of the A. A. A.

In my opinion it will be worth many times what it will cost for dues for any newspaper to be on the select list and, once for all, separated from the doubtful class.

In order to meet situations where one publisher thinks that another, by juggling accounts or other falsification, has made an audit ineffective, the A. A. A. plan now provides for a second and third review of the findings and outside investigation of routes and other delivery.

The suggested basis of annual dues for affiliated members is:

In cities over 500,000 population $100
"   "   "   250,000 to 499,000 population 75
"   "   "   100,000 to 249,000 population 50
"   " under 100,000 population 25

SUMMARY

This plan means:
1—Affiliated membership and listing for all papers which will stand for audits and verification.
2—Provides for having quarterly reports of circulation of affiliated newspapers placed in the hands of all large general advertisers—saving circularization and received as official data.
3—Larger volume of business from members.
4—First consideration in making up all lists.
5—Closer relations with large advertisers.
6—Effective separation from those papers which obtain big copy by falsely claiming more circulation than they can prove.
7—Enabling the advertiser to cut out the purchase of circulation that never existed and to spend more money effectively with you.
8—Provides a strong effective organization for all interested in the purchase and sale of advertising.

As stated above, please give this matter your careful consideration and favor me with a reply.

This plan is no part of the Bureau of Advertising of the A. N. P. A., but a purely personal effort on my part to stimulate more advertising for ALL REPUTABLE NEWSPAPERS that will stand for circulation verification and sell advertising as a commodity.

Yours truly,
JASON ROGERS.

After submission of the plan, with the approval of the board, I sent the letter herewith to the 2,600

BUILDING NEWSPAPER ADVERTISING

daily newspapers in the United States and Canada and started the movement which has grown until it includes 1,000 publisher members and its service reaches every worth-while advertiser in the country.

The plan of Graphic Commercial Surveys previously referred to and described in detail in Chapter XXI of *Newspaper Building* was another of my efforts to get the newspapers to make it easier for the manufacturer to use their newspapers.

That the idea was valuable is proved by extracts from a few of the many letters received from advertising agents:

> If such reports that could be thoroughly relied on were made all over the country, it would simplify matters very much and would give valuable information not now obtainable.
> H. N. McKINNEY,
> N. W. AYER & SONS,
> Phila. and N. Y.

> This ought to be valuable information for manufacturers and agents and you are certainly to be congratulated upon the undertaking. Such surveys of all the leading cities would be of immense advantage.
> C. H. PORTER,
> TAYLOR-CRITCHFIELD CO.,
> Chicago.

> You certainly are entitled to a great deal of credit in connection with the Graphic Commercial Survey of New York City. This is one of the most helpful propositions that has come to my desk for some time.
> G. C. SHERMAN,
> SHERMAN & BRYAN,
> New York.

> We find your Graphic Commercial Survey very useful every day, and it is just the sort of informing matter which I would

274 BUILDING NEWSPAPER ADVERTISING

like to see more publishers produce, because it helps the agent cultivate his full with so much more intensiveness.

>   ROBERT TINSMAN,
>   FEDERAL ADVERTISING AGENCY,
>   New York.

This is one of the most comprehensive propositions of its kind that has ever come to the writer's notice, and your organization deserves great credit for its enterprise.

>   GERALD B. WADSWORTH,
>   FRANK SEAMAN, Inc.,
>   New York.

These surveys come nearer taking the place of a man on the ground than anything that has ever come to our notice.

>   J. O. O'SHAUGHNESSY,
>   O'SHAUGHNESSY ADV. CO.,
>   New York.

Your plan if carried through will be of tremendous benefit to advertisers.

>   F. J. HERMES,
>   BLACKMAN ROSS CO.,
>   New York.

We asked that you send this to some of our clients because we felt it is very practical and valuable. When a manufacturer can get a full comprehension of a market, it is much simpler to adjust his advertising and sales plan to the work of that market.

>   PAUL E. FAUST,
>   MALLORY. MITCHELL & FAUST,
>   Chicago.

To my mind it is the most constructive effort I have seen on the part of newspapers to further their own interest and that of the national advertiser, which are of course linked together.

>   GUY BRADT,
>   LEVIN & BRADT,
>   New York.

This is an admirable thing, and if kept up to date and made authentic, will be invaluable to men in my profession.

VICTOR L. CUNNINGHAM,
WILLIAMS & CUNNINGHAM,
Chicago.

The work you are doing should prove of real service to every one who is interested in national advertising and local daily newspaper advertising.

WILLIAM DAILEY,
CHELTENHAM ADV. AGENCY,
New York.

This is the most complete work of its kind we have ever seen. We sincerely trust that the example set in producing this survey of New York City for the use of advertisers and advertising agencies will be followed by enterprising publishers in other cities.

P. F. O'KEEFE,
Boston.

It is a great help to any man who will use it in a practical and consistent manner and cannot help but assist any sales organization to a remarkable degree, provided it is handled in an efficient way.

I. R. SPIEGEL,
LORD & THOMAS,
Chicago.

XLIII

Intensifying Reader Interest in Advertising

During the summer of 1915 we ran a series of three or four advertising contests in *The New York Globe* which probably did more to put that newspaper on the map as an advertising medium at a time when it badly needed stimulation than could have been accomplished by years of toil. Limited space precludes more than a brief summary of the most interesting venture in advertising experience I have ever seen.

Coming East through Chicago in March, I noticed the advertising contests being conducted by *The Chicago Tribune* for the purpose of demonstrating that people read the ads. in *The Sunday Tribune*. *The Tribune* bunched the letters regarding the advertising of any firm and forwarded them to the advertiser.

The thing looked good to me as a means of intensifying reader interest in advertising. On the train I kept turning it over in my mind, and by the time I arrived at New York I had worked out something I liked better than the Chicago method.

Afraid that some other New York newspaper would get ahead of me, I sat up most of the night preparing the announcement, which we inserted in the next

BUILDING NEWSPAPER ADVERTISING

day's *Globe* in three full columns, offering $390 in prizes to women in competition from April 19th to 24th, as follows:

> All you have to do to enter the contest is write a letter to *The Globe* telling which advertisement in *The Globe* interests you most and why that particular advertisement does interest you.

The response from our women readers was truly wonderful, including some 20,000 letters, of remarkable quality. Classified by departments of advertising, the record was:

Miscellaneous	22	per cent.
Pure food	20	" "
Department stores	11¼	" "
Apparel for women	7¾	" "
Luxuries	8	" "
Financial	6	" "
Automobiles	6	" "
Shoes	5	" "
Medicinal	5	" "
Apparel for men	4	" "
Amusements	4	" "
Travel	1	" "

The advertising of John Wanamaker drew more replies than any other; as a matter of fact, more than twice as many as any other department store, and that of Hearn & Co., who use only two columns a day, came second, just a bit ahead of R. H. Macy & Co.

The five first-prize winning letters, as selected by a committee—J. J. Geisinger, Harry Prudden, Walter A. Bunnell, Harold A. Lieber, and L. A. Van Patten—were as follows:

(FIRST PRIZE—$200.00)

April 22, 1915

DEAR SIR:—

For quite some time I have been carefully reading the advertisements appearing in *The New York Globe*, and have noted particularly those of the LOOSE-WILES BISCUIT COMPANY.

Their advertisement printed on the 20th inst. impressed me more than any other. In the first place, the name "Sunshine" is suggestive of health, of purity, and of trust, and is well chosen. In the second place, the advertisement is written plainly and simply, making no impossible pretensions. There are no bold statements to the effect that their biscuits are the only good ones on the market. In the third place, their honest invitation extended to all to visit their "spotless, sunflooded rooms, in the largest bakery in the world" and see personally how their products are made, is sufficient to convince me of the purity and excellence of "Sunshine Biscuits." The above three reasons have influenced me to order my grocer to bring me only "Sunshine Biscuits," and I have always found the greatest satisfaction with them.

Respectfully yours,
MRS. SALLIE DELLON,
147 Dumont Ave., Brooklyn, N. Y.

(SECOND PRIZE—$50.00)

April 24, 1915

DEAR SIR:—

The advertisement of the JOHN WANAMAKER STORE in *The Globe* of the 22d inst. interested me more than any other that appeared in your pages last week.

It impressed me so strongly first, because of its freedom from exaggeration. Nowhere was I told that here was the chance of a lifetime to buy goods at prices never before equaled or ever likely to be equaled.

Second, because each class of goods was described so fully, simply, and accurately that I was able to decide at once with the help of the subjoined prices just which of the advertised articles I wanted. A shopping trip to the store the next day confirmed these conclusions and saved me the usual weary round of the stores.

Third, because it proved easy and agreeable reading. I was not tired when I finished it.

Last but not least, because the foreword by Mr. Wanamaker on the evil of "boast and brag" in mercantile advertising made a powerful appeal to me. I must confess it biased me in favor of the store. When will all the merchants realize the futility of misrepresentation and exaggeration in advertising?

Yours truly,
ISABEL F. DEGEN,
215 Audubon Ave., New York.

(THIRD PRIZE—$25.00)

April 26, 1915.

DEAR SIR:—

I have read over carefully the ads. in *The Globe* during the past week, and find I am most interested in the KAYSER SILK GLOVE ad., in the issue of the 20th, for the following reasons:

1st: Because it is a timely ad., as most women buy silk gloves in April.

2d: Because it has an attractive illustration as well as a catchy heading.

3d: Because it clearly states the fourfold protection given each purchaser through the careful system of inspection. It suggests to my mind that this same care is given every other detail of the manufacture. We hear so much about machinery nowadays that we get the impression that manufacturing consists of merely putting raw materials in one end of the machine and taking out the finished product at the other.

4th: Because it distinctly states that a guarantee is given with each pair of gloves. It stands to reason that unless utmost care is used in making the gloves the manufacturers could not afford to give this guarantee. Nothing inspires a purchaser with greater confidence than an article sold with a guarantee.

This ad. leaves no doubt in my mind that every pair of Kayser Silk Gloves are serviceable with long-wearing qualities.

Yours very truly,
MISS BERTHA ISABEL ROSENTHAL,
132 East 15th St., New York

(FOURTH PRIZE—$10.00)

April 27, 1915.

DEAR EDITOR:—

Among the many splendid *Globe* ads. from which it is difficult indeed to select a decisive favorite, I respectfully submit as my choice that of the GORHAM Co., Silversmiths and Goldsmiths, Fifth Ave. and Thirty-eighth Street. It pleases and interests me for these reasons:

The form is distinctive, standing out among the more commercial, illustrated ads. with a certain classic severity like a well-dressed person.

The contents, too, are most delightfully appropriate for the line of merchandise offered, "We have with us to-night" that ever faithful friend of public speakers, how deliciously appropriate an introduction for a Loving Cup ad., gripping the reader at once with a sense of fellowship; and how finely the whole commercial appeal is submerged in the sentimental one, a fact the value of which is being increasingly recognized in the world of business. Yet withal the ad. is most complete, carrying to the reader's mind every essential fact in regard to the GORHAM house. To summarize: The Gorham ad. appeals to me as

> The least striking, the most pleasing,
> The least commercial, the most convincing,
> A splendid ad., humanized, and finely written.
> It is more, it is a piece of literature.

> Respectfully yours,
> MARGARET COTTER, 348 E. 18th St.,
> Flatbush, L. I.

(FIFTH PRIZE—$5.00)

DEAR SIR:—

An attractive, convincing ad. like that of CAMMEYER'S in *The Globe* of last Wednesday, in a word, solves the problem of correct style in footwear. It displayed the merchandise and gave the value. It acquainted me with the style and I knew what to expect when I called at the store.

I had been quite perplexed the early part of last week as to what style shoe would answer my purpose. Of course I wanted it to be quite the thing, yet staple and not too expensive. And the pump at $5 shown in the attached ad. spelled "purchase"—and I did.

The whole ad. breathes an air of refinement and states the plain facts in a most interesting and convincing manner so appeasing and refreshing after the large spreads and shouts of bargains. It suggests no bargain--but a good value to be appreciated.

That is why CAMMEYER'S ad. caught my eye and held my attention, so that I read it through carefully and decided that here was the merchandise for me.

Yours very truly,
MISS JOAN BLACK,
14 Koerner St., Elmhurst, L. I.

($2.00 PRIZE)

DEAR SIR:—

The most interesting advertisement in last week's *Globe* to my mind was that of BEST & Co., on page 9 of your issue for Wednesday, April 21st. It interested me because of its:

(1) Superior technique. Ample white space, large type, open lines attract the eye and invite reading. Modest illustrations lend charm. No frantic appeal for custom here; even the technical features suggest dignity and inspire confidence.

(2) Originality of purpose. Weight of emphasis falls upon moral values. Integrity of the firm, its key-note. Convinced of that, we may trust the quality of the goods sold to take care of itself.

(3) Effective organization of subject-matter. The advertisement has unity. It seeks, and I think successfully achieves its end, by reason of its definiteness and exclusion of irrelevant and confusing suggestions. It has coherence. First, a simple direct statement of policy, then the citations of a particular case in point, clinching the argument.

(4) Personal touch. Unlike surrounding advertisements, Best's "appeals" because it presents a vivid personality in "W. A. A." One feels that he will make good, that he is more than a machine. An efficient business man, oh yes, but also a human being who cares.

Very truly yours,
MISS MARTHA S. BOARDMAN,
17 Washington Pl.,
Bloomfield, N. J.

BUILDING NEWSPAPER ADVERTISING

($2.00 PRIZE)

April 25, 1915.

GENTLEMEN:—

Never before did I read over with such carefulness the advertising columns of *The Globe*, although I am a daily reader of your paper.

On Monday, April 19th, I was particularly impressed with an advertisement appearing on page 9 of *The Globe* by the JOHN WANAMAKER stores.

Of course I know the Wanamaker advertisements well, glance them over nearly every day.

The real attraction of this particular advertisement was the introduction. Who wouldn't be interested in reading an introduction such as was used as a headliner in that particular ad., "This day, April 19th, was a great day in America in 1783."

Patriotism was the moving spirit in more carefully perusing this ad., and after reading that this was the date on which, 132 years ago, hostilities ceased in this country, I was so inspired that the entire advertisement was so carefully read over by me that I found in said ad. several announcements, which impressed me so much that they prompted me to visit that particular store the following day and make my selections.

An advertisement which speaks of offerings only can never be as impressive as one which has an educational value besides.

CORA ABRAMS,
522 West 157th Street, City.

($2.00 PRIZE)

April 24, 1915.

DEAR SIR:—

I have carefully looked over all the advertisements in *The Globe* for the last week, and the most interesting to me is MACY'S advertisement of Wednesday night.

First: Because it is pleasing and restful to the eye, there being no excess of printer's ink.

Second: It shows a fine regard for the law of order. There is a place for everything and everything is in its place.

Third: Every item has a plain heading. If interested, you read it all; if not, you save time by passing on to the next.

Fourth: The little drawings are very good, giving life to the page and attracting the eye.

Fifth: The size of the spacings is so arranged as to give a well-balanced page.

Sixth: There is a large variety in the type used, thus doing away with monotony.

Seventh: and very important, if not most important, the description of each article is not a jumble of fine words, but impresses one as being a clear, honest description of the garment or thing advertised.

This is my impression of MACY's advertisement of Wednesday night.

Here's hoping I may hear from you.

    Very sincerely,
        LOU ALBERTSON COCK,
           (MRS. ROBT. E.)
      57 Gould Ave., Caldwell Cedars,
          Caldwell, N. J.

($2.00 PRIZE)

April 24, 1915.

DEAR SIR:—

As a busy housewife, with four little ones to do for, I found MACY's ad. occupying page 7 of *The Globe* of April 21st the most interesting ad. printed in *The Globe* this week.

First: This ad. fills a page and stands alone so one can read it comfortably, without the distraction of assorted ads. which are sometimes confusing.

Second: This ad., while it is arranged compactly and lists a large number of items, is most appealing to the eye. It is dressed in pretty type and each of the various offers, placed in its separate frame, is scanned without effort, much as one would examine goods on their separate counters.

Third: Most of the items offered are for women or children and nearly every one of the dozen small and tasteful drawings offer a suggestion that a busy woman should appreciate.

Fourth: This ad. does not demand the presence of the reader at the store in order to take advantage of the economies offered, as many other "bargain" ads. do. Many women who might wish to take advantage of special offers and could not visit the city on a specified day can order by mail from an ad. like this.

Fifth: Most of the items offered in this page ad. are real bargains, offered by a store in which one can place full confidence; thus all misgivings are removed, and satisfaction remains when the articles are in use.

Yours very truly,
RUBY BOYD ANDREWS,
Winslow Cottage,
Crestwood, Tuckahoe, N. Y.

($2.00 PRIZE)

April 26, 1915.

DEAR SIR:—

There are some things which are bound to appeal to a tired business woman. MACY'S advertisement of Wednesday, April 21, 1915, is one of them.

It stood out as a page of sane, common-sense business advertising. Every article received its own little compartment, with the name of the article in large type. How simple to find what I wanted!

Beneath each heading was a simple, honest description of the article, no lengthy eulogy or impossible description. Many illustrations helped the tired brain to picture the article with the least amount of effort.

But the best of all was at the bottom of each article. In small type was given the floor where each article could be found. Not only that—the section of floor where it might be found was also given. How often have I trailed around a department store floor, vainly hunting for an article which was somewhere on that endless floor, but where? To one suffering with the chronic ailment of "no time," this small boon was of no slight value.

My few precious minutes of shopping would now be profitably spent without unnecessary waste of time or energy.

I am,

Respectfully yours,
HARRIET S. AUSPITZ,
961 Avenue St. John,
Bronx, N. Y.

BUILDING NEWSPAPER ADVERTISING

($2.00 PRIZE)

DEAR SIR:—

In entering *The Globe* advertisement contest I beg to state that the B. ALTMAN & Co. ad. appeals best to my taste.

Goods advertised by B. ALTMAN & Co. are graded and priced so distinctly, and without any hypnotic inducements to bait the public with. In fact, their advertisement leaves little, if any, room for being skeptical as to the merit of the "ad." The result is, that a person may instantly judge whether or not the goods thus graded and priced come within the possibility of one's purse; consequently, people going to B. ALTMAN & Co. would appear to be business customers and not mere visitors, a phenomenon not altogether unusual in many a big store. In my opinion such an ad. is bound to make for a lasting business reputation.

MRS. ANNA HALEMEIER,
462 Grandview Ave.,
Ridgewood, Brooklyn, N. Y.

($2.00 PRIZE)

DEAR SIR:—

The advertisements of B. ALTMAN & Co. have always claimed my interest because they ring true and inspire confidence in the store, its methods and merchandise.

For instance, the "ad." of Tuesday, April 20th, featuring a sale of bed furnishings, does not insult the intelligence of the housewife by claiming that the blankets sold during the sale for three dollars formerly sold for eight, or that the twenty-five-cent pillow-cases previously brought a dollar each.

In this advertisement, wherever B. ALTMAN & Co. thinks a particular item is real good value, they say so, leaving it to you to decide, when you see the article, as to the actual money saving it represents.

Where a considerable reduction is made in any line, the reason for it is given. If the goods are shop-worn or in any other way not exactly perfect, you are told about it, so that you know what to expect and whether to take advantage of the price reduction.

This method of advertising has made me a firm believer in the store of B. ALTMAN & Co. and my experience so far has proved that my confidence is not misplaced.

Yours very truly,
MRS. JULIA GROSS,
940 East 173d St., New York City.

BUILDING NEWSPAPER ADVERTISING

($2.00 PRIZE)

DEAR SIR:—

In looking over the advertisements in *The Globe* to-day the one that appealed to me the most, in view of the approaching summer months, and the fact that it appears in the columns of the Pure Food Directory, a guarantee in itself of the purity and quality of the articles advertised, is the RIKER-HEGEMAN Soda Fountain Advertisement, an advertisement that attracts the attention of the majority of the readers of *The Globe*, especially Women and Children who are among the largest patronizers of Soda and Ice-cream Parlors.

The wording of the advertisement is plain and right to the point, no superfluous reading matter, just plain and concise statements that the reader can absorb at a glance. What more could the most fastidious ask for? Absolutely pure Milk, Syrups, and Cream, served in dry and polished cups and glasses, polite and courteous service, these are things that are fully appreciated by the most exacting.

From my point of view, that is what the advertisement suggests to me, and I know that when I feel the need of anything in their line, I will look for a RIKER-HEGEMAN STORE first before going elsewhere.

GRACE E. FLEMING,
276 West 119th St., City.

($2.00 PRIZE)

April 26, 1915.

DEAR SIR:—

The stores of New York afford profitable shopping opportunities for residents of near-by cities, because of greater variety for selection and often at lower prices than could be had at home.

Judging from an out-of-town shopper's standpoint, I consider the inclosed ad. of SAKS & Co., April 23d, the most interesting because of its completeness and comparative brevity. It gives essential details concerning the different lots of garments on sale, namely: quantity, quality, style, size, material, colors, prices, and the location in the store of the various departments where the articles can be found. Such details are a distinct advantage to prospective out-of-town customers, whose time is necessarily limited, for a perusal of the advertisements before starting enables one to determine at which store her money can be spent most profitably, thereby avoiding unnecessary loss of time and energy searching for her requirements, which should be pleasantly spent at some amusement until train-time. Detailed ads. are of equal value to local shoppers, for the prudent shopper finds out where the best bargains are to be had, thereby gaining the advantage of an early selection.

Wishing *The Globe* an increased volume of substantial advertising, I am, Very truly,

KATHERINE Z. FARRELL,
65 North Clinton St.,
Poughkeepsie, N. Y.

($2.00 PRIZE)

April 26, 1915.

DEAR SIR:—

The best ad. appearing in *The Globe* during the week ending April 24th was the JOHN WANAMAKER ad. in your issue of Saturday, April 24th.

The two unique illustrations, and the arrangement of the headline in large type, attract the attention, and are so distributed that the eye unconsciously travels over the whole ad., taking in instantly the important features.

The goods offered are of present need to both men and women, whether interested in the home or out-of-doors.

Each article is interestingly and clearly described, the prices quoted seem consistent with description, and the giving of the location saves both time and energy.

The general simplicity of all statements inspires confidence in the truthfulness of the assertions.

The quality of the language, and the general refined make-up of the ad., induce one to believe that he or she will find dependable goods and be served by competent attendants.

The daily message, signed "John Wanamaker," gives a personal touch, and indicates that there is a man with a heart and of highest ideals behind the business.

Yours truly,
MARTHA A. W. CHANDLER,
22 Post Avenue, New York City.

Instead of sending the letters to the advertisers I kept them all safely housed in my office and invited the executives of the big stores to come down and study them. I found they were not half so much interested in the letters regarding their own advertising as those commending the advertising of competitors.

These thousands of letters presented a new angle regarding advertising to them and to me. The consumer's point of view is the crucial test of all advertising, and I had produced a fund of real testimony greater and more conclusive than had ever been assembled before.

The Second Contest

The success of the first contest was so satisfactory that after some study I decided to launch a second aimed at another point of interest in retail advertising. I called it an "Ad.-testing Contest," asking each contestant to tell the story of her experience in buying goods advertised in *The Globe*, with $1,500 in prizes for the best letters.

Staged to run over the period from July 1st to 15th, usually a very dull time with us, and well advertised among the local retail shops, this contest attracted and brought to us nearly double the amount of business we had ever run at that time of year.

We received over 26,000 letters from readers, most of whom inclosed with their letters sales slips, proving their purchases. We never calculated the total of these slips, but they ran into enormous figures.

Again we produced a fund of material for the study of our advertisers and incidentally convinced them that we really had done something very important in intensifying the interest of our readers in the advertising printed in *The Globe*.

THE THIRD CONTEST

Not satisfied that we had exhausted the interest of our readers, and at the suggestion of one of our large advertisers, we conducted a third contest, which had as the test "What Style of Advertising Do You Prefer?" for $225 in prizes.

While to a certain extent this contest went largely over the ground covered in the first one, it produced better than 12,000 letters and confirmed the previous opinion of our readers, with the Wanamaker copy running far and away in advance of all others, and with Hearn and Macy next in order.

It reflected an increasing interest in the smaller ads., from general advertisers, but conclusively proved to us at least that there was abundant opportunity for improvement in the appeal of this class of advertising. Many a line of copy which I thought would get recognition from the body of readers failed to get a hand.

At some future time I am going to consolidate a selection from the letters received in the contests into a book which should be of immense interest to all students of advertising copy. I am convinced that until our advertisers get these angles on copy they will never get the results secured by the department stores who approach the consumer more nearly in the language and style he or she is accustomed to.

To dig into these letters for a few hours in conjunction with the particular ad. which produced the letters proves that our women readers make a study of the ads. for what they convey to them in profitable service or values.

The Fourth Contest

Again at the suggestion of an advertiser, I started a fourth contest for small prizes for the best suggestions from readers regarding improved store service. Over 3,000 letters from readers were entered and a finer collection of constructive material was never assembled anywhere.

A committee, representing the advertising managers of five large shops, spent hours and hours reading over and judging the letters. It was most interesting to me to see the way the letters appealed to these hard-headed business men as giving them valuable suggestions and views regarding their own business never before coming to their notice. More than 3,000 letters were received.

This group of about 100 letters, clearly indicating points of criticism regarding present store management and suggesting remedies, has since been loaned by me to store executives and merits the closest and most sympathetic consideration. Many of these men have told me that I had rendered them the greatest service.

Incidentally, by the merest study of a few of the thousands of letters, I found myself at a great advantage in my subsequent contact with retail advertisers. Armed with data regarding use of space by all advertisers, and knowing the consumer angle, I can nearly always secure the closest interest from the man seeking to get greater results from advertising.

BUILDING NEWSPAPER ADVERTISING

There is a world of suggestive value in this for the general advertiser. Until he can make his advertising approximate the appeal of local advertising he is wasting a certain percentage of his appropriation for copy which may or may not look pretty to him or his agent.

I believe that a study of this material when assembled will revolutionize the advertising policy of many general advertisers and conclusively prove to them the absurdity of spending large sums of money in general mediums such as the magazines, the so-called national weeklies, bill-boards, paint signs, street-cars, and such.

XLIV

Local Development.—J. Bernard Lyon

A YOUNG man, J. Bernard Lyon, has taken up a new phase of local advertising development for newspapers which has been very effective. Unlike other syndicate plans, Mr. Lyon furnishes personal and expert service in a way that establishes permanent accounts.

Primarily, Mr. Lyon's plan means placing at the disposal of the publisher a highly organized promotion department, which not only solicits the local advertiser, but solves his publicity problems, writes his copy, furnishes necessary art work, and starts him right on a regular definite schedule. Then the new advertiser is turned over to the local advertising solicitor, who can easily develop him into a steady, year-in-and-year-out space user. This means that advertising counsel, copy and art service are furnished to him in practically the same manner as to the national advertiser. This co-operative work is handled with newspapers on a percentage basis of the actual business secured, and its cost is at a much less figure than the publisher would need to maintain his own promotion department.

In every city there are many stores and manufacturers who should advertise on regular schedules and whose campaigns would be very desirable. Inducing these inactive advertisers or "hard nuts" to make a start is a most difficult problem. The local solicitor has his difficulties. He is generally compelled to pass up these "hard ones" because he cannot spare the time to work them properly.

Mr. Lyon has an organization that has studied throughout the United States this problem of turning spasmodic or occasional advertisers into regular users of a fixed volume of space. In his organization are high-class advertising men who have given particular attention to all the phases of the many problems confronting the newspaper publisher and the retail merchant, as well as the local manufacturer. At intervals Mr. Lyon sends to newspapers, with whom he has connections, one of these specialists, who makes a careful, thorough, systematic solicitation of the local firms that should be advertising on regular schedules.

This specialized solicitor is often better qualified to talk to the prospect than the local solicitor. Often the local solicitor is too well known. To him the prospect airs his troubles, all local and of small consequence, irritates his memory of old petty quarrels and the solicitor listens and sympathizes. This specialist does not. He has no interest in anything but advertising and permits no conversation on other subjects unless they bear directly on the main issue.

The benefits of this work are lasting — to the advertisers, the newspapers as well as to the newspapers' solicitors. The advertiser so instructed on Mr. Lyon's plan becomes an intelligent buyer of space, and is no longer the uncertain patron who has to be "sold" every time he runs an ad. He is sold the idea of the value of constructive advertising—of running a definite campaign, calling for certain space on specified days. On Mr. Lyon's plan advertisers are never sold space on feature pages, schemes or in special editions. The constructive campaign only is taught, as it is better for the advertiser. It is also better for the newspaper. It helps to create an ideal situation for the newspaper, as the publisher knows weeks ahead at least the minimum amount of space he will carry. This plan is also of great value to the publisher at this particular time, during the paper shortage and other conditions brought on by the war, as it tends to equalize the space used by the advertiser—it helps the publisher relieve some of his overburdened pages, as it calls for schedules of daily, and two and three times a week insertions.

The copy and art service, as usual, has the strongest appeal to the local merchant and manufacturer, as well as to the national advertiser. This is true in securing as well as holding and developing the advertiser. When the light of the advertising gospel has been made to dawn upon the consciousness of the local prospect, he is "signed up" and his campaign is prepared in Mr. Lyon's copy department, and his advertising is handled just as carefully as if it were a national campaign.

The plan is working successfully for the advertisers and the newspapers. It is making money for both, and develops absolutely new accounts.

PART V

XLV

The Pioneer Special Representatives

A CROWD of special newspaper representatives and general agents met at lunch not long ago, and drifted in a reminiscent atmosphere. Early days in the advertising business in New York were recalled, and vivid word-pictures of the men who were active as pioneers were painted by different speakers. Each incident, touching on the personality of some one who was well known in days that have gone, brought to light characteristics of the men who put the snowball of advertising in motion and watched it grow in size.

"It was different before the first special publishers' representative came into the field," one of them mused. "Then the general agent was the whole thing. He represented advertiser and publisher. The first special representative heralded a division of interest —a concentration on a single point. The man who originated the idea deserves a monument, for he laid the foundation upon which the small but efficient band of special publishers' representatives work to this day. His principles were sound, his reasoning correct, his methods accurate. The portrait of that man should be in every special and general agency office, and on the walls of the room of every foreign newspaper advertising manager in the United States."

"Who was the first special?" asked one.

No one could answer. *The Editor and Publisher* in 1916 investigated the matter, interviewing the oldest of the specials in New York to obtain this information.

L. H. Crall was the first special publishers' representative. The general principles he laid down in 1875 are adhered to by the small army of special representatives to-day. They have succeeded, in a large measure, in reorganizing the business in the foreign field, and they have developed newspaper advertising accounts to the point where nearly one thousand daily newspapers and over six thousand weekly newspapers are to-day represented in New York and Chicago. The business Crall established is continued under the name of the L. H. Crall Company. Crall outlined the course he was to follow while he was engaged as an advertising solicitor in Cincinnati. He was in the habit of making trips to New York to keep in touch with new accounts or the renewal of old contracts, and on those occasions he came in contact with E. B. Mack and F. T. MacFadden, of the same city. Comparing notes, they discovered that the business was developing so fast that it would soon require the presence of a man in the metropolis all the time. The publishers, however, could not see it that way. To maintain a special representative in the East was an expensive luxury—he might just as well be spending some of his time drumming up business in Cincinnati.

Then Crall, who had faith in the future, conceived the idea of representing a group of newspapers. As the managements were dubious as to the success of the plan, he exhibited his confidence by offering to work on a commission basis, setting 15 per cent. as his compensation, he to pay all expenses. To the "I'll try anything once" publishers of that day this appealed in the nature of a cinch, and in the summer of 1875 Crall rented a room in the Bennett Building, which still stands at the corner of Nassau and Fulton Streets, tacking on his door the names of *The Cincinnati Times, The St. Louis Globe-Democrat, The Chicago Inter-Ocean, The Milwaukee Sentinel,* and *The Cincinnati Enquirer.* A month later E. B. Mack, representing *The Cincinnati Gazette, The Chicago Times, Louisville Commercial,* and *The Missouri Republican* (now *The St. Louis Republic*), came on and took a desk in the same room, to be followed in a few weeks by F. T. MacFadden, another Cincinnatian, who had *The Cincinnati Commercial* and *The Chicago Tribune.*

They all used the same office until the completion of the present Tribune Building, in 1876, when they took separate rooms in that structure, being the first occupants.

In those days the general agencies controlled the advertising business. They placed it when and where they pleased, at commissions that ran from 15 to 25 per cent. The amount of advertising they sent to weeklies is beyond belief. Then the weekly editions of *The Toledo Blade, St. Louis Globe-Democrat, New York Tribune,* and others, were enormous factors. Rates were cut in the most flagrant manner, the artists along that line being the space-buyers of the agencies, who paid about as much attention to rate cards as a Texas steer does to local option in the Rand. Because papers were fewer, their owners well known, and everything was bustling, it was possible for a space-buyer to know nearly all rates. There have been men in these days who are considered clever in this respect, but the old-timers were marvels. They knew not only what paper would stand a cut, and how much, but just how far they could go "beyond the limit," if the order were accompanied by a check. In those days it was more difficult to meet bills, and when a publisher received copy for 144 lines, that he couldn't possibly get into less than 200 lines, he banked the check and ran the business, notwithstanding the fact that on the basis of 144 lines he was taking the account at less than half his regular rates. Dailies carried very little foreign business, for the reason that they could not be induced to cut rates to the same extent that the weeklies would permit. Hence, there were general agents who cut the dailies off their visiting lists. The advertiser gambled with publicity. He knew nothing about the business, accepting the word of the agent. He seldom bothered to check up an account, and with an utter disregard for consequences, rarely attempted to prove insertion. Newspapers, dealing directly with general agents, came to look upon them as their representatives.

This was the condition Crall, Mack, and MacFadden faced when they came to New York forty-three years ago. The commission they were charging publishers was in addition to the amount the general agencies exacted. It was an uphill fight, against odds, and in a game where the cards were all held by opponents. Lottery ads. were quite the thing, and were among the best accounts that went out. Medicine advertising to-day is tame compared with the character of stuff turned out by the adjective manipulators of the '70's and '80's, who "piled up the agony" in a way that would convince the healthiest man who read their screed that he was tottering on the edge of the grave. Everybody was after the business, mostly by mail. These three men brought the personal element into the game. They went behind the general agency to the advertiser himself, told about their papers, what they were doing, the field they served, and the way they did it. They commenced to call for circulation statements, and to show the man who spent the money that they represented a class of publications that were growing rapidly, that were supplementing weeklies in the rapidity of circulation and popular favor. The pressure they brought to bear was tremendous. They invented keyed copy in order that the advertiser might check up results, and they kept humping.

Nearly all accounts in the general foreign field then were paid for quarterly—some semiannually. This furnished an opportunity for a number of fake concerns to sell what they had to offer, and go out of business before collection day came around. Crall, Mack, and MacFadden inaugurated the monthly settlement plan. One large advertiser in the late '70's failed, "sticking" every paper with which he did business, except those represented by these three men, who stationed themselves about his offices, taking up strategic positions commanding every entrance, from early one morning until after dark, when they caught the principal and collected every dollar coming to the papers they represented.

Crall was resourceful and original. He projected his mind into the future, and when the Centennial Exposition was held in Philadelphia, in 1876, he capitalized the rivalry between the various piano houses for exposition awards. He induced one firm to advertise its claims, and when the others followed, he invented the telegraphic reader, wiring his notices to the dailies, and beating competitors by from twenty-four hours to seven days.

Before very long each of the rival piano firms placed its business in his hands, permitting him to send its copy by telegraph nightly. It was a great stroke of enterprise that brought him a large amount of trade, for in those days special agents handled accounts themselves—just to demonstrate to the general agents that it was a game that two could play. A short time after this Crall obtained the advertising account of B. T. Babbitt & Co.

In the early '80's S. C. Beckwith came into the field, representing *The Omaha Bee* and *The Leadville* (Col.) *Chronicle*, and within a few years when a dozen more crowded into the field, the special agents confined themselves to newspaper representation, and relinquished accounts which they were handling in competition with the general agencies. They fought constantly for more business at better rates.

What was considered among the best copy of the '70's, however, was the reading notice. It was invented by H. L. Ensign, of Warner's Safe Cure fame. It was wonderfully worded and splendidly displayed, carrying the regular news head of the paper, and as the post-office department did not require newspapers to label reading matter "advertisement" when paid for, columns of this matter appeared daily. A man met with a terrible accident and was about to die, when some one in the crowd thought of a remarkable advertised remedy, got a bottle, administered a dose, and he was cured in a few moments—and so on, *ad lib.* The patent medicine men amassed fortunes.

Among the big men in the proprietary field at that time was "Pay in Advance Johnson." He would order a column, or a page, and either give a check to the agent or send it along with the order for "Dr. Johnson's Indian Blood Syrup." He got rock-bottom prices for advertising, made enormous sales, and retired with millions. He drove blooded horses in Central Park with W. K. Vanderbilt and other well-known men.

Crall, when he came to New York as a pioneer in his field, insisted that the Eastern field extended from the Florida Capes to Maine, the Western to Buffalo and Pittsburgh—a point he carried, and which the special without exception holds to this day.

When the proprietary medicine accounts had been developed to the snapping point, other lines were taken up, such as stocks, then bonds, financial, merchandizing, liquors—a hundred and one other accounts began to appear—and then the screws were again applied, this time to the patent medicine manufacturer, who fell back from first place as a patron of newspaper advertising. Higher prices came with new accounts, and with it the fearful and wonderful rate cards, amplified from the cut rates of the middle '70's and the early '80's, when newspapers boosted prices enormously, in the hope that the general agents would give them more when they applied their horizontal reduction process of 25, 33⅓, or 50 per cent.

Through all the changes the special publishers' representative has been a factor in developing business, in maintaining rates, in rendering service, improving credit, and weeding out frauds.

XLVI

The "Special" a Constructive Force.—
John B. Woodward

In order best to present the modern efficiencies of the well-equipped special of the present day, I have asked him to tell his own story in his own words and suggested that he prove his reason for existence. This, I am sure, he has done, for no finer group of high-grade men are engaged in any line of business than the specials.

John B. Woodward, with offices in New York, Boston, and Detroit, representing *The Chicago Daily News*, *The Boston Globe*, *The Baltimore Sun*, and *The Cleveland Plain-Dealer*, with a sound organization in the field, also is acting as Advertising Director of *The Chicago Daily News*.

I have known John Woodward since about 1894, when he came to New York to represent the old *Chicago Record*, the morning edition of *The Chicago Daily News*. During all these years he has kept abreast of every progressive movement for the betterment of newspaper advertising, and maintained the respect, confidence, and co-operation of advertisers and advertising agencies.

What Mr. Woodward says under the title, "The Special: A Constructive Force," is most informatory and valuable:

JOHN B. WOODWARD

"The 'special representative' is almost as old as the newspaper. The modern special representative is a more recent product of advertising. His advent in the field of 'foreign' business dates from the awakening of the great metropolitan newspapers and the lesser daily journals to the importance of developing business beyond the immediate influence of the home office.

"With this awakening on the part of newspapers there was a revolutionary change in organization and operation of the special representatives, to meet the more modern and exacting duties imposed upon them by the demands of their newspapers for constructive and creative work in the foreign field.

"In the old days, the special representative was a rather odd institution. He usually represented a string of newspapers, and the one vital purpose of his life was to unsell competing papers. He was a 'copy-chaser' of the first order, and the only creative activity of his life was that involved in discovering new arguments against his competitors. In a word, his activity was of a purely negative sort, and the constructive element was not in his book.

"The special representative of the present time is not an individual, but a highly specialized organization. The group plan has survived because it lends itself more effectively to the idea of specialization—to creative work—and offers each publisher on the list not only the individual genius of the organization's head, but the diversified genius of a staff of well-trained, keenly ambitious men, to whom the special agency now offers a prosperous and highly respected career.

"The old 'copy-chasing' idea is gone forever. The

men who dominate the 'special' field to-day are in every sense creators of business. Their old system of calling and agencies and other sources of advertising where personality played an all-important part in the success or failure of the 'special' have broadened and developed along substantial lines until to-day the relations existing between the 'special' and the agency, or between the 'special' and the advertiser direct, are based upon co-operation, mutual respect, and every other relation that is needful to well-turned and thoughtful business operations.

"The special representative is, in fact, his newspaper or newspapers abroad. His organization is a group of merchandizing specialists upon whom the advertiser has come to depend for first-hand knowledge of market conditions in territories which he seeks to cover with his publicity. This organization brings to the advertiser careful analysis of these conditions in general or particularized form upon which may be intelligently based plans which experience has proved profitable. In rendition of service, the 'special' is as well equipped as his home office. He can and does furnish the advertiser the proper solution of merchandizing, distribution, and dealer contract problems, and the various forms of sales assistance which has come to be a part of every well-ordered newspaper establishment.

"The special representative of to-day is in reality a composite of all branches of all the newspapers which his organization represents. He brings to his selling effort a high intelligence and knowledge of the communities that the advertiser is interested in, which he discusses constructively and intelligently. He is armed with statistics and works on a broader plan than the mere landing of an order regardless of the ability of his newspapers to give adequate returns to the advertiser.

"And, too, the aggressive special agency is finding a new field of endeavor in development work. It is no longer unusual, but quite an ordinary thing, to see a potential advertiser brought to the point from which he is carried forward by a good advertising agency, through the efforts of the special representative. In this work his purpose, primarily, is to make the prospect a newspaper advertiser; and, of course, being a good 'special,' he has constantly before him new lineage for his papers from a heretofore undeveloped source.

"I believe that the special, as a constructive factor in advertising, is only at the beginning of his development. The men who are associated with the profession are coming more and more to appreciate the lasting value of constructive work. They are coming more and more to understand that highly intelligent salesmanship, combined with full knowledge of every detail of the commodity which they sell, is a business asset that must be as carefully guarded and cultivated as the structure upon which any other business is built. He is no longer a 'copy-chaser.' He no longer hinges his hope for lineage upon his ability to unsell his competitor, but in every essential point of good salesmanship he measures up admirably to the high standards by which good salesmen of advertising are measured."

XLVII

Service Rendered the Newspaper.—Dan A. Carroll

DAN A. CARROLL represents *The Philadelphia Bulletin, The Montreal Star, The Indianapolis News, The Washington Star,* and *Baltimore News,* four wonderfully dominant newspapers always having recognition on any list for any campaign designed to cover their fields.

I have known Dan Carroll since the '90's. He led the way among specials in important statistical data regarding commercial conditions in the cities where his papers were printed.

His plan of serving a limited number of absolutely top-notch newspapers rather than a long string of strong and doubtful newspapers has been a winner from the start.

Mr. Carroll has won a place second to no one in the advertising field by his genial and effective service. Every one worth while in the advertising world knows Dan and knows that when he says a thing "it is so."

What Mr. Carroll says regarding "The Service the Special Representative in the National Field Renders the Newspaper Publisher" is worthy of close reading and study:

"The function of the special newspaper representative in the national advertising field has broadened and become definitely fixed. He renders the newspaper publisher an essential and economic service as important in its way as is the service which the general advertising agency delivers the national advertiser.

"The well-equipped special representative maintains an organization in close touch at all times with the development of national advertising, and it is this type of service that is generally recognized by astute publishers to be indispensable.

"Time is not far distant when various publishers had an idea that national advertising in itself was not of sufficient importance to warrant a well-organized force in the field operating from New York and Chicago, developing new business and working with advertisers and general advertising agents as a part of the service between the newspaper and the advertiser. To-day, however, it is pretty generally recognized that the special representative lends a certain speeding-up process in the transaction of business between the publisher, advertiser, and general advertising agent. His suggestions relative to the important part which the newspaper plays in a campaign are welcome and generally received with appreciation because the successful special representative who knows his field intimately can often render worth-while service in this way that makes his work in the field invaluable.

"There are three prime essentials in the make-up of a progressive advertising salesman. I rate them in the order named: Honesty, Enthusiasm, Concentration. Furthermore, every newspaper advertising salesman should know in advance as much as he can ascertain about the advertiser, his proposition and the general characteristics of his business, as reserve ammunition, before planning his sales argument on a prospective account. In addition, he should of course know all the important points of interest regarding the market where his paper is published. This refers to trade conditions, peculiar local business conditions which may or may not make a successful bid for new accounts. Cold facts, yes, but given the human touch by the representative who knows how to do it, become intensive sales argument.

"Manufacturers of trade-marked merchandise are interested primarily in market more than mediums, and it is the function of the well-equipped newspaper advertising salesman to 'sell' the market first to the manufacturer and fit in with his selling talk afterward the newspaper which he represents.

"On the advertising staff of *The Philadelphia Bulletin* is a man who for several years was advertising manager of a leading department store. He has charge of a merchandizing service department, and his job is to take cold, hard facts, such as circulation figures, advertising comparisons, market conditions—visualize them, making interesting charts to be used for the purpose of solicitation. Statistics merely as statistics don't interest anybody, but statistics worked out on a human interest basis can always get an audience.

"Likewise, *The Washington Star*, *Indianapolis News*, *Baltimore News*, and *Montreal Star* operate trade investigation departments, in charge of competent men who can make an advance analysis of market conditions for any manufacturer, thereby putting in the hands of their advertising representatives valuable information that helps them over rough spots in presenting their argument to the prospective national advertiser.

"The selling of newspaper advertising in the national field has materially changed during the past twenty years. In the old days ability in salesmanship was not the first essential, as a great many advertisers conducted their own advertising departments and doled out their advertising to such advertising agencies as could make the best price to them for a given list of papers.

"The newspaper commission for this agency service ranged from 10 to 25 per cent. Hence, the agency that made the biggest cut in commission generally got the order for placing the account. *Printers' Ink* says it was N. W. Ayer & Son among the larger agencies back in 1873 who first established a fixed commission rate of 15 per cent. for service. Heretofore many advertising agencies and newspaper representatives were nothing more nor less than space brokers, with all the attendant irregularities—indifferent service, cut rates, inflated circulation statements, etc.

"In recent years a marked development in national advertising in the daily newspapers is noted, both in the amount and character of the business and the way in which it is promoted. Leading advertising agencies have well-organized departments for the purpose of developing and handling newspaper advertising nationally in an intelligent manner; no longer is it the custom for advertisers to delegate certain lists to advertising agencies to place at a price. The preparation of copy and merchandizing service are big factors. Contracts are made with newspapers generally as per the card rates, because known rates and known circulations are standardized with all worth-while newspapers.

"Every national campaign in the newspapers is merely the sum and total of many local campaigns and the possibilities of the success of each local campaign are more manifest when the newspaper through its special representative is working in close co-operation with the advertiser or his agents in the carrying out of all the details pertaining to the matter of service, and the advice and suggestion of the experienced newspaper salesman are often helpful in the development of a new account.

"It is estimated that over 90 per cent. of the national advertising accounts are placed through general advertising agencies. This emphasizes particularly the necessity of close contact between the representatives of the newspapers operating in the national field and the general advertising agencies for the very best results. The special representative in the national field occupies somewhat the same position as the advertising manager of the newspaper in the local field. He must be alert, in close touch with all prominent accounts as well as the personnel of the leading advertising agencies who handle the principal accounts. He must have at his finger ends at all times correct and impartial information regarding the field which his newspaper covers and be prepared to consult with the advertiser and his agent relative to local marketing conditions.

"In total, the special representative renders to the publisher through the means of accelerating the work in the development of the business in the national advertising a definite and important service. He acts as an intermediary between the publisher, the seller, and the advertising agent or his client, the buyer of white space. He eliminates lost motion and reduces the possibility of friction between publishers and agents by means of personal contact. In no other way could the newspaper publisher get service of this character."

XLVIII

Foreign Business at Home.—John E. O'Mara

JOHN E. O'MARA, of O'Mara & Ormsbee, representing a group of sound evening newspapers including *The New York Globe, The Minneapolis Journal, The Newark News, The Brooklyn Eagle, The Milwaukee Journal, The Omaha World-Herald,* and *The Des Moines Capitol*, likewise needs no introduction to the advertising world.

Starting on *The Brooklyn Eagle*, he rose to be advertising manager and then came to *The New York Globe* in the same position. Mr. O'Mara, feeling that the selling of advertising for a single newspaper was not big enough work, entered the special field, taking as a partner Malcolm Ormsbee.

That he has worn well is proved by the fact that both *The New York Globe* and *Brooklyn Eagle*, two evening newspapers in the same city, and on both of which he had worked, have continuously employed his firm to represent them in the foreign field.

Mr. O'Mara's methods are along lines of patient and intelligent presentation of the case of the newspaper he is representing to the space-buyer. John knows his papers, their purposes, their strength, and their weaknesses, and has the respect of the buyers of advertising all over the country.

JOHN E. O'MARA

Of O'Mara & Ormsbee, A special representative of sound training and great effectiveness.

Mr. O'Mara is too modest to write me a paper, but in response to my request sent this letter:

"As long as competition exists, the manufacturer must have a competent sales force for the disposal of his product, whether it be soap, shoes, or advertising space. Without intelligent selling effort not one article in a thousand could be successfully exploited. There are, of course, a few isolated exceptions to the rule in the newspaper business, where a publication so dominates its field as to practically eliminate competition; if such a publisher only sold his space to advertisers who sought it he would receive but the minimum, not the maximum volume of advertising.

"I do not know of one newspaper in the country that does not employ solicitors in its own city. A local advertising staff is as vitally necessary to the successful existence of a paper as its composing-room staff, and will always continue to be so as long as newspapers sell to the retailer at from one-third to one-fifth of the manufacturing cost. And the need for good salesmanship in the national field is even more essential. A local merchant is in a position to judge with reasonable accuracy of the values of his home media, but how can the national advertiser hope to do so at, say, a thousand miles from his manufacturing plant? It seems almost needless to say that volume of sales cannot be made by correspondence. If such were the case, hundreds of millions of dollars now paid to American salesmen could and would be immediately saved. So much for the necessity for publishers' representatives in the national field.

"The bulk of foreign advertising cannot be secured

by newspapers without them, and this situation will remain unchanged till the government assumes control of all publications and pools their interests as it has done with the railroads. Taking it for granted, however, that the publisher's representative of any newspaper earns his remuneration by properly presenting the merits of his publication to regular advertisers, the functions of the publisher's representative do not end there. Newspaper advertising has steadily increased for many years. In the last half-dozen years this increase has shown wonderful growth. And it has been possible only because of the intelligent, persistent, and constructive work done by the publisher's representative not only with the advertising agents, but direct with the greatest business interests in the country.

"The publisher's representative not only secures the advertising already in existence for his papers, but is constantly creating new advertisers. Convincing manufacturers of the superior advantage of localized over scattering publicity, and then demonstrating the pre-eminent sales power of newspapers over all other forms of local publicity. The publisher's representative not only sells the individual papers, but newspapers as a whole. He sells his territory with an accurate knowledge of the trade conditions therein. The publisher's representative is responsible for the establishment in many newspaper offices of local service departments which have made possible the opening of new fields to hundreds of manufacturers.

"In the national field the publisher's representative is as directly connected with his paper as is any member of the local advertising department. The publisher's representative is in reality the manager of the foreign department, and differs from the local advertising manager only in that the paper permits him to represent one or more uncompetitive publications. Such a list, if wisely selected, adds to the strength of every paper therein and gives the publisher's representative the opportunity to render to his papers an efficient national service at a cost far less per paper than such service could possibly be secured by any publication that was handled individually in the national field.

"The publisher's representative is indispensable in no small way to the publisher and to the advertiser and agent as well in promoting and maintaining cordial relations, otherwise subject to strain by diverse viewpoints due to lack of actual contact. The existence of such relations is a means of greater business to the publisher and agent and greater results to the advertiser."

XLIX

Why the Special?—G. Logan Payne

G. LOGAN PAYNE, representing a group of smaller newspapers, is the man who entered the newspaper business as projector of a daily in a town of 6,000 population. That he made a success of his little paper and of the business of selling foreign advertising for the newspapers he has had on his list goes without saying.

What Mr. Payne says regarding the desirability of representation for newspapers in the smaller cities is most important. He knows. His statement that a good special can double the foreign business in such a paper in two years is merely a confession from his own experience.

"Let me preface my remarks by stating that if I were the publisher of a daily newspaper of only 3,000 circulation I would have a special representative for my paper and the best one possible for me to obtain. No daily newspaper having a circulation of 3,000 or more can afford to be without the services of a representative. A good special representative—one that has well-established offices in the principal centers from where advertising is placed—who is capable of taking full charge of foreign or national

G. LOGAN PAYNE

advertising of that paper is just as essential to the owner of the publication as a local advertising or business manager.

"That is a broad statement, and if not properly analyzed would seem extremely absurd—almost foolish —to the average publisher. To begin with, while the average volume of foreign or national advertising is about 30 per cent. of the total advertising lineage carried by a paper, it really represents about 50 per cent. of the net income. Remember, please, that a local advertising department costs about four times as much as foreign representation.

"First: There must be an advertising manager and at least two or three solicitors on the smaller daily, ranging from eight to ten on the larger daily.

"Second: Local advertising matter is all to be set and then corrected after proofs are read, and all at quite a little added cost to the paper, while 90 per cent. of the foreign or national advertising is sent to the paper either in mat or plate form, there being little or no composition.

"Third: While a number of the large metropolitan dailies have their foreign and local rate card on the same basis, the average daily paper in cities from 30,000 to 200,000 has a rate which is accorded department stores, which is on an average of from 20 to 30 per cent. lower than the foreign or national rate.

"When you average it all up, even though the volume of space does not measure up to the local lineage, I think you will find the net proceeds from the foreign or national field will practically equal the net proceeds of the local advertising.

"A publisher may say: 'Your argument is all right

from your viewpoint, but why can't I, with a wide-awake advertising manager, secure this foreign or national advertising without the aid of representation by covering the territory occasionally with a personal visit, and by direct selling of our market to agencies and national advertisers?' That is absolutely impossible.

"Let's presume, for instance, that the advertising manager of the publication makes one trip a year into the foreign field. He is compelled to spend at least two weeks in Chicago and nearby territory, three or four days in St. Louis, another week in Detroit, two or three weeks in New York and a week or ten days in New England, which would cover a period of practically two and a half months. Before he has concluded his Eastern itinerary a dozen campaigns may have been made up and possibly have appeared while he is in the East, that come from the West and were formulated after he left the Western territory on his trip and which he knows nothing about.

"The home office can know nothing about them because they have no way of obtaining this information until they have seen it appear in neighboring city papers or probably in the paper belonging to their competitor who has live up-to-date representation. Then think of the cost of this special trip. The railroad fare, special entertainment, etc., and the time of the advertising manager who is away from his duties at home and the time lost there in directing the efforts of the local force, probably would be double the cost of a good special, and he cannot secure more than 60 per cent. of the business that a good live special would send them.

"You ask, 'How would a special know? he is not omniscient.' He is constantly in touch through his different offices and through his men on the road the minute a new campaign is contemplated. He sells in advance—before the door is closed—his market and his publication.

"It seems to me that the most perfect illustration that I can possibly give of the service of a special representative and what they can do for their publishers is best illustrated by my own experience and my study of foreign or national advertising.

"I had to leave the Wesleyan University in Iowa in my sophomore year when I was nineteen years old, and always having had an insane desire to become the owner of a daily newspaper, I started one in Washington, Iowa, a town of less than 6,000 population. I started it on extreme nerve and $1,400, and by working day and night and filling the different offices of City Editor, Managing Editor, Reporter, Society Reporter, Bookkeeper, Auditor, etc.

"I really made a success of it and in five years' time had made a record in both circulation and advertising that attracted state-wide attention, and was made secretary of the Iowa Evening Press Association. At these meetings of Iowa's dailies we always discussed the ways and means of securing national lines of advertising that the large city papers and the many national mediums were obtaining and always at these meetings—which, mind you, were over seventeen years ago, when there were few specials in the game—I advocated the theory of having a good man to establish offices in Chicago and New York to represent us.

"After selling my daily newspaper I came to Chicago for broader experience with the thought in mind of not remaining here, but to gain experience and go back and buy a larger and more important daily newspaper in Iowa. My experience was with *The Chicago Journal* under the best training ever given a young man—Mr. John Hunter, now connected with your splendid medium. I was always hungry, really hungry for work, and Mr. Hunter, after I had gained much experience in the local field, permitted me to handle some of the less important matters with the agencies in the foreign field. I was successful in getting in some of these smaller national accounts for the *Journal* in calling on the advertiser director and the solicitor of the agency handling the account, and I could readily see why our Iowa papers did not get in on them; simply lack of representation.

"Having gone as far as I could on that paper, in other words, having gotten to where I was sort of assistant to the business manager, I changed my mind about going back in the Iowa field, and one day I said to Mr. Hunter: 'I am going to offer my resignation, and with your permission dictate a letter to the evening newspapers of Iowa asking them to appoint me as their representative of Iowa's Leading Dailies.' My letter was addressed to the principal papers of our old association and practically all of them responded.

"In less than five years' time I not only established a good rate for these publications, but carried 90 per cent. of all national advertising going out even to the big city papers; as a matter of fact, by that special effort centralized on these publications, I had the agencies both East and West use Iowa's Leading Dailies on experimental accounts, because of the special co-operation that the publishers offered them, and it got to be sort of a slogan: 'If you don't know where to start with a daily newspaper campaign "Try it on the Dog," Iowa's Leading Dailies.' That seems to me to be most positive and concrete evidence of the value of a special representative.

"In closing permit me to say that no daily of any importance can afford to be without representation, and that any daily, large or small, can double their foreign business in a period of two years if they will properly co-operate with their representative and support him in the right manner by answering promptly all inquiries and keeping him well informed as to the market conditions and changed conditions and the growth of the city and community wherein the paper is published."

L

Mutual Confidence the Keynote.—R. E. Ward.

ROBERT E. WARD, with offices in New York and Chicago, has specialized in representing in the foreign field a strong group of Ohio newspapers known as the "Ohio Select List." I have known Mr. Ward for many years and have watched his work, which has been consistent and dependable for his newspapers.

I asked Mr. Ward to give me a short contribution, which I am presenting in his words:

"Soliciting of national advertising is becoming almost as specialized as some of the other professions, and the organization that represents newspapers published in the smaller cities makes a different appeal, and provides somewhat different service to its publishers, than those who solicit for the larger-city newspapers.

"Advertisers and agencies gain their impression of the smaller-city and less familiar newspapers from the publisher's representative himself, and for that reason the qualified solicitor saturates himself with the local situation by personal visits and frequent queries and investigation, all of which give his daily work authority, conviction, interest, and freshness of appeal.

"The recognition of agencies and the question of

R. E. WARD

credits and collections is unusually important for this class of representative, because the smaller publisher is not as closely in touch with general agents, because he has a smaller amount of business and less frequent relations with them than do the larger publishers. Therefore, the representative must be fully alive to those features all the time.

"While the representative spends a great deal of time looking after copy, electrotypes, schedules, supplying rate cards, circulation statements, checking copies, etc., those functions are of secondary importance compared to the creative work he does with the general advertisers and the general agents.

"This intensive development of additional business takes two forms; first, the representative increases the amount of space being used by present advertisers through the co-operation, the stimulating of new ideas, and strong personal work.

"Probably the most important feature of the creative work is what the representative does with new advertisers who have never been in his publisher's columns before. That is the basis of the publisher's judgment as to the representative's effectiveness, and is the source of the greatest satisfaction and financial income to the representative himself.

"The representative constantly suggests to his publisher the proper form of circular matter to be used, and, being on the firing-line, he knows what sort of printed appeal makes the strongest impression with the advertiser and agent and is the most timely. He reports to the publisher prospects for local co-operative work, suggesting products and surveys, and how the publisher can go about furnishing the advertiser with a better local service.

"The representative watches his competition and papers in near-by territory for matters of policy, rates, methods, etc., that he may suggest to his publisher the necessary changes to keep his particular newspaper in line or in advance of what is done by other smaller and near-by newspapers.

"The publisher supports his representative by frequent voluntary letters of information regarding local conditions, the prosperity of his community and trading territory, the development of industry, increase of pay-rolls, and anything that increases buying or trading possibilities. The publisher issues from time to time well-prepared printed matter, supplementing and amplifying what the representative does. He issues circulation statements, comparative advertising records, etc., for the representative to use and distribute by hand while he is calling on advertisers personally. In some instances the publisher can do a great deal of good by visiting the national advertisers from time to time in company with his representative.

"The publisher reports to the representative when salesmen, representing national advertisers, have visited his city, and he learns from the dealers just what the salesmen have outlined as to the advertising policy of their respective manufacturers, and he also furnishes the representative with copies or information taken from letters sent by manufacturers to local dealers announcing forthcoming advertising campaigns.

"The publisher avoids hampering the work of the representative, arising from arguments and differences of opinion with agents and advertisers. When such instances arise, as they inevitably do, the publisher refers the whole matter to the representative for adjustment, knowing that a few properly selected words, delivered personally, are greatly preferred to bitter letters.

"The relationship between the publisher and the representative must be close and based on mutual confidence, because their interests are mutual and nothing is effective without the other."

LI

Assisting Space-buyers.—Charles H. Eddy

CHARLES H. EDDY, likewise representing a wide group of important small city newspapers, is a man standing absolutely at the top of the ladder in his line of activity, and is known throughout the advertising field as a tireless worker and a man of absolute dependability.

Mr. Eddy touches upon phases of work coming within the scope of the service rendered the newspaper which is most interesting and informatory to those who are inclined to think that the special does not earn his salary or other compensation:

"From an experience of many years, I am convinced that the competent 'special' renders a service to the newspaper, the general agency, and the advertiser which could not be secured so economically or efficiently by any other means.

"The 'special' enables the publisher to extend his personality everywhere outside the home field, where national advertising is to be secured. He gets his publisher's message over as he wants it put over.

"He is provided with complete information and data regarding his newspaper and its home city, and presents his case to the advertiser, or to the agency,

CHARLES H. EDDY

exactly as his publisher would do were it possible for him personally to canvass the foreign advertising field.

"The 'special' is of constant assistance to agency space-buyers, who are frequently overburdened with the mass of detail which their work of dealing with thousands of publications entails. He stands ready to furnish all necessary information in regard to his newspaper and its field to facilitate the space-buyers' work.

"In numerous instances the 'special' is required to canvass the sales of advertising manager as well as the agency, and inform him fully as to the claims of his newspaper and its home city.

"After securing the advertising contract the 'special' is expected to see that the necessary instructions and copy reach the paper, that the advertiser or agency is furnished with copies containing the advertising, and to handle any complaints as to service until the order is completed.

"The 'special' also acts as a collector of delinquent accounts and keeps his home office informed as to credit conditions which may concern the interests of his newspaper.

"More and more the selling of newspaper advertising trends toward the elimination of competition between the various newspapers in a city, and to the selling of the city itself to the advertiser as a desirable market for his goods. This is promotion work for the home city, and much of the effort of the 'special' representative is devoted to this work.

"All of the foregoing represents a personal service to the individual newspaper which is performed by the 'special' representative and which could not be rendered so economically or with such satisfactory results by any other agency.

"To perform this service a complete organization is necessary, as the field is wide, embracing the whole United States, with the number of advertisers and agencies to be covered running into the thousands. This makes a vast amount of work for the 'special' who thoroughly covers the field. He must command a highly trained staff of solicitors and office help and must maintain offices in New York and Chicago, and possibly other cities in order to render this widespread service to his newspaper.

"Altogether, the 'special' is, and has been, one of the prime factors in building up the business of newspaper advertising, and he will, I believe, so continue.

"The closer the co-operation between the agency, the advertiser, and the 'special,' and the higher the business standard of their dealings with each other, the better will be the results to the great business of national newspaper advertising."

PART VI

LII

New Sort of Co-operation with Advertising Agencies and Words of Advice from Notable Agents

THE design of this part of the book was to provide an opportunity for those generally accepted as leaders in best agency thought briefly to show the newspaper publisher how through greater co-operation with the agencies he could help develop new business.

Since writing the earlier chapters regarding agencies and plans for developing more advertising for the newspapers, it has been my advantage through close contact with many of the leading agents to discover the fatal weakness which for years has kept newspapers from their full share of national advertising.

The failure of newspapers generally to pay advertising agents a commission on "local" as well as "foreign" business in my opinion is more largely responsible for their failure to get all the business they should than any other factor.

· Hundreds of advertising agents located in cities all over the country who should be primarily interested in developing "local" accounts in the newspapers which would gradually grow into sectional accounts and then national, cannot afford to do so, because the newspapers fail to arrange conditions

❡ *What advertisers think of a newspaper is more interesting than what the paper thinks of itself. And when such thought happens to be expressed in terms of dollars spent for advertising space — there can be no question of its sincerity.*

16 of New York's Leading Retail Stores

Here they are:
Altman & Co.
Arnold, Constable & Co.
Best & Co.
Bloomingdale Bros.
Bonwit Teller & Co.
J. M. Gidding & Co.
Gimbel Brothers
Hearn
Lord & Taylor.
R. H. Macy & Co.
Oppenheim & Collins
Franklin Simon & Co.
Stern Bros
Stewart & Co.
Worth
John Wanamaker

used a larger volume of advertising in the New York GLOBE during the past five years than in any other New York paper.

Why did these leading stores

Use More Advertising in the Globe?

There is only one possible answer.

To be the choice of one or two such shrewd buyers of advertising space would be a compliment to any paper, even though inconclusive as to that paper's leadership. *But to be chosen by sixteen such merchants* —SURELY THAT IS PROOF POSITIVE!

❡ Write for facts and figures that tell why THE GLOBE offers the best opportunity for reaching the one-tenth of NEW YORK'S people with money to buy goods.

America's Oldest and Most Virile Daily Evening Newspaper

73-83 Dey Street
NEW YORK

JASON ROGERS,
PUBLISHER

This advertisement won $1000, the first prize in the Globe's Advertising Agency Competition. It was prepared by C. W. Page, of C. W. Page & Co., Richmond, Va.

BUILDING NEWSPAPER ADVERTISING

so that the agent will be compensated for the service he renders.

The agent is forced to charge local advertisers using local newspapers a service charge on top of the gross rate of the newspaper, which the advertiser naturally resents, and more often than not the newspapers do everything they can to eliminate the agent from the relation which he has established.

Under these circumstances the agents in most places find themselves working for business for magazines and general mediums which pay them a commission or give them a net rate on business which they stimulate, handle, underwrite, and care for.

Therefore we as newspaper publishers must change our business policy and allow these developers of business to secure a brokerage fee between the net rate we must receive and the gross rate to be paid by the advertiser, if we are to get the facility of this powerful selling factor.

Here in New York our newspapers for years have allowed commissions to agents on both local and foreign, and I have always had our rates the same for both local and general advertising.

In July, 1918, I started a campaign of education among newspaper publishers urging them to go and do likewise, and thus set loose as selling agents of newspaper advertising these hundreds of men best qualified to produce results for those who buy space in our columns.

I am reproducing some of the advertisements which we printed in the trade papers in this section of the book.

Even where newspapers are not disposed to allow agents a commission on local business, it strikes me as absurd that they should stand in their own light by refusing to pay him his fee on business coming from an outside manufacturer hooked up to names of local dealers.

A leading agent recently told me that he had switched $100,000 of a $300,000 account from the magazines to the newspapers and lost $13,000 in commissions as a reward, because the newspapers had refused to pay him commission on the business inserted over the names of local dealers.

Localized National Advertising is newspaper advertising linked up to the names of local dealers, and is the most effective form of printed salesmanship. The advertising agent who prepares the campaign, gets up the cuts, and devotes the energies of his organization to the selling-plan, is certainly entitled to compensation.

For best results the medium should sell its product—advertising—for the same price under like conditions to all customers, whether local or distant. By protecting agents on all business running less than, say, 25,000 lines a year, the newspapers would be bringing to their aid powerful promotional forces of limitless potential.

If our friends, the advertising agents, would bill all space at the newspapers' gross rate, and our newspapers would consider their "net" rate after allowance of commission their real rate, much needless confusion would be avoided in closer co-operation in other directions produced.

In going over the figures of a small city newspaper doing an advertising business of $265,000 a year, I ran across the item, $13,000 "commission," as an expense. If he had entered his earnings at $252,000

BUILDING NEWSPAPER ADVERTISING 337

from advertising, he would not worry about the imaginary payment of commission.

The advertiser pays both "our net rate" and "the agent's commission."

By closer and more harmonious relations with the dependable service agents of the country our newspapers will not only increase the volume of business in their columns, but be making the advertising which they print more resourceful.

The contributions in this part from leading agents, and their views as expressed in speeches before advertising clubs, etc., regarding effective co-operation, will be found most instructive and interesting.

LIII

*The Advanced Agency Service of To-day.—
Robert Tinsman*

ROBERT TINSMAN, president of the Federal Advertising Agency, New York and Chicago, in response to my invitation to contribute a paper on modern agency service, has produced the most comprehensive presentation of the case to be found anywhere.

Mr. Tinsman is an advertising man of sound and most effective experience, who when he takes on an account renders a sort and degree of service that is far and beyond the power of mere money to buy. He is a close student of merchandise and human nature and knows how to ring the bell time after time.

We will let Mr. Tinsman tell his own story:

"'Service' is a well-worn, much abused word in advertising parlance. It should be hitched to its yokefellow 'co-operation,' and the team driven off the dock. The language of advertising would be the gainer thereby, for then we would have to search sincerely for new words, more expressive of to-day's thought in advertising practice.

"The last ten years have witnessed a marked revision in the agency method. We all know the evolu-

ROBERT TINSMAN
President of the Federal Advertising Agency, New York City.

tion of the agency—first the space broker, then the space filler, and finally the merchandise advertiser of to-day.

"This evolution has brought us to a point where an advertising agent, to be truly successful, must be able to advise authoritatively on merchandizing matters as well as on the selection of media or the preparation of advertisements.

"He must be able to analyze market conditions and draw deductions therefrom; he must be qualified to organize selling and advertising campaigns to the trade, understanding the particular approach most effective in each special industry; he must be able to create names for most effective appeal for each product and to each audience. Also, he must originate packages to outshine competition, whether it be a tin can on a grocery shelf, a perfumery package on a druggist's counter, or a silk wrapper in a drygoods store.

"Thus, you see, it is not sufficient for an advertising agent merely to be a good general advertiser. He should be a specialist in each trade and know a great deal about something rather than a little about everything, otherwise he is apt to scatter the shot aimlessly, or miss the mark altogether.

"The successful agent generally knows how to handle salesmen for his clients, how to enthuse them for the campaign about to be conducted, how to answer their questions when they want to know how to sell reluctant trade, and how to communicate the policy of the clients' business with the salesmen so as to develop the *esprit de corps* of the house and thereby make the trade-mark advertising increasingly resultful.

"In addition to all this, the agent's work to-day comprehends a far closer analysis of the power of media than was hitherto thought necessary—not only circulation, but the character of circulation, its division into class and mass appeal, its sex, age, and racial percentage—all this must now enter into the discussion before the space allotment is made.

"Finally the advertising itself, not merely a pretty picture and clever text, but an interrupting idea that dominates the space and memorizes itself with even the careless reader so that each advertisement repeating this interrupting idea accumulates an investment value that the old-fashioned general publicity advertisement never did.

"Of course the production of such interrupting ideas, harmonious with the product advertised, calls for a creative sense of the highest development, requires an artistic presentation of extraordinary force and sensible originality, and, finally, a copy or text treatment quite different from the old-time rewrite effort of the copy hack.

"Such advertising possesses a sparkling brilliancy and permanent interest that multiplies results far above the usual, but the casual reader does not appreciate the infinite time, patience, experience, and research involved in its production.

"As to the newspaper's part in agency service, I would suggest the following:

"*First*, let the newspapers study the personnel and qualifications of each agency. Then when any new account is started, the newspaper will be able to advise the advertiser which agents should be considered, and then the advertiser can make his own comparisons. This will eliminate most of the mistakes due to the careless recommendation of misguided acquaintance.

"*Second*, the newspapers should know a lot more about an account before soliciting it, so as to make recommendations both suitable and sensible. This requires advance application and some study, but it will pay in the long run.

"*Third*, the newspaper is in a position to render unusual service, which often is the most valuable introduction to an account. For example, *The New York Globe* assisted the Federal Advertising Agency in securing the custom and friendship of the hair-dressers, which led to *The Globe's* securing the advertising of Fashionette Invisible Hair Nets. So when a newspaper carries business, it might show some concern to make extra good for that business by reason of its connections, such as the service rendered Mallinson's Silks de Luxe by *The Globe* when they secured advertising of Mallinson's Silks de Luxe from the New York merchants, using same to accompany the Mallinson advertising in their fashion issues.

"*Fourth*, in the make-up of the newspaper there is also lots of room for improvement. If the make-up man has some advertising sense as well as typographical skill, he will not only see to it that the page is a good type balance, but also that the advertising is placed, if possible, where it will secure some additional advantage, running near reading matter of similar interest. This is a rule that the magazines observe with great profit, but which the newspapers overlook even when it is possible, as is frequently the case.

"*Fifth*, the most interesting development in newspaper service is the newspaper's power to act as a go-between with the national advertiser and the retail trade. Here is indeed a place for great and profitable development which the newspaper is in a position to fill as no other medium.

"With the new advertiser particularly, emphasis, reiterated emphasis, should always be placed on the value of repetition, the keep-at-it policy that is the first fundamental for the beginner's success.

"Finally, the newspaper should present its circulation, preferably audited by an independent concern such as the A. B. C., and classified not only to show the distribution of its circulation exactly, but also its character down to the most precise detail.

"The flat rate, simplified rate card, the A. B. C. audit, and a definite help policy, as outlined above, all combined in one newspaper, must mean success for its advertisers, leadership for itself."

LIV

Co-operation.—Stanley Resor

SUPERFICIAL temporary outside service which a publisher's Production Department can give an advertiser does not constitute, from the agent's point of view, any part of the real value of the paper as an advertising medium. The paper's value can be determined only by fundamentals of service which I shall outline.

The extent to which agents avail themselves of many of the forms of co-operation offered to-day is no indication of the value they set upon them. As buyers, we have taken, and shall continue to take, much that is offered because it is included in the rate. It must be paid for, anyway, and whatever of value it may contain is used. We should be quick to welcome, however, the use of the publisher's money that this work represents in channels that would be genuinely productive.

Let us see exactly what it is we are trying to accomplish with any piece of work. The part that the advertiser, agent, and publisher should perform and are equipped to perform will then be clear. Can we not then check the tendency to encourage situations like one that recently arose between a publisher and one of the largest advertisers in the United States?

A leading American manufacturer established a

new record in the amount of co-operation asked for from the newspapers. One of the newspapers which had given full co-operation sought a renewal of the contract and volunteered to co-operate again in every way. The advertiser would not admit that he had received Class A co-operation. He said that, in addition to doing all of the many things requested, the newspaper publisher should suggest new methods of co-operation which the advertiser could not think of or did not know of.

In order to introduce a new product in a territory, to maintain sales and to increase them, it is necessary to determine, not what minor things would help this or that campaign, but to establish the big permanent values.

For the sake of clearness, let us consider a definite problem—the introduction of a thirty-five-cent coffee into a new city.

Let us admit the product has been tried and proved sound; that it will repeat in markets for which it is adapted; that the machinery for securing distribution is adequate; that deliveries will be made promptly and in proper quantities. This is the kind of service the manufacturer must give.

The next step is to realize very clearly the conditions that are to be met. The following elemental functions are typical of those that must be definitely answered:

Are women the primary purchasers?

Is there a natural indifference on the part of the consumers and a consequent inertia to be overcome before a sale can be established?

Does the price offer real resistance?

What is the character of the population?

STANLEY RESOR
President of the J. Walter Thompson Advertising Agency, New York and Chicago

BUILDING NEWSPAPER ADVERTISING 345

Is the city primarily an industrial one, such as Lowell? Mainly a trading center, such as Wichita, Kansas, or residential town, such as Pittsfield?

Is the city a cheap food market, such as Milwaukee or St. Louis?

Wherein lies the strength of competitive brands already established in the market?

What should be the nature of the appeal on this new product?

How should it be conveyed?

What should be the size and frequency of the insertions?

If newspapers are to be used, shall they be daily, Sunday, or both, and which ones?

Upon the correct determination of these and many other points, and upon the proper execution of the plan worked out to meet them, depend the success or failure of the campaign.

This is the type of service that the agent must give.

We now come to the co-operation to be rendered by the newspaper.

For the newspaper to attempt to sell merchandise or to send with the salesman a solicitor to introduce him to the trade, to give window displays, or to assume the responsibility of deciding whether or not the city is a good market for a thirty-five-cent coffee —for a newspaper to attempt work of this kind is in reality as much beyond its function as for the advertiser to publish a newspaper and for the agent to solicit subscriptions for its circulation.

Even if one grants that the paper can sell some merchandise, the complications that arise from its attempting to sell first one article and then another are too obvious to need any discussion, and to designate a solicitor to accompany a salesman is a reflection upon the salesman the manufacturer has placed on the job.

To attempt to judge the possible market a city affords for a wide range of products is to assume very grave responsibility. Only those who do not know the multitude of problems involved would lightly undertake it. Every one knows how easy it is to prejudice the answer of either housewife or dealer in favor of the point he is trying to prove. For this reason people capable of securing the real facts cannot be hired and fired. It has been our experience that absolutely impartial investigators, thoroughly familiar with the product and with the conditions which make for or against its use, are the only ones who can get information that is truly indicative of conditions.

Before recently introducing a new grocery product, our investigations in eight cities under consideration represented an outlay of one thousand dollars. Incomplete investigations may prove as dangerous to the future of a product as an incomplete or inaccurate diagnosis by an operating surgeon to a patient.

Newspapers cannot do this work efficiently for all advertisers. Furthermore, the burden is so great that the attempt to do it must ultimately be reflected in the rate, and the rate must be borne by all advertisers alike, whether they use this kind of service or not. The properly equipped agent does not need and does not wish to encourage this type of co-operation because for his clients it comes to mean virtual subsidy, covering the deficiencies of other ad-

BUILDING NEWSPAPER ADVERTISING

vertisers whose only claim upon such charity is their inefficiency.

There is co-operation, however, which the newspaper can give, and should give—co-operation which is really effective for advertiser and agent, which is permanent and profitable to all concerned. Much of it is the service for which the paper charges a legitimate rate. In addition to the cost of materials and production, the advertising rate of a newspaper is figured to cover the following essential items:

Cost of selling the advertising space on its actual merit.

Cost of handling copy.

Cost of bookkeeping and billing.

Should the agent do less than demand the fullest co-operation in these particulars, which constitute the very basis of effective space buying, and are very definitely included in that for which his client pays? Let us list these forms of co-operation together with others under five heads:

1. Complete information on the circulation and character of the paper itself and its readers.
2. Standardized rates and standardized rate cards.
3. A very marked improvement in the handling of the business details of the advertising department.
4. A greater influence on the business in a community; a greater effort to stimulate buying interest on the part of the consumer.
5. A broader attitude toward American business.

Definite progress toward these points would be of great help, would be lasting, and would establish a basis for future growth.

The first thing we need from a newspaper is a genuinely accurate statement of the amount of circulation, of the distribution of this circulation in the city and outside, etc. This work is being done through the A. B. C., whose reports we feel are of very definite assistance. We also need just such simple facts about a paper as the volume of local advertising carried, its division among the principal lines represented, its division by days to indicate any peculiar local customs, such as the tendency in some cities among good stores not to use Sunday papers.

The second service for which we believe there is a conspicuous need is standardized rates, standardized rate cards, and a flat rate. The great variation in the amount of circulation that a dollar can buy is a condition that is impossible for any one to defend. We do not refer here to the variation between a paper of established quality circulation and a paper of popular circulation, but to the variation among papers of similar standing.

For 10 cents a line it is possible to buy 23,000 circulation in Birmingham; 37,000 in Bridgeport; 62,000 in Atlanta; 87,000 in Omaha.

For 15 cents a line it is possible to buy 55,000 circulation in Washington; 98,000 in Baltimore; 130,000 in Detroit, and 170,000 in Kansas City—over three times the circulation in one city that it is possible to get in another.

For 50,000 circulation in papers of similar standing, the prices range from 7 cents to 18 cents a line.

Freight rates and production costs cannot explain the great variation.

An equally amazing variation appears in the discounts allowed. Of three papers approximately alike,

BUILDING NEWSPAPER ADVERTISING 349

one gives a 26-time discount of 2½ per cent. and a 52-time of 5 per cent.; the second, 5 per cent. on 5,000 lines, 10 per cent. on 10,000 lines, and 15 per cent. on 15,000 lines; the third gives discounts on both time and space.

Furthermore, a strange resourcefulness on the part of publishers in concealing these vagaries is qualifying many a rate clerk to be a Philadelphia lawyer.

Can we hope in our generation to be blessed with a flat rate?—not of course the flat rate of the minimum discount.

The American Association of Advertising Agents has prepared and recommended a standard form for rate cards which greatly simplifies the work of estimating. A wider adoption of this form is one very definite and simple way in which publishers can co-operate.

The third service is a very marked improvement in the handling of the business details by the advertising department of the newspaper. Only the agents, I think, can appreciate how much we need this.

A fourth of the entire correspondence of our company is necessitated by the avoidable mistakes in the newspaper office—insertions not according to schedule, wrong key numbers, checking copies not received, bills wrongly figured, deductions not noted. These and many minor laxities cause an endless and for us a very expensive correspondence. The growth of newspaper advertising, in spite of the looseness of business departments, is a significant tribute to the genuine value of newspapers as a medium.

Then there is the question of typography and make-up.

In a moment of optimism should we ask even a large city newspaper to see an advertisement, following copy exactly—Heaven forbid! Agents have long since realized that advertising has developed its own typography which demands compositors trained in advertising setting. Have the newspapers, especially in the larger cities, ever stopped to consider what an economy it would be to have advertising compositors?

Those papers that have a logical basis for the make-up of their advertising columns constitute a very small proportion of the nineteen thousand eight hundred published. Yet such papers as *The Philadelphia Public Ledger* and *The Christian Science Monitor* have demonstrated that mechanical excellence in a newspaper is a possibility.

The progress that has been made toward the elimination of objectionable advertising has been marked, and there is hope that all of it will eventually be dropped. Then there is need of more discretion in the arrangement of advertising copy, so that competitive and non-competitive advertisements will be intelligently grouped or kept apart.

Every economy in time in making standard and automatic these obvious and paid-for services of the newspapers will save just that much more of the agent's time and money for creative effort.

The fourth service that we suggest, of becoming a greater influence in building up business in a community and of stimulating buying interest on the part of the consumer, is a great deal more concrete than appears.

Any given number of people do not necessarily constitute a good market. The value of the market to the advertiser is in direct proportion to the standards of living in the community and to the progressiveness of the dealers. John Stuart Mill's statement that "Wealth is not money, but utilization of resources" is amply proved every day in the marketing of commodities. The difference in the situation in two towns of approximately the same size—Ogden in the central part of Iowa, and Lancaster in central Kentucky—is an excellent example of the market's dependence upon the spirit and development of the community. In Ogden the buying habits are a full decade in advance of those of Lancaster. Is it not a very obvious function of the newspaper to develop on the part of readers and dealers an appreciation of newspaper advertising and newspaper-advertised commodities? The newspaper should certainly not yield first place to any other medium as the power for developing both dealer and consumer.

In the magazine field the value of a departmentalized magazine has been established beyond question. Readers of such magazines whose buying interest has already been developed by the medium show a conspicuous responsiveness to advertising. The question of departments in a newspaper is a very big one; but the fact that departments can be a permanent force in developing markets for commodities, and that they will produce a large volume of advertising, is proved by the many columns of automobile advertising carried by newspapers to-day.

The fifth and last service we suggest is a broader attitude toward American business.

An English traveler of note recently commented on a significant factor in American life. Abroad, he said, the well-known buildings are cathedrals; in this country it is the Metropolitan and Woolworth towers, the railroad terminals and business monuments which are shown the distinguished traveler.

In America, business is the dominant interest, and in America business articles, intelligently handled, constitute news.

The Saturday Evening Post and *The American Magazine* have proved that the triumphs of American business interestingly presented arouse a wide interest.

The newspapers seem to have had difficulty in finding any middle ground between the extremes of running obvious "readers" to an unwarrantable degree and of failing to present interesting facts about large industries. The service of the canning industry in saving 50 per cent. of the fruits and vegetables raised in America, and that of the mail-order industry in raising the standard of living in farm districts, are two developments that have come within our own knowledge.

The attitude of the small-town newspaper toward the mail-order industry has been anything but intelligent. Instead of trying to help the small retailer establish himself in his rightful field, they have merely encouraged him in his hopeless effort to stop the tide of mail-order buying.

Briefly, then, these five forms of co-operation, I believe, offer the greatest permanent value to the advertiser and his agent:

A clearer picture of the paper, its readers and circulation;

Standardized rates and rate cards;

Better business departments;

A greater influence on the trade and consumers of the community;

A broader attitude toward American business.

BUILDING NEWSPAPER ADVERTISING 353

This is the work that all publishers are eminently fitted to do. And can there be any doubt that the performance of these functions is profitable to the publisher in direct proportion to the thoroughness and ability which he applies to the task?

Agents naturally will favor papers which are making conscientious efforts in this direction. Such papers become more responsive advertising media, and from the start deserve all the encouragement the advertising agencies can give them.

But there is a more important reason why the co-operation outlined will be profitable to the publisher—a reason they apparently have not thought of.

If newspaper publishers will earnestly try to stop that waste of the agencies' time and money, now caused by deficient co-operation, then the agencies will find it possible to devote a much larger portion of their time and money to *creative* effort, to the preparation of more effective campaigns that are bound to result in an increase of present business and to the development of new business. This is co-operation agents are able and eager to supply just as fast as the publishers' co-operation makes it possible.

LV

Effective Co-operation.—Paul Faust

A REALLY remarkable explanation of Co-operation from the advertising agency standpoint was presented by Paul Faust, of Mallory, Mitchell & Faust, of Chicago, in the Newspaper Departmental of the Associated Advertising Clubs of the World, at Philadelphia, in June, 1916, in part as follows:

"For Co-operation to be intelligently considered, or for Co-operation to be dispassionately viewed and discussed, it cannot be defined as many people have defined it.

"Trade papers have called it graft. Some publishers have called it a new way of cutting rates. Some advertisers have regarded it as a free lunch.

"If Co-operation is any of these things, it cannot endure. If it is none of these things, what is it, and why is it necessary?

"There must be merit in it, or some of the most ethical, intelligent, and far-sighted newspaper publishers in this country would not advocate Co-operation with advertisers so positively; neither would they continue the service that they are now rendering so enthusiastically.

"We have nothing to do with the misuse of the

PAUL E. FAUST
Of Mallory, Mitchell & Faust of Chicago

word Co-operation. It has been misused. We are concerned with the legitimate possibilities of a service from the publisher to the advertiser which must be based (1) on the self-interest of the publisher; (2) on helping the advertiser to succeed so that he is perpetuated as a customer of the publisher. Co-operation, as we view it, is merchandizing, is merchandizing aid or merchandizing service. It is not the actual sale of goods, but, rather, helping to organize a market so that selling is simplified to the dealer and to the consumer.

"Perhaps the most general attitude of the newspaper publisher toward a service to the foreign advertiser is the objection to doing anything beyond the publication of a good newspaper, delivering it regularly to the subscribers and giving the advertiser a fair measure of circulation for the rate charged.

"If a publisher believes in publishing news only, he is likely to find himself very much alone in a viewpoint a good many years old.

"This is because the newspaper is constantly becoming more than a purveyor of news. News can properly be defined as 'daily happenings.' If a newspaper to-day were limited to that, it would be decidedly restricted in its scope. Publishers have found that news, as such, does not interest 100 per cent. of the people. So that for the newspaper to be of universal or 100 per cent. interest, something more than news had to be printed.

"In many metropolitan dailies there are accordingly various features, such as editorial pages, fashion departments, household pages, automobile sections, real-estate sections, book-review sections, magazine supplements, and so on. These are all variously valued for their information, entertainment, and for the attraction and holding of subscriptions.

"In a nutshell, the publication of news alone is not enough and there has to be added literary merchandise to keep pace with the competition from other publications and periodicals and, in a word, to keep up with the times.

"Twenty years ago newspaper publishers would have reviewed the present-day newspaper as being just as unethical as many of them call misunderstood 'Co-operation' unethical to-day.

"The fact is, the newspaper business is developing. The point of view of ten years ago, or even five years ago, must be revised if the newspaper is going to keep up with literary competition and finally with advertising competition.

"When the newspaper elected to carry advertising, the newspaper assumed a responsibility to the advertiser as well as the subscriber. The publisher cannot long prosper and take money from the subscriber without giving ultimate satisfaction to both.

"In the past, publishers have felt that their responsibility terminated with printing the advertisement of the advertiser. This was well enough until it was found that in an alarming number of instances advertising contracts, published under these circumstances, probably would not be renewed at their expiration.

"It has finally developed with observing publishers that it is a far-sighted policy to concern themselves in the real success of the advertiser for the purely selfish newspaper reason that in so doing they could renew business and increase business at less expense than they could possibly keep up their revenue by

BUILDING NEWSPAPER ADVERTISING

getting a new crop of foreign advertisers every year.

"We come, then, to the point that if the newspaper advertiser succeeds, he renews his contract and perhaps increases his appropriation. If he fails, it is one more black eye for newspaper advertising, one more advertiser delivered to the magazines or to the billboards, or to the agricultural papers, one more blow to the efficacy of newspaper advertising.

"If we admit the truth, we must start with the power of the newspaper as an advertising medium. It is safe to say that the newspaper which markets the millions of dollars of merchandise for the big retail stores of America is the most powerful local selling medium we have. It works the quickest. And we have documentary proof, in sales and subscription records, of the number of persons it actually reaches.

"But this high-powered, quick-acting, universal advertising medium is an expensive one as ordinarily used. It is not expensive if thoroughly used. And it must be thoroughly utilized to be made to pay.

"Every one of you have had experience with advertising campaigns of five, ten, and fifteen thousand line contracts being undertaken by foreign advertisers with a most unsatisfactory or disastrous result. Apparently attractive copy has been printed. Apparently the schedule was fairly adequate. Apparently the product was good. Apparently the salesmen were energetic. But the final outcome was not successful. So the campaign petered out and was not renewed.

"You may have wondered, for a short time, why. If you gave it thought you probably concluded that maybe the people in your section did not want the goods. You may have thought the price was out of line. You may have thought the product was not meritorious. Anyhow, you found some alibi.

"And I know that down in your hearts some of you wondered if your own medium might not have been a little bit weak for that class of product or that quality of trade or for that particular merchandizing undertaking.

"If you thought your medium was not an effective seller of this class of goods, you tried your best to forget it, your advertising manager did, too, and your foreign representative did his best to explain the failure of the campaign.

"I wonder how many publishers have investigated the whole merchandizing process of getting such products from the factory to the consumer.

"If you had started with the premise that you had the most powerful medium, that you were probably selling that very same item for some grocery store, or department store, or hardware store, or furniture store, or market in your own town, you would probably have come to the same point of view that we have reached as merchandizers.

"We know of a certainty that the newspapers are successfully selling for retail stores the class or kind of products that we undertake to advertise in them. It is very simple to find out why, for example, the department store gets results. The department store advertises to-day. It displays the goods to-day. The clerk is informed of the advertising to-day. When the consumer comes in, the product is available. It is displayed. It is intelligently discussed by the salesman or saleslady. There are no gaps between

BUILDING NEWSPAPER ADVERTISING

the advertising in the newspaper and the delivery of the product to the consumer. The advertising has an opportunity to attract attention and aid definitely in the sale of the product. The advertising medium, the advertising manager, the window trimmer, and the clerk all operate in unison when the department store advertises.

"When the foreign advertiser advertises, the sales condition may be exactly the opposite. On the one hand we have a forceful advertisement appearing in the newspaper. In many cases the goods are in the hands of dealers. Certainly they should be. There is a serious question whether any one in the dealer's store, excepting the dealer himself, knows that the goods are there. We know of cases where the dealer was unaware that the advertised product was in his storeroom. We then have the situation that (1) the product may not even be distributed; (2) it may not be known to the clerks; (3) it may not be known to the dealer; (4) it probably is not displayed in the dealer's store.

"Contrast the two opportunities for results from newspaper advertising. With the department store they are almost 100 per cent. perfect. With the foreign advertiser they may be almost 100 per cent. imperfect.

"Now you may say that this is no business of the newspaper publisher. You may say that this is no concern of any one but the foreign advertiser.

"Well enough if you are prepared to do without the revenue that can be yours for reaching out a reasonably helping hand.

"This 'helping hand,' as stated in our definition, does not mean selling goods.

"The fact to be looked in the face is that in successful advertising the Consumer, the Salesman, and the Dealer are of almost equal importance. It is not enough that advertising reaches the maximum number of consumers in any locality.

"The dealer must be in a position to supply the goods when they are demanded, and he must be in the frame of mind to offer the goods to the willing consumer. He must do justice to the product in store or window display. His clerks have to show a reasonable interest in the requirements of the consumer for the product advertised. In turn the salesman who places the product with the dealer must make use of the advertising as one of the reasons for the sale. He must be reasonably interested or enthusiastic, and for him to work with sustained interest and enthusiasm he must find the dealer reasonably approachable on the subject of the advertised product.

"The newspaper publisher may perhaps feel that this concerns the manufacturer; that it does not concern the publisher. The answer is that advertising does not grow on barren ground. If the dealer resists advertised products, as thousands do, there is a handicap placed on the advertising that almost neutralizes its value.

"Whether we like it or not, we must realize that in every locality there are dozens of good dealers who take a very unfriendly attitude toward advertising and advertised goods. We may not be able to know just why this is. But I personally believe it is because advertising has always been presented to the dealer as something that would 'force a tremendous demand.' There have been countless circulars sent to dealers telling the story of advertising, all emphasizing the crushing power of the demand that the advertising would produce. Writers of circulars have for years gone on without restraint talking about what advertising would do in creating consumer demand. No one has stopped them, until the advertising world realized that the old formula of talking to the dealer about advertising would no longer serve the purpose.

"This is because the predictions of demand do not always come true. In fact, they very seldom come true in the manner outlined in the various statements that have been made to dealers.

"This was the condition that brought about the principle of 'Consumer Acceptance,' which was the combined work of Mr. H. J. Winsten, sales manager of Black Cat Hosiery; Mr. William Laughlin, advertising manager of Armour & Co., and Mallory, Mitchell & Faust.

"In a nutshell, the principle of Consumer Acceptance is that advertising produces two kinds of results —one is positive demand on the dealer; the other is willingness on the part of the consumer to accept certain products when the dealer offers them. This has been covered in articles in *The Armour Magazine*, and specifically in one discussion, by Mr. Forrest Crissey, in *Printers' Ink*, May 18 issue of this year.

"Hereafter in talking to the dealer about advertising we must tell the dealer the plain, unvarnished facts. Because the dealer must always be the important factor in the final distribution of the advertised product to the consumer.

"We have found with letters and circulars which have covered the point of Consumer Demand and Consumer Acceptance that the dealer welcomes this new idea. It is therefore easy to predict that it will be but a question of time until the words 'Consumer Demand' almost pass out of the advertising language, and when advertising campaigns are submitted to the dealer they will be presented with a full recognition of the fact that advertising does not create stampedes, nor work miracles, but performs its benefits in a very understandable, non-mysterious manner.

"In the mean time, however, the dealer must be educated to the proper appreciation and the proper view of advertising and its results. When we say 'dealer' we mean all dealers — grocers, meat markets, dry-goods stores, department stores, furniture stores, drug stores, bakeries, and so on.

"If these dealers are brought to the proper recognition of advertising, they will take a much more friendly and receptive attitude toward advertised goods. Incidentally, they will do a great deal more local newspaper advertising.

"But we can put this down as Rule No. 1: In towns where the newspapers have educated the dealers to the real significance of advertising in the newspaper, it is a simplified matter for the foreign advertiser to get distribution, to get window displays, store displays, and finally results. Where the newspaper publisher is hard-headed and refuses to believe that the education of the dealer is vital to himself first, to the foreign advertiser second, it is difficult for the foreign representatives of the newspaper to sell advertising space.

"Item No. 1, then, in newspaper co-operation, is bringing the dealers in the newspaper's locality to a proper appreciation of advertising. This will benefit all foreign advertisers. But it will, first of all, benefit the newspaper publisher.

BUILDING NEWSPAPER ADVERTISING

"We find in observing a great many localities that the art of store arrangement, store trimming, and window decoration is too little understood or appreciated by dealers. Following the education of the dealer to the value of advertising will come greater activity on the dealer's part in scientific or sales-making window and store trims.

"All the contests and advertised product weeks and food shows and similar undertakings are working great good in this direction, and there can hardly be any co-operation developed or extended by the newspaper of more practical aid to the foreign advertiser.

"Item No. 2, therefore, in newspaper co-operation, is to get the dealers to trim their windows, arrange their stocks and make store displays in co-ordination with newspaper advertising.

"Then there comes the question of the manufacturer's and the jobber's salesmen. These men, in many cases, are hard to reach, hard to get the newspaper message to. But it is important that the manufacturer's salesmen receive from the newspaper complete information about the scope, power, and peculiar values of the newspaper the advertiser is using. We would go so far as to say that a newspaper can do no greater good for itself than to get the advertiser in the foreign field using their newspaper, and at least once—better still, regularly—tell the story of the newspaper to these men. This is because some manufacturers, in taking up advertising, have to depend upon veteran salesmen to co-operate with the advertising, and often they are men entirely unused to advertising, its value and its real utility to the salesman. If such a man is properly coached in the value of the newspaper and the leverage it can be in holding old dealers, selling them large stocks and in getting new accounts, that salesman becomes an earnest booster for advertising and for newspaper advertising.

"If the salesman does not use the advertising, he ceases to study it, he loses interest in it, and it is but another step to active opposition to newspaper publicity.

"Who, then, would benefit most by teaching the salesman how to utilize the newspaper campaign? On the one hand, if the salesman is trained to use it, the business is insured perpetually for the newspaper. If the salesman is not trained to utilize it, in time the advertising must become a questionable value to the salesman and finally to the manufacturer, who gets much of his impression from the men in the field.

"Item No. 3 in co-operation, therefore, becomes the practical education of the salesman in the newspaper's territory to the utilization of the newspaper advertising.

"Finally we come to the consumer. There are available all kinds of records of traced-result advertising to prove that where a written response is expected from the consumer, publications with text kindred to the article advertised produce the greatest measure of returns as a rule. That is to say, there are a great many different class publications in which class advertising will pull extremely well. This has been demonstrated over a period of years, by inquiries and sales, whether the sale is finally made by correspondence or through a retail dealer.

"To illustrate: You can advertise wearing apparel in publications having authoritative fashion departments and secure a remarkable result for the readers in definite inquiries, all because the reader has been

BUILDING NEWSPAPER ADVERTISING 365

educated to the fashion viewpoint. There are a number of publications that pay particular attention to houses and house-furnishings, and without exception these produce remarkable responses for building-material and house-furnishing advertisers. They are the regulation household journals. But because they have aroused the readers' interest in houses and house interiors, the readers of those publications are peculiarly responsive.

"A number of journals have given special attention to foods. So that any kind of attractive mail offer in connection with food-product advertising will show immediate expression of interest by traced-result responses from the readers of these publications.

"We perhaps have not yet analyzed the full significance of all this, but it goes to show that as you educate the consumer you stimulate the consumer responsiveness to advertised goods.

"The magazines have found this a very legitimate thing to do. In fact, as a class, the most successful publications to-day have made a business of so departmentizing their text as to pay the maximum attention to the diverse household interests—particularly of the woman.

"It is not out of place to repeat the comment of a newspaper-man that the lack of attention to household interests by newspapers made the opportunity for this specialization work, editorially, by the magazines.

"The final result to the advertiser is that the advertiser of wearing apparel, building material, fashion goods, food products, and furnishings can very accurately judge in advance the productiveness of a periodical by the character of its text. The result is that the kind of text a magazine publishes, which is determined entirely by the editorial department, becomes one of the selling resources of the advertising department.

"At our office we receive regularly from various magazines most interesting analyses of their text pages to indicate their particular fitness for various accounts we may be handling.

"While we believe that this material of a strictly household nature must be published by newspapers, if they are to have the keenest interest of their women readers, we are not willing to debate this point. We only bring it before you for consideration. We do know that a number of newspapers have made great successes of special departments, enabling them to build up, first of all, a wide reader interest in these special text pages, and finally to utilize this reader interest in creating and holding highly desirable special advertising.

"I think, for example, Mr. Owen Moon, and his associates of *The Trenton* (N. J.) *Times*, would say that the editorial department of food matter is one of the best subscription winners *The Trenton Times* ever used.

"We know that this daily has four women editors who produce food pages and household pages of highest merit and broad scope. Mr. Moon feels that these household and food pages have been most effective in circulation building. We may or may not consider it incidental to this that *The Trenton Times* publishes a half-million lines of food advertising per year. One thing is sure—that after the food text has been published for a considerable time in *The Trenton Times*, it was very easy for *The Trenton Times* to get profitable advertising from local stores and from foreign advertisers and carry a three to five-page food section on a light day each week. The test is that when a foreign advertiser goes into Trenton he finds the dealers of Trenton in the frame of mind to place the advertised products in stock; so that the text pages of *The Trenton Times* devoted to household and food interest ultimately have a bearing on the success of the advertiser. And that is what concerns our company.

"If the publisher of a newspaper elects to disregard the woman reader, to carry no household departments, to carry no fashion or food pages, we have no quarrel with him. But we do say, that if the newspaper publisher desires to compete for advertising it is fundamentally necessary for the newspaper to help put his readers in a sufficiently responsive frame of mind so that the advertiser can use the paper efficiently.

"This cannot be construed in any degree as an argument for illegitimate text; that is, text that is not, first of all, of definite news interest to women readers.

"We can put this down as a fact, I think, that if a newspaper expects to pay the specialized advertisers over a long period of time, it is absolutely necessary to pay some attention to the frame of mind of the newspaper audience toward that class of product. This is true of foreign advertising or local advertising. It is true of investment publicity, or advertising for automobiles, fashion goods, wearing apparel, food products, household appliances, and so on.

"This is not to be taken as an argument that the newspaper shall assume magazine proportions or that it shall publish every day this magazine-like material,

Neither is it intended that all such material shall be assembled in a gigantic issue, publishing such features only on Sunday. There is a middle ground which will enable the newspaper to publish material of maximum interest to the woman, and when a newspaper arrives at this point of view it is not difficult to analyze the feminine or household interest, based on income and the percentage of the income that goes for various lines.

"If a quarter of the income goes for wearing-apparel products, it is evident that this is of great interest to the home. If 50 per cent. of the average income goes for foods, then food products can be seen to be a very live issue. If 10 per cent. of the income goes for furniture and house-furnishings, it is reasonable to believe that these items are entitled to editorial attention, so that the reader may be guided, counseled, and given very much desired information on the subject.

"As the newspaper is developing to-day, it seems inevitable that it cannot be a purveyor of news of happenings only. As the newspapers reach the point of view that departmentized text matter is desirable, they will perform co-operation of the utmost value to the foreign advertiser, because the newspaper will then be educating the market, which, when it falls entirely upon the advertiser, is an expense that makes newspaper advertising practically prohibitive.

"In this connection it is interesting to note that an analysis of the text of some of the leading woman's magazines reveals the following percentages devoted to various topics:

"Thirteen per cent. of *The Ladies' Home Journal* text pages in 1915 was devoted to fashion; 33 per cent. of

The Delineator was devoted to fashion; 29 per cent. of *The Pictorial Review* was given to fashion, and 14 per cent. of *The Woman's Home Companion.*

"Eight per cent. of *The Ladies' Home Journal* was devoted to cooking and household items; 9 per cent. of *The Delineator;* 6 per cent. of *The Pictorial Review;* 6 per cent. of *The Woman's Home Companion; McCall's Magazine* devoted 7.3 per cent. to menus and recipes, 11 per cent. to household items, such as building and remodeling, furnishing and decorating, labor-saving devices, and so on. *McCall's* devoted 32.9 per cent. to personal appearance, 6 per cent. to embroidery and fancy-work, 25 per cent. to fiction.

"*Good Housekeeping*, a magazine of wide interest to women, published in 1915 enough material to make 528 pages of a standard size book on the care of children and raising the family. *Good Housekeeping* published enough material to make a standard size book of 358 pages on foods and their preparation, a book of 260 pages on building material and houses, a book of 234 pages on wearing apparel. This material was supplied the reader at from eight to twenty-two pages per month and is an interesting commentary on the amount of text that can be originated and assembled for a discriminating woman audience in one year.

"*The Chicago Tribune* in the past year published text in departments as follows: Fashions—344 columns daily, 520 columns Sunday; Foods—173 columns daily, 80 columns Sunday; Automobiles—173 columns daily, 272 columns Sunday; Financial—3,300 columns daily, 632 columns Sunday; Real Estate—1,058 columns daily, 390 columns Sunday.

"Many other publications offer interesting figures for the observation of the newspaper publishers.

"Many of these woman's and household magazines have achieved extraordinary successes for their owners in recent years and they have produced startling results for advertisers. They offer, therefore, something for the consideration of both the editor and the advertising manager of the daily paper.

"To repeat, co-operation with the advertiser is service to the advertiser. The word 'co-operation' cannot be frowned upon or put aside because many newspaper publishers profess to misunderstand it. As we have stated throughout this discussion, service to the advertiser is desirable, primarily in the newspaper publisher's own interest. And if the newspaper publisher is to render service, it is well to look about him and see what other publishers are doing to aid the advertisers to succeed to find what these other publishers are doing to help the same advertiser that the newspaper's representative is looking to for business.

"Do newspaper publishers find that service to the foreign advertiser is profitable to the newspaper? We suggest that you ask Mr. R. H. Cornell, of *The Houston Chronicle;* Mr. Henry Doorly, of *The Omaha World-Herald;* Mr. C. C. Rosewater, of *The Omaha Bee;* Mr. Clarence J. Pyle, of *The Wilmington* (Del.) *Journal;* Mr. E. L. Clifford, of *The Minneapolis Journal;* Mr. Owen Moon, of *The Trenton Times;* Mr. L. B. Tobin, of *The Lincoln Star;* Mr. W. A. Elliott, of *The Jacksonville Times-Union;* Mr. George F. Booth, of *The Worcester Gazette;* Mr. Charles S. Diehl, of *The San Antonio Light;* Mr. Clayton P. Chamberlin, of *The Hartford Times;* Mr. J. S. Mapes, of *The Beaumont Enterprise;* Mr. Harvey R. Young, of *The Columbus Dispatch;* Mr.

M. B. Reed, of *The Bangor News;* Mr. John D. Plummer, of *The Springfield Union;* Mr. W. L. Williams, of *The St. Paul Dispatch;* Mr. Fred H. Drinkwater, of *The Portland Express and Advertiser;* Mr. H. C. Rugg, of *The Fitchburg Sentinel;* Mr. Hugh B. Kennedy, of *The New Haven Register*, and Mr. H. H. Horton, of *The Muskogee Phœnix.*

"There are scores of other live wires who have seen the opportunity for themselves, to the foreign advertiser and in making earnings by giving this co-operating or merchandizing service.

"Right here we want to acknowledge the inspiration as well as the co-operation we have secured from our contact with the many advanced thinkers and real reformers we have found in the newspaper and special representatives' ranks. It is that spirit which is making such a record for newspaper advertising as to make advertisers, advertising managers, and advertising agents keen to place business with the newspapers where they know it will surely win.

"We can profitably consider the case of The Curtis Publishing Company. We select them, believing that they typify high ideals and practical common sense and combine both with a phenomenal record of success for their owners and with readers and advertisers. The Curtis Publishing Company has believed that the success of the advertiser depends to a large measure on exact information which provides accurate guidance of advertising and sales plans. To that end, The Curtis Publishing Company has organized and financed a department of Commercial Research, which has been, from the first, under the supervision of Professor C. C. Parlin, who has come to be recognized as not only an expert investigator, but as a man whose deductions from his investigations have been turned into reports that may be considered almost text-books, because they are so highly authoritative in the lines treated upon.

"In The Curtis Publishing Company's Commercial Research Department there are a number of experienced investigators who have traveled in practically every country in the United States, getting accurate data on jobbing, retail, and consumer conditions. In a word, The Curtis Publishing Company has endeavored to analyze the market for manufacturers as no one has done it—even the manufacturers.

"As a result, when important advertising campaigns are under consideration, this market information is submitted to the advertiser in such concrete and accurate shape as to often absolutely determine the manufacturer in his publicity plans.

"Furthermore, the speakers of the Commercial Research Department have met with scores of sales organizations to lay facts before them and to enthuse them to the true possibilities of the plans in hand.

"The Curtis Publishing Company has not stopped in its duty to itself or to the advertiser or to the advertising agent on questions of ethics or expense. Instead The Curtis Publishing Company has been a great influence in standardizing advertising procedure, dignifying advertising and putting it on a solid basis.

"Many other publishers are working along the same highly organized and scientific lines. We have had instances where publishers have placed in our hands information on trade conditions that has insured the success of campaigns and perpetuated business that must otherwise have failed.

"Furthermore, the work of magazine publishers in

arousing in dealers, salesmen, and clerks a proper appreciation of advertising and advertised products, has been of incalculable value. This has not only been undertaken, but it has been continued for many years persistently and systematically.

"We do not mention magazine advertisers here to be an irritation to newspaper publishers, but because there exists for a fact a service to advertisers that must have the cognizance of many newspaper publishers who are lagging.

"In these days of newspaper associations there is opportunity for organized effort that means a great deal for the future of advertising in daily papers. Advertisers now know that through the Audit Bureau of Circulations they can buy definite value. They can get circulations analyzed accurately and dependably, so that they can plan sales scientifically both in the town of publication and in surrounding territory. Service of this character is in itself most practical co-operation.

"In our opinion, if it is in order here, we feel that such auditing has put newspaper advertising on a definite basis of purchase, and has given the foreign advertiser such confidence in circulation and rates as to have made one of the most significant steps in recent newspaper advertising developments.

"When rates for foreign advertising are standardized on a par with local advertising, it is our opinion that this will also be a point of radical improvement.

"In summarizing our view of newspaper co-operation, our merchandizing experience with a number of advertisers is that the newspaper publisher has it in his power to assure the success of the foreign advertiser through making ready and keeping normal his local market. This calls for education of the consumer, the dealer, and the education and stimulation of the sales force that places the goods in the newspaper territory.

"Furthermore, there must be forthcoming from the territory of the newspaper accurate information on distribution, market conditions, progress of sales work, that will enable the advertiser to know exactly what considerations affected the inauguration and progress of the advertising campaign.

"It is, in our opinion, within the province of the newspaper, in its own interest and that of the advertiser, to manage this. It goes without saying that when the newspaper can show that the market it covers is in cultivated shape for the invasion of the advertiser, it makes much more effective the work of its own foreign representative and all advertising agents.

"Perhaps in time it may be necessary to adjust advertising rates so that co-operation with the local advertiser and the foreign advertiser shall be included as a customary performance.

"One thing, in conclusion, we recommend to the consideration of newspaper publishers, is that advertising is seldom bought for publicity value alone. Certainly our company sells advertising for its merchandizing value, which is its value as an aid to selling—its value as an aid in getting the product from the factory to the consumer. If the newspaper publisher realizes that the foreign advertiser regards the newspaper strictly as a merchandizing medium, then service and co-operation become part of the regular business of the newspaper. When this merchandizing service or co-operation is scientifically or-

BUILDING NEWSPAPER ADVERTISING

ganized, it will be found to be, not an expense, not a drain upon the resources of the newspaper, but it will be found to reduce selling expense, entrench the newspaper with its readers, dealers, and local and foreign advertisers, and, in the final analysis, increase the newspaper's value to its owners, readers, and advertisers."

LVI

The National Agency.—H. K. McCann

WRITING from the viewpoint of a national agency, it would be hard to exaggerate the value of genuine, consistent co-operation between newspapers and agencies. It is gratifying, too, to look back, even over the space of a few years, and note how this spirit of co-operation has grown. There still remains, however, much that newspapers and agencies in general can do for one another to promote the prosperity of advertising, and we may be able to see a little more clearly how fundamental is this community of interest if we first examine a little more closely just where the agency really stands in the scheme of things.

At first glance it may seem to the newspaper publisher that most of this co-operation, of which the agency men seem so fond of speaking, is on his side, as if it were an excuse for asking him to do more, and more, and more. He is apt to regard the agent merely as a buyer of his space, who is always trying to drive a close bargain. Would his feeling in the matter change if he came to consider the agent, not as the buyer of his space, but the man who sells his space for him?

From that point of view the agent who asks co-operation is not simply trying to get something for

H. K. McCANN

President, H. K. McCann Advertising Agency, New York, who won his spurs as advertising manager of the New York Telephone Company and the Standard Oil Company.

nothing. He is trying to develop easier and surer ways of selling the newspaper's advertising space.

To the publishers of a paper a thousand miles away from the agency headquarters, no less than to that publisher's local representative, who goes directly after the business, the agent comes to seem the closefisted guardian of an appropriation which he hoards as jealously as a miser from those who try to get space orders from him.

As a matter of fact, in first getting an appropriation, the agent was himself selling space. And on what basis did he have to sell it? Advertisers are shrewder buyers of space than they were some years ago. They do not buy "blue sky" any more, neither does the high-class modern agency think of trying to sell it to them.

When the agency man goes to an advertiser and asks for a newspaper appropriation, the advertiser at once asks back, "What do I get?" And it soon becomes apparent that he expects to get something more than a list of papers with their circulations and rates.

What, then, is the big thing that the newspaper can offer? Direct local influence, of course; wider distribution; more intensive sales activity. But the advertiser still asks for proof of this, and the agency comes direct to the point where it has to produce that proof in the form of newspaper co-operation in order to sell that newspaper space.

What, then, does the agency need from the paper, and for what is it entitled to ask? In the first place, the agency should be fortified with a thorough appreciation of the commercial possibilities of any given town through the accumulation of statistical matter, which gives a fair and comprehensive view of wholesale and retail trading conditions in a community, the buying power and characteristic needs and tastes of the community, and all information on the policies of local trade associations which might affect distribution and sales.

Such definite information as the number of drug or grocery stores in a town, their approximate ratings (as an index of the volume of trade they command), is most helpful. This enables the agent to put before the advertiser a definite picture of the opportunities which that town offers, and to convince him that it is a field which is worth cultivation.

The editorial policy of a paper, the class of readers it reaches, and the confidence which the editorial columns inspire in the advertising columns, are also points of great value. While politics, local or national, are no concern whatever of the agency, broad ethics are questions which involve and determine the class of readers the paper reaches, their mental attitude and receptivity. This brings in very definitely the question of the censoring of the advertising columns, the elimination of all objectionable matter and of all extravagant or misleading claims. A paper, whose readers have learned by sad experience to discount all they read in its advertising columns, has not a great deal to offer the foreign advertiser who comes in with a straightforward, honest story, and has not yet had an opportunity to build up a personal confidence in his product.

This brings us directly to the question of dealer influence and the promotion of dealer good-will for the advertiser. As a matter of general policy, a paper should keep the dealers within its circulating radius thoroughly sold on the value of its advertising space. Some employ service men who call on the dealers, not primarily to solicit business, but to keep these dealers always convinced of the demand-creating power of the paper's columns. They strive to get the dealer's assistance in making an advertising campaign a success, something which is really to their mutual advantage. The dealer can be induced to give prominent display to the goods during the run of the campaign, to use window displays or counter cut-outs, and to instruct his clerks to get behind the campaign and push the goods, and so cash in on the advertising.

In some cases newspapers have been of the very greatest assistance in actually helping distribution, advising dealers of the campaign that is to be launched, and persuading them to stock the goods in anticipation of it. This does not mean so much that the paper is asked to go out and sell the goods as that, for its own sake, it should insure against the advertising being a failure. If the campaign is launched, and the dealers, not being stocked, cannot meet the demand that arises, the story soon spreads itself on the manufacturer's sales sheets back home, and the paper is tagged as "not pulling" and the community as "dead."

Co-operation of this kind should not be asked too freely, and cannot fairly be asked at all unless a substantial advertising contract goes with the request. But it does sometimes happen that a national campaign is launched of such a scope that it is impossible for the manufacturer's salesmen to cover all the ground—all points—at once, and the whole success of the campaign, which means the continuance or the withholding of subsequent campaigns, may depend on the extent to which the newspapers do this work.

The manufacturer's argument is simple. "I am told," he says, "that advertising in this paper will induce the dealer to stock my goods and the public to buy them. If the paper has not enough influence with the dealer to stock in advance on the strength of the advertising, what reason have I to suppose the advertising alone will ever do it?"

Where salesmen do make a town there are many ways in which the local papers may be of help to them. If the salesman is a stranger, he may be saved much time and labor by a little advice on his routing, the layout of the town, how he can arrange his calls in a more or less straight line, and take most advantage of the existing transit facilities. Letters of introduction to particular dealers of prominence, calling attention to the advertising that is running, or planned, and expressing confidence alike in the goods and in the power of the paper itself to move them, are often very helpful.

Here, again, where a paper employs service men for such work, they can be tremendously helpful in calling on dealers, either with or without the manufacturer's salesmen, and working for the installation of the window and counter displays.

It often happens that there are certain conditions in a town which call for special treatment in advertising or merchandizing a product, and in these cases, too, service men can be very helpful in that they have at their fingers' ends information which it might take a salesman several trips to accumulate and digest.

Some papers have regular show windows in their

offices, just like the show windows of large department stores, and in these, while an advertising campaign is running, the publisher will set up a display, either of his own or of the advertiser's manufacture, showing the article being advertised, and calling attention to the notices of it in his paper. There are, however, comparatively few newspaper offices so located or constructed that they can do this, and warmly as an advertiser would appreciate such co-operation, he would hardly feel justified in asking for it.

The main point is that all such work as has been suggested in the foregoing is of very direct and definite help to the agent, not only in selling a particular paper or a particular campaign, but in making the manufacturer a consistent and confident user of newspaper space in future campaigns. The agent and the newspapers are, after all, on the same side of the fence—both interested in the development of advertising—and when the agent asks for co-operation he is showing the publisher easier ways of selling space, or surer methods of selling more space, and not simply trying to make the publisher work extra hard for his money.

LVII

The Vital Things.—John Lee Mahin

JOHN LEE MAHIN, a man whose reputation as a successful advertising expert extends throughout the country, has for years been a strong advocate of close co-operation between the buyer and seller of advertising and is entitled to speak as an authority.

He built up a big agency business in Chicago, which he sold and came to New York seeking wider fields, and finally became associated with Mr. Tinsman in the Federal Advertising Agency. Mr. Mahin has written several important books on advertising and is always read with interest.

What Mr. Mahin says on the subject:

"The most vital thing that a newspaper publisher can do to help advertising agencies create new advertisers for newspapers is to understand what a creative advertising agency is.

"Mr. Jason Rogers's purpose in publishing this book commands the most hearty co-operation of every advertising agency, because it is a long step forward in that direction.

"Mr. Robert Tinsman's article in this book is the most comprehensive presentation of the functions of the modern creative agency that it has ever been my pleasure to read.

JOHN LEE MAHIN
Now a Director of the Federal Advertising Agency of New York and for years identified with advertising at Chicago.

BUILDING NEWSPAPER ADVERTISING 383

"The next most vital thing that every newspaper publisher can do is to equip himself to furnish, at a moment's notice, up-to-date information regarding the field he covers.

"If, in addition to the population, occupation, earning power, manufacturing and agricultural statistics furnished by the United States Census Bureau, the publishers could give lists of dealers engaged in various kinds of business, together with their addresses, commercial ratings, and the name of the man who in each instance is interested in pushing well-advertised goods, he would indeed perform a great service.

"A publisher must remember that no advertiser can afford to use space in his paper unless adequate distribution can be secured. To get this distribution now often requires the services of expensive specialty salesmen, who are hard to get, costly to train, and who must work hard and fast in order to pay their way.

"I have worked with a number of newspaper publishers in various try-out campaigns, and all agree with me that a publisher's trying to sell the advertiser's goods to the merchant is a mistake. It gives both the advertiser and the merchant the wrong idea about advertising. Goods should be sold because of their merit, and not because they are advertised.

"If the advertising increases the cost of the goods to the final consumer, it is in a precarious condition, and is certainly not worthy of the same kind of coöperation on the part of publisher and agency as advertising which reduces the *cost of distribution* by increasing the volume of sales and stabilizing market conditions.

"Advertising which is done on goods handled by

only one dealer in the territory where the newspaper circulates is not worthy of much co-operation on the publisher's part. It usually results in the dealer's asking for the control of the advertising—taking it out of the agency's hands—and frequently the appropriation is not spent in the newspapers at all, but in the many catchpenny schemes which are daily presented to retailers everywhere. The advertising that means most to the publisher is that which is put back of goods on which universal distribution is sought and exclusive selling arrangements are refused.

"The department stores of the United States do less than 5 per cent. of the total business in the lines which they handle. The small specialty shops, the neighborhood grocery, the drug store, the retail jewelry shop, the hardware store, the lumber yard, the paint store, the haberdashery, the millinery parlor, the news-stand, the cigar store, the lunch counter, and the house-to-house canvassers do the other 95 per cent. The mail-order house may get a little of this business, but certainly less than the department store.

"The biggest problem confronting the general advertiser is to show these small shopkeepers—who rarely do or could advertise in the newspapers—how to cash in on the advertising which appears in the daily newspapers that they themselves read. The newspaper publisher who can make these small retailers feel that the general advertising appearing in his paper is the *dealer's own advertising*—if he uses it —will be rendering a great service to advertisers and dealers, and certainly to newspaper publishers.

"Right here it is advisable to emphasize an error that some publishers have made in urging dealers to handle advertised goods. They have told the dealers *that the advertising will sell the goods.* This is one of those 'partly true' statements that do much more harm than good.

"For every sale made for an indifferent dealer by advertising at least twenty sales—which the advertiser has started and carried along at least half-way—can be made by the dealers who display, push, and enthusiastically get back of the goods advertised.

"Two of my clients have positively forbidden my asking publishers to call on dealers with reference to the goods advertised in their columns. One manufacturer said that the publishers talked too much about the advertising, and knew nothing of the intrinsic worth of the goods themselves, giving the dealers the impression that it was advertising rather than quality that the goods represented.

"Both these advertisers duly appreciate the newspaper-man's knowledge of their respective fields, and now instruct their salesmen to call upon the publisher whenever confidential information with regard to an obdurate dealer is desired.

"Publishers can and should refuse to permit any cut-price dealer to offer goods at cut prices when these same goods are advertised on a quality basis in their columns. They should insist on this for their own sakes, because cutting prices on staples is the surest way of curbing sales with dealers who make a legitimate profit.

"If a publisher is in a position to make an adequate, intelligent canvass of goods already distributed in his section, on which no advertising in his paper is being done, he can often start advertising under the most favorable auspices.

"In making such a canvass he should be careful to have the information gathered by men who will not ask the dealer leading questions, or suggest the kind of answer desired. Most advertisers are of the opinion that dealers favor the publisher in answering such questions, and particular care should be taken that these questions are framed and asked in the same way in each store. Also, the correct name and address of each dealer should be given, whether the proprietor or clerk answered the questions, and the kind of trade to which the store caters—high-class, medium or low-wage earners.

"A good method of approach is as follows: 'I am not going to buy or sell you anything, but will greatly appreciate a little information which I am sure you can give me.' Then questions like these might be asked:

(1) What is your leading laundry soap, washing-powder, cleanser, roofing, grape juice, etc.?
(2) What sells second, third, fourth, etc.?
(3) What prices do you get for each?
(4) Is the trade on —— increasing?
(5) How much do you sell weekly now?
(6) How much more do you think you could sell if the manufacturer would put an advertising campaign in the (name your paper)?

"A canvass with short, terse answers to questions like these (all alike to each store), arranged in logical and convenient form, would be welcomed by practically every manufacturer.

"Free publicity is not desired by the best advertisers or by creative agencies, but it will be asked for and expected as long as it is granted at all. On the other hand, articles which tend to build up the idea of sound merchandizing, and to teach what a well-advertised trade-mark represents, must always be regarded as a beneficial and desirable form of publishers' co-operation.

"There are many existent things that agents would like to see changed, but they are of minor importance when compared to the great general purpose of developing only such advertising as permanently benefits the readers of the newspaper, which, consequently, must be the best kind of advertising when considered from the selfish standpoint of both newspaper publisher and the creative advertising agency."

LVIII

Cost of Space in Newspaper Campaigns.— *William H. Rankin*

WILLIAM H. RANKIN, president of the W. H. Rankin Advertising Agency, Chicago, presented a most interesting and instructive consideration of the cost of space in newspaper campaigns at the San Francisco Convention of the Associated Advertising Club in July, 1918.

Mr. Rankin bought out the Mahin Advertising Agency, and with his associate, Wilbur D. Nesbit, has been performing big successful feats in exploitation of business through advertising.

The work of Messrs. Rankin and Nesbit in Chicago for the Red Cross and Liberty Loans was the best and most effective in the country, and was ultimately adopted and duplicated in many other cities.

Here is Mr. Rankin's wonderful presentation reprinted from *Printers' Ink:*

"The volume of newspaper advertising will be increased as those who sell advertising and those who use it learn more about its value. The local advertisers—department stores and purely local producers and dealers—know its value and economy. Lots of them, however, in my estimation, do not

BUILDING NEWSPAPER ADVERTISING

know its full value, but simply use their local newspapers because they have no other way of reaching the people and feel that they must advertise.

"Too many advertisers look at the cost per page or per insertion and never get far enough along to analyze what they buy when they buy newspaper space. Generally they conclude: 'Newspaper advertising is expensive. If we have to use it, let's use it sparingly.'

"There are exceptions to this. These exceptions are the most successful business men in any community, and the most successful distributers of nationally known products.

"The department stores know what newspaper space is worth to them, and that is why you see them using full pages and double pages right along. They know that the impressiveness of a full page compared to small space is just the difference between a public meeting and an individual visit.

"Recently I had the opportunity to analyze the cost of newspaper advertising for one of the big governmental departments in Washington. I have always felt that I was fairly well posted on what newspaper space means, and have always sold it enthusiastically—but I was surprised at the facts and figures and the sales points the analysis brought out. I found that a quarter page in every newspaper in the country—dailies, weeklies, bi-weeklies, and tri-weeklies, could be bought for less than $200,000. This gives a circulation of over 46,000,000—or about two copies to every home in the whole United States.

"Think that over. This means reaching 92,000,000 homes twice with every dollar spent, or a cost of seven-tenths of a cent for carrying your message twice to every home in the land.

"Here are some more vitally interesting figures:

"I found the advertising rate in newspapers like *The Chicago Daily News*, $1,200; *The Chicago Sunday Tribune*, $971,29, and *The New York Times*, $829.12, and per page per home delivery—*Chicago News*, less than three-tenths of a cent; *Chicago Sunday Tribune*, 159 thousandths of a cent, and *The New York Times*, 201 thousandths of a cent.

ECONOMY IN THE SERVICE

"I found that these newspapers pay their delivery boys more for delivering each paper into a home than they charge the advertiser for furnishing the white paper, setting the type and printing and delivering the advertiser's full page into each home. That if the advertiser should attempt to print a one-page advertising dodger the white paper alone would cost almost as much as the newspapers charge for a full-page advertisement in a newspaper that the publishers pay thousands of dollars per day to the best editorial news writers and war correspondents—to edit.

"Take, for instance, *The Chicago Daily News:* Victor F. Lawson has spent forty years of his life building up the prestige, character, and standing of *The News*—as a result over 400,000 families in the city of Chicago take *The Daily News* because of its dependability and because they know they can believe what they read in both the news and the advertising columns of *The News*.

"Mr. Lawson has spent over $25,000,000 in building up *The Chicago Daily News*, and has gained the confidence of *The News* readers—and yet every advertiser who uses *The News* can buy that good-will for

BUILDING NEWSPAPER ADVERTISING 391

his product when he advertises in *The Daily News*—all he has to pay for is the space, the white paper, the printing, and the delivery of his page is less than three-tenths of a cent per page per home.

"Can you imagine anywhere you can get as much for so little money?—and what is true of *The News* is true of *The San Francisco Examiner, Bulletin, Call, News*, and *Chronicle*, and of nearly every newspaper in the United States.

"But how many of us have used these arguments to help us increase the volume of newspaper advertising?

"It took the war to bring out forcibly to the government, the business man, the banker, and the advertiser the full value, force and dominance of the full-page ad. in the daily newspaper.

"There have been more full-page advertisements in newspapers during the past year than any previous three years—used to promote the Red Cross, the Liberty Loans, the Y. M. C. A., Smileage, K. of C., W. S. S., and every war activity.

"Frank R. Wilson, advertising director of the Liberty Loan, Washington, has just sent out a letter from which I quote:

"'Display advertising space contributed by merchants and publications throughout the United States has become one of the most important avenues for the dissemination of government appeals to buy Liberty Bonds.

"'During the first, second, and third Liberty Loan campaigns these contributions of advertising space amounted to millions of dollars. Practically every publication in the United States carried many of these advertisements urging the people to buy bonds.'

"This is certainly a strong indorsement of what advertising men at the St. Louis convention have done at that.

CHICAGO'S RED CROSS RECORD AN ENVIABLE ONE

"I had the great privilege to tell you of the pioneer Red Cross campaign and to exhibit the forty-two full pages that made it possible for Chicago to increase its Red Cross memberships from 17,000 to 416,000 in four weeks' time. The total cost for all expenses was 7½ cents per member—compared with the best previous record (made without newspaper advertising) of 16 cents per member; thus proving for all time to come that advertising is an economy and not an expense when properly used, and that advertising lowers the cost of distribution.

"You will remember, too, that your newspaper-men took this same plan and used it in nearly every city and town in the United States—to awaken your people to their responsibilities in this war and to show them why they should buy Liberty Bonds, support the Red Cross, Y. M. C. A., W. S. S., K. of C., etc. As a result of that great convention in St. Louis over $5,000,000 worth of newspaper advertising has been bought and paid for by business men, bankers, and others and at least a like amount has been bought and paid for by the same patriotic business men in magazines, farm papers, trade papers, billboard and painted signs.

"These men realized the necessity to the government of dominant advertising, and because of their faith and confidence in advertising they went down into their own pockets and paid cash for this adver-

BUILDING NEWSPAPER ADVERTISING

tising space and cheerfully did so for their country to help *win the war*.

"And to the members of the Associated Advertising Clubs of the World belongs the credit for making these men realize the great value of full-page newspaper advertisements to mold public opinion and bring about results and sales never before realized in all the world's history. To show you the small cost for the results obtained I quote from *The Washington Star:*

"'Only 65/1000 of 1 per cent. was the Percentage of Cost of Advertising.

"'$23,050,550 worth of bonds were sold. $20,000,000 was Washington's maximum allotment.

"'3,050,550 was the amount Washington exceeded its allotment; 84,388 were individual subscribers.

"'$15,000 was the total amount spent for advertising.

"'Newspaper advertising is the dynamic force that helped the bankers and business men of Washington make the Second Liberty Loan a tremendous success. This was only made possible by the wonderful work done by the Liberty Loan Committee of Washington and the hundred or more volunteer speakers and workers drawn from Washington's splendid citizens.'

"In Chicago the Second Liberty Loan advertising was financed by leading business men who voted not to have their names mentioned in the advertising, and $85,000 was raised by a committee headed by Henry Schott, vice-president of Montgomery Ward & Co., and here is how it was spent and the results:

"'In Chicago we sold over $177,000,000 to 239,500 people at an advertising cost of 27/1000th of 1 per cent. or 2.7 cents per $100 bond sold, Chicago having the advantage over Washington because of our many advertising campaigns. Over one-fifth of the total subscribers to Liberty Bonds were from the Chicago district; 1,950,000 out of a total of 9,500,000. There are twelve Federal Reserve districts.

"'Costs of advertising in some of the cities per $100 bond sold were as follows: Muncie, Ind., 2.4 cents; Chicago, 2.7 cents; Saginaw, Mich., 2.7 cents; Davenport, Ia., 2.9 cents; Utica, N. Y., 3.9 cents; Clinton, Ia., 5.4 cents; Adrian, Mich., 5.5 cents; Columbus, Ohio, 6.8 cents.'

"There should be a movement set on foot here to promote the idea of raising a War Chest fund in each city and state to take care of the advertising for all war activity, and I know this would meet with the approval of business men. During the last Red Cross drive one of our big-hearted Chicago business men paid for the entire expense of newspaper advertising and supplementary work—$50,000, and that man's name is William Wrigley, Jr., one of the world's greatest advertisers and one that knows the value of newspaper advertising.

CAN BE APPLIED COMMERCIALLY

"Some day we advertising men and newspaper-men will use these same big ideas and big space in newspapers for popularizing advertised products, and when we do the advertising in newspapers will increase tenfold and the advertisers themselves will value newspaper space and use it as a sales force just as the government is now doing.

"There will be more full-page ads. from the foreign advertising field, and more satisfied users of newspaper space,

BUILDING NEWSPAPER ADVERTISING

"And we can do this better if there is more team work—less knocking the other fellow's paper.

"More confidence in each other and more care in the spending of the advertiser's money—to see that the advertiser's goods are in nearly every available distributing outlet—and the advertising can be used to help secure this distribution prior to the appearance of the advertising.

"In other words—the advertising must be merchandized and sold to the manufacturer's salesmen and to the wholesaler and the retailer—just as it has been done to the salesmen who have sold Liberty Bonds.

"To answer directly the question, How to Increase the Volume of Newspaper Advertising Now? I would say:

"1st. Divide the country into twelve districts, just as the Liberty Loan has divided the country into twelve Federal Reserve districts.

"2d. Have a newspaper chairman and Promotion Committee in charge of each district.

"3d. Have these men report to the Bureau of Advertising of the A. N. P. A. This bureau is certainly doing good work for the newspaper and can do even better if more newspapers support it. The newspapers are fortunate in having men of the business caliber of Wm. A. Thomson and Thos. H. Moore to direct this bureau.

"4th. Prepare campaigns based on expenditures from $10,000, $20,000, $50,000, and $100,000 in each district. Let advertisers know how many thousands of people they can reach and how often for less than the price of any other medium.

"5th. The zone system should work out to the advantage of newspapers—I mean freight zone—and manufacturers in each district should be educated to build up their businesses to the maximum in their own district *now*, and thus relieve the freight and passenger traffic congestion.

"6th. Find out what products the government wants to have sold. Just now 'Use More Milk' is the slogan of the Food Administration, therefore there should be more milk advertising—fresh and canned milk. Vegetable oils should and are being advertised to take the place of lard with the approval of the Food Department.

"7th. Another way to increase advertising just now is to have the produce dealers advertise fruits and vegetables that are plentiful in each locality, so that the people will buy local products and not make it necessary for farmers to ship their produce and fruit by freight or express. You can readily see how this will help the railroad situation just **now**.

"8th. Combination advertising campaign based on the same plan that has been so successful for the Red Cross and Liberty Loan may be extended to insurance companies, real estate, bankers, grocers, bakers, dairymen, laundries, and hundreds of other lines of business which have not yet 'let the people know' all about their business.

"And to you salesmen of advertising I will give my War Thrift Message to Salesmen and Advertisers, which, if followed, will help you increase the volume of space which you sell—**day by day.**

THE SALESMAN'S THRIFT

"Keep Busy!
"That's the power behind every success.

"Let's make more calls a day. Let's write more sales a day.

"Let's put more honest effort into every call and every sale.

"Then we'll sell in one day what we used to sell in two.

"That is thrift.

"Thrift of time—the salesmen's thrift.

"Time is all valuable, the most precious thing we have. We have abundant time, but only if we conserve it. Spend it carefully. Make each hour, each minute count. Make it count for ourselves, for our employers, and for our country.

"If we conserve time, we shall be helping ourselves and our families; we shall be helping business; we shall be helping to win the war, and preserve humanity.

"So work! And keep on working. Work moves mountains. Work makes the impossible possible.

"Work with your customers. This is team work. Help them breathe your spirit of work into their organizations. Help them make their workers time-thrifty. Show them by example the benefits of constructive, not destructive work.

"Therefore don't knock anybody. And don't let others knock. Don't criticize till you have a tried-out remedy. A knocker is a time spendthrift. He squanders the time of himself and his listener.

"Knocking has no part in a salesman's creed.

"Boost.

"Scatter optimism broadcast. You can't squander it.

"Be time-thrifty for your employer, for business, and your country, and you can't help being thrifty for yourself.

"Then you will lift yourself by your own bootstraps; you will lengthen your height and vision to reach whatever you work to get.

"To be thrifty you must be creative. To be creative you must work to do in one hour the work that we formerly did in two.

THE ADVERTISER'S THRIFT

"Keep Busy! Yourself and your advertising.

"Make your advertising to-day do twice what it did yesterday. It can.

"Advertising is the matchless messenger of wartimes. It speeds your message on wings fast as thought, and cries it in a breath from the housetops and steeples of the nation.

"Whenever the government must get quick word to our people, and an answer as quickly, it enlists advertising. The Liberty Loans, the Red Cross campaigns, the Y. M. C. A., Knights of Columbus, Smileage, all bear willing witness to the wonder-work of advertising.

"For it is the great time-saver, and time to do all we must do is the task of the times.

"Time-thrift is war-thrift. And advertising is time-thrift.

"It is the thrifty way to get your message to your country.

"It is the quick educator, the sure inspirer.

"Be thrifty with your advertising. Don't stint it. Make the most of it. First be sure of your message; then put the efficiency test to the means of spreading it. Scrutinize your space. Usefulness has the right of way over artistry.

"Some advertisers are making their advertising do double duty, working for their country selling Liberty Bonds and Savings Stamps as it sells for themselves. Think how you can make your advertising a two-mouthed salesman.

"Don't stop advertising. War-time is no time to stop anything, except wasted time. Advertising has uses it never had before. Look into its new and special uses for yourself.

"It will save time for you and your men in whatever you are doing.

"Use advertising to be time-thrifty and war-thrifty."

LIX

Some Ideals.—S. Wilbur Corman

(An address before the Southern Newspaper Publishers' Association at Asheville, North Carolina, June, 1915.)

The first plank of my platform is that newspapers constitute the greatest form of advertising media; the second plank is that you newspaper publishers have a gold-mine that you don't know how to work, and that, as far as national advertising is concerned, it is being accomplished without your aid in proper degree, because you Heralds of Modernity are the most behind-the-times men in appreciation of your own opportunities and your own value that the business world can exhibit.

Most of you will readily admit the correctness of my first plank, so I'll put that aside for later consideration and take up plank number two, with some attention to detail.

Basically, newspaper-men do not believe in advertising. With rare exceptions, the advertising agency and the publisher are the poorest advertisers in America. A newspaper-man had rather do anything else than spend some real money (all of which he has earned from advertising) for some advertising for himself. If he ever does get his courage screwed up to the point of printing an ad. in his own paper (where it costs him absolutely nothing, and generally earns him a reward proportionate to its cost), the ad. is usually the poorest example of advertising in the paper—poorly written and poorly arranged typographically—a bunch of brag and bluff and bluster of a sort that would send any business house into bankruptcy if it adopted publicity of a similar type. . . .

The newspaper publisher with his stock of merchandise (which is white space for the advertisers of this nation to utilize to their high advantage) does not, broadly speaking, fix his prices, terms, and conditions with any scientific regard for to-day or to-morrow, but with almost slavish fidelity does he face the past and ask, "How have these things always been done and what do my fellow-publishers do?"

The whole newspaper rate question needs disinfecting, fumigating, and deodorizing. You will gather from my remarks that I consider it to be in a bad state of decay. A similar price to all customers under like conditions is generally regarded as simple business honesty, and yet the newspaper which, under any circumstances or conditions, will not in any manner, shape, or form make any rebates, discounts, or concessions of any kind or character is a rara avis.

How many of you will not, for my house, give a free insertion or a reading notice or concession of some kind? Do you answer me that my house should not ask for such things, fight for them, demand them, yes, almost force them? Well, I reply that if we did not do so we should soon be badly in need of customers, because if we do not sell these things for our clients some other agent will; and as long as advertisers want such things and newspapers grant them, we, as an agent, must ask for them and contend for them as a simple matter of primary self-protection.

We never know what day we will lose a good account because we have tried to be fair and decent, and some less scrupulous agent has cooked up a plan whereby, with the connivance of a lot of weak-kneed newspaper publishers, he has assured our client of that glittering bauble desired by so many advertisers—"something for nothing."

Dilly-dallying with newspapers for concessions of various kinds costs us time and money, and earns no commissions. You gentlemen, I think, have no adequate appreciation of all the annoying angles of this proposition from the viewpoint of an advertising house which is devoting its entire time and talent to the creation and development of advertising, and yet is subject to the constant competition of other agents keen and skilful in the manipulation of newspaper rates and rules.

I recently failed in the solicitation of an automobile tire account, and the president of the company told me privately that he had been promised by the successful agent a definite number of inches of free reading matter for every column of paid space he used in his newspaper list. I had refused to promise anything but the best service my house could give him for every dollar he spent with us.

All the associations you can organize won't stop this sort of thing. Get together and resolute until you are black in the face, and you won't stop it.

We do not ask The Curtis Publishing Company for concessions, because we know we will not get them, and because we know no other agent will get them. This is true, not because Cyrus Curtis belongs to the Periodical Publishers' Association, but because he is Cyrus Curtis—able, independent, and square. We may not agree with him on some points, but we know just where he stands, and when we tell a client what we can do for him in *The Saturday Evening Post*, or *The Ladies' Home Journal*, or *The Country Gentleman*, we waste no time in wondering if some other agent can promise or deliver more. . . .

Let's look at another phase of the newspaper rate situation that is very discouraging to the national advertiser. Even assuming that rates are fully maintained, there is to my mind a gross injustice done under the present system of rate making. No one shall surpass me in my admiration of the modern department stores as a great merchandise distributing machine, and as a community convenience of high order; but its cost to the community it serves, and particularly the newspapers of the community, should also be taken into consideration.

That the big buyers should have the best price is a very well established principle in many lines of business, but in some other lines it is absolutely unsound, uneconomic, and hurtful. The big customer of N. W. Ayer & Son gets his advertising advice and service at no lower rate of commission than the advertiser of small size. The big user of advertising space in many of our highest class periodicals pays exactly the same rate per line, per inch, or per page that is charged the most modest advertiser in the publication.

Department stores themselves are great advocates of the "one-price-to-all" theory, and in many first-class stores you or I would pay the same price per yard for one or a hundred yards of lace—the same price for one or a half-dozen neckties.

I am advocating no impractical, Utopian ideals, and I do not mean to offer the suggestion that conditions are ripe for such a revolutionary move, but it is very clear in my mind that the flat-rate principle is right, and that newspapers are great sufferers because so many mediums of general circulation are proving it to be right.

Under a flat rate the little fellow has a square deal. Beginners in advertising, like beginners in anything else, are apt to start small. Protection and help for the beginner are very desirable. Advertising badly needs the beginner. The death-rate is alarmingly high, so let's keep up the birth-rate.

You use the amount of department-store advertising that your paper carries as a big argument in soliciting business from me, but because a department store used your paper at five cents a line is no reason why my client, with possibly only a partial distribution in your town, can use it at five times as much, which is probably the rate he will have to pay for the amount of space he can use.

Now here is another point. Possibly my client sells his goods through dry-goods or men's-furnishing or hardware or drug stores, and the department stores, and the department stores handle such goods as he produces. Department stores are notoriously difficult to induce to stock a branded and advertised line, but having taken it on, one of their pleasant practices is to cut the price to smithereens, and by advertising it in your papers at the dainty little private rate extended to them, disgust other merchants with the line and ruin the market for your client.

Under present rulings a manufacturer may not, by contract or agreement, fix the price at which his wares shall be offered to the consumer. Suppose you owned a trade-mark name on a valuable line of silks, and had spent a half-million dollars in advertising until the consumer of such goods knew it and respected it. Suppose that department stores here and there, recognizing that your goods were standard, cut the price in half for their own glorification, and to attract customers to buy other things on which they make a good healthy profit. Suppose department stores advertised their cut prices on your goods widely in the newspapers of their towns (paying for such advertising about one-fifth or one-sixth the rate that you would have to pay for the amount of space you could afford to use). Suppose some newspaper man came to solicit your advertising, and used as his chief argument the amount of department-store advertising his paper was carrying. What would you have to say? Your answer to him is my answer to you, when you inquire why the newspapers do not get more foreign business.

Short rates, foolishly extravagant discounts for space, local rate arrangements to meet the requirements of some one store or class of store—all these things must pass away before the correctness of the flat-rate principle—if not now, eventually.

Some attention must be given to the actualities of the requirements of national advertisers if the newspapers want the business of national advertisers. I, for one, do not think you will have to lower rates, but an evening process must come about; gross inequalities must be ironed out; some must pay more, others less; the peaks must be trimmed down and the valleys filled in. You can make money by bringing about the change.

As far as dry-goods lines are concerned—in our 100 largest cities five stores in each city do over 75 per cent. of the business; in the 2,500 next largest cities three stores in each city do over 85 per cent. of the business; in the same 2,500 cities one store alone does 40 per cent. of the business; in 1,200 small cities one store does not 50 per cent. of the business.

In most American cities most newspapers are "stymied" by the department store, and the wise publisher will do well to face the facts and think of the future.

If I were soliciting advertising for a newspaper from the general agencies of this country, or from the national advertisers direct, I would quit bragging about the amount of space some department stores used with me, and tell how many hardware stores or drug stores or grocery stores there were in my town. I would be prepared to tell what kind of merchants they were; what branded lines of goods they carried. I would equip myself to talk about the people of my community; what kind of homes they had; their employment; their standard of intelligence; their scale of earnings.

Advertising is shifting and changing very rapidly. No worth-while agent talks much about the glittering generalities of advertising nowadays. The best advertising man is neither a literary genius nor a spellbinding solicitor. He is a student of the flow of merchandise. He is investigating the purchasing habits of stores and consumers.

The making of a modern advertising plan involves a study of distributive methods and channels and

BUILDING NEWSPAPER ADVERTISING 407

a proper understanding of trade relations or lack of them. Advertising is now generally considered as an item of sales cost, and may only be made fully effective through intelligent retail co-operation, sales efficiency of roadmen, and numerous other contributing factors. Even when publications of national circulation are exclusively employed, in an advertising campaign, very exhaustive charts of their circulation in various communities or districts are compiled as a basis of operation, and newspapers are far behind their opportunities in the extension of the sort of co-operation that is practical and helpful.

Newspapers will not develop their foreign business by opposing other forms of advertising. They are natural aids to periodical publications, and periodical publications can greatly improve the resultfulness of a newspaper campaign.

Quit knocking the magazines. The most successful periodical publisher in America answers that sort of thing by spending a few hundred thousand dollars per year advertising in your newspapers and building his own splendid subscription lists larger and larger, and his prestige with business men stronger and stronger—making his wonderful publications more and more essential to the general advertiser and making it constantly less essential for such advertisers to use your papers to cover the country.

Running a newspaper is a simon-pure business proposition, like running a laundry, or a coal mine, or a shoe-shining parlor, or a street-railway system. Business in any line succeeds in almost direct ratio to the efficiency with which it understands and meets the requirements of its customers.

The biggest asset that any newspaper can have is

the confidence of its primary customers—that is, the readers. Next, it must consider the claims of its secondary customers—that is, the advertisers. If it wants the national advertiser it must pay some attention to his needs, his difficulties, his rights.

There probably isn't a man within the range of my voice who couldn't take my place and tell as many wrong things about the advertising-agency system as I have pointed out concerning the newspapers. I will save him the trouble, however, by admitting them in advance. The main difference is that you make the agent by your recognition of him, while, on the other hand, if your paper is right and deserves to win, I do not believe that any agent or combination of agents can whip you.

Every one knows there are far too many advertising agents—newspapers, magazines, and the agents themselves all admit it. The business promises of half the advertising agencies in this country aren't physically large enough for a real file-room of the leading newspapers, but take it by and large, "any one who can get an account can get a commission."

This simply results in most agencies devoting their time to taking accounts from others instead of creating new business. You transfer the account from one agency to another on your books, but your revenue isn't increased.

Newspaper recognition should be a highly prized franchise. It should be impossible of obtainance except on a basis of demonstrated ability to create and develop new advertising accounts and unquestionable financial responsibility.

There are not above a score or so of agents with whom you are doing business who could pay their

BUILDING NEWSPAPER ADVERTISING 409

bills to-morrow if their leading client were to fail, but this great business of newspaper publishing takes no heed of that fact.

And so I say again, as I said at the outset, that what the newspaper business needs is business principles on its conduct and management—a realignment of rates, rules, and regulations to the requirements of this present hour.

Now I haven't forgotten, even if you have, that there are two planks to my platform, and that one of them is a pleasant plank.

I made the statement that the newspaper is the foremost form of advertising media, and I mean every word of it. Many of the greatest national advertising campaigns had their start in the newspapers of one city or one state or one section. As production, capacity, and distributive ability grew, the zone of advertising widened until the country over was covered, and national publications could be used with maximum resultfulness.

The house that I have the pleasure of representing does a very large business with the newspapers, and is successfully conducting many sectional campaigns. I believe we will see more national advertising in newspapers, simply because all logic and all sanity and all experience are behind the newspaper as the ideal advertising medium for everything, from the five-cent soda-cracker to the five-thousand-dollar automobile, and because I believe that the newspapers are beginning to see the national advertisers' side of the case.

The American newspaper owes its strength to its local sufficiency. It is the palladium of local interests. It is the reflector of local sentiment. It is the stimulator of local enterprise. It is the booster of local talent. It is the recorder of local endeavor. It is the reporter of local accomplishment. It is the herald of local ambition. All these things it is, should be, and will continue to be.

But a spirit of nationalism is in the air. Men are thinking with a national mind. What the nation eats, wears, does, and feels is reflected in Decatur, Alabama; Decatur, Illinois; and Decatur, Texas.

If a man produces an excellent breakfast food in Battle Creek, Michigan, and educates a nation of men and women to demand it, and a nation of storekeepers to supply the demand, the attitude of the New Orleans newspapers toward it should be that they will advertise it for him at a fair rate, compared with what they would charge one of their big stores if it should bring out a breakfast food under its own brand—they should help him get it into stores in their town—they should give all the local aid and help they can to those employed by the advertiser in opening and developing the New Orleans market. Incidentally, the papers of Battle Creek ought to do just as much for some gentleman of the Crescent City who works up enough courage to put a first-class package of rice on the market when he reaches their town with his campaign.

Who cares where goods are made? The average man doesn't know or care if Prince Albert Smoking Tobacco is made in Westfield, New York, or if Welch's Grape Juice is bottled in Winston-Salem, North Carolina. The newspapers are getting the advertising of both products because they have been nationalized, and intensified selling means local application of the forms of publicity.

BUILDING NEWSPAPER ADVERTISING

Don't be afraid of national advertising mediums. Love them for the good they have done. The very best national periodicals are only sublimated newspapers, anyway. They are fast developing news features and approaching newspaper standards. The greatest advertising mediums are getting away from the purely fiction idea and are approximating great national, weekly, or monthly newspapers. They are doing infrequently, in a national way, just what you can do frequently in a local way. You fit together in a national advertising campaign like peas in a pod.

Why this question of newspapers or magazines? What reasons under the sun are there, except your own self-erected barriers, why newspapers should not have more and more national advertising?

We have seen a lot of thinly spread out, so-called national advertising campaigns, designed solely with the idea of bluffing the dealers into stocking the goods, but this is only just one little picture in the ever-shifting, fast-moving kaleidoscope of advertising experimentation.

Advertising fundamentals are safe. Advertising principles are certain.

LX

Making Newspaper Space Pay.—Wilbur D. Nesbit, Vice-President Wm. H. Rankin Company, Chicago and New York

"NEWSPAPER co-operation" is a term that has been bandied back and forth so much that in the minds of a great many people it means running free reading notices. There is a certain amount of legitimate publicity that may be given any firm, whether it advertises or not. That certain amount is confined to actual news. Any other kind of publicity is hardly worth the ink and paper it consumes. When I speak of newspaper co-operation I have in mind, however, neither free puffs nor actual news stories. A real editor knows news when it comes in and abhors the palpable puff.

A newspaper is of value to an advertiser according to its strength. Its strength is based upon its circulation—and its influence with that circulation. Given the confidence of its readers, a newspaper becomes immediately a profitable investment. Reader-confidence, to my mind, means that the man or woman who subscribes regularly to a newspaper has just as much faith in what an advertiser says in the space he has paid for as in what the editor himself says in

WILBUR D. NESBIT
Vice-President, William H. Rankin Company, Chicago.

BUILDING NEWSPAPER ADVERTISING 413

the editorial columns. More than that, the advertising space should have just as much opportunity to inspire action as has the editorial urging of the newspaper. In other words, the reader of that newspaper believes the news it prints, trusts its editorial policy, and has faith in its advertisers. He has faith in its advertisers because he believes that newspaper believes that in protecting him it is fortifying itself.

Every newspaper, large or small, is the crystallization of a market for many people. It is the connecting link between seller and buyer. As a general thing, most newspaper representatives can tell you more about the possible buyers who read their paper than they can tell you about the ways and means of getting the goods into the hands of those buyers.

Newspaper space is bought and used to get dealers to sell goods and to get readers to buy those goods from those dealers. Space in a newspaper becomes more valuable to an advertiser when he finds that the newspaper not only has the confidence of its readers, but the support of its dealer-readers. Tell a dealer, for instance, that a certain product is to be advertised in a certain widely known weekly, and he puts in a stock. He has been educated to believe that articles so advertised will have a consumer demand. There are newspapers which enjoy a similar confidence, in a more intensified form, on the part of the dealer.

Save that it is the custom, there is no real reason for buying newspaper space by means of a yardstick. Space in a good newspaper can be made worth just as much as the advertiser will pay for it. And, when he is shown what the combined influence and circulation of that newspaper can do for him, his judgment will do the rest.

First of all, however, it is necessary for the newspaper itself to know the market it opens and to be able to show this market intelligently to a manufacturer or advertiser. A producer of carburetors is not convinced by a lot of broad generalizations of the number of groceries, meat-markets, show stores, or hotels in a city. He is interested in tangible evidence of what that newspaper can do with the motor-car trade.

It is a good rule, when soliciting a man's business, to assume for the time being that his is the only business on earth and that his is the only firm in that business. If he manufactures hats, show him what your paper does with the hat dealers. Map your city. Mark each hat store. Show him how many hat stores handle his hats. Show him how many can handle them. The manufacturer knows that if he gets dealer distribution his advertising space in your paper is made 100 per cent. better for him.

The consumer is going to find more people than ever trying to sell things to him now that the war days are over. He is going to find a more concerted, more determined selling effort. Practically everything advertised in a newspaper must be bought through a dealer. The dealer, then, is the first step. Newspaper space will pay better when it is known and shown that the dealers in that newspaper's territory will stock and push goods advertised in it. That sort of confidence will mean that the dealer will not only sell the goods to readers of the particular newspaper, but to every other customer he has.

BUILDING NEWSPAPER ADVERTISING

Circulation certainly is a good standard of value in a newspaper. Circulation and influence generally go together.

Much may be written or said on this point, but the thought I have in mind is that a newspaper can make itself the key to a given market. To do this it must know that market in all its phases, so that it can say to the advertiser of any product, "Here is exactly what we can do for you here."

It is hard to get the support of some dealers—but it is not hard to get the support of any live dealer when he sees a profit ahead of him. The newspaper publisher who can make the dealers feel that there is a consumer demand for goods advertised in his publication is helping create the market the advertiser must find.

One thing more a newspaper can do, and should do. That is to preach the value of advertising to its readers. There is a real benefit to the reader in advertising. He or she should be taught and told how to read an advertisement, why to look for advertised goods, why advertising is an economy that benefits manufacturer, distributer, and consumer. My experience with big national advertisers teaches me that none of them will say in an advertisement what they would not say in a letter over their own signatures. Their good faith, their good repute, and the good-will of the public are all embodied in their advertisements. Fair play to the dealer and to the consumer is the keynote of successful advertising and instils the sentiment of fair play toward the advertiser and his product.

Newspaper advertising pays when the newspaper is the key to the market, when it knows its market and its possibilities so completely that it is the selling link between dealer and consumer. This sounds as though 1 meant that a newspaper should be able to sell the dealer harder than it does its readers—and maybe that is exactly what I do mean.

LXI

Improved Solicitation.—Richard A. Foley

A VERY interesting and frank statement to the text, "How Newspapers Can Improve their Solicitations with Advertising Agencies," was delivered by Richard A. Foley, of Philadelphia, before the Associated Advertising Clubs of the World, at Philadelphia, in 1916, as follows:

"One day early this month at the Poor Richard Club, where we were all discussing 'preparedness,' the sales manager of a large manufacturing concern—a man who had handled advertising for several years past in connection with his other work—said to me:
"'Why don't the representatives of newspapers and magazines give more time to preparedness?'
"'What do you mean?' said I.
"'Well,' he replied, 'a lot of them come to see us without really preparing their story as thoroughly as they should. They come to see us, in many cases, without any real reason for asking for the account.'
"Two methods of solicitation seem to be open:
"First. 'We should have your advertising because the other fellow has it.'
"Second. 'You ought to advertise with us because your competitor advertises with us.'

"This sales manager further said to me that he had often asked representatives why they had never called upon him before his house became an advertiser. Usually this question took the solicitor off his feet. Sometimes he would try to make up a reason while he thought about it, and sometimes he would be strong enough and acknowledge he was following the line of least resistance by soliciting space users rather than helping to create them.

"'What solicitors need,' said this sales manager, 'is more of the up-to-dateness, real information and greater preparedness.'

"This comes direct from a man who is solicited several times a week, and to some extent it covers the criticism that might be offered by the advertising agents. The solicitor should prepare his story thoroughly in advance and know what he is talking about both from the standpoint of the advertiser and from his publisher's viewpoint as well.

"Of all solicitors for newspapers, those in the foreign field are, in most cases, the most thorough and the best informed.

"Newspapers sometimes make the mistake of sending out men who are not capable of meeting on the same plane of business knowledge those upon whom they are to call. A newspaper representative should be a man of presence, of ability and tact. Too many solicitors stop in to say 'Hello' in passing, and do not come in with something definite in mind.

"To make a proper impression, a newspaper solicitor should know all about his paper, should know ALL its rates, should know local conditions thoroughly, how the paper stands among the various lines of trade, what the paper will do to help the advertiser among

RICHARD A. FOLEY

his trade and also what the paper can do in the way of position.

"Position is a very important factor in advertising and many representatives are not acquainted with conditions of their own paper or papers. They do not know what they can do until they have taken the matter up especially with the publishers. This may be necessary in some cases, but the representative should have the confidence of his publisher to such an extent that the publisher will abide by practically whatever he does. Of course, the representative cannot be expected to be posted all the time on local business, so that he can know just what he can promise in the foreign field, but he should be sufficiently in touch to approximate what can be done.

"In the matter of position, when an advertiser or an advertising agency wants something specific, too often the solicitor will say that it cannot be done without extra charge, when it should be the aim of the newspaper to give an advertiser full position every time it can possibly do so. It is a part of the newspaper's service to work along this line, and unless it is absolutely impossible to give full position no extra charge should be made.

"We sometimes think that the newspaper publisher and his representative look upon the advertiser as an enemy rather than a friend. His requests and his desire to make a good showing in the newspaper, so far as position goes, are often looked upon with the same suspicion as the second-story man making a midnight visit.

"We do not believe in the indiscriminate giving of space, but the newspapers have themselves to blame if advertisers seek their help in putting across their story, and by this I mean in reading matter in the news columns, for they see the columns about baseball and other things and wonder why they, too, cannot be among the favored of fortune who have editorial assistance rendered in their business quest.

"Why, your newspapers are filled with the most inconsequential items about automobiles, automobile manufacturers, automobile representatives, and every time a new manager comes to town his picture is in the paper with a column and a half of fulsome nothingness about what he has to say. Sometimes it looks as if a vacuum cleaner were used to get the matter that goes into newspaper columns, and yet when the president of a great tobacco company invents a brand-new type of tobacco, something that every man is interested in, if he gets a stick, by the time it reaches him it wears the royal mantle of kingly favor, so much stress is placed upon the special conditions which the representative has obtained. And we appreciate the representative's effort, but at the same time the advertiser and ourselves observe that the baseball advertising seems to have been put under a trip-hammer before it reaches the newspaper, while the gossip is blown up with a force pump.

"We realize that baseball is news, and perhaps this is all beside the question of solicitation, but it is just such things as this that the representative should be prepared to discuss. We agents are between the upper and the nether millstone. We have on the one side the advertiser's wonderment that he must pay for every little privilege when others gain so much with scarcely an effort, and on the other side we have your rules and regulations and the non-acquaintance of your representative with many of these.

"Again, some solicitors also are so thoroughly imbued with their own proposition that they cannot recognize the merits of any other, and are extremely put out if they are not favored with practically every line of business that an advertising agency issues. Fortunately, that is not true of all solicitors.

"In local solicitation, many an account is often killed or stunted practically before it has got any real start, through over-solicitation. We will say, for example, that an advertising agency prepares a campaign for a product that has never been advertised. One paper in the city may be used, and if there are three or four other papers in that city the representatives of these papers will call on the advertiser and treat him to a large amount of argument as to why he has made the mistake of his life in not using their papers. After that, it is only because of double work on the part of the agency that the advertiser does not lose confidence and either want to stop or cut the advertising.

"Often in calling on agencies solicitors are overly insistent on seeing the space-buyer when he is particularly busy, and it often happens that at that time the space-buyer is busy figuring a campaign in which this solicitor's paper is or will be involved and he doesn't need to see him. A written message is sometimes at least as good as a needless publication.

"Another type of solicitor is the one who always wants to see the president or one of the high officials of the advertising agency, and does not think the man designated by the agency to deal with him is sufficiently important for him to see. This type of solicitor is really standing in his own light and he should recognize the fact and keep away from the president or any other high official, because an agency doing business along this line will soon have very little or no business to place. For agency producers must be left alone and sooner or later solicitors will find that if they cultivate the space-buyer they will positively secure more business than they could through any other channel.

"No newspaper or publication of any sort should make a practice of sending three or four men to an agency on different lines, such as school advertising, etc. One man should be big enough to cover all, so far as that agency is concerned.

"The newspaper solicitor should aim to take up just as little of the agency man's time as possible, yet keep him well informed.

"These criticisms, of course, do not apply to all solicitors or to all newspapers, as, fortunately for the agency, there are in the advertising field a great many very intelligent men who know how to work properly.

"The other day a publisher said to me:

"'How would you really define or describe an advertising solicitor?'

"Permit me to essay the task:

"An advertising solicitor is a man who believes his paper ought to have every advertisement that is printed and several hundred that never were printed and aren't likely to be. He is a man of intense likes and dislikes. He likes the advertising agent who gives him a new advertising order to-day, and dislikes him when he doesn't give him another new one that goes out to-morrow.

"He always knows why Jones lost an account and

Smith got it, and is the first in at the death and the earliest visitor to compliment the new baby.

"The advertising solicitor carries a pleasant air, a circulation statement, and a fine old assortment of tips, many of them handed down from generation to generation.

"The advertising solicitor is a man who never 'knocks'—he just walks in—and uses a sledge-hammer on the other fellow's rate card and sworn statement.

"The sworn statement most used is—

"'It's a damn shame the judgment some men use in selecting mediums!'

"Politically, most advertising solicitors are socialists. If the representative of the morning paper gets a contract the representative of the evening newspaper comes in and says, 'Can't we have some of that?'

"Equal division of property—that's the socialistic creed, isn't it?

"The advertising solicitor's life is full of surprises. He is invariably surprised that you used the other newspaper.

"He always knows his P's and Q's, but he isn't always sure about his A B C's.

"The advertising solicitor is the only man who has ever proved that figures can lie—in fact, that old man Ananias must have invented mathematics, for the advertising solicitor can take the other fellow's lineage statement and show that instead of gaining 100,000 lines last month the darned old paper is headed for the bankruptcy courts.

"If you advertise tobacco the advertising solicitor will furnish statistics showing that his paper carries more tobacco advertising than any other, and if you advertise woman's apparel he'll prove that 90 per cent. of his paper's readers are women.

"The advertising solicitor can call on a man with one local account and make him feel as big as Fred Ayer; and he can impress the space-buyer of the biggest agency with the feeling that he has inside information necessary to that lordly being's future happiness.

"But taking him all in all the advertising solicitor, after all, is a good fellow. Loyal to his newspaper, he'll fight for it, he'll die for it, he'll live for it—he'll —well, he'll *almost* lie for it.

"He gets to know the agency that plays the game fair, and he plays just that way. He appreciates honesty more than the average man. He likes to hear the truth—even if it's a monologue. He despises bunk, even where it isn't policy to say so; he is something of a toreador, for he is expert at dodging the bull.

"He has to meet all sorts, many of them out of sorts. He carries around a lot of confidential information and seldom, if ever, leaks. He's a digger for nuggets of business often where the lode runs light, but he keeps on digging. He must be a big man, for he represents a big proposition—the American newspaper.

"And in conclusion, gentlemen, please remember that your solicitor represents *you*. So far as we agents know, he *is* you—he *is* your newspaper. Give him full credentials, with power to act. And if he is not the man to be trusted with plenipotentiary powers, don't send him out at all. Make envoys of only those men whom you can trust in all the delicate adjustments of diplomacy; who will meet with dignity and clarity of vision the problems that daily arise in the clash of business.

"Such men—and there are many of them—find ready welcome in the offices, and sometimes in the councils, of those who make or buy advertising."

LXII

*Relations Between Agencies and Newspapers.—
W. B. Somerset, of A. McKim, Limited, Montreal*

It seems to me that most of the misunderstandings existing in the past between newspapers and agencies has been the result of a fundamental misconception as to their relations. Instead of realizing that the agencies are their national solicitors and co-operating with them and even regulating them as such, many publishers seem to have regarded agencies as outside of their control and inimical to their interests.

Let it be once fully realized by the publishers of this country that the advertising agencies are their employees in the same sense as are their own individual solicitors, and all misunderstanding will disappear. That newspapers would consider it good policy to pay their canvassers inadequate remuneration for good work, or to harass or obstruct them, is unthinkable.

In taking the ground that the advertising agencies are the national solicitors of the newspapers, I do not think that any controversial issue is raised. Any view that any properly constituted advertising agency is other than this cannot stand serious examination. While it is true that agencies perform many valuable services for the advertisers whose

W. B. SOMERSET

General manager, A. McKim, Limited, Advertising Agency, Montreal, Toronto, Winnipeg, and London, England.

BUILDING NEWSPAPER ADVERTISING

accounts they secure for the publishers, none of these services—recommendations as to plan of campaign, business counsel, selection of mediums, preparation of copy, checking, accounting—can be classed as anything but good salesmanship on the part of the publisher's solicitors, or as not being done in the interests of the publisher in the course of the agency's efforts to initiate and increase business.

The work of an advertising agency is to develop and build up national advertising in the press— by which is meant all regularly published periodicals, including daily and weekly newspapers, magazines, farm and religious publications, trade papers, etc.— and placing these before advertisers as superior advertising mediums to all other classes of advertising, such as billboards, street-cars, painted signs, direct advertising, etc. The agency believes in its work, it believes that press advertising is by far the best and cheapest method of reaching the public, and that until the money that can be spent to advantage in the press of the country is available for that purpose some supplementary forms of advertising should be left in abeyance.

The task of the advertising agency in soliciting business is more complicated than that of the individual publication. The individual paper is only concerned with securing business for itself. "Let the buyer beware" is still the motto to a large extent so far as individual newspapers are concerned. I do not think that the individual newspaper can be expected to consider other publications in its canvass, neither is it expected by the advertiser to be responsible to any degree for the advertiser's decision to use the publication, and to a large extent it is not responsible for results produced, which, if poor, may often be blamed on the copy used or some other circumstance. As long as the individual publisher tells the truth and plays the game fairly, and the harder he tries to get business for his own paper, the better is he thought of.

The advertising agency, on the other hand, is the national solicitor of all the publications. It is commissioned by the publications as a whole, not only to develop business, but to protect their interests. Too often in the past has the irresponsible agency, by foolish or ill-advised recommendations, through which a potential large and steady advertiser has been permanently lost to the publications of the country, cost the publishers many thousands if not hundreds of thousands of dollars.

The result of the advertising agencies' work is far-reaching and they should be held responsible by the publications of the country for the results of their work with any advertiser. The publications should hold themselves responsible for the advertising agencies they recognize and thereby appoint to do this work. To do their full duty to the publishers the advertising agency must get results for the advertiser, for what doth it profit an agency or a publication to get an advertiser started only to lose him again?

An advertising agency can only be properly and successfully conducted through building up a clientele of well-satisfied advertisers who remain permanently in the press of the country and increase their expenditures year after year. Agencies which are equipped and able to do this constructive class of work should be helped and encouraged, and the other sort of agencies should be required to live up to the same standards of business. The satisfied national advertiser is one of the best assets the publishers of this country have; he sticks by the press through thick and thin and can be relied upon for that backbone revenue so comforting to every publisher in times of crisis and stress.

The work of an advertising agency is long range in character. It takes months and even years of patient, hard work to develop a new account. It may be thought that any fairly successful solicitor employed by an agency can be expected to earn his salary from the start. As a matter of fact, it takes six months to determine if a new man is going to be able to produce business at all, and nearly always a year, if not more than two years, before a good man's work can be determined to be profitable. Not only that, but his work, all the time, can only be effective when backed by the efforts of the whole agency organization.

A national advertiser cannot be made in a day or a month. It often takes years of painful groundwork to bring him to the point where he first appears in the press of the country. Every well-equipped agency spends thousands of dollars every year in listing, investigating, studying, writing, learning, recommending, estimating, and doing other development work on firms they consider to be potential advertisers and only a small proportion of whom actually become users of space. This is the unseen and therefore unappreciated work of the advertising agencies to which the newspapers' commissions contribute.

No part of the publisher's commission goes toward

paying for the preparation of advertiser's copy. The advertiser pays for this himself, including all sketches, etchings, electros, plates, etc. The advertiser does not pay, perhaps, for the ideas the agency develops to induce him to become an advertiser, but he does pay for everything aside from this, in addition to paying for the space in the publisher's paper. This point is important: publishers should understand that advertising agencies should not rebate any portion of their commissions to advertisers, inasmuch as these commissions are given to the agencies to enable them to develop business. To such extent that any agency fails to use the commissions paid it by publishers, for the purpose of full legitimate advertising development, just to such extent are the publishers and other agencies unjustly treated. The commissions paid to the agencies are: First, to cover operating expenses, and for the purpose of developing new business and the enlargement of current accounts.

Possibly this article seems more largely written on the proper relations of the agency and publisher than on the advantages that properly constituted agencies can be to the publisher. The point of view, however, from which the publisher approaches the subject very largely governs the conclusion he will come to in this regard. The only organizations that the publishers have through which they can reach the national advertiser are the advertising agencies. The only way in which they can preserve for themselves and foster the growth of national advertising in their publications is through the agencies. That the publishers should co-operate with the agencies, should, I think, be fairly clear. First, let them appreciate the agencies as their national solicitors

Co-operation

of a new and more effective kind is going to mark the coming of a vastly increased volume of advertising for the newspapers.

The new co-operation will include a more harmonious relation between the newspapers and the advertising agents for better and more profitable service to the advertiser.

This will be produced by a better understanding between the newspapers and the agents through the elimination of recognition to the irresponsible, and adequate protection and reasonable compensation for the degree of service rendered.

The New York Globe believes in these broad principles and the undersigned is working with many hundred newspaper publishers and leading agents to produce greater traffic for all at interest.

Must Help and Protect the Agent

Through their erroneous conception of the agent's commission as an expense, many publishers have developed the practice of trying to minimize the volume of business from agents.

Instead of seeking to encourage the agents to develop more business for newspapers, many publishers have continuously sought to drive these agents out of business, by failure to compensate them for service which they alone are able to render.

Few, if any, newspapers are equipped to render the advertiser or prospective advertiser, the sort of service the agent can render; and yet many have not recognised this condition and have thus been led to nullify the great service that might have been added to their own promotional service, had they done so

We must help the agents develop more business for us and protect them from the competition of irresponsible individuals and firms seeking to parade as advertising agents.

JASON ROGERS,
Publisher New York Globe.

New York, July 18, 1918.

Series of Trade-paper Advertisements Inserted for the Purpose of Stimulating Newspapers to Closer Co-operation with Advertising Agents.

Co-operation

As viewed in many newspaper offices, co-operation too often takes on one of the many varieties of promises of things to be performed, rather than broad, effective service of the sort the experienced space buyer knows must be had to make his projected campaign a success.

Co-operation of the old style is a thing that most of our space buyers flee from as they would the promises of dreamers and incompetents. The new co-operation is being built upon sounder foundations than "conversation" and "glowing promises."

The best thought in the advertising business is being directed to the construction of greatest service to the advertiser for the purpose of making advertising more profitable and more definite in results.

We Must Co-operate With the Agents

The day is close at hand when a sufficient proportion of the newspapers of the country will commence to see the advantage of closer and more effective support of the worth-while advertising agents for the stimulation of increased volume of business.

The scarecrow "commission," when charged as an expense on our books, has in my opinion done more to nullify the great service the agents could do for us than almost any other factor in our business

I am coming to the belief that it is foolish to withhold agents' commission on local business when the agents can render a service that is helpful alike to the advertiser and the newspaper, and a service which the average newspaper cannot render By considering our net rate as our only rate, carrying all business as net, we can more readily bring ourselves to pay the agent for the service he can render.

JASON ROGERS,
Publisher New York Globe.

New York, July 24, 1918.

Effective Co-operation

will be the outcome of the big thought that is now in the minds of those who unconsciously are viewing the large future of newspaper advertising rather than its immediate present. It is the making of constructive dreams come true that is most interesting in business or other endeavor.

Before we are ready for effective co-operation we must carefully prepare the soil for the seed which we will plant. Both newspaper and agent must be brought to more fully appreciate their mutual interests and responsibilities for the results from the advertiser's investment.

The newspaper solicitor must be encouraged to temporarily forego deeds of achievement in the mere sale of space, and he must be made devote his energies and efforts to co-operating with advertising agents and advertising managers, to make advertising more productive.

Advertising agents must learn that in order to get the whole-hearted support of the newspapers in serving the advertiser's interests, they in turn must give to the newspapers that consideration and treatment which their merits not only warrant but absolutely demand now more than ever.

Must Co-operate With the Agents

Big increased volume of advertising is in prospect everywhere. We newspaper men are seldom equipped to successfully go beyond the development of a local account and even then are not rigged to continuously handle it successfully.

By recognizing responsible and competent local agency and service men to the extent of paying commissions on new local business we will be bringing to our help new and forceful machinery for the stimulation of new regular business.

With newspapers in all the leading cities thus co-operating in the development of new local business which in time will grow into general accounts, there will be produced a larger volume of profitable, resultful business for all.

JASON ROGERS,
Publisher New York Globe.

New York, Aug. 1, 1918.

The Spirit of CO-OPERATION

must be more generally established and practised by our newspapers before they will commence to secure any appreciable part of the advertising which rightfully should come to them from merchants and manufacturers seeking trade expansion.

Selfish attempts to secure temporary advantages over a competitor seem a favorite practice among our newspapers. Small-bore men should be replaced with those able to see beyond the day's profit.

As the Curtain Rises

upon the scene of the new developments in advertising, those able to discern the indications for the future see two big basic principles among many others which we must assimilate and practise:—

1. *Cut out the knocking of a competitor and boost newspaper advertising regardless of whether we get it in our own newspaper, or not.*
2. *Frankly pay the advertising agent a commission on new business which he creates for us, whether it is local or foreign.*

Let us first adopt and practise these two simple rules and we will find that our foreign business will more than double in a year. Then we will be ready to undertake still greater refinements such as the flat rate, no free notices, etc., etc.

JASON ROGERS,
Publisher New York Globe.

New York, August 28, 1918.

The Spirit of Co-operation

urged by necessities of war conditions is growing by leaps and bounds in every direction. Selfishness and destructive competition are being crushed out by powers more forceful than in peace times. This is going to be one of the great benefits growing out of the war,

For best and soundest business it is desirable that all important factors in any situation get together to iron out wastes and expensive bucking up against conditions, often very easily adjusted when all at interest approach a problem in the proper spirit.

Between Newspapers, Advertisers and Advertising Agents

there is abundant opportunity for effective co-operation which will reduce selling costs, create immensely enlarged markets for standard advertised goods, and double or treble the volume of general advertising in the newspapers.

So long as newspapers withhold commissions from advertising agents on local business, the agents will continue to be forced to seek other mediums that will pay for service rendered by them. The new advertiser more often than not will refuse to pay full newspaper rates plus a service charge to the agent caring for his business.

If our newspapers will gradually come to an understanding by which commissions will be paid on local "new business" they will be going a long way toward helping the real service agent to live and enable him to use their columns.

JASON ROGERS
Publisher New York Globe.

New York, Sept. 5, 1918.

Let Us Get Together
for Maximum Results

During the past two months the NEW YORK GLOBE has been using space in the newspapers and advertising trade papers "Printer's Ink," "The Editor and Publisher," "The Fourth Estate," "Advertising News," "Newspaperdom," and "Judicious Advertising" for the purpose of urging newspaper publishers and advertising agents to get closer together for greater efficiency and improved service to the advertiser.

We have indicated that an important reason why agencies cannot afford to throw more of the local business which they create into the newspapers is because the newspapers in few cities pay a commission for such service.

We have indicated that few newspapers are equipped to continuously serve a large group of customers in similar lines, while the agencies can render such service

We have indicated that local business going out from its home town becomes general business and that in nearly every city or town there is some industry capable of being so expanded.

We have indicated that through the sane and fair treatment of responsible advertising agents the newspapers can greatly increase the volume of their advertising.

The Globe has shown the way and sent thousands of letters and ads to newspaper publishers and agents. The Globe will continue to urge greater co-operation.

JASON ROGERS,
Publisher The Globe.

New York, September 17, 1910

appreciate the work that the agencies can do for them and take full advantage of it, pay the agencies reasonable commissions and work with them. At the same time regulate the activities of the agencies and insist on all agencies that are recognized and commissioned to act as national solicitors living up to the reasonable requirements of their responsibilities.

Established national advertisers are the shining marks for all other kinds of advertising solicitation. "You are spending enough in the publications of this country," is their cry; "you should use billboards, street-cars, painted signs, or direct advertising," as the case may be, and the advertiser is inclined to listen, for these other advertising propagandists are well organized. They, too, have their national solicitors whom they support in ways undreamed of by the publications. They refuse to accept national business save through their properly equipped national solicitors. Their association carries on a constant supporting propaganda, directed not only at the advertiser, but to the wholesaler, his travelers, and to the retailers in every line, in favor of their own particular line of advertising. These same advertisers that they are approaching usually have been developed in the first place by the national solicitors of the publishers of the country, the agencies, but the publishers only partially support their agencies, and an advertiser is very prone to be influenced when he is urged by his trade and his travelers to consider forms of supplementary advertising, to the detriment of the publishers with whom a larger portion of his appropriation should be spent.

It would almost seem as if the press of this country was indifferent to the situation. From the attitude of some of the publishers we might gather that national advertisers were anxious to get into the publications and that agencies were stepping in between them and such advertisers to their detriment. These national advertisers were not anxious to advertise when the agencies developed them; it took courage on their part and mighty hard work on the part of their national solicitors to get them to venture their money, and it takes hard work to keep many of them from placing other forms of advertising first. How hard it is to convert a man to advertising every advertising solicitor knows. Most advertisers can only judge their results in a broad and general way, and, moreover, they constantly "fall from grace" and have to be converted over and over again. Even when finally convinced it is the hardest sort of hard work to get the advertiser to increase his appropriation use larger space and to add more mediums, rather than dissipate his efforts in other kinds of supplementary advertising before what should be his main effort is really adequately provided for.

The publishers need the work of all properly constituted advertising agencies of this country in a most urgent way. The advertising agencies need the support and co-operation, and the regulations and protection that the publishers of this country can give them, if they would only do so.

PART VII

LXIII

Advertising Brilliants

My only excuse for drawing so copiously on the work of others in this section is to put into the permanent records of constructive advertising a selection of the most notable bits from scrap-book records which I have been keeping for upward of thirty years.

The two contributions from Thomas E. Dockrell, "Superiority of the Newspaper as an Advertising Medium" and "The Law of Repetition," are brilliants which should be fresh in the minds of every advertising man.

In "Advertising an Unknown Want" William R. Hotchkin touches upon a phase of the psychology of advertising seldom understood by newspaper-men. "Barnum as an Advertising Writer," by Bert Moses, presents a consideration of the greatest showman who ever lived as interesting as it is important.

"Henry Ford the Super Advertiser" is a study of the quantity production genius of the age from my own point of view, showing unlimited range for the application of the basic Ford idea.

In "The Time Element in Advertising" J. F. Jacobs, a Southern advertising expert, presents a phase of advertising research and experience which most of us realize exists, but which few of us have ever taken the time to work out as interestingly as he has done

Herbert Casson, for a time associated with the H. K. McCann Agency, leaves a bright spot in my memory of addresses on advertising. In "Efficient Newspaper Advertising" Mr. Casson is seen to full advantage as a close student of printed salesmanship.

In "Selling Costs" J. George Frederick, editor of *Advertising and Selling* and manager of the New York Business Bourse, presents ideas of suggestive value to those selling newspaper advertising space.

"Modern Advertising," a historical review from a special issue of *The London Times*, deserves a place in a permanent record of advertising and pays a striking tribute to the superiority of American advertising efficiency.

In "Killing the Beginner in Advertising," written by me in 1910, I relate some of my early experiences in selling advertising and trying to keep it sold in spite of the knocks and destructive efforts of solicitors representing other mediums.

The remaining bits are just thrown in for good measure and to round out the picture I have tried to develop regarding the building of newspaper advertising and the psychology upon which it is founded.

LXIV

Henry Ford the Super Advertiser

HENRY FORD, the automobile manufacturer, who, from a standing start, has developed a business of 3,000 cars a day or about a million a year for a gross profit of nearly $100,000,000 a year, stands as the advertising genius of the generation. It is not fair to say that Ford is not an advertiser; he is more than that. He, by instinct, more precious than almost any other business possession, knows how to cash in on words and acts in a way that others cannot equal by the expenditures of millions of dollars.

I well remember Ford's exhibit of his crude little flivver at the first big New York Automobile Show, in 1899. It was the laughing-stock of that show of freaks of which less than half a dozen lived to tell the story. Ford got lots of space in the newspapers for his assertion that he wanted to make in large quantities a car to sell for less than $750 each. Every one said that he was crazy. Of course, as it turns out, none of them knew what the cars they were trying to sell at various prices really cost them to build, and Ford had skinned them a thousand ways.

Ford, who had grown up a mechanic, had an engine that he knew was all right, and as soon as he hit upon the design of a body that suited him he went straight away on a quantity-producing basis that recognized no change of seasons or styles. One hundred dollars a car for profit was all he wanted. An output of 1,000,000 cars a year with $100 a car profit means $100,000,000 net, a sum to conjure with, but just as simple and logical a result as adding two and two together if you get the Ford conception into your head.

Naturally, the whole country watched with interest the developments of the man who was going to turn out automobiles for less than $750. He hadn't spent a cent for advertising to get that fact well grounded into the minds of the New York public. Newspapers everywhere picked the item up, for it was real news and it is fair to suppose that Ford was more sought after by those wanting cheap cars than if he had been able to spend thousands of dollars in advertising. His every attempt to solve the problem and produce cars for $750 was news and continued to be news.

Naturally, under such circumstances, Ford has never had to advertise to any great extent to sell cars. He has never had a serious competitor. Every one else who started after him got side-tracked and switched off the big idea just the way imitators usually do. Some dude or efficiency expert throws sand in the gear-box by suggesting seasonal changes and refinements which mar the performance and turn it into pure experimentation. Here is where Ford stands in a class by himself, and against all advice and pressure has stuck to his knitting.

A simple announcement in the daily newspapers of a new reduced price for Ford cars made possible, as explained in the ad., by large production, served a larger and more effective purpose than would many pages of carefully prepared arguments regarding novelties, new design, and such, prepared by other makers. A 360-line advertisement inserted in 142 daily newspapers sold 338,771 cars, as shown by the statement of C. A. Brownell, advertising manager of the Ford Motor Company.

No matter how long I live I never expect to hear of the equal of Mr. Ford's methods of meeting a demand on the part of Ford agents for a larger commission than he was allowing them. He simply showed them proofs of some ads. he proposed to run offering three cars for $1,000 to as many blocks-of-three people as would order them direct. The agents went back in their boxes without a complaint. Ford would have secured several million dollars' worth of new publicity from the newspapers for another reduction to users had the agents failed to see the point.

Ford's axiom, "Any man who can make anything in the public demand better and cheaper than any one else can sell all he can turn out," is a basic truth which is as simple as it is effective, and which by his works he has abundantly demonstrated. Many newspapers have sought to laugh at the Ford car, but, as we all know, the result has been just so much free publicity for it. Ford's experience goes to prove that advertisers who are prone to fear every adverse current or criticism must have a screw loose somewhere in their armor.

Ford, like Thomas Lipton, the famous British tea man and yacht owner, has found that every time his name gets into print is worth just so much to him; when a man has the goods a knock is a boost. Anything but the silence of the tomb regarding his product is desirable by a manufacturer with something to sell. The trouble with too many makers of things is that they stifle all possibility of enormous sale by their greed for heavy profits.

There is a whole world of sound common sense behind a success like that of Henry Ford. It is present to a degree in the success of many other men of this generation, but there is always something missing to equal that of Ford. "Make something that people need and make it so good that they will buy your particular product; actually render them a service by selling them the article. I tell you the man who has the idea of service in his business never need to worry about profits." What a world of value this Fordism possesses to those seeking to know how to advertise a product for which there is a general demand and which they want to make known!

The following interview with C. A. Brownell, advertising manager of the Ford Motor Car Company, reprinted from *The Fourth Estate*, tells of a record probably never equaled for results from a single insertion of copy in a group of newspapers:

"We analyze our advertising when we buy space.

"We seek the lines of least resistance and the best media to approach the most people.

"We aim to carry our message to the maximum number of people at the minimum of expense.

"To attain this end we found that 360 lines in 142 newspapers in 51 different cities of the United States (taking N. W. Ayer's Directory as a basis) would reach an aggregate of 15,477,422 individual subscribers, not three readers to each paper, but individual subscribers.

"Our advertising agents investigated at the same time and found that the individual subscribers of

BUILDING NEWSPAPER ADVERTISING

The Saturday Evening Post and *Collier's* in the same 51 cities aggregated only 878,538.

"Now 360 lines in 142 newspapers cost us less than $6,000.

"One page space in *The Saturday Evening Post* and *Collier's* would have cost us $7,500, and the difference in the number of people who would receive our message.

"We spoke to 15,477,422 people through the newspapers, and through these two weekly magazines could have reached but 878,538 individual subscribers.

"I want to say right here that I am not saying anything against the advertising in the magazines referred to. They are both excellent mediums. But every man who reads *The Saturday Evening Post* and *Collier's Weekly* gives undeniable evidence that he surely is a reader of the daily newspapers. We reached the multitudes, and we sold 338,771 cars. Why speak to the few when you can talk to the millions for less money?

"Be practical in advertising.

"We found that course to be profitable in the Ford Motor Car Company. In this case we reached 15,477,422 people in one advertisement of the Ford Motor Cars.

"We did not use page space because we could say all we had to say in 360 lines. We had reached in our production 248,307 cars a year. We had the facilities by which we could make 300,000 and more cars just as well, and I said: 'Make them. There will be a sale for them.'

"We advertising men always figure we can sell anything.

"We could have reduced the price of the car because

our facilities were such that we could make it cheaper. Not cheaper in quality, but cheaper by methods of production, but we didn't reduce the price of the cars.

"Instead of that we said we will make 300,000 and sell them within the year if we can, and if we do, we will rebate or give back to every buyer of the Ford car within the twelve months from $40 to $60 on each car, provided we make and sell our production of 300,000 within the twelve months of our fiscal year.

"We sold 338,771, and we rebated to every one a $50 check.

"We had run one advertisement of 360 lines, and what did it do? Why, it told 15,477,422 individuals scattered all over the United States (speaking in 142 newspapers in 51 great cities) the prices of our cars and our proposed cash rebate if we could sell 300,000 cars in twelve months. We put our advertisement where the people expected us to advertise. We went to the people and the people did the rest.

"It further established the stability of our company and the stability of its advertising. No one questioned that advertising at all. The word of the Ford Motor Company goes. We promise and we deliver our promises.

"Then we set out to make 500,000 the next year, and made 501,275. The pace grows. Last year our production was 785,426 cars, and our estimate for this year is 900,000. Present production averages 2,700 cars daily. We expect to reach 3,000 daily in November, or a million a year.

"Ford advertising is still confined to the daily and weekly newspapers. When we once got started we couldn't stop. We employ 33,000 men. We are now turning out 1,000,000 a year, over 2,700 a day."

LXV

Advertising an Unknown Want.—W. R. Hotchkin

W. R. HOTCHKIN, one of the clearest thinkers on the subject of newspaper advertising as a selling force, who for years had charge of the advertising of John Wanamaker, and later of Gimbel Brothers in New York, recently made another notable contribution to the cause of advertising in an address delivered before the Nashville Advertising Club on March 7, 1917, part of which was as follows:

"When we advertising men take a survey of the great public, our customers and prospects, from the windows of the Woolworth Building, or from wherever our watch-tower may be, we have to think of the thousands of millions of people as belonging to two main classes:

"1. The people who know that they want our kind of goods; and

"2. The people who don't know that they want our goods, or who don't even know that our goods exist.

"Most advertisers burst right into the hot turmoil of competition, to get the dollars of the people who know what they want, but don't know yet where they are going to buy it, or perhaps don't know what trade-mark, if any, is going to be on the goods they will select.

"This is a fascinating field for advertising and salesmanship. No good merchant, and no smart advertiser will neglect it for a moment. It is spectacular, inspiring, resultful effort.

"Our day's work is there. Our regular business is there. We must get those sales. We don't need to be urged to do our utmost to get that business.

"But we all want increased business.

"We want new customers.

"We want to sell our product for new uses.

"It is all very well to get the sales of things that people want to buy; but that is too small in volume. We must make people want many other things, in order to get a big increase in business. So the advertising manager must have two things constantly in mind:

"*First.* What do people want?

"And his advertising must let them know that he is able to supply that want. That is one vital side of advertising.

"But the other side is not less important, and is too often either neglected or only half done, and that vital question is: What do I want to sell, that I must make people want to buy?

"Commerce is constantly demonstrating that millions of people need things very badly, though they don't even know that the things exist. This point is very graphically illustrated by a commodity that I have been doing a lot of writing and talking about recently: It is Pyrene, the well-known fire extinguisher.

"It is an unknown want in the home that never dreams of fire.

"Yet, how vital it becomes when advertising sug-

W. R. HOTCHKIN
A worker in the world of Advertising who has made a national reputation.

BUILDING NEWSPAPER ADVERTISING

gests the importance of having it at hand for instant use when, at midnight, you smell the smoke and find the flames leaping up the stairway.

"It may be an unknown want—we hope that it will be forever an unused want, like the life insurance, where we win in life, when we don't cash in, in dollars.

"It is an unknown want, when the automobile is running beautifully with your foot on the accelerator; but it is a vital need when an explosion under the hood sets the whole works on fire and destroys your car.

"Pyrene is only one article among thousands that have a definite usefulness, that would give a definite service to the people who should buy them, but who do not realize the need and hence are not provided when the article is wanted for use.

"There are thousands of manufacturers who are working upon this principle, because they have to create an entirely new market for their product. They are producing things that are unknown wants.

"The manufacture of very few articles is attempted unless the manufacturer sees the place where it definitely can serve a purpose; but the ultimate consumer may neither know that such an article is manufactured nor contemplated.

"'This means that the article itself must not only be advertised, but its use must be advertised in a manner which will compel the reader to feel the need of it.

"For instance, the manufacturer of Dioxogen has exactly the same thing to do as the manufacturer of Pyrene. Nobody thinks about Dioxogen until he has a bruise or a cut.

"But the want is not realized until the accident occurs, and yet it is a very definite service on the part of the manufacturer to insist that Dioxogen be put in every home.

"In the old days everybody thought it was perfectly all right to drink two or three cups of coffee at every meal. Mr. Post came along, and, through his advertising, reduced the market for coffee and created an enormous sale for a commodity that was unknown and unused before.

"To-day the Standard Oil Company has found another way to get a high price for oil, besides jumping up the price of gasolene, and so they put a petroleum product in a bottle and call it 'Nujol,' and are now making thousands of people think that it is a necessity of life.

"Kellogg is going after the same market, with Bran.

"A tremendous new market has been created in the kitchen by developing the desire for kitchen cabinets, fireless cookers, aluminum wares, and other articles.

"The enormous power of advertising in creating new business may be attributed directly to the continuous clever suggesting of the merchandise to the public, creating an intense desire for the goods advertised on the part of people who would never have thought of wanting them.

"This result is totally overlooked by those advertisers who rely on such general publicity as a pretty picture, or a unique design, in connection with the name of the commodity, in order to stimulate its sale.

"For instance, one tobacco concern will simply print the name of its cigarette or tobacco in connection with the illustration of the package, or with the picture of a beautiful woman. On the other hand, the concern that realizes the power of suggestion will tell such a story of the delights that come from smoking that particular brand that every smoker will want to try it, and thousands of non-smokers will be tempted to learn to smoke, in anticipation of enjoying the delights that have been exploited.

IT IS THE UNUSUAL THAT MAKES BIG SUCCESS

"The store which simply prints a list of prices day after day may win the attention of people who have their minds made up to buy certain things at that time; but such advertising has no more influence in creating desire for the merchandise than a railroad schedule has in tempting people to travel.

"The vital thing for the retail advertising man to think about is: how many things have you got in stock that people either rarely think about or do not even know exist?

"How are these things going to be sold if the story is not told in the newspapers?

"Did you ever realize how helpless merchandise was while lying back in the shelves, with no display in the windows, no word about it in the newspapers, and rarely being shown by the salespeople?

"All of this merchandise was made to meet some definite want; but advertisers are neglecting to get together the goods wanted and the people who want it.

"A great many merchants think that certain goods won't sell, when the goods have never had a chance.

"The first way to increase business in a store is to sell more things to the present customers of the store.

"People have a great many known wants, but you are only getting part of the business when you satisfy them alone.

"You must educate them in reference to the unknown wants that you can also supply, and thus sell more goods to every customer who comes to your store.

"Again you must make people buy oftener.

"A vastly greater quantity of hosiery could be sold by a store if people didn't darn their stockings so continuously. Many people darn their stockings until you can scarcely see any of the original soles, heels, and toes. They need only be educated to the fact that the same amount of labor would be worth vastly more than the small saving from continuous darning. If a man were told what a labor and tax he was putting on his wife by compelling her to continuously darn his old socks, he would have enough compunction to buy the new ones that you want to sell.

"With the proper kind of advertising a great many more corsets could be sold. The figures show that, on an average, a woman buys only one corset a year; while many women buy more, thousands of women do not buy one a year or one in two years. The proper educational advertising would prove to women that an old corset makes her best gowns look badly and spoils her own figure.

"A similar educational campaign would sell vastly more shoes, blouses, and tooth-brushes.

"If business were confined to the sales that would be made to people who woke up in the morning with definite wants on their minds most department stores would have to go out of business.

"If manufacturers confined their production to the filling of the wants of the public, for things for which they themselves found the need, American commerce would shrivel and the country would be filled with the unemployed.

"The unknown want is a most powerful factor in making sales, and hundreds of industries depend upon it entirely. We all realize it, when we think about it; but most of us are prone to overlook it in the rush of our day's work.

"I am inclined to the belief that one of the greatest wastes in promotion work comes from failing to get the impelling argument for the use of our goods placed in the most effective manner before the eyes of the people who really need it.

"When goods don't sell readily the storekeeper is inclined to blame it on the price and make a reduction that kills the profits. At least half the time I believe that diagnosis is wrong. I don't believe that the merchandise has had a chance. Either its story has not been well told or it has not got the attention of the people who need the goods.

"So this is the great advertising problem:

"1. To analyze the uses of the commodity and determine to whom the goods should be sold.

"2. To tell the story of the goods in an intelligent and alluring manner—to interest and arouse the desire of the people who actually want your goods.

"3. To get your advertising printed in the best possible mediums to reach the people who you know will want them, or to get your printed matter mailed to the list of names of people who want the goods.

"In other words, it is the problem of both merchant and manufacturer to bring together the goods and the people who want them.

"To tell the people why they want the goods, and to convince them of their need of them.

"After that is done the matter of price becomes a secondary matter. A cut price is unnecessary; and a fair price is entirely satisfactory to the customer, and the merchant fills a want of his customer while he makes a profit for himself. Everybody is happy because a real constructive piece of selling has been done."

LXVI

Barnum as an Advertising Writer.—Bert Moses

THE following from the pen of my old friend Bert M. Moses, in *Newspaperdom*, under the title, "Barnum an Advertising Writer Before He Became a Showman," is a brilliant contribution to the literature of advertising which every newspaper-man and advertiser can well afford to study:

"I may be wrong, of course, but when I say that Phineas Taylor Barnum was the greatest all-round advertiser who ever lived I am expressing a deep-seated opinion. This man Barnum wrote a book about himself, fifty years ago, that tells more of advertising than all other books bunched. It is most refreshing to turn from latter-day advertising books diluted with dilettantism and go back half a century to this Connecticut Yankee whose name and fame ran all the way around the earth. He has been dead long enough so that a correct perspective of his character and accomplishments can be seen. The time is here to analyze Barnum's work and to clear his reputation of the taint that he was a dealer in humbugs and made his money by fooling and hornswoggling the public.

"This shall be a sincere effort to bring Barnum back

to public view in advertising circles. His life should be an inspiration to every man who aspires to succeed in business, for he began with nothing, made and lost several great fortunes, and touched the lowest and highest spots in the journey from cradle to casket. He never worked on the theory that the public liked to be humbugged, and it is doubtful if he ever expressed such a sentiment. I have just finished reading the book of his life, and throughout its eight hundred pages he lays down the fundamental principle that 'the surest way of deriving the greatest profit, in the long run, is to give the people as much as possible for their money.' The quoted words are his own.

"Barnum, it seems, was the first professional advertisement writer who followed that precarious avocation. He states in his work that, in 1841, he wrote ads. and notices for the Bowery Amphitheater, and drew down the fine salary of four dollars a week. I have no doubt that the work he then did at 'four per' was more effective than anything Charles Austin Bates did in the heyday of his fame, when his income from words he fished out of his ink-bottle was reputed to be around \$25,000 a year. Some time ago a Chicago agency boasted that it had on its pay-roll a writer who was paid \$50,000 yearly, but this man's name is lost to memory in a few fleeting months, while the name of Barnum, whose salary for writing was less than an office-boy's, is graven deep in the granite of time. Thus do we see that to judge a man by his salary is as uncertain as to judge a woman's mentality by her millinery.

"Barnum's humor was perennial. He knew the uplifting influence of the laugh, and could go off in a corner and enjoy a laugh at himself. He mingled wit with work, and the fun he got out of success counted as big as the money. His eternal energy plunged him into interminable turmoil, but his fine sense of humor never failed to point a way out. The pages of his autobiography are dotted with stories of jokes he played on others and that others played on him. And always did he turn a funny situation into an advertisement. Whatever he did—whatever the predicament—whatever the occasion—he made news matter out of it, and the papers flung his fame to the four corners of the earth. Triumphs, successes, failures, catastrophes—all went as advertising into his perpetual grist. Nothing he did or failed to do passed out into oblivion. He supplied the atmosphere that made each trivial happening an occasion and each occasion an event. The time of Barnum marked an advertising epoch.

"The term 'humbug' was an epithet that jealous competition hurled at Barnum, and it was an epithet that stuck. And yet this so-called 'humbug' was nothing but psychology under another label. It was that element in advertising which arouses curiosity, and irresistibly urges the public to yield to its influence. Barnum's 'humbugs' were thrown in free. People paid to see his real show, and no showman ever gave so much for the price of admission as this Yank from Bridgeport. Some of the freak things he advertised were unquestionably hoaxes, but the genuine things outnumbered the fictitious as a thousand to one. The hoaxes gave the people a chance to laugh, and a laugh is always worth many times what it costs. In Barnum's case the cost was nil. The hoax was piled on to make the measure run over.

And no one who attended Barnum's shows ever said he got less than his money's worth.

"The humbug and hoax are with us yet, but they are now more cleverly camouflaged. Billy Sunday's work is honeycombed with humbug, and in some degree he duplicates Barnum as an advertiser, but Barnum gave more for fifty cents than Billy ever gave for fifty dollars. 'You press the button; we do the rest,' is humbug, and so is 'Let the Gold Dust Twins Do Your Work.' We have humbug in 'The Ingersoll watch is the watch that made the dollar famous,' and we have it again in 'Beecham's pills are worth a guinea a box.' Humbug of the 22-carat variety is found in the working formula of *The New York Tribune*—'First to last, the truth—news, editorials, advertisements.' I even venture to say that in this year of our Lord, 1918, you can find more or less of this form of humbug in every conspicuous success in any line of human endeavor. The richest man in the world is perhaps the most colossal humbug of them all, and yet he is admitted into church and held in high esteem in respectable circles.

"Barnum lived in a time when it was considered proper to fool and trick the people. The buyer was expected to be on the lookout for deception and fraud. The more success a tradesman had in deceiving his customers the better was his reputation as a shrewd business man. If you bought sugar and found it mixed with sand, you had only yourself to blame. You should have examined your purchase carefully before accepting it. If you found a brick inside a tub of butter, the man who tricked you was simply more clever than you. If the nutmegs proved to be wooden when you got them home, the joke was on you. If the 'all-wool' suit you bought was half cotton, why didn't you detect the deception before you bought? *Caveat emptor* was a legal warning. Horse-trading tricks permeated every line of business, and if the buyer didn't beware, why, he ought to be cheated! Such were the times when Barnum lived, and yet he rose superior to the times and laid his cards on the table face up.

"Let Barnum tell of his methods in his own words:

"'In some respects I fell in with the world's way, and if my " puffing " was more persistent, my advertising more audacious, my pictures more exaggerated, my flags more patriotic, and my transparencies more brilliant than they would have been under the management of my neighbors, it was not because I had less scruples than they, but more energy, far more ingenuity, and a better foundation for such promises. In all this, if I cannot be justified, I at least find palliation in the fact that I presented a wilderness of wonderful, instructive, and amusing realities of such evident and marked merit that I have yet to learn of a single instance where a visitor went away from the museum complaining that he had been defrauded of his money. Surely this is an offset to any eccentricities to which I may have resorted to make my establishment widely known.'

"The only protest or criticism I have to enter against Barnum is because of his exquisite skill in manipulating the free reading notice. He was the prince of press agents. No man ever got within gun range of his genius in this direction. Coming events cast their press agents before whenever Barnum was out in quest of dollars, and the papers of the world gave him more space on the first page than can ever be computed. He reduced space panhandling to a fine art, and while he paid thousands for display advertising, he annexed millions' worth of advertising for nothing in the news columns. He magnified trifles into sensation and supplied more readable copy to reporters than all other showmen put together.

"Some one once asked Artemus Ward, the old-time humorist, what his principles were, and he replied, 'I have no principles; I am in the show business.' Barnum was the world's most successful and most conspicuous showman, and it is interesting to read what principles governed him. This is what he has to say on that subject: 'The qualifications of a showman are these: He must have a decided taste for catering to the public; he must have prominent perceptive faculties; he must have tact, a thorough knowledge of human nature, great suavity, and plenty of soft soap.' Barnum knew human nature far better through his Yankee instinct than any professional psychologist ever knew after wending his devious way through all the technical institutions of the world.

"Barnum's philosophy of advertising is condensed into the following extract taken from his book that was written half a century ago. Nothing better has been written since. He exhausts the whole subject of advertising in these brief words, and we must admit that we know nothing new to add to Barnum's creed nor can we cut out any part of his philosophy and improve it.

"'We all depend, more or less, upon the public for our support. We all trade with the public—lawyers, doctors, shoemakers, artists, blacksmiths, showmen, opera-singers, railroad presidents, and college professors. Those who deal with the public must be careful that their goods are valuable; that they are genuine and will give satisfaction. When you get an article that you know is going to please your customers, and that when they have tried it they will feel that they have got their money's worth, then let the fact be known that you have got it. Be careful to advertise it in some shape or other, because it is evident that if a man has ever so good an article for sale, and nobody knows it, it will bring him no return. In a country like this, where nearly everybody reads, and where newspapers are issued and circulated in editions of five thousand to two hundred thousand, it would be very unwise if this channel was not taken advantage of to reach the public in advertising. A newspaper goes into the family and is read by wife and children as well as the head of the house; hence hundreds and thousands of people may read your advertisement while you are attending to your routine business. Many, perhaps, read it while you are asleep. The whole philosophy of life is, first sow, then reap. That is the way the farmer does. He plants his potatoes and corn and sows his grain and then goes about something else, and the time comes when he reaps. But he never reaps first and sows afterward. This principle applies to all kinds of business, and to nothing more eminently than to advertising. If a man has a genuine article, there is no way in which he can reap more advantageously than by sowing to the public in this way. He must, of course, have a really good article and one which will please his customers. Anything spurious will not succeed permanently, because the public is wiser than many imagine. Men and women are selfish, and we all prefer purchasing where we can get the most for our money; and we try to find out where we can most surely do so. You may advertise a spurious article and induce many people to call and buy it once, but they will denounce you as an impostor and swindler and your business will gradually die out and leave you poor. This is right. Few people can safely depend upon chance custom. You all need to have your customers return.'

"Having now made a preliminary attempt to resurrect Phineas Taylor Barnum, I suggest that the advertising clubs of the world lay aside the modern books on advertising written by men who never succeeded in business and take up the study of Barnum, who was a colossal business success and whose knowledge of advertising touched bottom. No one will ever know the essentials of advertising until he reads the life of this phenomenally brilliant man from Connecticut, who was the welcome guest and friend of presidents, kings, emperors, sultans, and czars, as well as of the common people of the farm and the town. His intellect reached out and swept every channel of human endeavor. He is best known as a showman, but in all essentials and characteristics he was perhaps the greatest all-round commercial genius that this country ever produced. He is to be measured, not by the exact total of dollars he accumulated, but by the expanse of his imagination and by the creative powers of his mind."

LXVII

*Superiority of the Newspaper as an Advertising Medium.
—Thomas E. Dockrell*

UNDER the heading, "The Greatest Sales Force—
The Newspaper," Dockrell, in an article in *Advertising
and Selling*, for November, 1910, produced a gem of
brilliancy which should be treasured by all advertising
men, as follows:

"Among the oldest memories I have are of the days
when my father took me for long walks on Sundays,
the last parts of which were often spent riding picka-
back on his broad shoulders, in the twilight; and the
interesting stories he told me on those walks. They
were interesting stories—of fight and courage, of human nature; never fairy tales, just plain stories of
business.
"At that time my father was building a business
which is to-day one of the largest of its kind, but in
those days it wasn't the largest, it was small, and
fighting its way to the top of the heap. The stories
were of why this employee was winning, or that one
was failing; how one department was being nursed
along, how another had brought off a big coup, and
how each department and each man fitted into the
whole. But the stories were to me as full of courage

and fight and vivid interest as any Indian tale or titanic struggle.

"I suppose I never will know how valuable those walks and talks were in teaching me to love business and all its ramifications as a chess-player loves chess, a chemist his laboratory, or a doctor his cherished cases.

"To this good fortune was added that of always being thrown into contact with heads of businesses, and having the opportunity all my life of watching the wheels go round. This intimacy with the inside machinery developed a habit of dissatisfaction with a mere superficial view of the machine. I always wanted to see the inside works. When I was only a youngster and ill-health demanded that I live in a warmer climate, I went to South Africa, provided with introductions which were responsible for tremendously valuable experience. I can look back to a couple of dinners in Cape Town, seated opposite Barney Barnato, of Kimberley diamond fame, as he told the youngster just out from home how he should conduct himself in order to find success. Another never-to-be-forgotten evening was when the powerful introduction I bore brought me a long interview at Groot Sehuur with Cecil Rhodes. I spent over two hours on the veranda listening to the kindly advice of the great South African empire-maker.

"Since then I have met many a great mind, and, looking back, see that one of the concomitants of the big man is the habit of straight thinking, past superficialities down to fundamentals, a clear reaching through to underlying causes; a constant, habitual, analyzing attitude; an ability to see not the whole, but the sum of all its details, and in imagi-

BUILDING NEWSPAPER ADVERTISING 461

nation to marshal widely separate facts and vividly visualize them into a whole.

"There is no better method of mental conduct than that of conforming to the practice of the most successful individual or principle, and constantly searching for the laws that always accompany cause and effect.

"A man manufactures something. The best method of selling it is to sell it himself. The next best method is to have a good man sell it for him. The next best method is to write to somebody who he knows is interested. The next best method is to use a newspaper. After, but not until after he has exhausted the possibilities of the newspaper, there are many other media he can use with profit.

"If we seek the most profitable medium for reaching a majority of people in any one locality we must guide ourselves by the experience of some business which has been compelled to appeal to the majority of people in one locality, and learn by its experience.

"In any locality in the United States the department store appeals to a majority of the people, and in order to reach the majority of the people uses the daily newspaper practically to the exclusion of any other method. The department store also uses the newspaper to a greater extent than does any other advertiser. It is, therefore, absolutely apparent that the experience of the department store has been that the newspaper largely used is the best method of reaching the majority of people in any one locality.

"We still, however, have to find out whether the department store is modern, progressive, and highly successful. If it is, we have practically found an ideally successful business, which has learned from its experience the ideal medium for reaching the majority of people in any one locality.

"Since every man knows that the department store is a branch of merchandizing which has developed more rapidly than any other direct method within the last ten years, the law is practically established that a business to be ideally successful in reaching a majority of people in any one locality must use the daily newspaper largely.

"Having established by one proof, although there are many others, the necessity of the use of the daily newspaper in any one locality in order successfully to reach the majority of the people, it would seem that we would have established its supremacy in dealing with all localities. Certainly.

"'Then,' you ask, 'why do national advertisers endeavoring to cover all localities use any other medium before they have exhausted the possibilities of newspapers?' There are many reasons.

"Among them are inexact knowledge of underlying advertising principles by the advertiser; inability or disinclination of newspapers to put their proper claims before the advertiser; competition or other media which, while not so effective for the advertiser, put before him apparently very strong arguments for their use; lack of true co-operation of the agent with the advertiser.

"Let us examine these causes which befog the advertising business.

"The main reason for the lack of straight thinking on advertising by the average advertiser is psychological. He has been trained to think of advertising as something apart from his business. He has been told that it is something that cannot be handled by business men. He has seen advertising handled by men outside of business—an alien race to commerce—a race of men peddling what to him seemed dreams, and which he yet realized were actualities when used by other business men. Not thoroughly understanding advertising, he handed it over to a man outside his organization. In most cases, once he allowed his advertising to be handled by an organization apart from his business, he grew to consider advertising itself as being apart, something alien and foreign, a magic force which, working entirely apart from the business, would have wonderfully beneficial results.

"From this mental attitude of the advertiser of allowing himself to lose touch, his business has also lost touch with the real fundamentals of advertising.

"Successful advertising cannot be handled apart from the business.

" An agency which, although its system of remuneration is wrong, still stands high in its ideals and efforts, shows that it realizes the point just mentioned. In a recent advertisement it says, 'We don't know how to define " advertising service " other than to say that it is so closely akin to salesmanship that it begins with the conception of the thing to be advertised, and goes step by step along its course of manufacture, through the dealer to the consumer."

"Advertising must be interlaced, interwoven, bound up with every activity of the business, and the business in turn must be permeated and saturated with the advertising. Advertising can do nothing without the business behind it. You can have a business without advertising, but not advertising without a business. Therefore, the business is the more important. Advertising cannot precede a business at a distance, but it may lead it by the hand. Advertising, to be successful, must be affected by and based upon every other department of business, raw material, finished product, credits, sales department, shipping, local conditions, competition, timeliness, and in fact every activity which is present in merchandizing.

"To reach the people in any one town in the United States a man must use a newspaper. In every town, large or small, you find the retailer using the newspaper with which to build his business. He uses the amount of space which brings him the maximum of profit with the minimum of waste. What is good in any town must obviously be good for all towns. And yet, the newspapers carry but a small fraction of the advertising to which they are entitled.

"Why?

"Because the advertiser does not realize the importance to each community of its daily newspaper. If somebody had told him that the paper he read circulated every day in every town and hamlet in the United States, you couldn't have got him to use any other medium with a battle-ax. But they didn't tell it to him. It was the absolute, unshaken truth, but the newspapers didn't know how to put it up to him. The same newspaper that any one man reads in any one town, in any part of the United States, is read every day by nearly every literate adult in every other town and hamlet. But the newspapers didn't tell it that way. Because every daily newspaper has a different name, that doesn't change the underlying fact that every worth-while literate adult in the United States reads the same daily newspaper. The name may be different, but the daily newspaper that he picks out for his information on everything that goes on in the world around him is the same newspaper that every other man reads.

"What does the name matter? What does the city matter? You, whose eyes glance at this page, read a daily newspaper, a publication published every day, upon which you rely to keep you informed of all that makes life worth living.

"Practically every other man in the United States does the same thing. He reads his daily newspaper, the paper that every day brings him the news that makes life worth living. 'Oh, it has a different name,' you say; 'it's published in a different city.' What does that matter? To the men who read it it brings not only the news of the world, but the news of their neighbors, of themselves, of their town, their community, their street, often of the very house they live in.

"The man who lives in New York and reads the evening *Globe* goes to Philadelphia, misses *The Globe* and is offered *The Bulletin*. He thinks it's a different paper. It is not. To the man in Philadelphia *The Bulletin* is what *The Globe* is to the New-Yorker. It's his evening paper. Same thing to the man in Buffalo. *The Buffalo Evening News* is the same evening paper to the Buffalonian as *The Bulletin* is to the Philadelphian or *The Globe* to the New-Yorker. The same thing applies to every other city. It doesn't matter what is the name of the paper in any city, it's the paper that the man who buys it picks out in order to make him a human being. A paper must appeal to its readers, or it couldn't be published, and a reader must consider a paper his paper or he wouldn't buy it.

"There is the point. Advertisers have been led

astray through inability to see clear through to this fundamental. The great advertisers saw it. The greatest advertisers that ever were saw it. The men who ran patent medicines certainly knew advertising. They used the papers and made millions. I once placed advertising for one firm with four thousand papers. 'Different papers?' you ask. Not on your life! The same paper. Because each one was the paper to each of its readers, and, consequently, all taken together were the paper that everybody read.

"The department stores know it. They've got every locality by the throat in volume of business. And yet they're the largest users in the world of daily newspaper space. The volume of business done by all the department stores in America compared to the volume of business done by any other industry is almost incredible, and it is bound like a Siamese twin to the daily newspaper in every locality in the country.

"Mr. Thomas Balmer, whose advertising experience 'needs no bush,' recently wrote, 'I say it advisedly and with conviction, that more than 60 per cent. of advertisers nowadays are failures—many of them doomed before they begin. It is time we based our efforts in advertising along the lines of demonstrated experience and facts.'

"Why did not the advertiser see this? Because he let somebody else do his thinking for him. And because he was blinded by the false gods of pretty typography and appeal to his vanity. Other minds, thinking for him, showed him 'a false vision and divination and a thing of naught and the deceit of their heart.' The advertiser wanted to reach out all over America, and said, 'Give me something that goes all over America.' They gave it to him in mediums, like flies on a window-pane, whent he dew is on it in the early morning. The flies are bigger in spots because they loom large to the eye. Four or five flies seem to cover the pane. The dew is not so noticeable, because each separate atom is tiny and almost invisible. But while the very visible fly just covers a few places on the pane, the almost invisible dew lies so thick that it is practically a part of it. The advertiser for a moment thought, 'I wish my own paper went everywhere.' He was told it didn't circulate outside his own city. He was told half a truth but all a lie. It did circulate. Every man's newspaper circulates everywhere, circulates everywhere men and women read. Only the name is different; the influence and grip are everywhere the same, but the advertiser didn't know it.

"A few advertisers said, 'We want to use the daily newspaper.' But they were told it would cost too much to use all the newspapers. That's true, perfectly true, if the advertiser wasn't ready for them. But this is what he could have done:

"He could have said to each retailer in a town who held his goods, 'I'm going to back you with advertising—real advertising—advertising in the medium you rely on to build your own business. I will advertise in the newspapers that are read in your community, your town, your ward, your street, and in your own house.' And then the advertiser could have done the same thing in other towns. Instead of scattering his energy all over the United States, whether or not he had distribution and used the medium that would have built real sales. What matter if he had only money enough to cover one state with newspapers? Provided he got more business out of it, and more profit, one state was better for him than the whole country. Then he could use his profits to go on to another state.

"The total amount of dollars a man spends in advertising does not matter. The aim of every advertiser is to make every dollar pay a profit, and the minute he gets every dollar working at a profit his constant prayer is to put more of those profit dollars at work. The minute a man finds an investment making a profit he'll keep on investing. The aim of the advertiser is to spend $10,000,000 a year in advertising, provided the last $5 of the $10,000,000 will bring him as big a profit as the first. Localization, specialization, analysis, consideration of the importance of the unit will squeeze the hot air out of the whole proposition.

"Advertising has been handled by a class of shrewd, keen men, men who ran their business as progressively as any other business. Men who realized that in order to keep their profits up they must keep their expenses down, and very soon realized that it cost them far less to place advertising with a few general publicity mediums than with one hundred newspapers, and that their use didn't require any knowledge of the sales statistics of the business, statistics the average agent doesn't know, and couldn't handle if he did know. Imagine what it would cost him if he had to put the caliber of man required to deal with statistics on to every account he handled. Look at the time and money it would cost to find out local conditions. No, sir! The agent kept at the thing that cost the least to handle. But the newspaper's coming into its own. It is a demonstrable fact, and the advertiser sees it for himself the very moment it is put before him, that the medium that allows him to suit his appeal to each locality, the medium people must read if they are going to be human beings, is the medium to use to get close to the people.

"As the advertiser gives his own attention more closely to advertising, he will rapidly eliminate a lot of the present waste and loose thinking. The trouble is that the advertiser has been letting other people have too free a hand in the spending of his own dollars.

"That shrewd old thinker, Decimus Junius Juvenalis, gave a man a hint on this subject nearly two thousand years ago. The friend was complaining of a breach of trust through which he had suffered, and Juvenal asked him, '*Nescis quas habeat Veneres aliena pecunia?*' which, freely translated, is, 'Dost thou not know the charm there is in spending money that isn't your own?'

"The cost system that has been so successful in helping every other department of business is beginning to be applied to advertising, and it is hurting the scattered medium. Hand in hand with the cost system go localization and consideration of the unit, and with localization and consideration of the unit comes the daily newspaper. I get hot when I write on this question. I've seen so much of it that I want to know why any man merchandizing through retailers ever got away from the use of the daily newspapers. I talk to business men, small and large, every day of my life, and every time a manufacturer picks up his sales ledger and goes through it with me the veins in his neck swell, and he wants to know how he can use any other medium than the newspaper with its intense localized selling energy.

"It's all a matter of straight thinking. The newspaper's beginning to get the business now, but to get it more rapidly it must change its method of solicitation a great deal, stop talking only circulation and give reasons why it is a localized selling force. It will come more nearly right in the end, but, in the mean time, it's hard on a lot of advertisers, who could be making great profits with newspaper campaigns based on the varying sales statistics of different localities."

LXVIII

The Time Element in Advertising.—J. F. Jacobs

SPEAKING of the subject of "The Time Element in Advertising," J. F. Jacobs, of Jacobs & Co., Clinton, S. C., in an address before the Lynchburg, Virginia, Advertising Club, on September 14, 1915, presented an argument which must find a place in this book, as follows:

"I am an enthusiast on advertising as a science. I believe that the time is rapidly approaching when the natural laws of advertising will be accurately defined as a science.

"Two hundred years ago there was no such thing as the science of economics. To-day the study of that science has its place in every well-regulated college the world over. A thousand years ago there was no such thing as the science of astronomy. A false astrology prevented its development. There was also no such thing as the science of chemistry, a false science of alchemy taking its place. And just as the modern sciences of chemistry, astronomy, and economics have emegred from the ignorance of the Middle Ages, so in coming years will the new science of advertising, worked out in the experience of thoughtful men, be recognized as a real science, and the underlying principles upon which successful advertising is based will be taught and recognized universally.

"I invite you this evening to the thoughtful consideration of one of these underlying principles—The Time Element in Advertising. A proper recognition of this principle may be expected to conduce to more successful advertising. Ignoring the principles invites disaster in advertising expenditure.

THE IMPATIENT ADVERTISER

"There are not a few advertisers who, on contracting for advertising space and putting out their advertising copy, expect immediate results commensurate with the contemplated outlay. Others expect the results to have been attained by the time the invoices are rendered for the advertising. In other words, many advertisers are impatient of results, feeling that when they lay down a bank-note upon the counter they should receive the value of the bank-note in goods. They purchase so much advertising space, and expect that space to immediately produce sufficient to pay them back what they spend plus a profit. This expectation is seldom met by any type of advertising. The proposition advertised may be a thoroughly merchantable one. The media selected may be the very best for the purpose. The advertising copy may be convincing, interesting, and effective; the illustrations may be attractive and illuminating; the execution of the advertising may be as nearly perfect as human affairs will permit, and yet the results on the completion of a given advertising order may not be commensurate with the expenditure. In such case many advertisers—I might say the majority of advertisers

BUILDING NEWSPAPER ADVERTISING

—are seized with disappointment, condemn the media and copy, become discouraged, and immediately declare that advertising does not pay in their business, or that the copy or media used were worthless. I have known this to occur many times in an advertising experience of the last seventeen years, and in a large percentage of those cases I have known the conclusion to be an incorrect one, and the disappointment unjustified by the facts in the case.

"The reason for this disappointment is lack of recognition of the fact that the time element in getting advertising results is just as essential as the intellectual element or the money element.

SUCCESS TAKES TIME

"Permit me to announce the principle in a formal statement. Successful advertising involves lapse of time as well as investment of money and application of thought. In other words, you may have a thoroughly merchantable proposition and apply the best of brain in promoting it. You may invest a reasonable sum of money in financing the promotion, but you must also be ready to wait for the results.

"This statement might be accepted by every one, but at once the question arises, 'How long must we wait?' And on that question there is a wide divergence of opinion due to lack of appreciation of the process of the propagation of information through publicity. It is essential that we understand the process in order that we may reasonably estimate the lapse of time necessary before a conclusion can be reached as to the effectiveness or inefficiency of an advertising campaign.

THE MENTAL PROCESS OF THE READER

"Now, in order to produce results in advertising, assuming that you have a thoroughly merchantable proposition—one which, when understood, is recognized as attractive—and assuming that your copy attractively presents the proposition, and assuming that you have spread that copy through the proper media before the class of people who would normally be customers for the proposition, you must recognize the fact that it is necessary, first, to get the attention of the reader before you can get results.

"The Parable of the Sower teaches us that when grain is scattered upon the field some of it falls among thorns; some of it is eaten by the birds of the air; some of it falls on stony ground, and hence quite a proportion of the seed is unproductive.

"This is the case with advertising. It is not possible to secure the attention of every reader of the publications used. Very few readers begin at the beginning of a publication and read to the end, including reading matter and advertising. Popular reading is usually done in a selective manner. One reads what one wishes to read and skips what one wishes to skip, and the material skipped is always, or usually, much more considerable than the material which is read. Consequently a large percentage of the readers of any given publication or line of publications do not at first see your advertisement; that is, their attention is not attracted to it. The smaller the advertisement the larger the number of people who are less likely to see it at the outset, but the more you repeat the advertisement the larger the percentage of the readers who are likely eventually to see it and read it. If you wish quick results it follows that large copy should be used. If you are willing to be very patient, and you wish to be very economical, it follows that you may use very small copy, provided only that it is large enough to carry fully a statement of your proposition; but in that event you must be more patient in waiting for the results, and must be more persistent in the repetition of your copy.

INITIAL SALES

"The first prime idea, then, is that a large percentage of the people are inattentive to any proposition advertised anywhere, and that their attention must be secured before they can be induced to become customers. Hence, at the outset of any advertising campaign relatively but few people read the advertising; fewer still are convinced by it, and enthused by it to the point of purchase, but those few represent the vitality of the advertising campaign. They purchase the goods. If the goods are deserving of advertising they will please the customers, and pleased customers propagate advertising, so that while you might reach a million readers with your advertising campaign and interest and sell only a few dozen of them at the outset, that few dozen is increased proportionately in subsequent advertising, and if the advertising is persistent the initial purchasers become more and more numerous. However, it is seldom the case that initial purchasers buy sufficiently in their initial purchases to justify the advertising expenditure.

"We must look beyond the first purchases by the first purchasers in order to secure sufficient results to justify the advertising appropriation, and here comes the necessity of recognizing the time element.

"Let us return to the Parable of the Sower. When the sower went forth to sow, he did not go forth the next day to reap. He waited for days and weeks and months before his crop was ready. Then he went out and harvested it. He did not harvest a crop from the seed which fell upon stony ground, or among thorns, or the seed which were eaten by the birds of the air. His crop resulted only from the seed which germinated, and reproduced, some thirtyfold, some sixtyfold, some a hundredfold. That seed when garnered was in the next season resown and multiplied itself again, and in the third season resown again, and multiplied itself again. The result, of course, is not an arithmetical, but a geometrical development of results.

"The case is paralleled in an intelligently directed, persistent advertising campaign. The initial customers buy, but buy lightly, and they are few and far between. They recommend the goods, however, to their friends. They are enthusiastic over their purchases. They boast of their bargains of quality or price. The consequence is that other buyers are induced on their recommendation to make purchases. They in turn are pleased, and they also recommend other buyers to buy, so that each pleased customer becomes a walking advertisement of the proposition, spreading the news of the quality of the proposition far and wide.

HOW THEY GROW

"Each initial purchaser might be regarded as a sort of inoculation of the community in which he lives with the virus of the proposition, that inoculation resulting in the spread of trade just as inoculation with a virus results in the spread of germs throughout the body, and the propagation of millions of other disease germs of the same type. Moreover, pleased customers when they find themselves pleased with a purchase are likely to repeat their business year after year, or from time to time, as their needs occur.

"The advertiser then has three sources of income from his advertising: first, the initial sales of initial purchasers. This is a small source of income. Second, repeat sales from time to time from initial customers, which is a much larger source of income, and third, first purchases and repeat purchases from people to whom the proposition has been recommended by other purchasers. We will call these sales collateral sales, and this constitutes the big crop of results from the advertising.

"In order to secure collateral sales in large quantity it is, of course, necessary, first, for the advertising to be printed, to be read, to interest the reader, to result in initial purchases. It is further necessary for the goods to be delivered, to be used, to please the customer, and then for sufficient time to elapse for that customer to advise his friends and relatives that he was pleased. That advice may be repeated through years and years, to scores of individuals, who in turn become purchasers and repeaters.

"The impatient advertiser is not willing to await results in the way of collateral sales, nor even willing to await results in the way of repeat orders from initial customers. He expects a flood of orders from every reader of his advertisement, and assumes that

478 BUILDING NEWSPAPER ADVERTISING

every reader of a publication necessarily is a reader of his advertisement. Hence the disappointment.

AN ILLUSTRATION

"Hasty, impatient advertisers are likely to give up their advertising campaigns and get very little out of them. They are likely also to fail to attribute what they do get to the advertising which they have done. To illustrate: Some years ago a metal shingle manufacturer in Ohio placed with my house an order for something over $4,000 worth of advertising. The copy was prepared, designs made, electros sent out to the papers, and the advertising developed up to the value of about $2,000. Invoices were rendered for the first and second months, and when the advertiser received the second month's invoice he ordered the advertising canceled, saying that his inquiries were costing him about $8 each, and that he had only sold $500 worth of goods, while the advertising invoices amounted to $2,000. I wrote him, pointing out the fact that he had only waited two months for results, that he had not given sufficient time for the advertising to bring results, that his inquiry cost would no doubt be reduced from $8 to something like $6; that $6 was not a high price to pay for inquiries on a proportion where the sales would probably average in excess of $100 per sale, and where the percentage of sales to inquiries would probably be at least one out of two, and where the repeat orders would likely come in from a large percentage of the initial buyers. However, my customer insisted that the advertising was no good, that he had lost a lot of money, and didn't care to lose any more. Sixty days later I asked him for information as to the cost per inquiry, number of inquiries and quantity of sales. He replied that the sales were over $2,000, and his inquiry cost was down to approximately $6 per inquiry. Six months later one of our salesmen called on this advertiser, and was told that his factory was working overtime, and was sold beyond capacity, that the only advertising he had done was the $2,000 worth of advertising done on the contract given to us; that he was much pleased with the advertising; many dealers in the South had stocked the line; sales were magnificent, and that he never expected to advertise with any one else; and would begin advertising again when he could get his factory enlarged so as to produce more goods.

"Thus, within eight months from the time when the advertiser thought his advertising campaign a complete failure his point of view was changed to the theory that it was a magnificent success. That particular advertiser was most fortunate. There are not so many who can get results so rapidly as he did.

ANOTHER ILLUSTRATION

"I have in mind another advertiser—a mineral-water proposition in South Carolina. The advertiser was persistent. He was determined to popularize his proposition. He guaranteed the quality of the water, money back if not satisfied. He had never sold a drop of water until he placed an account with us, an expenditure of $600. The results came in quite slowly, and at the end of the year the combined result of the advertising and the sales effort of the owner of the spring was a total of only about $3,000 of sales. On the face of it the campaign was not a success, if judged from the standpoint of one year's experience, where a large part of the sales had been made by the personal efforts of the owner of the spring; sufficient time had not elapsed for the water to become popular in the area in which it was advertised. The second year he spent with us $3,000. His sales exceeded in the second year $20,000. The third year he spent over $6,000, and his sales were $102,000.

"Now the first year a large percentage of the mail-order sales were initial purchases, carrying the keys shown in the advertisements, and hence identified as initial purchases. These buyers, however, repeated their order from time to time. The second year the traceable keyed business was much smaller in ratio to the total business, and the third year the ratio was twelve to one; that is, twelve times as much repeat business and collateral sales as initial business. This year it is anticipated that the total sales will exceed a quarter of a million dollars on an advertising appropriation of something over $12,000, and it is likely that the percentage of repeat business and collateral business will be even larger in proportion to the initial keyed mail-order sales, for as the expenditure of advertising increases the territory has to be widened, the express rates are higher, and greater handicaps therefore apply on getting business, so that the advertising cannot be expected to be as effective initially, though fully justified by the magnificent results in repeat and collateral business.

"I might give you scores of other illustrations of like character where results are at first disappointing,

BUILDING NEWSPAPER ADVERTISING 481

but later increase in volume and eventually swell into such proportions as to make magnificent successes.

PSYCHOLOGICAL EFFECT OF ADVERTISING

"But the point which I wish to accentuate is that the advertiser should be patient, as patient as a successful fisherman. A fidgety fisherman catches but few fish. It takes patience; it takes long waiting to get the right results, and persistent advertising, in order to build the biggest results. For every time you reach a reader with an advertisement about your proposition you add something to the conviction which that reader already perhaps possesses from having read other advertisements in previous issues of his paper. The more often he sees your advertisement the more he comes to have confidence in your proposition. Indeed, you may take any proposition, even a falsehood, and if it is repeated sufficiently often you will find not a few people who will not come to believe it simply because it is a reiteration. The statement of a truth may be at first advanced. The repetition of the statement adds strength to it, and a reiteration of the statement over and over again gradually accumulates conviction. It is on this principle that the imperative in advertising copy is effective. You tell the public to do a certain thing, a simple imperative; for instance, 'Drink Coca-Cola,' only two words, but repeat it millions of times. Have the public read it over and over, and over again. Eventually, without any good reason for drinking Coca-Cola other than that they are told to drink Coca-Cola, people will begin to try it. If they like it they will repeat. If they continue to repeat they may become perhaps extensive users of the drink. Or, take another illustration: You walk up to a soft-drink counter. Your friend asks you what you will have. There are scores of soft drinks from which you may select. You have been reading Welch's Grape Juice advertising. You have no particular favorite drink. You have seen the Welch's Grape Juice advertisement time and time again, so much so that it has impressed itself upon you, and you are carrying it in memory without really realizing it. Your subconscious memory comes to your assistance and you say, 'Give me Welch's Grape Juice.' It is because you have seen the advertising repeated time and again. The iteration and reiteration made you call for Welch's Grape Juice rather than somebody else's grape juice, or rather than merely ask for grape juice.

PERSISTENCE AN ABSOLUTE ESSENTIAL

"Persistency in advertising, the iteration and reiteration of your proposition, gradually interests more and more of the possible customers in your field of operation, and the more customers you secure, if they are pleased, the more they repeat the news of their satisfaction to others, lead others to adopt your position and use it. It is in this way that business is propagated. Every one recognizes the necessity of brain in business propaganda. Every one recognizes the necessity of money in business propaganda, but every one should also recognize the necessity of time in business propaganda, before checking up for results, and it is that point which I wish to accentuate before your club, because so many really successful campaigns are quashed in their infancy through the impatience of the advertiser, and through lack of recognition of the fact that it takes time to make an advertising crop, just as it takes time to get a crop of pecans from a pecan grove, or a crop of oranges or grape fruit from a citrus fruit orchard. Not so long, perhaps, as it takes for securing results in nut growing or citrus fruit growing, but nevertheless it takes a considerable period, on some propositions perhaps six months; on most propositions, where the goods move through second hands, from a year to two or three years. Indeed, to put a proposition on a fine financial basis, making it a big dividend payer, I should say that the advertiser ought always be willing to wait three years for his maximum results, or, in other words, dividend-paying results, for maximum results are never reached until a line of trade is monopolized.

"I have had the opportunity in the last seventeen years to analyze thousands of advertising experiences. Many of them were remarkable successes and so recognized by the advertisers. A considerable percentage, however, were superb successes, not recognized by the advertisers, and not a few of those became failures simply through the impatience of the advertiser and his unwillingness to back the proposition to a productive basis, his unwillingness to recognize the fact that it takes time to grow a crop, and that it takes time to propagate information about any proposition, commercial or otherwise.

"Have you not frequently observed that a candidate runs for office, is defeated, runs again, securing a larger vote, but is defeated, and, running a third time, wins out? I have observed this to occur in scores of instances. The persistent candidate almost always wins. Why? Simply because he is persistent. He recognizes the time element in advertising. He knows that his friends, once having voted for him, are likely to repeat their vote, and are likely to influence more and more people to vote for him as he repeats his candidacy. The advertiser is a candidate for trade. If he fails to be elected the first year and runs again the second year he will get a larger volume of trade. If he runs the third year he is likely to be elected. In other words, is likely to get results fully commensurate with and more than commensurate with his total expenditure. After that it is an easy thing to keep on spending and keep on receiving much more than is spent.

"If I can impress upon the advertisers, present and to come, in your club this important basic condition of successful advertising, I feel that I have brought you a message worthy of being remembered and one which will be of value to you in all of your advertising experience."

LXIX

Efficient Newspaper Advertising.—Herbert Casson

UNDER the heading, "Efficient Newspaper Advertising," Herbert N. Casson contributed a really notable article to *Newspaperdom* of December 12, 1912, the major part of which I reproduce:

"After many years of being lost in the bushes, the daily papers are now finding the straight, broad road of advertising efficiency. For the past five or six years at least, in the higher grade daily papers, there have been many advertisements that are just as efficient and just as effective in every way as any of the ads. in the national magazines.

"The fact is that good and skilful advertising began about fifteen years ago in the monthly magazines. The magazines were first to weed out the trash They were first to have a sense of responsibility for what they printed. They were first to protect the public from dishonest advertising. They were first to shut their doors on patent medicines, whiskies, and real-estate explosions.

"Through the statesmanship of several very competent magazine proprietors, advertising became clean, responsible, and efficient. It came to be regarded as an asset instead of an expense and a nuisance. It became a business-builder, and achieved so much national respect that to-day no manufacturer can hope to be nationally successful without the assistance of advertising.

"So, the credit for the development of advertising may be properly divided up to the present time between the newspapers and the magazines. The newspapers came first. They proved that any kind of advertising was better than none. Then came the magazines. They have proved in the past fifteen years that the better and cleaner advertising is the greater are the results.

"But the time has now come, I believe, for a third great step. The magazines will lose their present commanding position. The newspapers will now begin to clean up and become responsible for their advertisements. They will find, as some have already done, that for every disreputable ad. they have the nerve to reject other ads. will come—ads. that are decent and beneficial to the community.

"More and more we are moving into an age of speed and specialties. Here is where the newspaper comes in. It is the fastest of all mediums. It strikes thirty times to the magazine's once; and each newspaper strikes its own people in its own special community.

"The recent improvements in newspaper presses, the invention of new methods, and the betterments of paper stock, all these have prepared the larger and more progressive newspaper for a forward step in the march of advertising.

"At the present time there is no one man or no one newspaper that can claim to be a national authority on efficient newspaper advertising. No one has

BUILDING NEWSPAPER ADVERTISING

worked out the problem as to exactly what a newspaper advertisement ought to be. There has been discussion, and plenty of it. Every ad. club in the United States is expressing opinions and giving experiences concerning newspaper advertising.

"But as yet there has been no exhaustive study of the proposition. No one has taken ten thousand newspaper ads. and classified them. No one has made a two years' study of results, except perhaps from his own personal point of view. Practically all the data that we have at the present time is of a purely personal or local character.

"In the first place, it is plain that an ad. in a newspaper should not be built on the same lines as an ad. in a magazine. As the magazine men have taught us to say, 'A magazine ad. lives for a month, while a newspaper ad. lives only for a day.' A magazine carries a large amount of waste-basket insurance. It is not apt to be thrown away. Its readers are apt to have more leisure and to be in a more receptive frame of mind.

"A magazine ad. is bound in the same cover with the best of reading matter. Accompanying it are articles and illustrations, which represent the topmost pinnacle of skill on the part of both writer and artist. All this, of course, adds greatly to the value and to the prestige of the advertisement in the magazine.

"A newspaper, on the other hand, is read with less leisure but more interest. It is a less perfected but much more urgent and intense publication. People may read magazines, but they must read newspapers. The newspaper, by its very nature, suggests immediate action. It is vivid, stimulating, electrical. It does not give us articles and essays and works of art. It gives us the quick and dramatic news of the day.

"A newspaper, and nothing but a newspaper, can awaken a local community to quick action. Nothing else besides a newspaper can strike the iron of public interest while it is hot.

"In short, I think we may fairly say that magazine advertising is best for education and national prestige, while newspaper advertising is best for local follow-up work and for making the actual sales. There is, of course, no conflict, and there never should be any dispute between magazines and newspapers so far as advertising is concerned. Each does its own work in its own way. Each does its work differently; and each will be used for advertising purposes as long as business lasts.

"In making a few suggestions as to what an efficient newspaper ad. ought to be, I would say:

"First, it ought, above everything else, to be conspicuous. Suppose a man takes twenty minutes to read his morning paper, and suppose the paper has twenty pages. He has only one minute to give to each page. He has only ten seconds to give to a column. He has only one second to give to a three-inch ad.

"A newspaper ad., therefore, must not be on a basis of minutes, but of seconds. It must tell its story in a space of two or three heart-beats. In a word, a newspaper ad. must be a glance ad. rather than an ad. which must be read with care and attention.

"Also, it must be conspicuous because it has to compete with the full-pages of the department stores. These full-page ads. are the lords of the newspaper. They are so large and so interesting and so specific that it is very difficult indeed to get any attention for an ad. of any other kind. How to compete with the full-page department store ad. on one hand and the day's news on the other hand—that is the problem which we have to solve.

"To compete with the full-page every other ad. must be conspicuous, and to compete with the news of the day every other ad. must have a certain amount of news value.

"I doubt if there is any profit whatever in advertising a mere trade-mark or the same old set of words over and over again in a daily paper. A newspaper is not a billboard. The people who read it read it to get the news.

"Whatever else a newspaper ad. is, it ought to be fresh.

"Nobody buys yesterday's papers.

"Nobody lives on last year's breath.

"Not even one paper a day will satisfy us in this impatient age.

"We must have a morning paper and an evening paper, and sometimes two or three 'Extras' in between.

"If we naturally resent it when our news is a few hours old, do we not also instinctively resent it when the ads. are old and stale? The man who would increase the efficiency of his newspaper advertising must pay constant attention to the front page of his paper. He must watch the headlines. He must keep in touch with the whole swing of events. He must know what people are talking about. Then he must fit his ad. to the news of the day and swing it into efficiency with the tide of public opinion.

"After a great national disaster, for instance, the

man who jumps into the daily papers with an advertisement of accident insurance is sure to reap great results. After a great fire in a city the man who comes to the front at once with advertisements of fireproof apparatus is sure to win success. During cold weather the public is in the right humor to buy coal, and during hot weather it is in the humor to buy ice-cream. During a period of increasing prosperity almost everybody is in the mood to buy real estate, and during a period of panic and depression it is in the mood to buy bonds or any other reliable income-bearing securities.

"The especial value of a newspaper is that its readers have the habit of looking in the paper to-day for what they want to buy to-morrow. Whenever the impulse of buying seizes them there is always a newspaper on the spot; and thus, while a newspaper ad. can never be as beautiful as an ad. in a magazine, it always has the value of being recent.

"Generally speaking, men buy goods because their minds have been impressed recently or vividly or often.

"The vivid impression is more likely to be that made by the ad. in the magazine. But the recent impression and the repetition of impressions come more naturally from the newspaper. A newspaper is not the best place for an advertisement of sentiment. An ad. of the 'heart-throb' variety is not likely to be very effective in the daily paper. Neither will an ad. of the 'art-gallery' type be found to prevail on the poorly printed pages of the daily. Nothing can be more forlorn than a would-be artistic ad., which comes out in the paper looking like the splash of a shoebrush. An advertisement that is designed to give prestige—an advertisement of the 'dignity' species—always looks somewhat out of place in the hurry-scurry pages of the newspapers. In fact, all ads. of sentiment, beauty, and dignity are placed much more fittingly in a magazine than they are in a daily paper.

"On the other hand, an ad. which is an announcement, or which names the price, or which is an intimate face-to-face talk about the goods, is much more effective in a newspaper than in a magazine. There is not, and there never can be, very much rank and prestige in a newspaper ad., but there can be interest, efficiency, and force.

"Picking up a copy of *The New York Morning World*, I notice that there are 32 display advertisements; 11 of these have the name of the firm as the headline; 5 of them have as the headline the trade-mark name of the article, such as 'Royal' baking powder; 9 of the ads. were written in the form of an announcement to the public. Out of the 32 ads., 24 are either conspicuous or have a certain news value, while 8 are neither newsy nor conspicuous. Therefore I would say that the display ads. in this copy of the morning *World* are 75 per cent. efficient, which is certainly an unusually high percentage."

LXX

Selling Costs.—*J. George Frederick*

It has been proved that advertising reduces the selling cost of commodities in general use and demand, and that an effective advertising campaign has given many concerns doing merely an ordinary traffic in an article a national and international market many hundred times larger.

The following by J. George Frederick, editor of *Advertising and Selling*, gives some definite cases regarding the cost of selling worth consideration by students of advertising:

"If the muckrakers ever stumble on to the facts about the selling expense of some concerns, there will be a series of sharp literary explosions.

"There is a manufacturing concern in New York whose product is enjoying an international market, and is regarded as having achieved success in every way, yet its selling cost is still five times its manufacturing cost!

"Now if this product were a luxury, or even a specialty novelty as yet not universally used, there would conceivably be some justification for this selling cost; but the article referred to is a typewriter which has come to be practically a staple.

"There is another highly successful typewriter whose

selling cost is still four times manufacturing cost. There are several other very successful typewriters which have selling expense down to three times cost of manufacture, which may be regarded as fairly normal for typewriters or any well-known semi-staple mechanical device where repair and service after purchase are additional factors.

"But, gazing generally over the field of manufacture, selling cost in a surprising number of cases is excessively high. Only in the most staple of staple lines does it come down to a more sane proposition. One or one and a half times the cost of manufacture is a general average for selling staples, while in the drug lines, and specialties in all lines, grocery, textile, hardware, etc., the selling cost rises to four, five, and six times the cost of manufacture. Sometimes, for some articles (and not all of them like Colonel Sellers' Eyewash, either), the cost of manufacture is a mere nothing, and almost the only expense is selling expense.

"The estimates of selling expense just made include office and overhead expense and everything else chargeable to the 'selling end.' To examine selling cost in single detail, let us take purely the cost of salesmen and sales departments, exclusive of whatever else might be chargeable to selling.

"In hosiery and underwear lines this selling expense (frequently the only kind there is) runs to 6 and 10 per cent. of net return. In men's clothing it runs from 4 to 7 per cent. In office equipment lines it runs to 25 and 33 per cent., and in drug and hardware lines it runs up from 25 to 40 and 60 per cent. and higher. In purely luxury lines selling cost has no roof at all—it is as expansive as the empyrean blue

—according to the article, competition, and method of distribution. The branch agency is mighty expensive machinery of sales, but it produces volume and keeps sales contact with consumers keyed up (things which are vital in competition). It frequently costs $500 to sell an auto, and the average is $100 to sell a piano. In many cases, especially in the piano business, there is precious little profit left after this high selling cost is expended.

"This matter of increasing selling cost is becoming more and more vital all the time, because of two things, the widening of markets and the growth of competition. The bigger a manufacturing concern becomes the greater usually does the selling cost become. This may seem paradoxical, but public accountants will testify to its almost invariable truth. A selling organization adequate to the territory, the policies, and the product of a large concern increases selling cost considerably over that of a smaller manufacturer, chiefly because the large manufacturer needs more executives and must meet competition at more points. He has more baskets of eggs to be watched than the small manufacturer.

"In the last decade or two, therefore—ever since the beginning of big markets and big enterprises—selling cost has been rising steadily and become a problem with manufacturers. Some have agreeably deluded themselves about the true state of affairs by figuring loosely that reduction of cost of production was 'helping' to lessen selling cost. But inquisitive modern cost accounting turns the light on such delusions for those manufacturers (none too many) who are modern enough to have thorough going cost systems.

"The one significant thing about selling costs is still blindly overlooked by many manufacturers, while, meantime, those keener ones who do understand it, and have applied it long ago, are the big gainers. Selling cost goes down in proportion to the reputation of the goods and the favorable conviction in the mind of the buyer. You don't have to work nearly so hard to sell me Baker's chocolate as you do to sell me Jones's chocolate. Neither do you have to work so hard to sell dealers and jobbers. In fact, in such exceptional cases, like Baker's and a few others, you could shut down on all selling expense for a time and make a lot of money nevertheless."

LXXI

Proclamation and Persuasion
(From *"The London Times," September 10, 1912*)

It is singular how little is known, theoretically speaking, of what one may call the commonest of all the objects by the wayside. It is more than by the wayside, it is by the bedside, on the breakfast table, in omnibuses, in trains, and by the railway lines. It waits for us in restaurants, in hotels, and in theaters. It follows us abroad and lives in our books at home. It shuns not altogether either the cradle or the grave. It begs us to borrow money. It urges us to buy everything under the sun. It implores us to accept, free, medicines, powders, soaps, and every sort of household necessary or food. Whence come this shamelessness, these perpetual intrusions, this ubiquity? What is their moral justification, if any? What is their economic explanation?

These questions are rather hard to answer, but it is peculiarly within the province of a newspaper to solve these problems. The commodity which a newspaper has to dispose of, by which it lives, is the most valuable in the world—publicity. This commodity it dispenses freely and for no consideration whatever in its news columns. It has the power to set generals, politicians, and artists on pinnacles of success and glory by holding them up prominently before the public eye, not necessarily favorably in all cases. On the other hand, three lines in the paper may cut short the career of the public servant, of the society leader, or even of the humblest individual having pretensions to character or respectability. Now, it is by the sale of the same commodity for purposes of business that the newspaper acquires the revenues which enable it to bear the enormous costs of its modern news-collecting system and of the payment of its skilled staff. Advertising enables the newspaper proprietor to sell for threepence or a penny what it has cost him far more to obtain. In return, all he requires from his pampered readers is the minutest fraction of their attention to his advertising columns. They have been paid for it beforehand in kind.

The elements in the value of advertising are two, of which one lies in the reader himself or the onlooker, whichever he may be; the other is embedded in the conditions of modern industry. The stress and hurry of modern life, the increasing calls on his time, and the appeals of his various pleasures are daily raising the price of the attention of the ordinary individual. It is, moreover, not only the mere pressure on his mind of his amusements and his occupation which have increased the difficulty of approaching him; but the man in the street has lost his receptivity, he is warily on guard against his own impressions, and he has schooled himself to petty harshness and frugalities. Yet the silent struggle goes on. Sooner or later he must spend his money, and generally in the direction of those who have wooed him most skilfully and, perhaps, most expensively. In the price which he ultimately pays for his goods or his enjoyments is presented, among other constituent costs and profits, also the little bill for advertising. So it is the public that pays for all in the end, as we might expect.

The other, and even more important, half of the question lies in the fact that, while the individual buyer is every day harder to approach, the conditions of modern industry require more and more that he shall be hustled or bullied or bounced or coaxed into buying, and buying quickly. That is the characteristic difference between the advertising of ancient days and modern advertising. When production was slow and costly, the seller found customers eager and waiting for his goods as soon as they were finished. The world was always a little hungry then. Few stomachs were entirely filled. Fasting was easier, and repletion a less common sin. This cardinal fact applied no less to luxuries than to necessaries. The natural consequence was that advertising never found itself obliged to go beyond the proclamation stage. People would throng to Cheapside to buy shoes at the sign of the Golden Lion, because they had heard when they were young that John Geddes made the best shoes at a reasonable price, and it was known generally that his sign was a Golden Lion. Arrived at the Golden Lion, they would hear from John Geddes that nowadays he could not turn out shoes fast enough for the people who came to him, and that, what with the price of leather and his failing eyesight and the increasing taxes, he could not afford to ask less than 6d. a pair more than his old prices. His trade and connection were made for him by simple industry and honesty, so long as he preserved easy means of identification by remaining on the same spot.

John Geddes would find trade different in the twentieth century. If he had inherited an old stand turned into a new and luxurious shop from earlier Geddes ancestors, together with a goodly supply of Geddes capital wherewith to buy large stocks and hold them against the market, he might follow the old prescribed routine. But there are very few merchants in this happy position; and a new and fresh John Geddes without any ancestors behind him would not be able to sell any shoes at all, except at current prices fixed by the laws of supply and demand. The prices he would find would be so low that he could only manufacture them by buying the latest machinery at the prices required by the Boston trust. The new machinery would be all that it was supposed to be, and would turn out shoes at 500 times the pace that the old John Geddes could reach at his best. The simple result would be that the new John Geddes would make a fortune if he sold all his shoes in good time, and would be ruined if he did not. Between one alternative and the other there would be an interval, which nothing but good selling and good advertising would bridge over.

That speculative interval between fortune and ruin is growing wider and wider every day; and the sum of money which it represents becomes steadily larger. It is the fund available for advertising and selling in one way or another. In the United Kingdom at the present time it has been estimated to be 100,000,000 pounds—about 25 per cent. greater than the net output of the iron, steel, shipbuilding, and engineering trades in this country together. Central Europe would spend about as much. Latin Europe and Russia would also do the same. North America would probably equal all Europe together. South America and Asia, with Africa and Australia, would amount each to a unit of the size of the United Kingdom. Let us take the whole available fund for advertising of all kinds to be about 800,000,000 pounds annually. Of these in most countries, including ours, something less than one-half goes to the newspapers.

It is the paradox of modern industry that production has outstripped demand. All the markets of the world are glutted with goods from time to time, and the adjustment of the rate of output to the needs of buyers is the greatest practical problem of our day. There is an inherent opposition between the requirements of rapid and immense production for the purpose of securing cheapness in manufacturing cost and the equally urgent necessity of putting these floods of goods on the market as slowly as possible in order to maintain prices. Since it is often impossible so to arrange production and marketing as to get rid of this fundamental contradiction, it becomes worth while to spend large sums of money in order to hasten on sales, to stimulate demand, and to rouse desire. The modern seller can seldom afford to wait for his customers to come to him. He must go out into the highways and hedges and compel them to come in before his manufactured stock depreciates and is wasted, or before the bills drawn on himself by his wholesale house become due.

The business of modern selling is carried on in three ways. The first and oldest is the plan of living within the circle of your customers and establishing intimate personal relations with them. It is the common practice of many old-fashioned firms; but the circle of customers controlled in this way is generally too small for the needs of modern extended business. The second is to set out to solicit your customer by means of trained agents and canvassers —a very effective way, but again confining trade to a small number of transactions. This method can be made to pay only when the orders are valuable enough to stand the heavy rate of commission required to reward capable agents; for the business of selling is a highly skilled one, and exacts generous remuneration. Since in the greater number of modern businesses the tendency is to seek a small profit on an immense number of transactions rather than a larger profit on a restricted business, the net has to be spread more widely and an appeal has to be made to the public at large by advertising.

Advertising embraces two distinct processes, proclamation and persuasion. The first is the older, and consisted merely in announcing that one had such and such goods in stock or was prepared to offer services for a specified reward. These announcements in modern newspapers and periodicals come under the head of classified advertising. In every paper there are special headings for them, to guide the eye of the customer who is looking out for that kind of service or commodity. Up to the time of the industrial revolution, as Arnold Toynbee called it, it was practically the only form of publicity attempted in a commercial sense. There were perhaps in it occasionally the germs of persuasion, yet this was a subordinate element of which the intention was not fully acknowledged. One would be safe in putting the covering dates of this period of change as occurring between the Napoleonic and the Crimean wars. Until the end of that period and a little later advertising remained rather in an embryo state; and it began to develop rapidly about the time that the tax on newspaper advertising was entirely removed. In 1832, when the tax was at the higher rate of 3s. 6d., the amount collected from all the newspapers in the Kingdom was £170,650, of which in some years *The Times* alone contributed as much as £70,000. After the reduction of the tax, in 1833, to 1s. 6d., the receipts fell to £131,000, and rose again in 1853, the year of the repeal, to £180,000.

The golden age of newspaper advertising may be said to have begun in the Victorian sixties in this country, and in America after the close of the Civil War. It is probable that in the early days the ordinary devices of commercial advertising originated in this country and were adopted, carried to greater lengths by American enterprise, and returned to us amplified and improved. Until very recently the bulk of newspaper advertising belonged to or assumed the form of the proclamation pure and simple. This was to some extent due to the extremely conservative habits and regulations of the newspaper managers of the time—habits which undoubtedly resulted in considerable injury to the properties they controlled. At a time when the public was accustomed to look chiefly to its newspapers for general advertising the insistence on small type and column rules, the imposition of an antiquated scale of charges and queer penalties on any irregularity of insertion succeeded ultimately in driving away to a wide and more liberal field the natural flood of advertising which could not allow itself to be held in perpetual shackles. To this desire and even compulsion to escape from hampering restrictions was due the tendency during the last twenty years of the last century toward mere blatancy which at the time was so offensive. This blatancy will probably prove to be a passing phase due to temporary tendencies and to the fact that all freedom to advertisers was at first denied in the more reputable and dignified channels of the press. It is already tending to decrease, and is being succeeded by a much more formidable foe to our pockets—the art of insidious persuasion. But in the course of the change many a valuable newspaper property has been severely damaged and even destroyed. The wide opportunities found by advertisers for themselves in the cheaper press or in technical publications are now to some extent habits stereotyped in both advertisers and readers, and it is improbable that the old monopoly of the daily press which once existed in this country will ever be restored.

Let us examine a little more closely the development of advertising from proclamation to persuasion, remembering always that all advertising must contain some elements of both, and that of persuasion there are many forms. Probably the first discovery made by the primitive advertiser was that proclamation repeated sufficiently often itself became persuasive. The iterated appeal to the eye stamps its form on the brain without any special connotation, and in the absence of any opposition remains there until some favorable occasion or recollection brings it into practical association with the wants of some individual. Since this idea of mere iteration is not at all an obvious one, it did not occur to many people, and it was thoroughly exploited by a few pioneers, who made often immense fortunes if the goods they were offering were really wanted by the public, and sometimes even when this was not the case. These early advertisers, having each his own field largely to himself, did not trouble to couch their appeals to the public in any but the crudest of forms so as to reach the largest number of customers. The temporary immunity from competition, together with the effect of the restrictions mentioned above by conservative institutions, reinforced the tendency to blatancy, vulgarity, and mere insistence. But this stage to some extent carried its own corrective tendency with it. Advertising was rightly accused of preposterous vulgarity. Vulgarity to many minds is synonymous with poor quality and distasteful presentation of pleasure; and, although the popular classes were themselves unconscious of the presence of vulgarity in advertising and would not probably resent it if they did recognize it, these habits of distaste and criticism descended to each class gradually from the class above it, since the public in every stratum is nothing if not imitative. Such a critical feeling toward advertising was quickly reinforced by competition.

As other sellers came streaming into every kind of market, and there were numbers of advertisers offering articles of the same kind, the public began to make distinctions and draw inferences. One of the first effects of this improvement was that vulgarity in the form of appeal became associated with inferior quality; and a steady amelioration in this direction is well on its way. Even the commonest articles—such as washing-soap, beer, patent medicines, and cheap clothing—are rapidly improving in this respect. The poorest classes as well, who have little purchasing power as individuals, but whose custom is so important owing to its mass, are showing signs of requiring a similar fastidiousness. Although they can hardly ever afford to buy commodities of really good quality, they like to be persuaded that the quality which they can afford to buy is really good, and generally they prefer to be assured that it is the best.

In the United Kingdom we are considerably behind-hand still in the prevailing fashions of advertising as compared with the United States of North America or even with Canada. The vulgar appeal carries more weight with it than it should do. An easy opportunity of judging this can be obtained by buying two popular sixpenny magazines of each country, which are on sale everywhere, and then carefully comparing the method of appeal in each case. About twice as much trouble is spent in preparing the material for American advertisements as is the case with us. An English advertiser considers that the cost of buying space in magazines and newspapers is so considerable that he cannot afford to spend more money in getting his advertising prepared for him by an expert. The American will argue differently; having spent forty or fifty dollars in buying expensive space, he feels he cannot afford to waste it by presenting his case badly to the public at the critical moment; otherwise he has simply thrown his money away. There can be no kind of doubt that the American point of view in this matter is right. The result is that, while three times the amount of money is spent in America as here, probably they get five times the benefit out of it that we do. Many public men and the King himself have made impassioned appeals to this country to rouse itself and prepare for a severer competition in the future with the great progressive nations in the world. Commercially speaking, there is no direction in which vigorous and intelligent energy is more required than in this: that we should train up a class of intelligent, well-educated, alert, young men to spread our commerce in competition with the strong corps of travelers which Germany annually sends out; and that we should learn to advertise as lavishly and as brilliantly as the Americans.

Let us take one concrete example of good advertising and analyze its elements so as thoroughly to extract their meaning. There is a well-known American biscuit manufacturer, who endeavors every day and week to persuade the public that his toasted corn-flakes are the best in the market. Let us see how he uses magazine space on a colored cover. In the first place he fulfils the primary obligation of proclaiming his name clearly by using his own signature, which is picturesquely written, as a trade-mark. By an iteration which is innocent of annoyance, he has got his signature stamped on the mind by repeating it on every box and in every advertisement. In the advertisement in question it is printed conspicuously in red with a white line around it. The secondary requisite is the presentation in the picture, clearly but not too large, of two or three boxes of his biscuits with a clever colored picture of a small child with a suitable inscription in an inclosed panel.

Now the object of this advertisement is to present the trade-mark, describe the goods, and create in the ordinary mind a pleasant association of ideas. It is the simplicity of the scheme which makes it effective. Mere praise would be of no use. Even flattering testimonials have fallen into disuse, as no one reads them. Observe also that all artistic effect is carefully avoided. The suggestion of pleasure in that particular way would be not only useless, but harmful, as it would cause pleasure in itself and not in association with the simple idea presented by the advertisement. On the other hand, blatancy or any unpleasant association of ideas would be equally deadly. What is wanted for this class of appeal is a pleasant impression combined with a suggestion of cleverness of presentation, which insinuates itself into the unwary mind and bears fruit next time the usual stock of biscuits has to be laid in.

We are entitled to hope that this inoffensive but acutely persuasive form of advertising will prevail over and destroy the usual vulgar and obstreperous methods, which have been unpleasantly prominent with us during the last twenty-five years. Of these the most offensive—and possibly quite incurable—form is the display board in the open fields. The reason why this detestable outrage to our more sensitive feelings is possibly incurable except by legislation is that the opportunity of presentation to the individual traveling in a train or motor is so momentary that nothing but a shocking and assaulting appeal to his eye and attention can possibly succeed in making a lasting impression on him. The writer on advertising in the British Encyclopedia does not exaggerate the offense in calling it a violation of one's mind and attention; and, as there is no natural remedy for its perpetration, it offers a clear case for the government of the country to step in and tax it out of existence. It has a tendency to degrade advertising of all kinds and to keep it on a low level. The prevailing and mistaken notion that all advertising is necessarily vulgar is kept alive by this monstrous public trespass on our sensibilities.

Another widely useful form of persuasiveness in advertising is the educative offer. This is probably more employed in the engineering trades than in any other, and it is legitimate and highly successful. For this there is a very good reason. The chief objects offered for sale in engineering papers and magazines are machines or tools for specific purposes; and, as the buyer will only buy and use at most a few machines of any given kind, his experience of any particular type of machine is inferior generally to that of the maker. It is a case of the reversal of Aristotle's maxim that the best judge of cooking is not the cook, but the eater. Any one trying to sell a machine-toll will be the most successful if he can persuade the prospective buyer, not only that he can sell an article which will save money to the other in the cost of manufacturing his product, but that he has in addition a fund of experience in cheapening manufacture in this particular way, which he can impart to any one who buys his machine-toll. Such a suggestion and such a claim must be, as the Americans say, "made good"; and, as this class of goods is bought only by the most highly skilled and trained experts in the world, it has to be and generally is, or the seller goes out of business. In these circumstances it is a striking testimony to the real value of advertising that such an enormous amount of money should be profitably spent as is the case in the engineering trades. Here we have a group of skilled and alert buyers, eager and anxious to spend money in every possible way to reduce the costs of manufacture and to find the best methods of doing so. Here, if anywhere, it would seem to be unnecessary to waste money in showing off one's goods, in explaining new methods, in doing the other man's work for him. Yet it is precisely here and in these circumstances that the largest appropriations are set aside for advertising and the largest revenues are earned by technical journals. It would startle some of the advertising managers of big daily papers in this country if they knew the gross advertising revenues of the weekly engineering papers in America, here, and to a lesser extent in Germany.

The plain truth is that a heavy expenditure in advertising is not, as the Socialists pretend, a disease of an old and effete world, a plain waste of good money, but a new method of progress, which is far from its full stature of development. As the world expands and industry becomes more complicated, production advances by leaps and strides and leaves exchange behind it. It has now become more difficult and expensive to sell things than to make them. So we find capital turning more and more to develop its selling and marketing agencies, and looking everywhere for the most efficient methods of bringing together manufactured commodities and those who desire them. We have a further paradox that the cheapest way of selling one's goods is to spend large sums in doing so; in order to save money in advertising it is necessary to make large appropriations for buying space, to engage the best artists and writers, and to advertise in the most expensive papers. Cheap advertising is money thrown away.

The most valuable form of publicity is that which comes from a gratuitous source, such as the chance puff in the columns of a newspaper or the genuine commendation of some person of rank or assured reputation, or, better still, the accidental advertisement of some good fortune or minor catastrophe turned to good account. One of the biggest general supply stores in London was built up on the fruits of a curious accident of this kind. The kernel of this business was an ordinary corner grocery in the West End, the proprietor of which had stacked up a large consignment of heavy cheeses in the upper stories of the house. The building did not prove equal to the weight. The upper floors broke down, bringing with them the exterior side of the house, so that the whole stock of cheeses fell out into the street. The incident earned an amusing paragraph in the papers next day, so that for some time considerable crowds were attracted there out of curiosity. The proprietor was clever enough to see his opportunity, and took fortune on the bound. He seized the chance of advertising and extending his business, succeeded and built up a considerable fortune.

No one knows better than the professional advertiser and his agent the unique value of such a chance publicity, and also of one obtained through the favor of some friend on the press, or by bringing pressure to bear on the management of a weak paper. It therefore becomes one of the trials of a newspaper manager's life, and of an editor's, to hold out against these free puffs and keep watch against their surreptitious occurrence. If a newspaper begins to make weak concessions in this direction, it will find it very hard to retrieve its character and regain its independence.

The free use of this aid to advertising, even when granted only to considerable advertisers, lowers in reality the commercial value of the advertising columns proper, and seems to proclaim to all and sundry that it is not very well worth while to buy legitimate advertising space in the ordinary way.

Modern advertising is rather at the parting of the ways. It was largely created by newspapers, and will always continue to make use of them; but, either by accident or by the fault of newspapers themselves, a considerable section has been diverted into other channels. Hoardings, placards, and decorated panels are one class of advertising; circulars, pamphlets, and even books are another. Among periodicals themselves almost as much business goes to special technical publications as to newspapers proper. There is no doubt that the newspaper proper, in spite of its immensely greater circulation and wider range, is relatively losing ground compared with other methods; and newspaper managers will have to give a great deal of thought to the problem of inducing the stream of future advertising to return to its pristine favorite source. Probably the direction in which improvement can be chiefly expected is the plan of getting into direct touch with the customer. Advertising departments must be much more specialized than they are now; experts of all kinds will have to be kept ready to advise on difficult points; artists and special writers should be retained to give their services free. Advance in this way, however, will be seriously hampered by the power already acquired by the profession of advertising consultants, who have become a very powerful body able to divert business in any channel they please. Some way must be found for newspapers to come into touch with their customers and assist them professionally as to the best methods of publicity without antagonizing this influential group of middlemen.

There is one class of advertising which will always remain with newspapers, because it comes to them direct now, and must continue to do so, that is, classified advertising, such as auctions, property to let or for sale, situations vacant or wanted. This is one of the very earliest forms of newspaper advertising; and it continues under conditions which are very similar to those under which it started. The revenues derived from it are the backbone of the penny press. It is the one respect in which they have hitherto held their own against the competition of cheaper and more widely circulated papers. The business is stable, because it depends on the acquired habits of the public, who have become accustomed to look in a certain direction when they have a certain want. It is almost entirely independent of circulation, for the reason that a man looking for a given thing which he is confident of finding in a given paper will buy that paper for the few days in which he continues the search. There is a well-known case of two daily newspapers in a large town in the provinces who found themselves in the following relative positions: The one had almost lost its circulation, but it still published regularly the great mass of what newspaper people call the "small wanteds" of the district; but these by themselves did not yield any great profit. The other paper had a vigorous and considerable circulation, which naturally carried with it the bulk of general advertising; but without the classified advertising its profits were restricted. Ultimately both proprietors came together and effected an amalgamation with strikingly successful results, as the double revenue was sufficient to maintain an extremely prosperous paper.

A relic of the old-fashioned advertising by proclamation still coming to newspapers is the stream of public notices, theater notices, losts and founds, and the "agony" column. For this class of business there is no rival to the newspapers, whose circulation immensely exceeds that of any other medium of publicity except that of general weekly periodicals, which are published at intervals too far apart to cover immediate needs. In this respect their function has become the semi-official one of being the universal gazette to the public.

LXXII

Killing the Beginner in Advertising

UNDER the head "Killing the Beginner in Advertising" I wrote the following for *Newspaperdom*, issue May 12, 1910, which, regardless of eight years' experience in broader ways since then, is not changed in a single word to sound an appeal for co-operative effort in the development of new accounts:

"Creating new advertising is one of the greatest accomplishments of the first-class advertising solicitor. To show a business man who has not advertised how a comparatively small amount spent in newspaper advertising will materially increase his business is not only making possible the development of a future large account, but brings a personal satisfaction of a good work well done that will be a pleasurable recollection as long as he lives.

"Some years ago I had the satisfaction of trying my hand at creating a line of women's tailors' ads. for the women's pages of *The New York Sunday Sun.* Up to that time only a few hair goods and proprietary goods houses were represented on those pages. I knew that the right sort of advertising would be profitable from the start, because it would not be buried out of plain view from women readers, no matter how small the copy.

"I well remember the hard time I had to get a tailor

close to Broadway, not far from Thirtieth Street, to pay me eighty cents a line for a thirty-line ad. on the first Sunday. I had a pretty little line cut of a suit copied from one of his fashion plates, and then in a very few words stated 'High-class tailor-made suits, from $35 up.'

"Before the ad. was published his store looked like a down-town lunch-room at midnight. The boss and a little girl sewing buttons on a dress were his only equipment. During the first week he admitted taking five orders from people who had called in response to the ad.

"On the Friday before the second Sunday, when I called with new copy, he commenced to talk about the rate being too high and that he could get the same ad. in other papers for one-quarter the price. I endeavored to show him that the women's page of *The New York Sunday Sun* stood in a class by itself, regardless of rate, and that no one could get an ad. there for one cent less than rates.

"I finally got the order for another issue and so on for three additional weeks. By that time he had four machines going in the rear of his shop and three or four girls working in the front. He commenced to use other papers for larger ads., and finally did his business through some small advertising agent, and moved on to Fifth Avenue, where he is doing a thriving business, if reports be true.

"Incidentally I worked up a number of similar new accounts which had to be carefully carried through the Doubting Thomas stages. While many of them stuck, I am sure that more than half of them were killed before they had really got above ground by copy-chasers and account-chasers, who knocked when they saw that they could not get immediate orders.

"Any plan to bring about a more concerted policy and better understanding between the solicitors of rival papers and advertising agents regarding the treatment of prospects is going to make the creating of new business more worth the effort and greatly broaden the scope of the advertising field, both in regard to the number of accounts and amount of space used.

"Those of us who have thus brought new light into the business lives of, perhaps, very small tradesmen at the start, and have seen them grow into great merchants of the present day, know the value of the seed we sowed years ago, and have good reason to be convinced and cry out at every turn the merits and wonderful pulling powers of effective newspaper advertising.

"The new-comer in the field of advertising must be induced to spend some real money for what seems to him to be a highly problematical venture. It is usually useless to talk to the prospect about the cumulative value of advertising. He must be convinced through almost immediate results that he has not been merely separated from his money just the same as on scores of occasions when he put an ad. in some church fair or ball program. He has been stung so many times when he thought he was buying advertising that he is wary of the hook of the genuine article, which would lead him to great future success.

"The solicitor cultivating the prospect must make a careful study of the situation and suggest a sort of copy which will most likely attract attention and produce inquiries, if not real orders, for the advertiser. Of course, the new advertiser must be induced to persist in his efforts for a reasonable length of time before passing final judgment on the merits of the advertising. It is absolutely fatal to hold out too rosy prospects for the first few ads., and it is much better to pretend that any immediate results are a surprise to the solicitor.

"Given a retail store on any main thoroughfare it is possible to get up a five-inch double-column ad. that will attract new trade almost immediately if inserted in a prominent position in any newspaper of general circulation in the neighborhood. For quickest results one or two big bargain prices for leaders will catch the eye and bring the people into the store. After a few insertions people will get accustomed to look over the ads. of the neighborhood store, just the same as they do other bargain announcements, and if they are sufficiently attractive and they require the goods advertised they will trade.

"At the start the budding advertiser is like a delicate plant just sprouting from the earth. He is so sensitive and doubtful regarding his venture that a breath of air is apt to make him lose heart and stop the seemingly frightful expense. It is while he is in this state that *many a promising prospect has been spoiled by oversolicitation* and the unbusiness-like methods of those seeking to get a piece of his money.

"While it is perfectly natural for solicitors on rival papers to seek to follow up every line of copy appearing in another medium, there should be an unwritten law established and practised by all that when soliciting the prospect of another's creating only words of encouragement be extended until the advertiser has become convinced.

"For the solicitor to pump the prospect full of adverse criticism of the medium he is using and to pretend to show him that his experimental advertising is costing him more per line per thousand of circulation than they can offer is only to confuse and discourage him. By the time he has heard similar stories from the representatives of several different papers he is very apt to quit the game as too difficult a proposition for him to handle.

"Advertising managers and publishers are more often than not really responsible for the oversolicitation of prospects, and thus often defeat the success of the good work of a creating solicitor on a rival paper which eventually would come into their own columns. It is done as the papers are clipped and assignments given solicitors. The report that it is a prospect should be sufficient warning to let the tender plant grow. Such a report does not satisfy the man who demands that the solicitor get every possible line in any other paper, even though he kill the goose that is starting to lay golden eggs.

"Still another handicap confronting the solicitor given to creating new advertisers in any of the large cities is the rivalry between local advertising agencies for the account. Immediately after the appearance of the first ad. the prospect is deluged by offers from adsmiths to really get him up some copy that is worth while. In towns where a commission is paid on local business, such as New York, the rivalry for new accounts is all the keener, while in other places the local agent seeks compensation for the preparation of copy over and above the cost of the advertising.

"While, without a doubt, a well-organized advertising agency is better equipped and qualified to ultimately handle and prepare the storekeeper's advertising in the absence of the services of a competent store advertising manager, overzeal after an account in the making may be just as dangerous for its wellbeing as the oversolicitation by other newspaper representatives.

"All prospective parties at issue should get together and wait for the prospect to see the light in his small experiment. Every one should preach the gospel of encouragement and congratulation: 'All advertising in any reputable newspaper is good advertising. Later on, when you are convinced, we will call around and show you how to still further increase your business.' Such a platform would bring the sort of fertilization that would promote the growth of the plant.

"The prospect is probably spending more money for the experiment than his mossback business training leads him to think he should. Later on, when he has seen the light and felt the benefits of advertising and is spending three, four, or even ten times as much money to make the goods move quickly, no one could stop him short of killing him.

"Then is the time, if ever, for rival papers to fight for larger shares of the business.

"Then the advertiser is in a position calmly to consider the relative values of the different mediums, which was impossible and confusing earlier in the game."

In Philadelphia *The Bulletin* has specialized in the cultivation of small ads., and William Simpson, the business manager of that paper, has told me they figure that it takes two years to get a prospect firmly on his feet as an advertiser. *The Washington Star* likewise has devoted much attention to the development of small advertisers who have grown into heavy users of space.

LXXIII

The Law of Repetition.—Thomas E. Dockrell

The Law of Repetition plays a very important part in advertising unappreciated by those who expect to advertise to-day for results to-morrow. Unless their advertising has become a matter of news interest by regular and constant insertion, a single one-time run will seldom produce results coming to the man or concern whose store news and announcements are looked for by those seeking information regarding goods they may need.

The late Thomas E. Dockrell, in his masterly pamphlet, "The Law of Mental Domination," on this point in arguing that the Bible interested, convinced, and forced action from humanity in a greater degree than anything else ever published, says:

First. It offered people something they wanted, or which, after its perusal, they realized they needed.

Second. It appeals primarily to the interest of its readers; that is to say, it talks more about its readers' wants and needs than of the remedy it offered.

Third. It always uses simple language.

Fourth. It constantly repeats its message and says the same things over and over again in the same or different ways. It does not consider that once

BUILDING NEWSPAPER ADVERTISING

is often enough to tell a message and expect it to be remembered.

Fifth. It is always dominant. It is always superior. It always affirms. It never argues. It never appeals to its readers for confirmation of its statements. Every line breathes dominance, superiority, and confidence in its power to dictate to its readers as to what their action must be in order to acquire what it suggests.

There is most precious background for a theory of sound advertising included in these five crisp conclusions. In summarizing Dockrell says, "In that last paragraph (the fifth) lies the difference between the successful and the unsuccessful leader, whether the leadership be conducted by word of mouth or by printed matter."

Later on in the same pamphlet Dockrell says: "The sacred writers brought the remedy for men's fears. Leaders of the masses always built upon the interests of the men they led. The advertising man—the writer of copy—must do the same. First in his mind must be the readers' interest. Never forget that. Man is interested in himself first. His ills are larger than the remedy. Desire is greater than its satisfaction. The present want or need which your goods fill is larger to your reader than the future satisfaction. First find your reader's interest and then interweave your goods with the interest.

"Copy that sells is not fashioned on what you want to say; it is founded on what your readers are ready and anxious to hear. As soon as this principle is grasped, the whole idea of copy is changed, the writer fades and the seeker of interest grows.

"In these days, when one man discourses on 'clever' copy, another on the necessity for 'art,' another on the 'human nature appeal,' others on 'publicity' and 'leaving-something-to-the-imagination,' it is refreshing to go back to the Bible and other sacred writings which did exactly what is demanded of advertising copy to-day, and did it so much better than any advertising man, living or dead, that there is no comparison. The Bible never is 'clever'; it is never 'artistic' in the present acceptance of the word; it never 'crawls' appealingly to its readers; it does not wander from its subject; it does not use unnecessary words; it does not disguise its thought.

"The Bible, while it changes the form of its message, does not change its simple language. It never changes its message so much that the underlying idea is lost. Above all, the Bible shows the intensity which possessed the men who wrote it; they were so saturated with the message which they felt themselves bound to convey that their minds could hold nothing else. They were incapable of straying from the point of their message; all they could do was to say the message over and over again in different ways."

LXXIV

*The Ten Commandments of Salesmanship.—
Dr. Frank Crane*

THE following, by Dr. Frank Crane, reprinted from *The New York Globe* of Saturday, June 3, 1916, which we have reprinted to meet calls from corporations all over the country, should have a place on the wall of every advertising or sales manager, as well as in every advertising manager's office:

"Some time ago I wrote an article on 'Salesmanship from a Consumer's Standpoint.' I have received so many requests from business houses to republish this that I have decided to rewrite it, make it more concise, and cast it in the form of Ten Commandments.

"It is to be kept in mind that these commandments are supposed to come from the consumer, and not from the sales expert. If you want to sell me or any other buyer goods, therefore, we pray you to keep these commandments.

"1. BE AGREEABLE. Other things being equal, I go to the store where the clerks try to please me. I buy clothing, typewriters, and automobiles of the man who acts as though he likes me. Exert yourself to make a pleasing impression on me, please. I appreciate it. Hence, dress well. Untidy clothes mean you don't care what I think of your appearance. But don't dress too well. That gives you an air of showing off. Dress just right. If you don't know how, find out. Cultivate a pleasing voice. Learn to converse entertainingly. Cut out all mannerisms. Give me the impression of a gentleman, honest, square, anxious to please, and good-natured.

"2. KNOW YOUR GOODS. Don't let there be any question I can ask you relative to the manufacture, history, distribution, or uses of what you have to sell that you cannot answer. If you're selling typewriters, know all about all the kinds. If you're selling coffee, find out all about where all sorts of coffee come from, and all the points about them. Put in your spare time making of yourself an encyclopedia of information about your goods.

"3. DON'T ARGUE. Go with me in your talk, not against me. Lead, don't oppose. Don't show me where I am wrong. Dodge a square issue, and show me wherein you are right. Suggest. Don't antagonize. Argument, as a rule, results in irritation, not conviction.

"4. MAKE THINGS PLAIN. Don't use any words I don't understand. You can explain the most complicated matter to a washwoman if you know your subject perfectly and practise using simple language. Don't air your technical knowledge and try to impress me. I want to be flattered, not awed.

"5. TELL THE TRUTH. Don't lie, or exaggerate, or mislead, or conceal. Let me feel that you are sincere, and mean every word you say, and that every statement you make is of par value. If you represent goods that need lying about, directly or indirectly, quit. There are plenty of articles that are straight and all right. Sell them.

"6. BE DEPENDABLE. Even in small things

create the impression that whatever you promise is as much to be depended upon as your signed note. If you make an appointment at 3 P.M. Tuesday, be there at 2.45, or telegraph. If I order goods of a certain grade, let them be found to be exactly of that grade when I receive them.

"7. REMEMBER NAMES AND FACES. If you have not a natural gift for this, acquire it. Get a little book and set down every day the names of those you have met, with their characteristics. Practise this until you become expert. No man likes to be forgotten or to have you ask his name.

"8. DON'T BE EGOTISTIC. Eliminate the pronoun I as much as possible from your vocabulary. Talk about me, not yourself. Don't tickle yourself, tickle me; I'm the one you want to win.

"9. THINK SUCCESS. Success begins in the mind. Why think fifty cents when it is just as easy to think fifty dollars? Tell success stories, not incidents of failure and hard luck. Radiate prosperity. Feel prosperous. It's catching. Keep your chin up.

"10. BE HUMAN. The reason you are hired to sell goods is that you are a human being. Otherwise your employer would have sent a catalogue. So be a human being, likable, engaging, full of human electricity. For I patronize as a rule the salesman I like.

"Selling goods is the greatest business in the world. It takes all there is in a man. You need to know psychology, you need tact, intelligence, self-control, courage, persistence, and inexhaustible good humor. It is not a job for a second-rater. You simply have to make good or go under.

"I admire a good salesman because I never was able to sell anything in my life. But I'm a good buyer."

LXXV

Successful Advertising.—George C. Sherman

A WONDERFULLY concise summary by George C. Sherman, of Sherman & Bryan, reprinted from *Printers' Ink:*

"There are as many definitions of advertising as there are kinds of advertising. Some call it 'Salesmanship-on-paper'—others, 'merchandizing-in-print.' The definition I like best is *'commercialized push,'* for advertising means *putting pressure* behind a business —shoving it *ahead*—keeping it moving *onward* and *forward.*

"Successful advertising consists of six equally important parts.

"1. A commodity already in demand or one for which a legitimate market can be created.

"2. An article good enough and priced to stand the gaff of competition.

"3. A trade-mark that explains at a glance (without pages of copy) the article that it identifies.

"4. An advertising agency that knows where and how the product should be marketed.

"5. The selection of proper media and forms of advertising to be adopted.

"6. A combination of interests (men) with backbone, and an advertising appropriation sufficient to blaze their own trail and wait for results—which must follow.

"A world-wide market can never be created for any article without advertising. Advertising is not a mystery. No man has the secret of advertising, because there is no secret to it.

"It is simply applied common sense, but applied along the right lines, meaning along the lines of experience. No manufacturer can make a world-wide market for his goods without taking the first step. He must take that step before he can get under way, and after he gets under way he must keep up speed if he expects to reach the desired haven. Any man who manufactures a good article and advertises it wisely can create not only a nation-wide market, but a world-wide market for his goods. But he must never say 'die,' even in face of apparent obstacles. Like any man in private life, a manufacturer of a trade-marked article must make stepping-stones out of stumbling-blocks."

LXXVI

Why the Salesman Fell Down

WHY THE SALESMAN FAILED

(*From the Bankers' and Brokers' Gazette*)

He wasn't neat in his appearance.
He lacked dignity in his bearing.
He used no tact in introducing himself.
He was late in keeping his appointment.
He had a conceited and arrogant manner.
He did not believe in his own proposition.
He disgusted his prospect with gross flattery.
He didn't know the fine points of his own goods.
He offended the prospect by undue familiarity.
He made a bitter attack upon his competitor's goods.
He openly ridiculed his prospect's ideas and methods.
He made no preliminary study of his prospect's case.
He relied on bluff instead of solid argument based on facts.
He got lost in the forest of details and couldn't stick to essentials.
He had been out with the boys the night before and showed the effects.

He talked too much. He gave his prospect no chance to explain his needs and position.

He couldn't answer questions and objections intelligently, concisely, and convincingly. He tried to close his prospect before he had worked him up to a point of conviction.

He lost his nerve because the prospect presented such an unyielding front, forgetting that battles are won by hard rallies at the finish.

He didn't know his business when he made the approach; didn't talk clean-cut business after he got in; didn't make it his business to fight all the way through, and didn't do business before he left.

LXXVII

Elbert Hubbard on Advertising

THE late Elbert Hubbard, who as well as any man of his time knew how to advertise and create resultful advertising, contributed the following to *The Commercial Union* of September 29, 1910, which is well worth recording in a book of this kind:

"The things that live are the things that are well advertised. The thoughts that abide are those that are strongly maintained, ably defended, well expressed.

"All literature is advertising, and all written advertising that grips attention is literature.

"The world accepts a man or an institution at the estimate it places on itself. To let the rogues and fools expound and explain you to the multitude, and you yourself make no sign, is to allow the falsehood to pass as current coin.

"As soon it becomes legal tender. According to the common law of England a path across your property once used by the people is theirs for all time.

"In America millions of dollars are now being expended by certain successful firms and corporations to correct a wrong impression that has been allowed to get a foothold in the public mind concerning them.

"Just remember this: It is not the thing itself that lives; it is what is said about it. Your competitors, the disgruntled ones, are busy. The time to correct a lie is when it is uttered. So the moral is: You must advertise, no matter how successful you are.

"You must advertise wisely and discreetly, so as to create a public opinion that is favorable to you.

"To stop advertising is to let your business run on momentum, and momentum is a gradual move toward a dead stop.

"The Zeitgeist is always at work, always rolling up as a big snowball grows. The best asset you have is the good-will of the public, and to secure this and hold it advertising is necessary. And the more successful you are the more necessary it is that you should place yourself in a true, just, and proper light before the world, ere the lies crystallize and you find yourself buried under a mountain of falsehood. For 'Be thou as chaste as ice, as pure as snow, thou canst not escape calumny.' And the more successful you are the finer target are you for rumor. The only man who is really safe is the man who does nothing, thinks nothing, says nothing, has nothing. He is the only one who need not advertise.

"To stand still is to retreat.

"To worship the god Terminus is to have the Goths and Vandals, that skirt the borders of every successful venture, pick up your Termini and carry them inland, long miles, between the setting of the sun and his rising.

"To hold the old customers, you must get out after the new.

"When you think you are big enough there is lime in the bones of the boss, and a noise like a bucaneer is heard in the offing.

"The reputation that endures, or the institution that lasts, is the one that is properly advertised.

"The only names in Greek history that we know are those which Herodotus and Thucydides graved with deathless styli.

"The men of Rome who live and tread the boardwalk are those Plutarch took up and writ their names large on human hearts.

"All that Plutarch knew of Greek heroes was what he read in Herodotus.

"All that Shakespeare knew of classic Greek and Rome, and the heroes of that far-off time, is what he dug out of Plutarch's Lives. And about all that most people now know of Greece and Rome they got from Shakespeare.

"Plutarch boomed his Roman friends and matched each favorite with some Greek, written of by Herodotus. Plutarch wrote of the men he liked, some of whom we know put up good mazuma to cover expenses.

"Horatius still stands at the bridge, because a poet placed him there.

"Paul Revere rides adown the night, giving his warning cry, because Longfellow set the meters in a gallop.

"Across the waste of waters the enemy calls upon Paul Jones to surrender, and the voice of Jones echoes back, 'Damn your souls, we have not yet begun to fight!' And the sound of the fearless voice has given courage to countless thousands to snatch victory from the jaws of defeat.

"In Brussels there is yet to be heard a sound of revelry by night, only because Byron told of it.

"Commodore Perry, that rash and impulsive youth of twenty-six, never sent that message, 'We have met the enemy and they are ours,' but a good reporter did, and the reporter's words live, while Perry's died on the empty air."

LXXVIII

Conclusion

I HAVE set down for consideration and possible application various views, suggestions, and practical demonstrations regarding the matter of newspaper advertising in a way to provide a guide for those who would go farthest in a most interesting and profitable business. I have sought to lay all the cards face up on the table, to explain what certain combinations mean and will produce, rather than to present a mass of theoretical matter much more difficult to grasp and put in operation.

I have sought to show that the manufacture and sale of newspaper advertising is a vastly different matter from the mere selling of space such as many very successful newspapers indulge in even to-day. The newspaper has a more serious duty to perform to its readers than to accept and print any advertising that is offered to it, and should have a greater interest in its regular advertisers than to compel them to compete with fakes and quacks.

I have merely glanced at the beginnings of newspaper advertising to point out from what crudities present-day efficiencies have grown and briefly considered some of the more interesting high spots of experience that have come within my observation

BUILDING NEWSPAPER ADVERTISING 535

during nearly forty years in the business. I have secured from leading experts in various phases of the business contributions which may be accepted as the present-day last word from acknowledged authorities.

I have found the study of newspaper advertising a subject worthy the painstaking research of all who would succeed in almost any commercial activity. I have found that those who really secured most lasting success through newspaper advertising have had to have "the goods" in order to establish permanency.

We have seen how Robert Bonner built up a story-paper with 400,000 circulation back in the '60's by giving the people "the goods" and advertising them in a bigger and more effective way than any of his competitors; how A. T. Stewart, Marshall Field, Benjamin Altman, from small beginnings, built enormous and enduring businesses which have continued to grow despite much heavier advertising by competitors, simply because the public had been convinced by long-continued honest practices that the advertising offerings of these firms were "the goods."

We have seen how Henry Ford, by the application of principles of sound common sense to quantity production of an automobile at a price within the reach of millions of people, frankly telling them that the more they bought the cheaper he could sell them, has proved himself the greatest advertising genius of the generation. Ford has always sold "the goods," and every one knows that he has, and that is why he stands head and shoulders above others less inclined to take the people into their confidence.

We have seen how John Wanamaker, both in New York and Philadelphia, by giving more serious attention to advertising in the organization of forces larger than are employed in getting out many a considerable newspaper, always making his advertising interesting and attractive, has won marvelous success. It is easy to prove that the Wanamaker advertising is more closely read and more readily believed than that of many of his competitors using other styles and much space.

I have considered the organization of the advertising department of the newspaper and the best type of men to employ both as manager and solicitors in order to make them co-ordinate with best thought and practices by both advertiser and advertising agent. I have shown how the advertising agent came into the problem, how the newspapers later had to develop special representatives, and how to-day we are at a point where greater co-operation between these various factors is going to double or treble the volume of newspaper advertising.

I have shown how the newspapers of the United States and Canada, operating as 2,650 separate units, each out for himself with foolish ideas that any one desiring to trade with it must do so on such terms as it demands, can never attain maximum results for any one of them or for all of them as an industry. I have shown how, through co-operation among themselves, standardization of practices and working in close harmony with other factors in the equation—manufacturers, retailers, and advertising agents—they can attain largest results.

The newspapers control the machinery or process by which, through sound merchandizing of honest goods with advertising which will win and merit public confidence, they can sell anything in general demand offered at fair prices in almost as large quantities as any manufacturer can turn out. This is a strong statement of an advanced position, but to the author and to any one who will take the trouble to dig out the underlying factors presented in this book it is logical and simple.

If I have proved that there is no possible substitute for "the goods" in successful advertising that builds enduring trade, that there is no royal road to wealth through advertising, and disproved the foolish notion that advertising successes are the result of chance shots and good luck, I shall rest satisfied. Unsound views of advertising are the rocks upon which hundreds of millions of honest advertising dollars have been shipwrecked by adventurers without proper equipment in the way of the compasses and charts of experience.

The graveyards of advertisers killed by the ruthlessness and ignorance of the representative of general mediums, who got serious business men to invest honest money in so-called national advertising before the firms had secured a distribution sufficient to make it possible for such publicity to be profitably employed, make up the most sickening exhibit in the history of advertising. Those best informed in the business now admit the superiority of newspaper advertising, and that it is the only sort of advertising that will sell the goods in the dealers' stores.

The author has no sympathy for those who would have him refrain from what they term "knocking" other types of media, on the ground that any criticism of advertising is bad for advertising. One would think, to listen to them, that advertising was a fragile, hothouse plant that must be nursed and coddled like an orchid, instead of the huskiest and most virile force in modern commerce and business, so sound, in fact, that it has been strong enough to lug along deadwood and parasites without limit.

My purpose has been to tell the truth, to acknowledge our weaknesses, to show how we can eliminate the germs of disease that may have crept into our system, and stand up like "go get 'em" men able to deliver about 100 per cent. efficiency. If shams and make-believe stand in our path we must sweep them one side or ride over them, as they have tried to do to us in the past, in the full confidence that as we are right and they are wrong we shall prevail.

To know our weakness is to be able to overcome it. To know our strength should make us desirous of utilizing it to greatest possible advantage both for ourselves and those who, through traffic with us, yield us profit and take it themselves. Knowledge is power if those in possession of it have ability to apply it correctly with advantage to the community and the nation. To have knowledge regarding advertising is to be able to perform what seem like miracles to the uninformed.

The conclusions and deductions from the basic truths laid down in this book lead us to believe the greatest stumbling-blocks in the development of vastly more advertising are the ignorance or insincerity of the seller or manufacturer of space and the lack of courage or meanness of the man with "the goods" which could be exploited a hundredfold through advertising.

The whole process is so simple and sure-fire that advertising may be said to have passed the experimental stage, provided it is done properly and with an absolute determination to succeed. Too many peck at it instead of carrying it through vigorously with the "I will" spirit. Too many go into it feeling that they are embarking on an experiment, and merely hoping against hope that it will succeed, but ever ready to weaken if everything does not come along on schedule time.

Wide observation has revealed to the author that many who pretend to have successful knowledge and experience in advertising are mere pretenders or erroneously think they know. To-day there is no need for depending on such, for there are many who can ring the bell nearly every time, provided the advertiser will stand game and see the battle through.

With men like Stanley Resor, Robert Tinsman, Wilbur Nesbit, H. K. McCann, John Lee Mahin, O. H. Blackman, W. R. Hotchkin, Joseph H. Appel, A. B. Freeman, to mention only a few in the class, he who would know whether his product is of the kind that can be largely developed through advertising will risk nothing by taking advice from those who by sound experience can render valuable counsel.

Few newspaper publishers have confidence in the goods they sell—advertising—as proved by the grudging way they spend their own money in advertising the goods they have for sale. A glance at the trade papers shows that only a handful out of the 2,600 regularly advertises in them. Yet it is mainly the newspapers which advertise in the trade papers that stand at the head of the procession.

Advertising is contagious in more ways than one. Those who know its power and how to use it constantly find new ways to use it for added profit. Among the newspapers, those which carry the volume in any line generally can be used successfully for that line with eyes shut. Advertising begets advertising, both for the medium and the advertisers, and the strange thing about the matter is that real advertising cheapens the cost of a commodity to the consumer.

I call particular attention to the part devoted to contributions from a selected few of the leading advertising agents of the country as giving best and most up-to-date views of soundest modern practices and indicating the degree and kind of co-operation which newspapers can extend to advertisers for greatest constructive purposes.

Having been in the newspaper and advertising business for many years, and having studied practices and methods in a national way during much of that time, I am now firmly of the opinion that, used effectively, newspaper advertising possesses powers and values which only a comparatively small number of our leading business men understand or utilize.

Summarized, successful newspaper advertising must be predicated upon:

1. An article in general demand.
2. An article worth at least what is asked for it.
3. An article at least as good as any other sold at the price.
4. Sound merchandizing methods.
5. Demonstrated customer satisfaction.
6. Money back if not satisfied.
7. Highest degree of service.
8. No overstatement or exaggeration.
9. Strong individuality in copy and treatment.
10. Forceful and persistent copy.

BUILDING NEWSPAPER ADVERTISING

Almost any of the great successes of the past, whether it be a department store, a story-paper, a circus, a line of undergarments, a show, or what not, can be reconciled with some or all of these basic checking points. There are other and probably just as important considerations among them:

1. Will it repeat?
2. Will it give satisfaction?
3. Can it hold its own against substitutes?
4. Will increased sale enable you to sell at lower price?
5. In what territory can market be most effectively stimulated?
6. At what point will saturation make further progress too expensive?
7. Is it an exclusive agency proposition?
8. The efficiency of the selling plan.
9. Dealer helps.
10. Special demonstrations and tryouts.

Real service advertising agencies, such as those represented by the contributions in Part VI, by reason of experience in the successful introduction of various articles, can furnish a degree of valuable advice and suggestion to the prospective advertiser worth many times what the service costs. In the next twenty years what we call efficient advertising to-day will seem as crude to the experts as that of the '60's and '70's does to us. We have discovered much concerning the truth and underlying factors, but it takes time for the knowledge to be accepted and applied.

APPENDIX

APPENDIX A

Table of Newspapers by States with Circulation, by Harry Pruden

VARIOUS estimates have been made regarding the average daily circulation of all the daily newspapers in the United States. It is probable that the total is now very close to 30,000,000 copies a day, or one copy to about every 3½ people. On the old established theory that the average household consists of five people, the newspapers would seem to fairly saturate the nation.

The following table, compiled by Harry Pruden, of Van Patten, Inc., of New York, for *The Fourth Estate*, presents very interesting data. It covers 2,044 publications out of probably 2,465 in the country:

For the convenience of readers of *The Fourth Estate*, the figures are tabulated herewith by state totals and papers in the principal cities. The table following gives full information on the subject in whichever of these forms is most desired:

	PROMINENT CITIES		OTHER CITIES		TOTAL	
	Papers	Cir'n	Papers	Cir'n	Papers	Cir'n
Alabama................	..	....	..	....	23	187,529
Arizona.................	..	....	..	....	17	40,026
Arkansas................	..	....	..	....	30	87,142
California.....San Francisco	5	469,750	126	430,498	137	1,302,092
Los Angeles..	6	401,844	..	....	..	....
Colorado......Denver.....	3	156,690	33	50,339	36	207,029
Connecticut.............	..	....	..	....	35	285,194
Delaware................	..	....	....	....	3	37,992

APPENDIX A

		PROMINENT CITIES		OTHER CITIES		TOTAL	
		Papers	Cir'n	Papers	Cir'n	Papers	Cir'n
Dist. Columbia		..	....	..	....	4	190,147
Florida		..	....	..	....	29	116,796
Georgia	Atlanta	3	135,156	25	135,989	28	271,145
Idaho		..	....	..	....	10	39,793
Illinois	Chicago	7	1,643,029	121	1,192,716	128	2,835,745
Indiana	Indianapolis	3	253,689	128	516,291	131	762,980
Iowa		..	....	..	....	49	522,560
Kansas		..	....	..	....	68	296,912
Kentucky	Louisville	4	161,980	23	82,202	27	244,182
Louisiana	New Orleans	3	160,350	12	20,569	15	180,919
Maine		..	....	..	....	13	109,781
Maryland	Baltimore	4	328,293	9	79,747	13	408,040
Massachusetts	Boston	8	1,419,418	62	482,955	70	1,902,373
Michigan	Detroit	4	497,111	60	442,621	64	939,732
Minnesota	Minneapolis	3	301,331	32	186,742	37	698,102
	St. Paul	2	210,029	..	....	..	....
Mississippi		..	....	..	....	16	40,894
Missouri	St. Louis	5	598,643	67	172,996	75	1,393,629
	Kansas City	3	621,990	..	....	..	....
Montana		..	....	..	....	18	89,267
Nebraska	Omaha	3	214,336	21	104,732	24	319,068
Nevada		..	....	..	....	10	17,186
New Hampshire		..	....	..	....	11	52,069
New Jersey	Newark	2	124,669	32	298,315	34	422,984
New Mexico		..	....	..	....	6	16,849
New York	New York	14	3,589,957	112	1,052,071	136	5,081,152
	Brooklyn	4	191,954	..	....	..	....
	Buffalo	6	270,166	..	....	..	....
North Carolina		..	....	..	....	33	143,560
North Dakota		..	....	..	....	12	55,231
Ohio	Cleveland	3	493,084	142	1,003,192	149	1,945,294
	Cincinnati	4	449,018	..	....	..	....
Oklahoma		..	....	..	....	51	232,555
Oregon	Portland	4	174,544	26	49,076	30	224,530
Pennsylvania	Philadelphia	8	1,100,949	171	1,083,683	190	2,752,818
	Pittsburg	7	568,186	..	....	..	....
Rhode Island		..	....	..	....	10	169,175
South Carolina		..	....	..	....	16	87,409
South Dakota		..	....	..	....	17	47,738
Tennessee	Memphis	3	142,948	11	175,760	14	318,708
Texas		..	....	..	....	94	569,612
Utah		..	....	..	....	8	88,232
Vermont		..	....	..	....	10	45,232
Virginia		..	....	..	....	30	267,619
Washington	Seattle	3	172,310	28	241,928	31	414,238
Wisconsin	Milwaukee	5	261,194	42	155,783	47	416,977
Wyoming		..	....	..	....	5	13,718
48 States	28 Cities	129	5,112,618	1,283	21,267,507	2,044	26,575,204

Only general English daily newspapers are included, all foreign language and class dailies being omitted from consideration, which accounts for the difference between that number and the total of 2,465 daily papers in the United States noted in Ayer's American Newspaper Annual and Directory for 1918.

APPENDIX B

Who Was the First Advertising Agent?

A LOOK BACKWARD THREE-QUARTERS OF A CENTURY

(From *Printers' Ink*, June 13, 1918)

DETROIT, MICH., May 31, 1918.

Editor of PRINTERS' INK:

Will you tell me, please, the name of the first advertising agent who started business in this country? Is he, or his successor, still in business? PHILIP W. REESE.

We are accustomed to think of the business of advertising as one that sprang up within a generation or two, and it is not to be wondered at if some of the younger members of the profession seek for the first agent among those now in business. Before the agency of N. W. Ayer & Son was founded, in 1869, perhaps a score of agencies had been established and some of them had made a perceptible dent in the business world. Geo. P. Rowell & Co. started in Boston in 1865, and there were in existence in that year agents in Chicago, Cincinnati, and San Francisco, as well as several in New York. But let us start at the root of the original tree and work up.

The first agent we know anything about was Volney B. Palmer, who started business in 1840 and soon had offices in Boston, New York, and Philadelphia. Appleton's American Cyclopedia in an addition that was current almost thirty years ago credits Orlando Bourne with being the first agent, giving him the date 1828, but no other record has been found of him, and Palmer was the first agent, assuredly, who left his mark.

Palmer's business in Boston passed into the hands of S. R. Niles. S. M. Pettengill, who worked for Palmer, established his own business in Boston in 1849. In Philadelphia, Joy, Coe & Co. succeeded to the business. Later the firm was known as Coe, Wetherell & Smith, and about 1876 what there was left of the business passed into the hands of the Ayer agency.

Palmer's business in New York likewise fell to Joy, Coe & Co., and in later years was passed over to W. W. Sharpe, whose death was recorded in *Printers' Ink* last month. Under the name of W. W. Sharpe & Co. this agency is still conducted in New York.

This much for the bare record of Volney B. Palmer's business tree. Let us now take note of another pioneer, and then return for a brief review of Mr. Palmer's personal traits and business methods.

HOOPER'S OFFICE WAS UNDER HIS HAT

This other pioneer was John Hooper, and he was, perhaps, the first agent in New York. Whether he was in this field ahead of Palmer history recordeth not. Certain it is, however, that early in the '40's of the last century John Hooper was executing commissions for a number of advertisers. He entered the employ of *The New York Tribune* in 1841 as an advertising solicitor. Quickly he secured a large patronage and a corresponding income. Quoting from the issue of *Printers' Ink* that chronicled his death, over twenty-eight years ago: "As his customers were often desirous of more general publicity than could be secured through the columns of a single paper, he was not long in perceiving the advantages that might be derived from an arrangement that could enable business men to secure, through him, a general appearance of their advertisements in whatever mediums they might choose to select. This idea was carried to a successful termination, and, by judiciously following it up, paved his way to wealth. Successful negotiations were made with the publishers, who willingly allowed him, from their net cash rates to advertisers, a fair commission for such business as he should secure for their columns."

For several years, apparently, Mr. Hooper's orders were mostly carried in his hat. His method of financing the business was simple: he would pay the newspaper's bill, take a receipt, carry the bill to his principal, and the transaction would be closed. He resided in Dutch Street, where he received orders, but rented no office. As business grew he took an office in Fulton Street, and when the old *Times* Building was erected at the juncture of Nassau Street and Park Row he moved there—then in the thick of all things of an advertising nature. In 1870 he sold his business to Geo. P. Rowell & Co. for $10,000. When he died, in 1889, he had for many years been a millionaire—which was much more of an achievement than now.

THE OLD IDEA OF "AGENCY SERVICE"

The most extensive account of Volney B. Palmer that we know about was written for *Printers' Ink* in 1890 by S. M. Pettengill, himself an early agent, and before that an employee of Palmer. The latter is described as a "short, thick-set gentleman of good address; genial and pleasant in manner, and had a good command of language, 'full of wise sayings and modern instances.' He was a capital story-teller—wore gold spectacles and carried a gold-headed cane, and was a first-class canvasser.

"He had more self-possession," said Mr. Pettengill, "than any man I ever knew. He would come to his office at about 9 A.M., look over the daily papers for new advertisements, which I would cut out and make a list of for calling on. At about ten o'clock we would sally out, calling on the most important advertisers first. He would march into the counting-room of the merchants, calling for the principal partner, and announce himself, and hand his card with a pleasing address, and with as much assurance as if he were a customer who was about to purchase a large bill of goods. If he found the merchant busy, he would politely excuse himself and inquire when he could have the pleasure of seeing him, and if possible would make an appointment for that or the succeeding day. Shaking hands and tipping his hat gracefully he would leave; but he was always sure of meeting his appointments.

"If he found the party he was calling on willing to listen, he would introduce me, and make a well-considered statement of the benefits of advertising in general, and to the party he was addressing in particular. He would mention parties who had made fortunes by the use of judicious advertising. He would show how he (the merchant) could easily double his business and profits by a like course. He would point out the places where he should advertise, and how he should do it. He would generally enforce his words by some well-told stories, and get all parties into good humor and laughing heartily. He would end up by asking if he might be permitted to make out an estimate for the merchant's advertisement.

"He would say he would charge nothing for his estimate or setting-up of his advertisement. The advertiser would be under no obligation to give him an order. If he did not like it, that would be the end of it, etc. I carried a list of the towns where newspapers were printed, and I checked off such towns as he wanted, and we recommended, and I would then go to the office and prepare the estimate. The next day, at the furthest, I would bring it to the advertiser, and we generally concluded a contract when we made out an estimate. . . .

"He would sometimes meet with men who said that they believed the benefits of advertising were all a humbug, and that the money spent for it was thrown away. He would ask such men if they had ever tried it, and if, as in one case, the reply was 'Yes, I once spent ten dollars that way and I never received a dollar in return,' he then told the old story of the Indian who had heard that sleeping on feathers made a bed softer and more comfortable, and he tried it by buying a handful of feathers, and putting them on a smooth rock, lay down on them, but he 'didn't rest any better, but was covered with the blank things in the morning'— that feathers were 'no good'—they are a white man's humbug."

Mr. Palmer's dealings with publishers were harsh in the extreme. He claimed to be the sole representative of the papers he acted for, and insisted that they state his exclusive agency at the head of their editorial columns, which many of them did. He charged the newspapers for postage stamps used, the losses he incurred through advertisers' failures and the non-collecting of bills. In his early years as an agent he would rarely pay any bill rendered until he had collected all the items it contained. He not only demanded a commission of 25 per cent. on all the advertisements he forwarded, but demanded the same allowance upon any advertisement that might be forwarded direct by one who had once been his customer.

Volney B. Palmer commanded considerable respect in his day, but he has been dead—yes, these sixty years.

No claim is made that we have run down the very first advertising agent. But if one really existed before the days of Palmer, it is very evident that he was not much of an advertising man.— *Ed. Printers' Ink.*

THE END

Titles in This Series

1.
Henry Foster Adams. Advertising and Its Mental Laws. 1916

2.
Advertising Research Foundation. Copy Testing. 1939

3.
Hugh E. Agnew. Outdoor Advertising. 1938

4.
Earnest Elmo Calkins. And Hearing Not: Annals of an Ad Man. 1946

5.
Earnest Elmo Calkins and Ralph Holden. Modern Advertising. 1905

6.
John Caples. Advertising Ideas: A Practical Guide to Methods That Make Advertisements Work. 1938

7.
Jean-Louis Chandon. A Comparative Study of Media Exposure Models. 1985

8.
Paul Terry Cherington. The Consumer Looks at Advertising. 1928

9.
C. Samuel Craig and Avijit Ghosh, editors. The Development of Media Models in Advertising: An Anthology of Classic Articles. 1985

10.
C. Samuel Craig and Brian Sternthal, editors. Repetition Effects Over the Years: An Anthology of Classic Articles. 1985

11.
John K. Crippen. Successful Direct-Mail Methods. 1936

12.
Ernest Dichter. The Strategy of Desire. 1960

13.
Ben Duffy. Advertising Media and Markets. 1939

14.
Warren Benson Dygert. Radio as an Advertising Medium. 1939

15.
Francis Reed Eldridge. Advertising and Selling Abroad. 1930

16.
J. George Frederick, editor. Masters of Advertising Copy: Principles and Practice of Copy Writing According to its Leading Practitioners. 1925

17.
George French. Advertising: The Social and Economic Problem. 1915

18.
Max A. Geller. Advertising at the Crossroads: Federal Regulation vs. Voluntary Controls. 1952

19.
Avijit Ghosh and C. Samuel Craig. The Relationship of Advertising Expenditures to Sales: An Anthology of Classic Articles. 1985

20.
Albert E. Haase. The Advertising Appropriation, How to Determine It and How to Administer It. 1931

21.
S. Roland Hall. The Advertising Handbook, 1921

22.
S. Roland Hall. Retail Advertising and Selling. 1924

23.
Harry Levi Hollingworth. Advertising and Selling: Principles of Appeal and Response. 1913

24.
Floyd Y. Keeler and Albert E. Haase. The Advertising Agency, Procedure and Practice. 1927

25.
H. J. Kenner. The Fight for Truth in Advertising. 1936

26.
Otto Kleppner. Advertising Procedure. 1925

27.
Harden Bryant Leachman. The Early Advertising Scene. 1949

28.
E. St. Elmo Lewis. Financial Advertising, for Commercial and Savings Banks, Trust, Title Insurance, and Safe Deposit Companies, Investment Houses. 1908

29.
R. Bigelow Lockwood. Industrial Advertising Copy. 1929

30.
D. B. Lucas and C. E. Benson. Psychology for Advertisers. 1930

31.
Darrell B. Lucas and Steuart H. Britt. Measuring Advertising Effectiveness. 1963

32.
Papers of the American Association of Advertising Agencies. 1927

33.
Printer's Ink. Fifty Years 1888–1938. 1938

34.
Jason Rogers. Building Newspaper Advertising. 1919

35.
George Presbury Rowell. Forty Years an Advertising Agent, 1865–1905. 1906

36.
Walter Dill Scott. The Theory of Advertising: A Simple Exposition of the Principles of Psychology in Their Relation to Successful Advertising. 1903

37.
Daniel Starch. Principles of Advertising. 1923

38.
Harry Tipper, George Burton Hotchkiss, Harry L. Hollingworth, and Frank Alvah Parsons. Advertising, Its Principles and Practices. 1915

39.
Roland S. Vaile. Economics of Advertising. 1927

40.
Helen Woodward. Through Many Windows. 1926